THE WINTER PALACE AND THE PEOPLE

THE
WINTER
PALACE

AND THE PEOPLE

Staging and Consuming
Russia's Monarchy, 1754–1917

Susan P. McCaffray

NIU Press / DeKalb, IL

Northern Illinois University Press, DeKalb 60115
© 2018 by Northern Illinois University Press

27 26 25 24 23 22 21 20 19 18   1 2 3 4 5
978-0-87580-792-8 (paper)
978-1-60909-247-4 (ebook)
Book and cover design by Yuni Dorr

Library of Congress Cataloging-in-Publication Data
is available online at http://catalog.loc.gov

Contents

Illustrations

FIGURES

TABLES

Acknowledgments

I am grateful for the intellectual, moral, and financial support of many individuals and institutions because, even though History remains one of the most individualistic of endeavors, no book comes together without assistance of many kinds. Above all I am grateful for the work of more than one generation of Russian archivists and museum professionals at the two institutions that inspired and facilitated this study: The State Museum of the Hermitage and the Russian State Historical Archive in St. Petersburg. I also spent fruitful and contented hours in the European Reading Room of the Library of Congress, the Rare Book Room of the New York Public Library, the manuscript division of the National Library of Poland, the Davis Library at the University of North Carolina, and the incomparable University of Illinois Main Library during more than one Summer Research Lab sojourn. It is a pleasure to thank their friendly and competent staffs and the taxpayers who keep them going. I am grateful to the American Council of Teachers of Russian for logistical support in St. Petersburg. My thanks also go to the circulation staff at UNCW's Randall Library, and especially to Christopher Malpass and Elisabeth Howland of Interlibrary Loan, for without the many hundreds of obscure books and reels of microfilm they procured I could not have written this book in Wilmington.

I am particularly grateful to the State Museum of the Hermitage for permission to reproduce several paintings and photographs from their collection, and to Anastasia Mikliaeva for her assistance. Thanks also to the editors of the *Russian Review* and *Canadian American Slavic Studies* for permission to use some material previously published in their pages.

I am pleased to acknowledge the financial support of my own institution, the University of North Carolina Wilmington, including a Cahill Award from the division of Academic Affairs, a Faculty Research Reassignment and other support from the dean of the College of Arts and Sciences, several Moseley Awards from the Department of History, and grants from the Office of International Programs. This project benefited in particular from the ideas and insights of my colleagues Bob Argenbright, Lynn Mollenauer, Lisa Pollard, Paul Townend, Mark Spaulding, Michael Seidman, Tammy Gordon, and Ken Shefsiek. To the rest of my History comrades at UNCW I owe a debt for the congenial atmosphere that makes it a pleasure to teach and write.

Thanks are surely also due to the spirited collective of the Southern Conference on Slavic Studies, where many of these ideas first met the light of day, and in particular to the comments and learned advice forthcoming there from Chris Ely, Colum Lecky, George Munro, Susan Smith-Peter, and Frank Wcislo. I am grateful to Eve Levin, to Christine Worobec, and to the two anonymous readers of this manuscript for clarifying my thinking at different stages of the project and for significantly improving the final product. Warsaw's Royal Castle hosted the splendid Rituals of Power Conference in 2016 and gave me the opportunity to present my work there. Like many other Russian History specialists, I am much indebted to Amy Farranto and Northern Illinois University Press for carrying on the tradition of Mary (and Bruce) Lincoln and so ably presenting our work to the wider world. For research assistance I must thank UNCW History students Katie Albritton and Sean King. Thanks to Shannie and Bob Moorman, Patti and Joe Neuhof, Natasha Orlova, Roza Starodubtseva, and Aida Zukowski for care and feeding during many research trips. All of these colleagues and friends have improved this study, and the errors of fact or interpretation that remain are entirely my own responsibility.

Closer to home my thanks are due, daily and hourly, to my husband, Beau, who spent the first year of his retirement staying very quiet on Tuesdays and Thursdays, to long conversations with my fellow historian Eddie McCaffray, to the moral support of Meghan Vicks who helped this project, and more, to gestate, and to Mara McCaffray, who still doesn't like history.

Finally, I thank the late UNCW "non-trad" Mike Jarrell, who succeeded on his second attempt to earn a History degree. Taking a break one afternoon from rebuilding roofs after Hurricane Fran, Mike revealed one of his many obscure fascinations—with the furniture of eighteenth- and nineteenth-century Russia. He brought tomes from his substantial personal library and piqued my interest in the Russian craftspeople who decorated the tsars' Winter Palace. The idea he planted many years ago has grown up to be this book. This is only the most obvious of the debts I owe to the people with whom I've spent the better part of the last three decades, and so it is to my students that I dedicate this book.

TO MY STUDENTS

Preface

On a gloomy March afternoon at the beginning of Leningrad's last decade, I am among the tourists lining up to enter the Winter Palace from the entrance on the Neva embankment. Ascending the flamboyant Jordan staircase to the maze of spectacular galleries and chambers above I learn my first Winter Palace lesson: if the endless clumps of international visitors obscure from view whatever your guide is pointing at, simply look up, where you are likely to see a colorful ceiling *plafond* depicting classical allegory, or down, where you can inspect at close range a parquet designed by the great Rastrelli himself. Even in drab late Soviet Leningrad, inside the Winter Palace there is always something beautiful to look at.

Glancing back at those gray days it is possible to view that lost city with something like nostalgia, its mud, thirst, and pervasive *neudobstvo* notwithstanding. Also on that first encounter I witnessed something that has endured through all the ups and downs of the last three decades: the dignified competence of the female guides. Apparently keen to ensure their own clatch of awestruck foreigners the best of views, these serious-minded women elbowed past others and took up posts in front of this or that Rembrandt or Leonardo, this hallmark of the "Flemish school" or the "Italian school," and regaled listeners who could hardly hear over the Babel echoing through the gallery with the finer points of art history. Too rarely for my taste our guide offered tidbits about the life of the Romanov rulers and servants who inhabited the place in its glory days. More proudly she spoke of the superhuman efforts to save the palace and adjoining Hermitage from Nazi air raids. I perceived on that first visit that the story of how these young Soviet women had come to be such experts on the paintings and decorations of the tsars' palace was a story in its own right.

Sixteen years later, in St. Petersburg, two friends and I toured the lovely Iussupov Palace, where we were richly rewarded for agreeing to take the tour in Russian from an exhausted guide who thanked us at the end for not asking anything about the palace's most famous event, the murder of Rasputin. Allowing this our guide to narrate stories about the stylish noble couple who had owned the place and engaging her in a rambling personal conversation as the four of us stretched out in the palace's elegant theater, I had an epiphany.

The story of these noble and imperial palaces—these architectural vestiges of a long-gone, and not altogether mourned, past—was not only, and perhaps not even mostly, the story of the people who built them. It was the story of the people who kept them going, including intervening generations who sank time, money, and talent into them and who treasured them in complicated ways. Palaces insinuate themselves into the lives of cities, or else they do not survive.

In time this notion infused a lingering desire to say something worthwhile about the spectacular building in the heart of Russia's imperial capital. Some find it gaudy, others find it beautiful, but most visitors and residents understand it to be emblematic of St. Petersburg. With my expertise extending at best to the history of imperial Russia, the plan that took shape in my mind focused on the Winter Palace, which was begun in 1754 and was ceded to new rulers in 1917. What follows is an account of interactions between the lords of the Winter Palace and the various constituencies who both served it and consumed the spectacle it presented: construction workers, servants, furniture makers, guards, veterans, merchants, artists, museum specialists, and ultimately, the people of St. Petersburg gathered before it on Palace Square. In these interactions lie important clues to what "monarchy" meant in imperial Russia.

All dates are given according to the Julian calendar that prevailed in Russia until the Revolution, unless otherwise noted. Russian words and names are presented according to the Library of Congress transliteration system, with exceptions made for famous names that have become customary. Unless otherwise noted, all translations are mine.

THE WINTER PALACE AND THE PEOPLE

INTRODUCTION

St. Petersburg's Winter Palace was once the supreme architectural symbol of Russia's autocratic government. Over the course of the nineteenth and early twentieth centuries it gradually became the architectural symbol of St. Petersburg itself. By the time of the Russian Revolutions in 1917 Russia's rulers no longer actually lived in it, and the most publicly accessible part of the great building was its appended Imperial Hermitage Museum of Art. The story of this palace illuminates the relationship between monarchs and their capital city during the last century and a half of Russian monarchy. The Winter Palace proved to be a peerless stage for monarchy and a place of ordered encounter between ruler and ruled. If we look into the lived experience of this place we will better understand the extent and the limits of the Russian monarchy's power to command public allegiance. We may also track the gradual process at the end of the nineteenth century by which the Winter Palace, the Hermitage, and their treasures attracted a constituency more oriented toward the public of the capital city than toward the monarchs themselves. This subtle usurpation of the buildings on the embankment is one of the many threads by which the fabric of monarchy began to fray.

Monarchy's legacy to the modern world is substantial.[1] In Russia and elsewhere the legacy includes above all the idea and the realization of a centralized polity and a durable network of cultural practices and institutions. Russian monarchs and subjects collaborated in building up a state, a national idea, and a cultural inheritance, although their collaboration was not that of equal partners. Rulers enlisted subordinates through means both coercive and attractive, but absolute monarchy is a two-way street. It is a system of government in which the monarch rules and reigns over a stratified society to which and for which it represents the public commonwealth. In his or her first function, as chief governing executive, the monarch is dependent on ranking nobles and an army of clerical and military subordinates. At the center of this book is monarchy's second function, its role in representing symbolically and ceremonially the people and the nation over which the monarch reigns. Here the crowned ruler also plays the leading role, assisted by legions of stagehands and supporting actors in mounting the display of monarchy to foreign and domestic audiences, who consume the spectacle. There is only one monarch, but monarchy is a joint undertaking. Richard Wortman has written a peerless study of the Russian monarchy's ritual and ceremony within St. Petersburg and across the empire.[2] While leaning on his work, the aim in the present study is to illuminate interactions between monarchs and supporting players within the palace household and within the capital city. Despite the difficulties and limitations of such a project, it is worthwhile to try to understand how things might have looked to the auditors of the Romanovs' scenarios of power.

While Russia's Romanovs survived as absolute monarchs later than any others in Europe, their monarchy did not endure unchanged. Until the early twentieth century Russia's rulers resisted both constitutionalism, to which Britain's Stuarts succumbed in the seventeenth century, and revolution, which swept away France's Bourbon monarchy in the eighteenth.[3] It is well established that in the last century and a half of Russian absolutism the imperial government grew denser, more repressive, and more effective, helping to ensure absolute monarchy's survival into the twentieth century. But what can be said about the effectiveness of the ceremonial presentation of monarchy? How did the rulers' notion of what they were trying to display, and to whom they needed to display it, change over the course of the long nineteenth century? How did the presentation shift during Russian monarchy's long denouement? Is there any way to assess the impact of this display on the people who witnessed it? The answers to these questions shed light on the relationship between monarchs and those they ruled and therefore on the effectiveness of monarchy in imperial Russia.

While monarchs and their humble subjects occupied different and largely separate worlds, a satisfactory understanding of monarchy and its legacy in modern Russia requires attention to the places of intersection between them and to the intermediaries who connected them. In eighteenth- and nineteenth-century Russia these points of contact occurred most regularly in the capital city of St. Petersburg, whose relationship to its rulers was unique among European monarchies. It was no ancient capital but a city Peter the Great founded in 1703 for the sole purpose of projecting a new idea of Russia.

When he decreed in 1709 that it would henceforth replace Moscow as the capital of Russia, St. Petersburg acquired its defining mission as the central locus for monarchical representation of the Russian idea. For two generations practically everyone who arrived in the fledgling town came to serve the monarchical court in one way or another.[4]

So how did St. Petersburg's people participate in the monarchical display their rulers produced and the changing relationship between monarchy and city? As a strategy for investigating the production and consumption of the monarchical idea in imperial Russia, the focus of this study is on monarchy's main stage, St. Petersburg's Winter Palace and Palace Square.[5] Built by Peter the Great's daughter Elizabeth and her court architect Francesco Rastrelli between 1754 and 1762, the Winter Palace was the Romanovs' principal official residence until the Revolution of 1917.[6]

St. Petersburg's Winter Palace was the last royal residence constructed in the heart of a major European capital, and the capital in which it was set was only fifty years old. As a setting for displaying wealth, power, and sophistication to foreigners and courtiers, the Romanovs' Winter Palace had few equals. But it turned out that the key relationship was the symbiotic one between city and palace. The historian Bruce Lincoln believed that "the palaces of Europe's kings and queens never conjured up moods and meanings in the way the Winter Palace did," and if this is so, perhaps these moods and meanings had more to do with the way the palace fit into its urban setting, its windows allowing ruler and ruled to gaze at each other at very close range.[7]

Certainly in anchoring a court and a royal household for most of the year, the Winter Palace resembled others such as the Hofburg in Vienna, Versailles in Paris, and Buckingham Palace in London. But the differences were more notable. Built in 1279, the Hofburg was the castle of a medieval duchy around which a city eventually accumulated. By contrast, the Winter Palace was built within half a generation of St. Petersburg's founding, and its square became the central civic gathering place of the capital. Versailles, completed in 1682, was a suburban palace, and it was followed by many other such royal retreats across Europe that allowed monarchs to escape the scrutiny of their lesser subjects. Russia's rulers also built spectacular suburban palaces, but until the late nineteenth century they all spent most of the year in the Winter Palace, closely observed by the city's people who marked their daily comings and goings. Even less was the Romanov residence a Buckingham Palace, purchased from an aristocrat in the nineteenth century and standing behind great iron gates that protected an expansive courtyard in front of the building.

The Winter Palace was the architectural expression of a bolder political claim: Russia's monarchy had chosen its place with intention, and the

Romanovs understood the city of St. Petersburg to be their own. The city itself surrounded the Winter Palace, enclosing it so tightly that people could stand right in its shadow, with no park, garden, or anterior courtyard separating them from the walls of the building. The imperial inhabitants could make private use of a large interior courtyard and, eventually, of a hanging garden. But if they wanted to cross through the gates and into the city, everybody could watch them do it.

The Winter Palace always *meant* something, but it also *was* something: a space of encounter, penetrated by the auditors of the imperial scenario, by people who bore attitudes and ideas into the ruler's household and who carried anecdotes and perceptions out. When Peter the Great situated his Jolly Company of courtiers in a brand-new city on the Neva River, he made St. Petersburg a company town, and the care and feeding of the imperial court became the city's main project. His daughter's Winter Palace came to be the concrete center of this enterprise, and thousands of people crossed the border between city and palace in the course of their lives. Here the monarch's court and the city encountered and conducted business with each other in carefully scripted scenes set on an elaborate stage.

The interactions between ruler and ruled on this stage reveal the monarchy's shifting ideas about what kind of imperial nation they ruled and what kind of people inhabited it. At the same time, to a more limited degree, these interactions offer a glimpse of how various parts of the urban public reacted to the monarchical display. It is easier to reconstruct the actions than the ideas of servants, merchants, tradesmen, Easter worshipers, and enlisted men who came and went from the palace itself, not to mention those of the great urban crowds assembled on the square. Nonetheless, describing the interactions of monarchs and public allows us at least to understand what images of monarchy the people of St. Petersburg had their eyes on.

Russia's rulers did modify their ruling scenario in the face of shifting political realities. While changes in representational style alone did not account for the long durability of the Romanovs' absolute "autocratic" rule, such changes did amount to an acknowledgment of ongoing cultural democratization and even a realization that the political foundation of Russia's government was shifting down the social ladder.[8] In the face of such challenges Russian monarchs gradually reoriented their display of imperial and national representation away from courtiers and foreign dignitaries and toward their own public. This reorientation did not include constitutionalism or power sharing. Instead, the Romanov monarchs sought to recast themselves as representatives of a loyal, obedient, and sacred national community, sovereigns who presided benevolently over a people who willingly accepted their authority.

A close examination of the lived experience of the Winter Palace also suggests that, over a century and a half, Russia's monarchy attracted what might be called a constituency. We need to be careful here, as serfdom, conscription, and political illiberalism imposed strong elements of coercion on many of the people who served and visited at the Winter Palace. Within these constraints, however, it is clear that people managed to extract employment security, education and training, positions for their children, social mobility, and profit from their interactions with the monarch's household and court. Among the people who attached themselves more or less advantageously to the imperial palace were construction workers, contractors, craftsmen, architects, city merchants, clerks, seasonal workers of Russia's northwest, servants, cooks, laundresses, liveried footmen, wealthy merchants with their wives and daughters, military veterans, art lovers, arts professionals, preservationists, and urban crowds entertained by imperial spectacles on the palace embankment and square.

Many things changed in Russia and the world between 1754 and 1917, and these changes can hardly be reduced to or summarized by a study of the life and times of St. Petersburg's Winter Palace. Russia's place in Europe, the breakneck speed of the expansion of the city's population, the challenges of industrialization, the rising prominence of an educated and engaged urban public, and the thwarted aspirations of many for constitutionalism and political modernization formed the broad context of Russian monarchy, the envelope within which the life of the palace unfolded. All of these subjects have attracted the deserved attention of generations of able scholars, and their efforts will not be repeated here. These studies make it clear that the government of late imperial Russia presented a mixed picture of reform and repression. However, we have thought less about that government's representational life and the audience that witnessed it. To undertake a close examination of the contacts between rulers and ruled on the symbolic stage of the Winter Palace also yields some clues to the long persistence, and eventual demise, of Russian monarchy: to the flexibility and durability of a ruling and representational system that succeeded for a long time before failing spectacularly.

Four significant conclusions emerge from this study of the relationship between the imperial Winter Palace and the city that surrounded it. First, it is clear that this building had as its original purpose a more grandiose performance of court-oriented monarchy than Russian rulers had managed up to that time. The palace was conceived and designed to impress foreign plenipotentiaries and Russia's great grandees, two groups who were capable in the mid-eighteenth century of joining forces to remove hapless rulers from the throne. Such a purpose was typical of royal building projects across the continent, but less typical was Empress Elizabeth's decision to install her great palace in the heart of the capital city rather than in the suburbs. In doing so, she and her architect Francesco Rastrelli finally bequeathed the young city an undisputed center. For the empress and the architect, this new city center was an afterthought, but it turned into one on which, quite literally, the monarchy and the public came face-to-face. Catherine the Great and her successors beautified Palace Square, mixing court-centered displays with an occasional nod to the urban public that assembled on the fringes to watch the show.

Second, during Europe's age of revolution Russia's monarchs gradually perceived that the principal audience for monarchical performance had shifted. Consequently they oriented their ruling scenario less exclusively toward Russia's highest-ranking courtiers and the plenipotentiaries of foreign powers and more intentionally toward rank-and-file troops as well as toward the inhabitants of the capital city. They made a more expansive effort to edify the people who served in their palace and to project the image of an exemplary household to the city at large. The Winter Palace and the Palace Square proved eminently adaptable to this new purpose.

The high watermark of this sensibility came at the proverbial apogee of autocracy. In the middle of the nineteenth century Nicholas I endeavored with mixed results to recast Russia's monarchy as resting on a dual foundation of divine providence and consensual popular deference. Instead of constitutional modernization, which he viscerally rejected, Nicholas strained to work a governing formula of orthodoxy, autocracy, and nationality into his practice of monarchical rule. He endeavored to preside over an exemplary palace household and to reify the bond between tsar and army in visual displays at the palace and square.

Third, Nicholas made a momentous decision that came to fruition in early 1852 when he opened his Imperial Hermitage Museum, inviting an advance guard of the urban public to enjoy the refined splendor of the imperial art collection on his own turf. Here, again, Russia's monarch did what others were doing, in opening his art collection to public view, but with a significant difference. Situating the new museum adjacent to the urban palace at the heart of the city gestured toward a putative hospitality in which the ruler seemed to invite the people into his very home. This gesture proved the single greatest legacy of the palace-city nexus. Over the remaining years of the nineteenth century an expanding cohort of fine arts experts and technicians gradually became the masters of the collection of European art initiated by Catherine the Great. To the museum buildings juxtaposing the palace flocked growing numbers of the city's people. When they visited the museum they crossed the boundary between imperial and public space, and under the conscientious tutelage of the city's cultural authorities this boundary slowly blurred.[9]

Finally, the climactic acts in the saga of Russian monarchy played out at the palace and the square, indicating that during the years of monarchy this place had become the focal point of the city's civic life. In the second half of the nineteenth century the fact that the Winter Palace was monarchy's main stage made it a target for the regime's enemies. Following the assassination of Alexander II, his successor's retreat from the palace brought the great imperial displays on the Palace Square to an end, but as the tsar retreated, the public claimed the space at the center of their city. It came to possess a dual centrality, and its symbolic meaning was contested. The Winter Palace and Palace Square had come to be the essential stage for representing not just monarchy but the civic life of the empire-nation. When the people of Petrograd finally rejected the monarchy, and then the Provisional Government that supplanted it inside the Palace in 1917, they asserted the publicness of the building, its art collection, and its square. Seizing the Winter Palace, the soldiers of Petrograd claimed the stage for Russia's people. The fact that this current analysis extends over such a long period of time makes clear the gradual accumulation of civic meaning attached to the Winter Palace and Palace Square, which speaks to the very gradual transfer of political legitimacy away from the monarchy and toward the public. By the twentieth century this central space no longer represented monarchy as such. It stood for the civic nation.

THE POLITICAL ROLE OF THE CENTER

Efforts to articulate the political history of Russia have inspired many approaches. Recently scholars have engaged in the long overdue consideration of Russia qua empire. By virtue of their position on the western edge of a vast and mainly borderless Eurasian plain, Russian rulers' nation-making project involved subordinating an extremely varied complex of heterodox and linguistically distinct peoples. In Russia the idea of nation arose more or less contemporaneously with the idea of empire, giving rise to the image of an imperial-nation. A Russian core amalgamated itself while simultaneously establishing its precedence over subordinated others. There is much fruitful work being done unearthing the interconnected history of peoples, nations, and regions of Eurasia that came to be formally subsumed by the political entity whose center was St. Petersburg. From a somewhat different angle of vision a body of significant work on Russia's regions has also emerged.[10]

The present study engages a different, but related, problem: how did the Russian national-imperial state project power not *from* the capital city, but *within* it? This is an important question, because, as the Russian monarchy's aspiration to govern a vast country grew, the necessity of preserving authority at the country's heart intensified. Arguably, the Russian government's chief strategy for governing so large a territory was to strengthen the "technologies" of the center, including the political loyalty of those who lived in the empire's capital city. In the eighteenth and nineteenth centuries Russia's monarchs presided over an intensifying government—one that grew prodigiously as rows and rows of new office buildings arose around the hub of their formal urban residence.

Provincial Russia has often been described as under governed—but this has never been said about St. Petersburg. In St. Petersburg power was consolidated and concentrated. The monarch's authority was effectively concentrated in the center and reproduced in the regions, at least sufficiently for the demands of the age. Provincial authorities drew their power rather literally from the capital, which they were obliged to visit and where they might expect to be received in the Winter Palace by the monarch personally. The provincial officials, grandees, and merchants invited to the palace were meant to be edified by the many examples of wealth and taste, of dutiful service, of domestic order, and of self-confident authority they witnessed there—just as their brief proximity to the center of power would elevate them when they returned to their own cities and duties. The authority transmitted by an audience at the Winter Palace was the authority of a centralized monarchy, which, even before the railroad and the photograph, was imposing enough to be felt at a distance of thousands of miles.[11]

For all the skill that Russian rulers developed in reproducing central authority in the provinces, however, after 1789 the skill that was more relevant was the Romanovs' ability to maintain order in the center itself. The shocking fate of Louis XVI clearly worked on the tsarist imagination, and the Emperor Paul and his two reigning sons all pondered Louis's mistakes.[12] They concluded that the Parisian crowd had been suffused with rootless vagrants, with people unwisely forced out of wholesome pastoral communities, loosened therefore from their duty both as subjects and as responsible parents.[13] In response, Nicholas I adopted an energetic program of modeling the exemplary household and displaying it for city folk from the palace facades and even from within the palace galleries themselves.

The Winter Palace would not have proved useful as a stage from which to project lessons if it had not attracted the city's attention. Step by step the palace, and the Palace Square that eventually took shape on its southern flank, became the center of St. Petersburg's formal civic life. The rulers' efforts to order this space encountered challenges, and on rare occasions the square was a place of public protest. More often it encompassed seasonal festivities and special performances. As the years went by, the personal and public experiences of St. Petersburg's people intensified the significance of the Palace Square in the city's life and created the possibility that ruler and ruled might contest its meaning and its use.

Henri LeFebvre believed societies shape public spaces that support the workings of their economies and the reproduction of their social relations.[14] He stressed the materiality of meaningful spaces, and this emphasis can be usefully applied to the monarchical center of imperial Russia. Great court-centered capital cities like St. Petersburg gradually drew to themselves every kind of regional resource like moths to a flame. However, many of those who populated these centers came not so much to worship the fire as to enjoy its warmth. Such folk found themselves in the proverbial shadow of the Winter Palace as they went about their daily business. People of the capital often had employment linked to the imperial government in one way or another, or they aspired to do so. The layers of nostalgia, memory, and significance that encrust the Winter Palace have at their base the lived experience of generations of people who worked, transacted business, and visited there as well as those whose daily lives required them to pass by its walls and cross its square and occasionally to converge on that square with civic intention.

The story of the Winter Palace in imperial Russia is a story of changing encounters between the state actors who controlled it and the expanding city that both surrounded it and penetrated it. In their efforts to resist political modernization Russia's monarchs claimed that the ancient structure of autocratic monarchy could still serve in the modern age. To advance this claim they strove to reorient the ritualized display of monarchical power away from courtiers and toward the urban public. They adapted the great stage of the Winter Palace, enacting feats of cultural democratization and military commemoration. On Palace Square they monumentalized the bond between tsar, army, and people, and here rulers performed civic ceremonies for city crowds. At times of national emergency or victory, urban crowds assembled before the palace begging the monarch to appear at the balcony. Russia's nineteenth-century rulers and St. Petersburg's public succeeded in making the palace and its square the city's central civic space. But the Romanovs could not hold the demand for political participation at bay forever. When revolutionaries joined that battle, the monarchy became a target with a well-known address, opening up a decades-long battle for control of the singular stage from which Russian sovereignty could be projected. It was a stage the people of St. Petersburg had built, tended, and attended, and which, in the end, they inherited.

A WORD ABOUT SOURCES

Specialists will already have suspected the principal difficulty of conducting this study. As is always the case when we try to understand relationships between the powerful and the powerless, the powerful dominate even in retrospect thanks to the overwhelming superiority of their documentary legacy. The lengthy bibliography to this volume does not begin to provide a comprehensive list of the archival and memoir literature produced by and about Russian emperors and empresses and their enormous court. In order to seek some balance between the players I have focused on materials that shed light on monarchs and courtiers at moments of public presentation. These include the court journals (*Kamer-fur'erskie tseremonial'nye zhurnaly*) maintained by palace officials throughout our period, palace housekeeping and staff records preserved in the Russian State Historical Archive, laws, certain governmental reports, and memoirs and letters of the imperial family and their intimates. The extant communication between Empress Elizabeth and Francesco Rastrelli is disappointingly sparse, but I was able to see what there is of a Rastrelli archive in the National Library of Poland.

The story of how humble people such as laborers, contractors, servants, and city guests interacted with the monarchs on the Winter Palace stage is far more elusive. To that end I have dug through the semi-official eighteenth- and nineteenth-century newspaper *Sankt-Peterburgskie vedomosti* (St. Petersburg gazette); the thumbnail biographies of palace servants buried in archival housekeeping records; and the similar life stories of Hermitage personnel of all ranks, published by the State Museum of the Hermitage. Indeed, this study would not have been possible without that institution's ongoing efforts to bring its rich history into the public light. Better-known figures left memoirs. Some of the best nuggets have been excavated more or less by luck—consulting the trove of personal memories compiled by P. A. Zaionchkovskii in his unparalleled bibliography of prerevolutionary Russia and leaning on the discoveries of my fellow scholars.[15]

The imbalance is significant. Upper-class literate people tell us what they thought and how they felt; they explain, or at least portray, their intentions and impressions. Working people—with little leisure, mostly unlettered, and at any rate, sworn to absolute secrecy and discretion—assuredly do not leave any such record. This is an old problem that has bedeviled historians since at least the 1960s when the first wave of social historians tried to turn their backs on elites. To some extent I have used the techniques of those days: if we cannot quote the words of a worker's memoir let us try to re-create how he or she spent the day, where he or she lived, how much money there was to spend. It is not necessarily sound to make any inferences about his or her ideas from this kind of material, but it may not be much worse than concluding that empresses were telling the truth when they wrote letters and diaries.

Today the old strategies of social history appear quaint if not naïve, and I have turned (as have others following a cultural analysis) to the symbols, language, and signs of the exalted and the humble whenever these are available to excavate. This kind of project led me to attend to the content of paintings, the decoration of galleries, the purveyors of fine furniture, the design of livery and uniform, the structure of monuments. I am not so sure inference is much safer with this kind of material, but things like these have the benefit of having been viewed simultaneously by both the high and the low.

The result of this analysis is that we are left wishing to know more about how palace servants and city people thought of the monarch and the Winter Palace. But combining such hard data as are available with the impressions of individuals where we can find them draws us as closely as possible to lives far removed from our own. In the end one hopes to be viewed in the terms of a notable epitaph once encountered on a coastal Carolina ramble: "She did what she could."

PART I

A NEW STAGE FOR THE THEATER OF MONARCHY

1

"A DIFFERENT WINTER PALACE"

Before monarchs ruled nations they presided over royal courts, and it was to such courts that the theater of monarchy was originally directed. In early modern times a ruler's court was an interlocking assemblage of powerful entities: his or her own household, including immediate and extended family as well as honor attendants and actual servants; the administrators of justice and finance; and the powerful nobles of the land, whom the monarch needed to enlist and subdue. The age of enlightenment added to these court entities a set of cultural institutions such as academies of sciences and arts. In learning to preside over courts rulers acquired the skills and resources to become the chief executives of consolidated national governments.[1] For a long time royal courts were peripatetic, but at the end of the Middle Ages monarchical courts gradually grew less mobile. Settling themselves within long established cities of special significance, monarchs eventually mastered the arts of central administration. These arts included the display and propagation of ruling scenarios.

The establishment of the ruler's court inside a principal or "capital" city was critical for the project of establishing a centralized national state. It gave the monarch a place of residence that was detached from the territorial claims of his own and rival clans. At the same time it allowed him to consolidate in space the several reins that a national ruler needed to grasp simultaneously: household mastery, administrative order, military command, ecclesiastical precedence, and eventually, mercantile wealth. Even as centralizing monarchs aspired to rule great territorial states, they attended to the older project of presiding over their courts. By the eighteenth century, court politics were complicated not only by the ongoing rivalries of grandees but also by the insertion of resident foreign emissaries into domestic intrigues. In order to rule, and sometimes in order to stay alive, monarchs had to master their own households, administrators, and nobles. Gathering the court entities inside their capitals made this task easier.

Peter the Great faced many of these challenges, and his strategies for addressing them were not so different from those of his brother monarchs. But when he founded a new capital city for Russia at the beginning of the eighteenth century and transferred the seat of power from Moscow to St. Petersburg, he did something unprecedented. By this gesture he meant for all to understand that he was reinventing the nation, among other things recasting it as an empire, proclaiming its essentially European character, and giving it a new center of his own making.[2] The riskiest part of the gambit was his effort to dislodge the Muscovite court from its ancient city. He succeeded, forcing the leading men of the realm to build new houses on the banks of the Neva River in what was barely a city, but resentment lingered. For Peter's successors even more than for other monarchs it proved necessary to display imperial mastery to this large cohort of restive courtiers who managed to dislodge several rulers from the Russian throne, sometimes with foreign assistance. Thus the principal display of Russia's eighteenth-century monarchy was toward the nobles and foreign emissaries of its own imperial court. The locus of this display was St. Petersburg, a purpose-built late baroque capital city. As such, its growth for the first century of its existence was connected almost entirely to the care and feeding of the Romanovs' expanding monarchical court, and this made for a particularly strong link between city and monarchy.

In practice, though, St. Petersburg resembled older capital cities. The technologies of centralization mastered by Peter and his successors meant that the country, however large, was increasingly represented by its capital.[3] These capitals housed the expanding apparatus of national states, including offices, parade grounds, military barracks and stables, as well as ceremonial spaces for increasingly splendid displays of monarchical courts such as grandiose churches, palaces, and public squares. Ceremonially, these capital cities were designed or retrofitted to display majestically the putatively all-powerful monarchies that represented them.

If Peter bequeathed St. Petersburg's skeleton, it was his daughter Elizabeth (1741–1761) who bestowed upon it a layer of gorgeous flesh. Falling between the pivotal reigns of Russia's two great eighteenth-century monarchs, the twenty-year rule of Empress Elizabeth Petrovna has begun to receive scholarly attention. The monarch herself has often been characterized as a vain and sybaritic spendthrift, and recent research documents the great expansion of her court expenses.[4] However, the mark Elizabeth left on St. Petersburg cannot be overstated. The city her father had founded would be the backdrop for a European style monarchical court and, if possible, a court that surpassed all others in elegance and wealth.

Her great collaborator in creating Russia's imperial capital was the chief architect of her court, Bartolomeo Francesco de Rastrelli. Rastrelli received the greatest commission of his long, illustrious career when Elizabeth decreed on January 1, 1753, that she would build a new "winter home" on the banks of the Neva. In so doing Elizabeth imparted a unique feature to the monarchy of late eighteenth- and nineteenth-century Russia: at a time when most other European courts were decamping for the suburbs, the principal formal residence of the Romanovs would stand in the very heart of town, unprotected from passersby by either fences or gardens. The empress and her architect meant for the new palace to house and host the imperial court, but their great project also planted Russia's monarchy firmly in what became the center of a booming capital city.[5]

The result of their collaboration was a grand stage for the court-oriented monarchy of late eighteenth-century Russia. They did not clearly foresee that their long and ultimately unresolved debate about how to treat the undeveloped stretch of land on the southern flank of the Winter Palace inadvertently laid the foundation for Palace Square, a new and vital city center. For Russia's eighteenth-century monarchs "the people" remained in the background, performing supporting roles in a scenario oriented primarily toward courtiers and foreigners. As it happened, the central stage they built proved adaptable for the public, urban monarchy of nineteenth-century Russia, something Catherine the Great pointed toward near the end of her reign.[6]

BUILDING THE BAROQUE CITY

Elizabeth, a notable beauty in her youth, is remembered now as a woman of lavish tastes who spent enormous sums on her wardrobe and, above all, on her endless building projects. Her taste for luxurious residences contrasted with the relatively simple accommodations created for her father, but though their tastes differed, Elizabeth was a founder and a builder, as Peter had been. She did invest in Moscow's imperial residences and presided over the founding of Russia's first university there in 1755. The empress also established schools and arts academies in towns all across Russia. However, St. Petersburg and its environs consumed most of her attention and the lion's share of her funds, as when she established the Imperial Academy of Arts there in 1757, for example. The most enduring imprint of Elizabeth's tastes and political thought lies in the buildings she commissioned in the capital city. Although the daughter was both less adept and less visionary than the father, she shared his instinct for deploying the symbols and architecture of power, and in the first three-quarters of the eighteenth century that architecture was, quite literally, baroque.

"The baroque" is one of those plastic European descriptors marked almost as much by diversity as by unity, a fact illustrated in St. Petersburg itself by two nominally baroque buildings that face each other across the Neva River: the Dutch-inspired Cathedral of Saints Peter and Paul, with its spire rising above the eponymous fortress, and Rastrelli's masterpiece, the Winter Palace. These buildings represent the different national traditions of their designers as well as different periods, but they share the underlying purposes of the baroque, which were the purposes of ambitious national rulers who exhibited military, political, and cultural power through urban design and architecture.

According to architectural historian Victor-L. Tapié, Renaissance principles gave way to a new tendency in the aftermath of the Council of Trent (1545–1563). Reinvigorated by its own reformation, the Catholic Church and its leaders initiated great changes in the city of Rome itself, where "the Popes were determined to give her a dignity which would be worthy of a 'country common to all Christian peoples,' as Pius V put it in 1565."[7] The triumphalist message written in the new stones of the eternal city was saying "more about celebrating victories over heresy than about penitence and meditation."[8] Long the fountainhead of European architecture and the inspiration of building designers across the continent, Rome henceforth dispatched to every corner of Europe architects able to produce monuments to the majestic power of triumphant centralizing monarchs.

For Lewis Mumford the roots of the baroque city lay in two overlapping tendencies. One was the gradual success of centralizing monarchs whose stationary courts took root in "absolute" capital cities that attracted commerce, craft, and wealth while curbing the multiplication of provincial cities. The second tendency was intimately connected to the first: the steadily increasing size of professional standing armies whose cannons brought to a close the age of independent cities that could withstand royal assault. By the eighteenth century the great armies that supported centralized monarchies required barracks, arsenals, and gigantic parade grounds inside capital cities.[9] The baroque city conveyed absolute political power symbolically, but it also accommodated the mechanisms of power spatially. Elizabeth's St. Petersburg was one of the classic examples of baroque city planning and design.

When Elizabeth chose to retain Rastrelli as the chief architect of the Russian court after seizing power in 1741, she extended Russia's tradition of employing Italian building masters. In fact, courts all over Europe had employed Italian architects since the late Middle Ages. Particularly strong ties had connected fifteenth-century Muscovy and Renaissance Italy, with Italian masters continuously at work in Russia between 1475 and 1539, "revolutionizing" Russian architecture.[10] Aristotele Fioravanti built the Kremlin Cathedral of the Assumption in the 1470s, and the Lombard brothers Marco and Onton Fryazin built new fortifications in Moscow's fortress (or kremlin) wall. The greatest extant monument to the impact of Italian masters in Muscovy is the Palace of Facets, which is all that remains of a palace complex built for Ivan III by Pietro Antonio Solari and Marco Ruffo in the late 1480s.[11]

Like his contemporaries, Peter the Great employed building masters from all over Europe. He assigned a leading role in St. Petersburg to the Swiss Italian Domenico Trezzini, who had arrived in Russia by way of Copenhagen. Trezzini was responsible for several of the chief buildings of Peter's time, the Cathedral of Saints Peter and Paul, Peter's Summer Palace, and the Twelve Colleges.[12] Peter also took advantage of the death of Louis XIV in 1715 to recruit talented builders who had been freed up from service at the court of the Sun King. The most famous such figure was Jean-Baptiste Alexandre Le Blond, a noted architect and garden designer, who arrived in St. Petersburg in 1716, where Peter bestowed upon him the new title of chief architect of the court. In the three years left to Le Blond before his death, he produced several city plans, none of which was ultimately approved.

A few months before Le Blond arrived in the city another émigré from the French court had already settled into his post. This was the Florentine sculptor, Bartolomeo Carlo de Rastrelli. Carlo Rastrelli had been inspired by the beauty of baroque Rome as a young man, but failing to find sufficient work there he had accepted a post at the court of Louis XIV and moved to Paris with his family before his son Bartolomeo Francesco was born there in 1700.[13] In 1716 Carlo Rastrelli accepted the invitation of Peter's agents and traveled with his teenaged son to St. Petersburg, where Rastrelli senior hoped to make a name for himself. One scholar characterized the elder Rastrelli as an inferior talent who had "purchased the title of Count in Paris" and whose efforts in St. Petersburg disrupted the design plans of the far more talented Le Blond.[14] However, if LeBlond's name would be forever linked to a (never implemented) plan to center the capital city on Vasilevskii Island, the name Rastrelli would be indissolubly linked to the place that did become its heart: the stretch of Admiralty Island that faces the Neva River, known simply as the palace embankment. Rastrelli senior helped to build two of the buildings that preceded his son's masterpiece on the same site.

For Peter the Great, the focal point of his new city was made of water: it was the great watery "square" of the Neva bounded by the fortress, the spit of Vasilevskii Island, and the Admiralty, with its busy ship-building wharves. What appears in retrospect as Peter's indecisiveness about where to concentrate cultural and governmental buildings might have been more clearly perceived in his own time as an effort to focus determinedly on the city's maritime character. Thus the first two great institutions, the fortress and the Admiralty, gaze at each other across an expanse that was alternately navigable and frozen. The tsar and his city planners considered the tip of Vasilevskii Island to offer the best prospect from which to view both of these architectural masterpieces, and they consequently launched important projects there, including the building that housed the governing Twelve Colleges as well as the Kunstkamera, built to contain the tsar's collection of scientific and artistic oddities. Nearby the city governor and chief arbiter of affairs, Prince A. D. Menshikov, built his own lovely Dutch baroque palace facing the water.

Peter, himself, erected quarters on both sides of the river. His first house—according to lore the very first built in St. Petersburg—was a wooden cabin (painted to look as though it were made of brick) on the Petrograd embankment, known as "the city side" in the vicinity of the Peter and Paul Fortress. By settling there as early as 1703 the tsar spawned residential building on Petrograd Island, particularly for the workers and craftsmen being concentrated in the new city in great numbers. By 1708, however, he apparently concluded that the separation of the workers from the Admiralty during the two annual seasons of the freezing and thawing of the Neva was too inconvenient. Peter decided to have workmen's quarters built on the southern embankment, and he similarly ordered a winter house for himself on the Admiralty side. This building, no longer extant, has been designated as the first winter home, or winter palace, on the general site where the Rastrelli building now stands.[15] The tsar's winter home separated the shipbuilders' settlement from the homes of the ranking naval officers and associates of the tsar. It was situated at the narrowest point between the Neva and the Moika (or M'ia) Rivers, today the site of the Winter Canal.

Living in the vicinity of the Admiralty soon proved so convenient that in 1708 Peter commissioned Trezzini to build him a summer palace a bit further east, within the fashionable summer garden that was taking shape along the river. This elegant building still stands. It included a system for providing running water inside the house as well as an up-to-date drainage system. Like other wealthy grandees across Europe and Asia, Peter was able to have both a winter and a summer residence. The latter was intended to house people only from the late spring through the middle of the fall, so it could be constructed with thinner walls and single -glazed windows. Even humble folk moved into summer quarters when they were able to do so, because the absence of monumental heating stoves rendered the interiors far cleaner and roomier than the winter quarters. Although Russia's rulers had cleaning staffs sizeable enough to deal with soot and smoke damage, they all preferred to spend summers in the airier summer palaces that took advantage of garden settings, terraces, and porches, without the looming presence of stoves in every room. Peter's summer palace was known for its innovative hydrologic heating system also, one of the first of its kind.[16]

Before long Peter also required a new winter home that would be better suited to house his growing family. In 1711 the tsar ordered Menshikov to have his small winter house moved across the river to the Petrograd side, and in April of that year Peter commissioned Trezzini to build his second winter home on the site of the first.[17] Taken together with the construction of his new summer home, this decision represents an important moment in the design of St. Petersburg. While the branched expanse of water bordered by three islands continued as the commercial and scenic center of the city, henceforth all of Russia's imperial rulers established their formal residences on the southern bank of the Neva, on or near the "palace" embankment. Peter had come to see the practicality of being able to come and go by land not only to his suburban residences but also to the country beyond them, along the Moscow road. If Peter bequeathed his successors a neighborhood, however, he did not bequeath a palace itself. For many decades to come, rulers engaged in great projects of destruction and reconstruction along this famous quay.

It was Francesco de Rastrelli whose long collaboration with Peter's daughter shaped the built environment of central St. Petersburg more than anyone else. After first arriving in Russia with his father in 1716, Francesco visited Russia periodically over the next dozen years, while studying primarily in Paris and Italy.[18] A few projects undertaken with his father launched the young master into the ranks of fashionable designers.[19] Francesco apparently returned to Russia permanently sometime between 1728 and 1730, as the number of commissions he and his father were receiving steadily increased.[20] During these years Emperor Peter II returned the court to Moscow, and Rastrelli worked there on designs for a palace for Prince Dolgorukii, among other projects. L. E. Torshina considers the time Rastrelli spent in the old capital, which may also have included a period of time in his youth, to have been critical in the younger Rastrelli's gradual invention of a decidedly Russian version of the baroque.[21]

The Rastrellis survived the coup that brought Anna Ioannovna to power in 1730 and soon secured her order for a new Kremlin palace known as the Winter Annenhof, and a Summer Annenhof in the Moscow suburb of Lefortovo the following year. After her coronation Empress Anna moved the

court once again to St. Petersburg, where the Rastrellis soon found themselves
working on the imperial stables (*manezh*) behind Nevskii Prospekt. While
much about their precise status in these years remains elusive, it is clear that
the careers of father and son were completely intertwined. Iu. Ovsiannikov
concludes that Carlo Rastrelli became Chief Architect in November 1730, a
post that passed to his son in 1736, before the elder Rastrelli's death.[22]

By 1732 Rastrelli the younger had married, and within the next few years
three children were born in quick succession. It became necessary to secure
a predictable income, something that noble and even imperial commissions
did not always provide. But when the empress's favorite, Ernst Johann von
Biron, hired him to build a palace in the Duchy of Courland, the younger
Rastrelli finally had the chance to demonstrate his independent talent and
originality. Rundale Palace, complete with its formal French garden and
outdoor amphitheater, was the first palace that Francesco Rastrelli designed by
himself, and whose construction he supervised directly. Recognition followed
this achievement, as he apparently began to receive a government salary. The
younger Rastrelli continued to hold this title until after the death of Empress
Elizabeth.

At the same time that Rastrelli the younger was working in Courland, he
and his father had also been put to work on a new winter palace for Anna
Ioannovna on the Neva embankment.[23] By the middle of the eighteenth
century, the building and rebuilding on this expanse of river bank verged on
mania, and it is worth considering why this was so. While it is often asserted
that St. Petersburg was "the most intentional city," the history of this one
place suggests something else.[24] Over the course of just thirty years Russia's
rulers found it necessary, first, to settle on the southern bank of the Neva only
reluctantly because the absence of permanent bridges rendered movement
during spring thaw and fall freezing all but impossible; second, to establish
both summer and winter homes facing what was emerging as the formal heart
of a maritime city; third, to rebuild the winter home in order to accommodate
the more conventional family life eventually embraced by a grown-up tsar;
and later to remodel this home extensively in accordance with the tastes of
Peter's widow.

Then, in the 1730s came the opportunity to create a palace that was more
up-to-date and far grander, which could take advantage of the fact that the
imperial family had recently inherited what was widely considered the city's
most beautiful palace, that of the chief of the Admiralty and governor of
Estonia and Karelia, Count Fedor Apraksin, whose palace stood just west of
the imperial winter home.[25] A handful of grandees had built palaces on this
embankment in Peter's time, and it was Le Blond who in 1717 had designed

for Apraksin "the most magnificent of all the aristocratic palazzos of that time; its façade facing the Neva, [over three hundred feet long] had a terrace built on twin ranks of columns and covered with an awning of colored canvas."[26]

Soon after ascending the throne Anna Ioannovna commissioned Trezzini to remodel the Apraksin mansion as her primary St. Petersburg residence. The scale of this reconstruction project was unprecedented: Trezzini reported that carpenters alone numbered one hundred men.[27] Before long, however, the empress saw the need for an even more splendid building on the site, which could incorporate the admiral's palace into the existing imperial winter home next door. The court extended an order for the production of 155,000 bricks in January 1732, and the Rastrellis took over the project in April. Their experience in amassing the requisite skilled laborers and materiel was tested by the need to employ over fifty bricklayers and to provide tools for several hundred tradesmen. Anna Ioannovna demanded that the work proceed quickly, and the building arose along the riverfront between May and November 1732. The Rastrelli creation that served as the rulers' formal winter palace for twenty years has been judged more ingenious than elegant.[28] The restless Anna never stopped decorating and remodeling the edifice that her talented court architects had assembled out of disparate parts.[29]

By the time Elizabeth came to the throne in 1741 the tradition of perpetual renovation was well established, but the new empress's sense of sovereign grandeur extended far beyond remodeling the imperial home on the embankment. Elizabeth Petrovna reigned during a period of considerable international flux. The ascent of Frederick II to the throne of Prussia at virtually the same time as her own ascent profoundly destabilized European international relations at mid-century. Determined not to relinquish her father's Baltic acquisitions, Elizabeth countered Swedish military efforts in the first two years of her reign and eventually extended Russia's northwestern boundary to include almost the whole of Finland. The complexities of the War of the Austrian Succession consumed most of the 1740s. These years saw Russian armies fighting from Latvia to the Netherlands, and the power of Russian arms commanded respect abroad.[30] At home, Russia's complex foreign policy produced entanglements at court and foreign intrigue in St. Petersburg.

Maintaining her throne in the age of palace coups required her to mount a display of monarchical power and graciousness to a combined audience of Russian guardsmen and foreign representatives who were often entangled with Russian courtiers through personal relationships, commercial interests, and romance. Thus Elizabeth's effort to create a more sophisticated court amounted to a political strategy. In the eighteenth century a monarchical court was a social and political world of its own, an expansive bureaucracy for administering the ruler's household and property, and a network of cultural institutions. For all the elaborate ceremony, luxurious living, and sartorial excess that marked its life, a monarch's court was the vehicle through which European rulers conducted international diplomacy and by which they implemented royal power at home. Elizabeth clearly believed that Russia required an imperial court that was grander in every way than the one she had inherited. She expanded it on every front: more dresses, more wines, more palaces, more servants. She reordered court ranks and regulated ceremonies.[31]

The court of a great monarch also needed to exhibit cultural refinement, and over the course of her reign Elizabeth associated her court with important new educational and artistic institutions. Like many of her fellow rulers Elizabeth particularly cherished theater, and she patronized the tragedies of the great playwright Alexander Sumarokov. Theater was an aristocratic activity that was central to the display of, and measured discourse about, monarchical power at the courts of eighteenth-century absolute rulers.[32] It was at the heart of Elizabeth's display of monarchy, which she oriented primarily toward great Russian nobles and foreign emissaries. The arts academies, educational institutions, and theaters established and patronized by her court reached into the city also. These institutions of the court required the identification and training of talented people, just as they sometimes welcomed the upper echelons of the relatively small educated public as members of the audience. Through this kind of patronage of a performance directed at courtiers, Elizabeth's imperial court managed to become the center of the city's cultural life.[33]

Above all, Elizabeth chose to manifest monarchy through her extraordinary investment in baroque churches, gardens, and palaces. If projecting power was the work of theater, theater required a stage. Entrusting her building program to the court architect she inherited from her predecessors, Elizabeth presided over the construction of an astonishing number of monuments to the kind of power that Peter the Great's empire meant to exert in Europe. In the language of stone, brick, and craft, Russia's monarch meant to testify to the might of a country that supported an imposing and beautiful capital city, which in turn served as a grandiose stage from which to demonstrate the all-encompassing power of Russia's autocratic monarch. What was true of the court's cultural institutions was even truer of its building program: it required the work of many hands, and it would attract the attention of the city in which it lodged.

A FRUITFUL PARTNERSHIP

Following her coronation sojourn in Moscow during 1742, Elizabeth lived in Anna Ioannovna's winter home on the embankment in 1743, filling its parade halls with guests observing all kinds of solemnities. Returning to Moscow for most of 1744, she directed the younger Rastrelli to make extensive changes to the Neva palace in order to accommodate new works of art and sculpture as well as richer decoration of cornices and alcoves, including the use of amber, imported mirrors, and parquet extracted from Biron's Courland palace.[34] Eventually Rastrelli was called upon to build two additional wings for this edifice. Apart from these renovations and expansions, Elizabeth made do with her predecessor's winter residence for the first decade of her reign, perhaps to mark a contrast with her predecessor, who had moved immediately to re-create her principal residence. Like many of her contemporaries, the Russian empress moved her court from palace to palace throughout the year, and she seemed to prefer her two primary suburban residences at Tsarskoe Selo and Peterhof to the patched together palace on the Neva.

Rastrelli's own summary of his chief works in this period indicate that Elizabeth commissioned him to overhaul Peter's palace at Peterhof (1747–1752), because "the empress has decided to make her residence in midsummer where all the foreign ministers and magnates of the country are regularly found twice a week."[35] In 1749 he began "Empress Elizabeth's favorite palace," at Tsarskoe Selo, named in honor of her mother, Catherine. After much discussion the architect and his patron arrived at an innovative design calling for two floors of columns mounted along a very lengthy primary façade, making it one of the few great palaces of the era that did not draw on the model of Versailles.[36] Rastrelli had important imperial and noble commissions in St. Petersburg as well in these years, such as Elizabeth's new summer palace (1741), the Vorontsov and Stroganov palaces on Nevskii Prospekt (1749, 1752), the Smolny convent and church (begun in 1751), and plans for a *gostinyi dvor* (merchants' court), which in the end was never built.[37] It was in the 1740s and 1750s that "the Russian baroque" came to full flower in the mind and work of the Italian-born architect who had spent his entire life in the service of the Romanovs.

The year 1752 dawned with a lull between military campaigns. It was during this respite that Elizabeth approached Rastrelli about building a brand new winter palace in place of the permanent remodeling of Anna Ioannovna's home. Her motives are recorded in the decree of January 1, 1753, that launched the project: "Our winter palace in St. Petersburg is not only inadequate for the reception of foreign ministers and plenipotentiaries, . . . and for the conduct of ceremonies with a grandeur appropriate to our imperial responsibilities, but also for the accommodation of the servants we require and the things needed; and so we have conceived the idea to build a different Winter Palace of great expanse in length, width and height."[38]

Elizabeth had found that, at great court occasions, the old palace simply was not big enough to hold all of the Russian and foreign guests at the same time. She may have had in mind the court festivities surrounding the wedding of her nephew and heir, the future Peter III, and his bride, the future Catherine II, in August 1745. Rastrelli's notes indicate that he had received the empress's commission to decorate the great hall of the old winter palace for this occasion, so that it could be "celebrated with all the magnificence appropriate to such an event."[39] To that end Rastrelli had installed cascading fountains in each of the four corners of the gallery, allegorical statues and vases all decorated with rich ornaments, and a bower of orange trees. The insufficient capacity of the old palace also came to light during New Year's receptions, when Elizabeth wished to host the entire court and all foreign ambassadors and their staffs. The court journal reported that she greeted Russian notables at eleven o'clock and foreign dignitaries at noon, but that some of the lesser guests would be received at the home of Count Shuvalov for want of space at the palace. Each of these instances suggests that Elizabeth was primarily motivated by her desire to mount larger and more lavish court spectacles for the traditional audience of foreign plenipotentiaries and Russian grandees than was possible in the existing building on the Neva.

If grander staterooms were fundamental to Elizabeth's vision, accommodation for her expanding staff of servants may have weighed even more heavily in her determination to build "a different Winter Palace." By the mid-1750s the staff of her court had grown substantially from its size at the end of her predecessor's reign. O. G. Ageeva cites records for 1756 indicating that, between the Great and the Small Courts (that is, Elizabeth's court and that of her heir) the staff being supported from court funds now consisted of more than 1,390 people compared to 968 in both courts when Elizabeth took the throne.[40] The expansion of the court staff by 50 percent in a decade and a half alarmed Elizabeth's officials, who provided her with a summary of the rising expenses in March 1755.[41] If this report gave the empress pause she did not allow it to deter her building plans that were now well under way. Her concern for the housing of a luxuriously large staff continued to manifest itself in her attention to Rastrelli's proposals for their accommodation.

Perhaps the most striking feature of Elizabeth's architectural vision was her apparent unwillingness to make one of her beautiful suburban palaces a year-round imperial residence. While she continued to hold court at Peterhof or Tsarskoe Selo during the summer months, it apparently did not occur to her to remain there, about fifteen miles from the city, throughout the year. At a time when the French court, among many others, had retreated from its capital city for more and more of the year, Elizabeth resolved to strengthen the bond between her court and the imperial capital.[42] The monarchy she wished to project was anchored in her father's willful establishment of his city on the Neva, and it was against this backdrop that Russia's claim to European eminence had to be portrayed. Russia's monarch required a stage in the heart of St. Petersburg.

So the building of a new Winter Palace was added to the welter of urban construction projects underway in the 1750s: the Cathedral of St. Nicholas the Mariner, the first St. Isaac's Cathedral, the Izmailovskii Bridge, the wallpaper factory, the reconstruction of the fortress church of Saints Peter and Paul following a fire, and the great Smolnyi convent and church near the bend in the Neva. The noise from building projects, none of which was nearly complete, rang out across the rivers and canals while smoke from construction fires choked residents in all quarters of the city.[43]

Not the least of the questions confronting Rastrelli was which way the imperial palace should face. In Peter's day it seemed clear that the front of the Neva buildings faced the river, just across which stood all of the buildings that supported monarchical power. The only exception to this rule was the adjacent Admiralty with its working wharves, surrounded on three sides by a moat. When Apraksin bequeathed the admiral's house to Anna Ioanovna, he

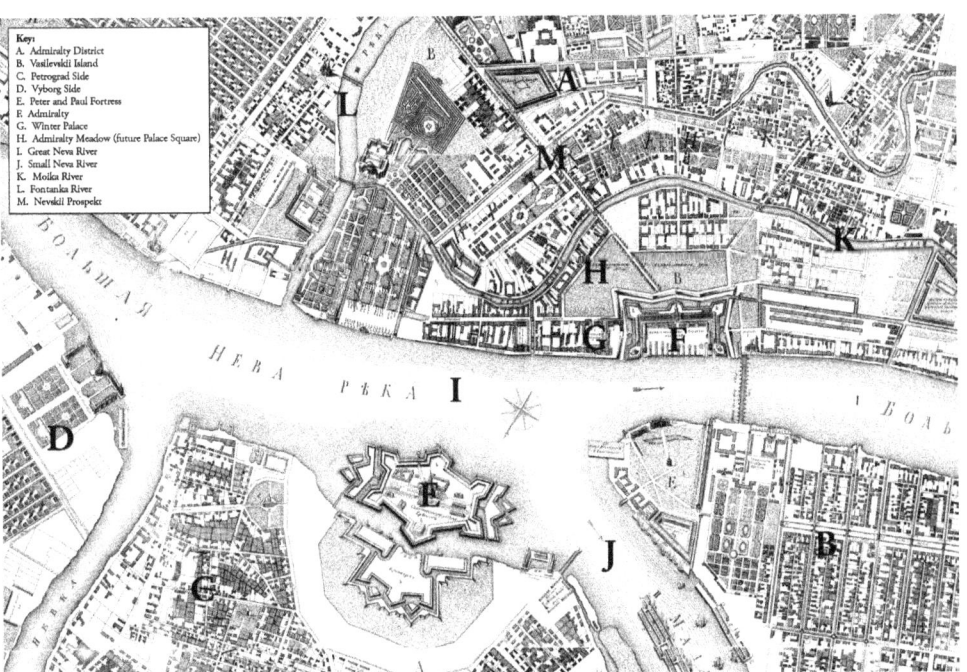

Key:
A. Admiralty District
B. Vasilevskii Island
C. Petrograd Side
D. Vyborg Side
E. Peter and Paul Fortress
F. Admiralty
G. Winter Palace
H. Admiralty Meadow (future Palace Square)
I. Great Neva River
J. Small Neva River
K. Moika River
L. Fontanka River
M. Nevskii Prospekt

FIGURE 1.01 Map by Kerry E. Stallings. Based on a 1753 map by the Imperial Academy of Sciences. David Rumsey Map Collection (davidrumsey.com).

not only raised the standards of architectural opulence on the embankment but also, quite literally, opened a new door for the imperial palace, which now might open to the west and face the Admiralty itself. Rastrelli decided to construct an impressive entrance on this side of the building, which became the main access for guests invited to balls or receptions. More challenging, however, was the question of what to do with the "back" of the building, the side that faced south. At the time it offered a gated entrance for pages and other serving courtiers.[44]

As was often the case with Elizabeth's building projects, the assembling of materials and first steps began before she approved a final design. Over the course of 1753 workers drove pilings for a new southern wall, although Rastrelli was still drafting ideas for imperial approval. At first he meant to incorporate the much-renovated Winter Palace and several large noble houses that abutted it, now owned by Elizabeth. But suddenly, in January 1754, the chief of the Construction Chancellery, Lieutenant General V. V. Fermor, ordered the work stopped because the chief architect had come up with one more, profoundly new, design.

It is all but impossible to know about the personal relationship between Empress Elizabeth and her court architect, but the record of the drawings produced in early 1754 offers a hint.[45] In her impatience to see the great project underway, she had prevailed upon the Senate to begin financing preliminary construction well before the great architect had decided on his final approach and before she herself had approved any of his designs. We can imagine Fermor's frustration when, after nearly a year of preliminary work, he realized that his men could proceed no further in the face of the wildly new proposals the architect was even now laying before his patron. At the beginning of 1754 Rastrelli seems to have decided that the simplest and least expensive approach would be to clear the entire site and erect an entirely new palace from scratch. He called for all the old buildings that stood on the embankment and behind them in the "meadow" south of the palace to be torn down.[46] The new Winter Palace would be raised on the cleared embankment and stretch all the way from the Admiralty to the Winter Canal. Elizabeth initially rejected this plan for reasons unknown, and it appears that the two were at loggerheads for the next several months. She indicated that she would reinstate the original proposal for renovating the Third Winter Palace with the addition of a small servants' wing on the Admiralty meadow, but Rastrelli was feverishly at work to produce a variant of his new vision that could win Elizabeth's approval. He succeeded in June, when she consented to what proved to be the final design for the Winter Palace.

Konstantin Pisarenko argues that Rastrelli and Elizabeth's collaboration on the innovative Catherine Palace inspired the final design of the new Neva residence. At the Catherine Palace besides the two ranks of columns along a preposterously long expanse, the other main distinction from the Versailles-inspired palaces of the time was the absence of wings protruding forward on each end of the central corpus.[47] Rastrelli now proposed to elaborate on the dual columned façades and again to eschew wings. Instead, the four sides of the rectangular new Winter Palace would enclose a central courtyard hidden from view on all sides.

Rastrelli had managed to preserve the heart of his novel idea, and the new palace would be built from scratch on an embankment cleared of all of its extant structures, including the existing palace. But an extensive system of courtyards that Rastrelli envisioned for Admiralty Meadow south of the

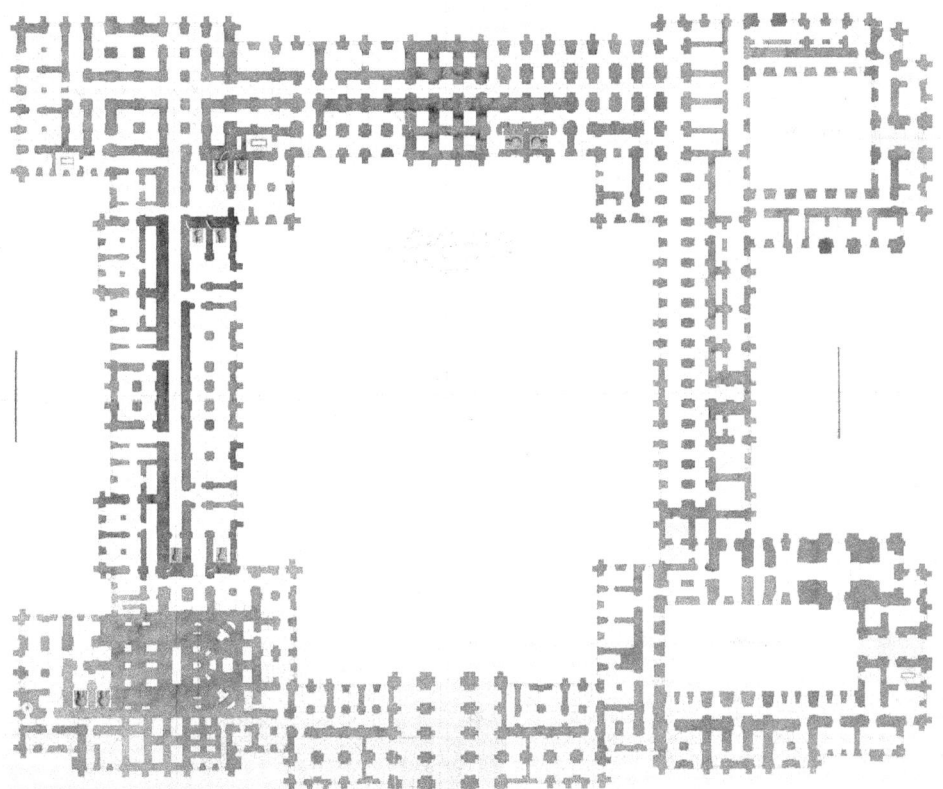

FIGURE 1.02   F. B. Rastrelli. Plan of the ground floor of the Winter Palace. Early 1760s. National Library of Poland.

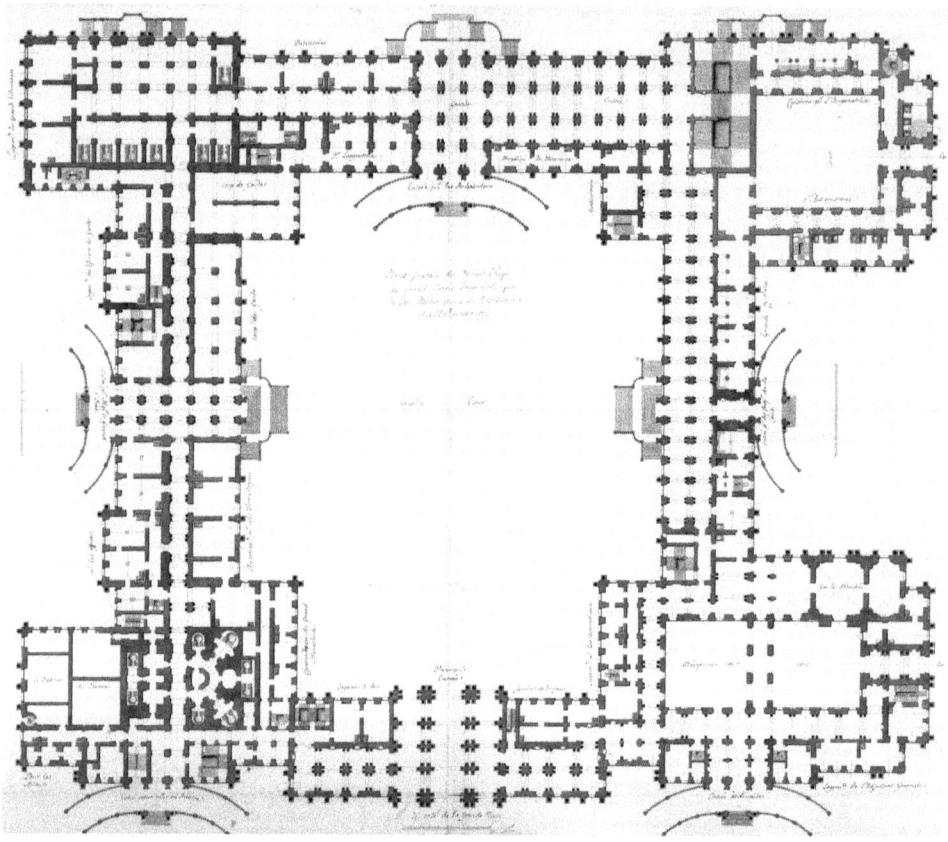

FIGURE 1.03   F. B. Rastrelli. Plan of the parade floor of the Winter Palace. Early 1760s. National Library of Poland.

palace was excised from his earlier scheme, suggesting that this had been at the heart of Elizabeth's objections.[48] Ultimately Rastrelli and Elizabeth did not resolve the question about what to do with a space they each intuited to be important, although Rastrelli's drawings strongly influenced, the monarchs and architects who did, as we will see.

For all the preparatory work that Fermor had already overseen in 1753 and 1754, it was not until some point in 1755 that Rastrelli recorded, "I have begun to build a large Imperial Stone Palace of three floors; this vast building has four façades with a grand courtyard in the middle, along with two smaller ones.... At the far end of one of the long façades, which looks out onto a great space, there will be a large Theatre with three ranks of loges, all of stone;... This great edifice, having already been worked on for two years,

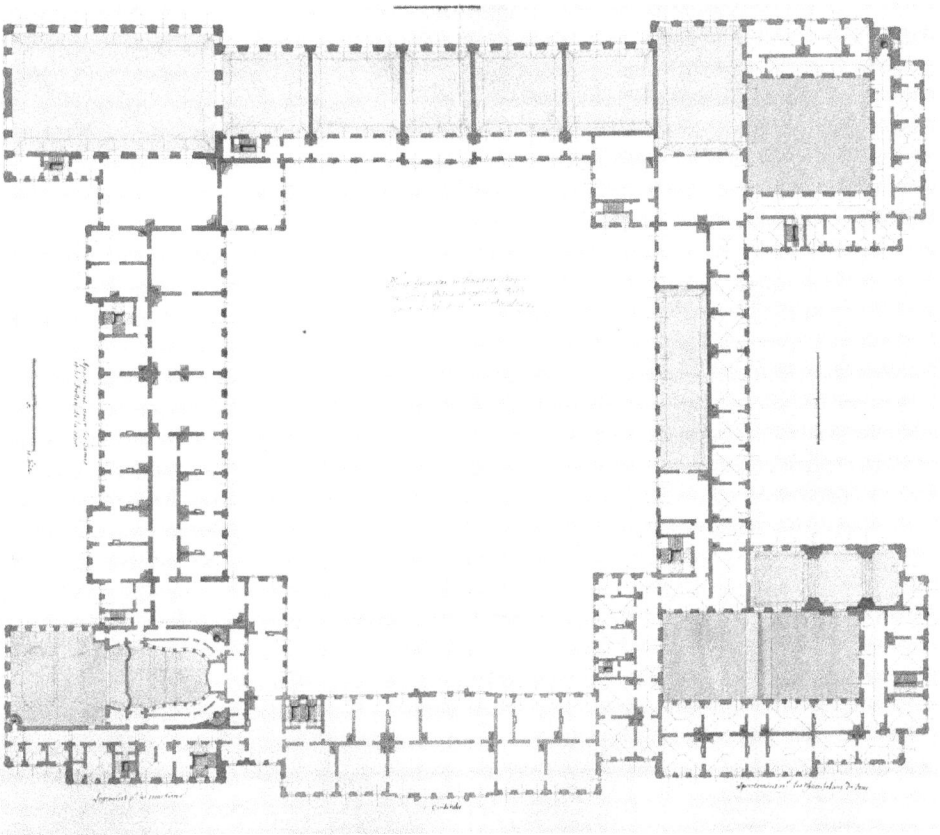

FIGURE 1.04   F. B. Rastrelli. Plan of the top floor of the Winter Palace. Early 1760s. National Library of Poland.

will require three more years for its completion."[49] This little hint suggests that 1755 marked an important turning point in the project: the point at which the empress and her court architect arrived at a meeting of minds. In March 1755 Elizabeth ordered the Senate to allocate 859,555 rubles for the project.[50] In summer 1755 workers tore down the large homes of Counts Iaguzhinskii and Raguzinskii that had stood along the embankment itself and began to shore up the foundation on that site.

The building Rastrelli finally created stretched on its northern and southern façades for nearly eight hundred English feet, and for six hundred feet on its eastern and western flanks. It comprised three stories with a grand central courtyard plus two smaller ones. Altogether the palace boasts 700 windows, excluding the interior courtyard. The original 460 rooms included four large reception halls, facing the Neva, and adjoining formal rooms on the main, so-called parade, floor.[51] The Great Palace Church supported its own cupola in the southeastern quadrant, and the southwestern block boasted an opera house, with four boxes for the imperial family. Elizabeth, her nephew Peter, and his wife were to have private apartments on the parade floor. All of it was built with the greatest of luxury in mind, although in the early years the stoves failed to heat the great halls adequately. The ground floor was dedicated to housekeeping and the second floor to housing courtiers and servants.[52]

The exterior of the building made a striking visual impression, especially from the opposite side of the Neva River. Comparatively low but remarkably long, the Winter Palace commanded its embankment and conveyed an impression of endless expanse. Rastrelli's rococo touches included 250 columns and a variety of window surrounds, which architectural historians invariably describe as imparting "rhythm" to the monumental edifice. The architect's great signature was his use of color; he painted the palace a sandy, light yellow color, detailing all of his columns and decorations in white. From the city side the palace was a bit less imposing, its façade broken by triple gates designed by the architect as well as a covered portico topped by a "lantern," or balcony.[53]

While overseeing this great project Rastrelli simultaneously built a temporary wooden palace into which Elizabeth settled during the construction. This building arose on Nevskii Prospekt, between Great and Small Morskaia Streets. This building, destined to be Elizabeth's final home, also received lavish decoration. She moved in in November 1754 and took up waiting impatiently for the completion of Rastrelli's final masterpiece.

Russia's brief lull between military undertakings ended when Elizabeth responded to Frederick's invasion of Saxony by declaring war on Prussia at the beginning of September 1756. Russia's fortunes in the ensuing Seven Years' War reflected the generally poor state of its military preparations and the empress's reluctance to spend money on her army.[54] The war's impact on Elizabeth's building projects, particularly the Winter Palace, was to slow them down, as the military siphoned off funds during 1756 and early 1757. But through the imperial treasury, Russia's taxpaying population continued to support both efforts, and Rastrelli's builders made progress.

It was not only taxpayers who lent themselves to this imperial project. The great endeavor was making itself felt at a considerable distance from the city, absorbing human and natural resources from every corner of northwestern Russia. As work on the palace dragged on, the stream of goods and people flowing toward St. Petersburg swelled.

2
A PALACE MADE OF WOOD AND BRICKS

Elizabeth Petrovna reigned over a city poised to take flight, thanks to several decades of infrastructural investment by her predecessors. With every brick the new Winter Palace gained luster as the concrete center of a court and monarchy whose capacity for consolidation expanded both tangibly and figuratively in its capital city. Between 1754 and 1762 thousands of people found their way to St. Petersburg to lend a hand in creating the great edifice or to cater to its appetite for contractors and suppliers. In turn, millions of rubles returned to the country from which they had been extracted. For all the foreign designers and craftsmen who contributed to the project, in the end St. Petersburg's Winter Palace was built and paid for by Russians. The impact of the palace project on laborers, contractors, factory owners, and other people who undergirded the economy of Russia's northwest was considerable.

The massive Winter Palace laid out in 1754 probably could not have been built any earlier. Half a century after the city's founding, Russia's northwest was now interlaced with transportation arteries along which timber, clay, sand, and stone found its way to the capital. Likewise, the bureaucracy that oversaw contractors and suppliers had taken shape. However, attracting a sufficient labor force with its requisite layer of skilled craftsmen continued to pose challenges to a court that presided over a complex society of obligated, bound, and free people.

In the second half of the 1750s, Winter Palace construction strained all of these labor and materials markets and revealed a state that was in open competition for resources with the nobles and merchants who were its chief supporters. In its demand for bricks, boards, and laborers the court irritated private builders. Heavy-handed in exerting its prerogatives, the court confiscated goods and labor while summoning all the manpower resources under

state control toward the Winter Palace embankment. At the same time, Elizabeth's court quickened the pace of trade, craft, and investment in the branches
of manufacture closely linked to construction and decoration.

Not the least of the prerequisites for building the capital city and its grand
palace was the Ladoga Canal, one of eighteenth-century Europe's premier
engineering projects. Begun in Peter's time to link St. Petersburg and the river
system of northern Russia, the canal facilitated traffic between the Neva and
Volkhov Rivers by skirting the southern bank of stormy Lake Ladoga. The
first leg of the canal opened in the spring of 1731, but the government was
still expanding the canal decades later. Along this canal sawmills and stone
quarries opened up, and St. Petersburg's builders gained access to the country's
resources. When the Winter Palace project got under way the court expanded
this transportation network. General Fermor was able to direct some of the
funds allocated for the palace in 1755 to inland infrastructure projects supporting the shipment of materials to Petersburg, projects such as sizeable new
bridges over tributaries of the Volkhov and Neva Rivers and the Ladoga Canal
itself.

Equally crucial in mobilizing resources for the new palace was the medium
for publicizing the court's needs. When the Construction Chancellery sought
bids to supply materials and labor, it issued proclamations in the back section
of the semi-official newspaper, the *Sankt-Peterburgskie vedomosti*. Dating from
the 1720s, by the 1750s this paper appeared twice a week and carried news from
home and abroad. Each edition also posted court and private advertisements,
announcements, and solicitations. Interspersed with invitations to private
musical evenings, requests to supply fuel for public and private factories,
and announcements about the comings and goings of foreign residents were
requests from the imperial court inviting proposals to supply comestibles
for the imperial table, hay and oats for the imperial stables, and construction
materials for the Winter Palace and other building projects.[1] During the 1750s
the court's greatest building project was accompanied by the steady expansion
of the gazette's announcement section. The paper's circulation expanded with
the palace, and by 1759 it had climbed to a thousand copies two times a week.
In fact, during the height of Winter Palace construction in the late 1750s, the
paper's circulation reached a peak not seen again until the early 1770s.[2]

Many of the imperial court's solicitations in the *Sankt-Peterburgskie
vedomosti* ran repeatedly, hinting at the strain that palace construction
was imposing on limited resources. St. Petersburg's boomtown atmosphere
intensified after 1754. Overlapping with the Strelna Palace, which was
reaching completion, and the simultaneous construction of the temporary
winter palace on Nevskii Prospekt, the new Winter Palace project demanded

prodigious quantities of a growing list of goods. All of these court projects competed, in the newspaper's solicitations, with the demand for construction materials and fuel from expanding factories—such as the state brick factories straining to fulfill court orders—and the endless appetite for construction and other supplies for the court stables.[3]

In the course of 1754, as the architect and the empress sparred over the question of whether to build the new palace from scratch, the Construction Chancellery was able to begin assembling materials. This office had considerable experience in organizing the empress's manifold projects, and at its head stood the capable General Fermor, a hero of the Turkish and Swedish wars. That summer an Office for the Construction of the Winter Home came into existence, subordinate to the court's Construction Chancellery. While the general awaited final blueprints, he set about procuring quantities of timber, brick, and stone.

ASSEMBLING WOOD AND BRICKS

At the end of January 1754 the court-owned Nazinskii sawmill sought twenty thousand pine trees measuring from twenty-one to twenty-eight feet in height and from fourteen to eighteen inches in girth, suitable for cutting into boards and square beams. Contractors who were prepared to supply these at the prices specified were to present themselves at the Construction Chancellery within the week.[4] In February the newspaper appealed to those "wishing to supply a large number of milled pine boards and squared timbers of various sizes."[5] By July it was soliciting smaller boards and beams, instructing contractors to appear at the Chancellery three days hence.[6]

Production of milled lumber was a relatively new thing in Russia, where the traditional practice of hewing timbers by hand had long held sway. From Peter's time onward officials labored to increase the number of sawmills, because cutting trees into boards was a more efficient use of timber than ax hewing. State agencies such as the Admiralty established their own lumber mills as demand for shipbuilding and other projects proliferated. Peter's faithful disciple Prince A. D. Menshikov established a sawmill at Izhorsk that was later subsumed by the Admiralty and moved closer to the city before expanding in the late 1720s.[7] This "Nazinskii" mill was a key source of milled boards for the Winter Palace project.

By the 1740s Elizabeth's government grew alarmed about the depletion of the forests of the northwest, which were increasingly pressured by ship and wharf building, export demand, and the expansive construction projects of St.

Petersburg and its suburbs. In 1748 Elizabeth decreed that henceforth boards
for vessels must be milled, not hewn. The next year this stipulation extended
to home building, and in order to make milled boards more broadly available,
the government called for the expansion of privately owned water- and wind-
powered sawmills. The sale of hewn timber would be permitted for only five
more years, while the mills were being built. It seems likely that construction
of both the wooden and the brick winter palaces in the mid-1750s contributed
to decrees extending the temporary sale of hewn timbers in 1756, 1757, and
1758, although in 1758 the law did specifically ban floating hewn timbers
downstream to St. Petersburg, "upon threat of confiscation" and lack of access
to the Ladoga Canal.[8] The next year Elizabeth extended her concern to the
supply of firewood for the city's factories, and she decreed that manufactories
that consumed large amounts of fuel, such as glass and brickmaking, should be
located well outside the city's precincts, in order to spread out the pressure on
forests near the capital.[9] The palace project gave the Construction Chancellery
an opportunity to support the government's forestry policies and encourage
the expansion of private sawmills.[10]

As the palace took shape, solicitations for plank and beam lumber appeared
several times every year, both for the temporary palace and for the Winter
Palace itself. By early 1756 the government forbade both merchants and
mill owners to export any kind of wood, milled or not, from the Narva port.
Such wood was to be reserved for public building projects in St. Petersburg,
Kronstadt, and environs, and those who had timber ready to export per
contracts were invited to sell their goods to her majesty's government instead.[11]
In 1758 orders for pine boards increased again, and by 1759 the Construction
Office sought "several thousand finished, dry, milled pine boards without
knots, cracks or shadows."[12]

When Elizabeth finally settled on erecting the new palace from scratch,
she issued a decree revealing the extent of coercion she was prepared to exert
in order to launch her great project. The decree issued on March 7, 1755, and
transmitted to the Senate the next day permitted Fermor to seize cut timber
lying along the shores of the Volkhov, Ladoga, Neva, Mst, Svir, and Sias Rivers,
regardless of who owned it, if it could be floated downstream to St. Petersburg.[13]
The fortunate proprietors whose timber needed to be towed upstream were
allowed to hold onto their building materials. Only the Admiralty could
continue to consume lumber, for shipbuilding, during the construction of
the Winter Palace. It is not hard to imagine the reception this announcement
received when it appeared in the *Sankt-Peterburgskie vedomosti* on March 14.[14]
The Senate now issued regulations that virtually halted the use of wood for
other building projects in the capital.

The call for "several thousand" bricks, of which most of the city's so-called stone buildings were made, first appeared in September 1754. The newly established Winter Palace Construction Office first solicited "the white type of bricks"—that is, bricks made from silicate—from several state brick factories situated in different locations.[15] Rastrelli preferred the silicate bricks because of their strength, which he pronounced superior to the bricks produced in France.[16]

Since the 1740s Elizabeth's government had taken pains to augment the older state-owned brickworks situated upriver from the city, including the Nevskii, Tosenskii, and Ilynskii factories, as the output from privately owned concerns could not satisfy the demand from her multiple building projects. Whether state or privately owned, a brick factory revolved around at least one skilled brickmaker (*obzhigal'shchik*), who knew how to bake the formed and dried bricks in a kiln. Around this one skilled worker a large number of others fulfilled the less skilled work of digging and hauling clay or forming and drying bricks. Throughout the eighteenth century the key to expanding St. Petersburg's brick production lay in attracting or compelling brickmakers to come to the city and settle.

In his day Peter the Great had compelled crown and monastery peasants, *posad* people in the towns, military recruits, and convicts to learn brickmaking, paying them the equivalent of eight to ten rubles per year, mostly in food and provisions.[17] Fully a quarter of the forty-four thousand annual workers drafted (though not necessarily delivered) to build the new capital and adjacent fortresses in 1710 were brickmakers.[18] Nonetheless, the number of brickmakers and bricklayers continued inadequate, leading to Peter's famous decree in 1714 banning all brick construction elsewhere in Russia. That law lured independent contractors to St. Petersburg, among whom were peasants and other skilled brickmakers who received permission to settle permanently in the city's vicinity. By 1720 the upriver brickmakers employed by the government numbered about fifteen hundred, who reportedly were producing three million tiles and twelve million bricks annually.[19]

THE CHALLENGE OF LABOR

So Peter's government had come to understand that the main bottleneck on the production of bricks was the dearth of skilled and unskilled brickmakers. Ol'ga Kosheleva has chronicled Peter's efforts to attract laborers to his new capital. She has demonstrated convincingly that while virtually all of the early settlers were peasants of one kind or another, including soldiers, servants, workers, traders, artisans, and even entrepreneurs, drawn from the unbound taxpaying population (*posad* people) of older towns and from state factories, there was one group not widely represented in St. Petersburg: the serfs of private landlords.[20] Peter aspired to compel and attract industrious workers with requisite skills and large families to settle permanently in the new capital, and those unable to elude orders to move to the Finnish gulf produced one of the original streams that fed the city. At the same time, Koshelova showed that other enterprising folk of the northern region often found their own way to St. Petersburg, where in time they formed another tributary of the pool of original St. Petersburgers. Kosheleva concluded that the early settlement patterns produced a "paradox between efforts to create a 'westernized' city and the spontaneous flood of its peasant population."[21]

This pattern continued through Elizabeth's time. Russian monarchs retained the power to compel crown peasants and soldiers to work on urban projects, but they also tried to attract skilled people to their capital for jobs that paid the going rate and conferred the potentially advantageous status of living in the capital city as legal residents. By the 1740s brickmaking in St. Petersburg combined elements of compulsion and incentive. Public factories made use of soldiers from the Voronezh Regiment, but it was during the 1750s that those presiding over the court's great building projects concluded once and for all that freely hired labor was vastly preferable to the unproductive conscripts. In 1756 the masters of the state brick factories sought to hire six hundred contracted workers "from distant places," but they wound up hiring many from St. Petersburg itself, where the supply of men looking for work was more ample.[22] One estimate suggests that by the end of the century the number of stonemasons and bricklayers in the city grew to about five thousand, although like most construction workers very few actually registered with the police.[23] Both public and private brickworks were organized around the skilled master brickmakers, many of whom were by now on the state payroll. The government leased out its factories to these masters, who contracted to supply a specified number of bricks annually and who did their own hiring and marketing of surplus product. These master-contractors had little incentive to invest in the business themselves, however, as their contracts permitted the government to reclaim the factories at any time, returning the contractor to the status of overseer. At the beginning of the 1740s there were nineteen such operations in the capital, working thirty kilns. In addition, eleven private brickworks operated thirty-two kilns.[24] At mid-century there were enough different brickworks to encourage manufacturers to begin marking their bricks.[25]

People at the Construction Chancellery were sensitive to complaints that it was siphoning off the region's entire supply of bricks and other building materials and driving up prices for whatever found its way onto the market. In April 1755 a long-winded court announcement in the *Sankt-Peterburgskie vedomosti* claimed its decree on bricks and other materials the month before had been misinterpreted:

> It has not escaped the notice of the [Construction] Chancellery that unfounded disclosures have been made to the people concerning brick goods and other manufactured materials, to the effect that it will not be possible for them to undertake private construction with brick, limestone, timbers, or wood under a prohibition from this Chancellery, and that this has caused the observed rise in prices; however, there has been no prohibition of any kind on the free sale of brick and other goods by the Chancellery on Construction, either last year, in 1754, or in this year, 1755, except for the limited demand, for the reconstruction of Her Imperial Majesty's Winter Palace in the coming summer, for only two million bricks. But since other manufacturers in their factories apart from the state factories were able to produce last year in 1754 up to eight million bricks, and if they are able to produce the same number in the current year, then for other public and private construction there remain available for sale six million bricks . . . ; and as for firewood, just as was the case last year, it all remains available for sale to the public, except for the purchases of the glass factories.[26]

Court projects had traditionally depended exclusively on bricks produced by state factories, but in the first years of Winter Palace construction the Construction Chancellery apparently also consumed a quarter of the bricks produced privately. Since the palace consumed sixteen million bricks by mid-1757, it would appear that it absorbed the majority of all bricks produced in the region between 1755 and 1757, protests to the contrary notwithstanding. Eventually the demand for bricks ebbed, and in 1757 the Palace Construction Office posted a notice that in the coming year it would not purchase any bricks from the private brick factories, and that purchase of such materials by private persons was not forbidden. Furthermore, the office of the Nevskii Brick and Tile Factory attested in writing that the price of bricks was not rising.[27] In July and August 1757 the court assured the public that the region's brick industry was producing five million bricks in the current year, of which the palace project would consume only four million "at an inoffensive price," leaving a sufficient number for other public and private building projects.[28] It is not clear why brickmaking capacity in the city had apparently fallen between 1755 and 1757, although it may have been due to labor shortages associated with supplying troops in the opening years of the Seven Years' War.[29]

Labor shortage is one of the great leitmotifs of Russian history, and the building of the Winter Palace offers a glimpse into the St. Petersburg regional labor resources of the mid-eighteenth century. All of the empress's subjects were categorized, as they had been for at least two hundred years, according to their susceptibility to labor and taxes. One of the distinctions most frequently referred to in court documents was between "fiscal [*kazennye*]" and "hired [*vol'nye*]" people. The so-called fiscal people were those on the state payroll, men attached to all kinds of government agencies throughout the realm, as well as thousands of soldiers and sailors. In Peter's day, provinces throughout the country had been required to send labor detachments to the great city building project, but in the face of chronic nonfulfillment of the quotas, this obligation was converted to a monetary tax.[30]

Construction officials in Peter's day bequeathed their successors the conviction that conscripted crown, monastery, and private peasants tended to be poor in quality since village communes did not send their best workers—and many of them drifted away long before they got to the capital. Thus from 1721 onward, Peter's government turned toward employing hired workers from nearby "non-black earth" provinces, where the generally low productivity of agriculture encouraged landowners to permit peasants to travel to the capital on temporary passports for wage work. Even though the Construction Chancellery continued to use convicts, soldiers, and prisoners of war, St. Petersburg slowly became "that place in the country where the large number of people in search of work came together."[31]

"Freely hired" people were thus preferred, but they, too, populated a variety of categories. In 1710 Peter had decreed that a specified number of skilled artisans were to come with their families for permanent settlement in St. Petersburg. They would receive twenty-two rubles per year, about half of it in food, but there was great resistance to this demand, and only about half the demanded forty-seven hundred had arrived in the city by 1712. Thereafter, Peter created the new social category of "free carpenter [*soslovie*]," offering twenty rubles per craftsman, ten for his wife, and five to ten rubles for each child, according to sex. Their first project was the construction of houses for the carpenters themselves.[32] Among the settlers in the city who received the status of permanent resident were also state peasants, private serfs on open-ended passports from their masters, and artisans who were attached to government agencies such as the Admiralty. Runaway peasants also comprised a significant portion of new carpenters, and although officials made an effort to return such people to their masters, their bosses often covered for them and many managed to continue hiding in plain sight.[33]

In the 1740s Elizabeth's officials were willing to resurrect compulsory labor, but they found, as their predecessors had done, that such recruits often lacked qualification.[34] The Winter Palace project makes it clear that the empress felt free to move people on the public payroll from one agency to another and to assign soldiers to her urban construction projects, but that the challenge of finding qualified people persisted.

Some of the fiscal people were numbered among the *raznochintsy*, or "people of various ranks." From early in the life of imperial St. Petersburg, laws categorizing the tsar's subjects by rank and taxpaying status used this designation for "low-ranking civil servants, administrative employees in government offices, and employees of the Court and stables."[35] Many were associated with one or another form of state service such as soldiers' children and canal diggers, people who occupied one of the city's bottommost layers.[36] These were the people who were available to be assigned a variety of jobs connected to building the Winter Palace.

When the empress formally announced her intent to build a new winter home in March 1755 she proclaimed that her Construction Chancellery would assemble an army of skilled craftsmen as well as unskilled laborers who were already on the government payroll, including:

> Good bricklayers, carpenters, blacksmiths, locksmiths, joiners, coppersmiths, foundry workers and caulkers, stonecutters, gilders, painters (*zhivopistsov*), framers, plasterers, and potters, wherever they are fiscal people, namely: on the register of the Military or Admiralty Colleges, at the Kronstadt Canal, dispatched from the Okhta Inspection, at the equipment factories in Tula and at the Sestr River, in the artillery, field, and garrison regiments; all of them are to be turned over to the Construction Chancellery.[37]

She also ordered three thousand men "from full regiments," as well as ten staff officers and ten noncommissioned officers dispatched "for supervision of all this work and the management of the public funds and all materials, and for ensuring the good regulation of all these matters in various places," for the duration of the project without interruption. Completing the military component of the workforce were one hundred "soldiers' sons from the garrison schools in the eastern territories" for training as various craftsmen. Moreover, "the Construction Chancellery may demand from any College, Chancellery, or Province any kind of amendment or assistance, which shall be fulfilled without delay and without further written instructions."[38]

But Elizabeth also intended to make use of "free people who worked by hire, those not from the merchantry or the *raznochintsy*."[39] Such people came from groups free to exchange their labor for room, board, and modest pay, such as townsmen (*meshchane*), especially from Iaroslavl and Kostroma, landlords' peasants on quitrent (*obrok*) who traveled with their masters' permission to the capital for seasonal and temporary labor, and people without passports, probably runaways, whose obscure origins were sometimes overlooked. The Construction Chancellery hired such workers through the mediation of contractors. A typical *Sankt-Peterburgskie vedomosti* announcement from the Palace Construction Office was the October 1754 note seeking "those wishing to supply bricklayers for the coming year 1755."[40]

The contractors (*podriadchiki*) constituted a particular kind of Russian entrepreneur, specialists in mediating the court's construction bureaucracy and the chronically sparse supply of laborers. They were themselves a varied group, hailing from the same mix of peasant and urban people they sought to enlist: merchants, factory owners, government personnel, peasants, and even serfs, who undertook small projects such as building window frames and wheelbarrows.[41] Archival data about them is scarce but suggest that in many cases contractors were simply spokesmen representing a group of workers agreeing to undertake a specific assignment for a specified period and price, whether chopping and hauling firewood or laying brick. As time went on, contracting became its own specialty, and no doubt court officials came to prefer men who had demonstrated an ability to deliver sober and reliable workers. Government contractors typically received big advances, and over time regulations proliferated to protect the Construction Chancellery against contractor bankruptcies.[42]

During the Winter Palace project, the Chancellery solicited thousands of workers through contractors, and the empress's initial interest in exploiting a hired workforce probably intensified between 1756 and 1762, as the campaigns of the Seven Years' War siphoned off tens of thousands of soldiers and new recruits.[43] At any rate, it was during the 1750s that the Chancellery and state brick factories alike grew to openly prefer contracted workers to the relatively unproductive, and at any rate increasingly scarce, conscripts. Apparently even *obrok* serfs came to be seen as less desirable than other people who could be hired on contracts, because such serfs could stay in the city only as long as their masters permitted. In its hiring practices the Construction Chancellery and Winter Palace Construction Office co-opted contractors to serve, effectively, as their own recruiters, combing the northwest for reliable skilled workers and enforcing such regulations as the empress saw fit to decree. The Construction Chancellery negotiated with contractors or leaders of worker-organized crews (*artely*), who supplied workers and oversaw details of their labor, including paying them out of what they drew from the Construction Chancellery.

There are hints in the *Sankt-Peterburgskie vedomosti* that the court's scrupulousness in requiring compliance with passport regulations waxed and waned, which amounted to undermining the most fundamental underpinning of serfdom. Having solicited numbers of skilled bricklayers for over three years, in November 1758 the Construction Office specified for the first time that it sought "skilled bricklayers with printed passports."[44] The Construction Office's appetite for laborers to build the great palace was substantial and ongoing, it coincided with the Seven Years' War, and the court was in direct competition with other builders. Sensitive to charges that it was extracting more than its fair share of resources, the court occasionally made a public show of following its own rules. Nonetheless, in the boomtown atmosphere of early St. Petersburg there were opportunities for men of murky backgrounds to find work, especially if they knew how to lay bricks.

It is worth noting that people from villages or estates belonging to the imperial family—their so-called appanage peasants—were not summoned for the building or, later on, for the staffing of the Winter Palace, with very few exceptions. The court did contract with peasants from villages in nearby provinces for woodcutting and various short-term tasks, but there is no indication that these laborers were from Romanov estates, and at any rate they were paid workers serving on contracts.[45] These labor relations reflected the fact that it was not the Department of Appanages that oversaw the growing number of imperial residences in the capital and its environs but members of the imperial court itself, and eventually the Ministry of the Imperial Court when it was created in the early nineteenth century. The Winter Palace was an imperial home with a court purpose; it was not part of the Romanov patrimony.

The Construction Chancellery having commandeered all the bricklayers it could, including two thousand from Kostroma and Iaroslavl, work on the Winter Palace began in earnest in the spring and summer of 1755.[46] However, the court does not appear to have been entirely scrupulous in respecting the status of those who were "freely hired," because Elizabeth now decreed that Moscow craftsmen were to be sent to St. Petersburg and not allowed to return home, "especially the bricklayers from Iaroslavl and Kostroma, who are needed, of course, this very March."[47] Over 850 Kostroma stonemasons soon set to work creating a socle, or wall base, composed of four hundred square *sazhens* of cut stone. This work took them until early October.[48] At the same time, workers began erecting the wall for the southern façade, and before winter slowed work for the year, they had completed the ground floor and roofed it temporarily so that various craftsmen could be at work inside. At its height the palace construction project employed some four thousand workers, including soldiers and apprentices. Many of them camped in the expansive Admiralty Meadow next to the site, while others bivouacked in settlements on the city's outskirts.[49] Just as it felt compelled to defend its brick consumption, the court was moved to illuminate its hiring practices in the spring of 1755:

> As talk has been going on about bricklayers, carpenters, and other skilled people, it is completely denied that on the strength of Her Imperial Majesty's Decree of 7 March 1755, such skilled people, who come on their own for work to St. Petersburg and who have then been freely hired, will be taken for construction of Her Imperial Majesty's Winter Palace, with only other workers available to satisfy the demand for other public and private construction in Saint Petersburg. Because for the construction of the said Palace for recruiting and bringing forward skilled workers of this kind the Construction Chancellery has purposely dispatched Staff Officers of the Life Guards.[50]

In the following years the chancellery continued to seek contractors willing and able to provide bricklayers and stonemasons in large numbers, as well as men to haul bricks or sand from the brick factories to the palace construction site and to haul away the buildings the empress finally agreed to have torn down. It also periodically asserted the court's willingness to share skilled workers with others, as when it announced in 1761 that it would not hinder those potters hired by the Winter Palace Construction Office from offering tiles for private sale.[51]

TABLE 1. Workers Solicited in the *Sankt-Peterburgskie vedomosti* for Constructing the Winter Palace

1755	3,000 soldiers 100 soldiers' sons for apprenticeships 2,000 bricklayers/stonemasons
1756	1,000 bricklayers 2,000 bricklayers
1757	A large number of free workers for driving piles Workers to haul fill dirt and debris Workers to haul bricks from the factories this winter 2,000 bricklayers for the next year
1758	Workers for hauling bricks from factories to work site Workers to clear Admiralty Meadow of several homes and debris 600 "skilled free bricklayers with printed passports"

1759	Workers for hauling bricks from factory to work site
1760	Unspecified number of "skilled framers" for interior work 700 bricklayers 100 stove makers
1761	Unspecified number of brass workers to make balustrades and vases and to work on the great parade staircase Carvers and goldsmiths who will work for less than "6,436 rubles"

STIMULATING ENTERPRISE AND MANUFACTURING

The palace project was also a boon for entrepreneurially minded contractors who could supply and ship stone, alabaster, and other heavy cargoes from elsewhere in Russia or from abroad. For example, in February 1757 the Construction Chancellery sought "those willing to haul bricks, tiles, clay and slabs . . . by their own means, in their own ships."[52] The infrastructure of private shipping was well developed by then, since from the early days of the city's existence contractors supplying state agencies accounted for over one-third of all mercantile shipments coming to the capital.[53] There was also plenty of work for haulers of bricks, boards, fill dirt, and debris. In the later years of the project the chancellery sought someone who could transport twenty thousand *poods* of gypsum stone, used for plaster, from Riga.[54] In June 1761 people were invited to haul in sand and other sorts of fill for finishing the meadow south of the palace.[55]

Those who could both supply and transport decorative stone and glass were likewise in high demand throughout the palace-building years. For example, in January 1754 the chancellery sought plate glass, and the next month it solicited "Kazan or foreign alabaster."[56] In the fall of that year the newspaper first hailed suppliers of Putilov stone, the famous Petersburg building material used to cover the lower portion of brick walls as both a decorative and a waterproofing material.[57] Thereafter to the ongoing call for Putilov stone were added solicitations for boards, iron nails, bricks, clay, wild stone, and white marble.

In the final years of the project, contractors were beckoned to supply quantities of fish-glue and finished wood required for furniture making. In the course of 1757 the Senate allocated 3,340 rubles to the gilding of decorations and by 1760 the gold work being done in the palace called for shipments of "Parisian poliment," "French chalk," and orpiment, an arsenic sulfide that served as a gold-colored paint. Later in the year the chancellery solicited curved moldings, French and Bohemian glass, transom windows, parquet floors, English locks of brass and iron, thirty-five brass stove dampers made to specification, and copper legs for stoves in the living quarters, one thousand gilded and six hundred not.[58]

The construction of the Winter Palace proved a boon to several existing and new manufactories, as well. The chancellery repeatedly sought cabinetry contractors who could supply doors, windows, panels, and cornices produced to specifications. It reinvigorated the wallpaper manufacturing business, particularly the firm of the Englishman Martin Butler, who held a ten-year monopoly granted by the Senate in 1751 for the factory he had established in Moscow with George Thompson. In 1755 the government reaffirmed this charter, while also reaffirming tariffs on imports of English wallpapers. Butler's factory could produce wallpapers of linen as well as the cheaper paper, a process the English first mastered.[59] The Senate also approved Saxon wallpaper manufacturer Johann Friedrich Leman's request to build a factory in St. Petersburg from which he could fulfill his commissions for the imperial palace, extending an advance of one thousand rubles. Leman built a state-owned factory on Vasilevskii Island and hired ten apprentices, who were to be trained according to the Senate contract.[60] The court was clearly interested in building up native skill even as it bought foreign products.

Elizabeth's overlapping projects and the strain on both fiscal and managerial resources combined to slow work on the palace and to frustrate its mistress. Fermor had been returned to active military service at the start of the war. By the middle of 1758, with the Winter Palace far from complete and her impatience mounting, Elizabeth issued a series of new decrees meant to hasten progress. She appointed Brigadier Dannenberg, successful builder of the Izmailovskii Regiment's barracks, as overall head of the Winter Palace effort.[61]

By the end of 1761 the imposing edifice now graced the upper left bank of the Neva River, facing the watery expanse that Peter had envisioned as a city center. The stucco covering the bricks was painted in the prevailing palette of baroque St. Petersburg, yellow ochre, with the columns and architectural details picked out in white.[62] Gazing from one of the expansive windows on the Neva enfilade a visitor could take in the city's most interesting and beautiful sights. Just downriver on the opposite bank stood Menshikov's elegant Dutch baroque palace and nearby the buildings housing Peter's Twelve Colleges and Kunstkamera. A bit to the right, on the Petrograd side, stood the impressive Peter and Paul Fortress with its elegant church spire towering overhead.

Carpenters, painters, goldsmiths, glassworkers, brass workers, and creators of the building's remarkable parquet floors labored to complete the interior of a home for which its patron had impatiently waited for seven years. The architect's shifting but meticulous vision, the empress's decorous pace of decision-making, her insistence on building a temporary palace simultaneously, and the fiscal and labor demands of the Seven Years' War had all converged to slow the progress on a building whose ground floor had been completed at the end of 1755. By the Feast of St. Nicholas in December 1761, however, the empress's household could foresee the impending move into the new edifice. Whether Elizabeth toured the building in these last weeks of the year we do not know. It would have been kind of history to permit such a visit, however, because she died on December 25 in the temporary wooden palace on Nevksii Prospekt.

THE PALACE'S FIRST MASTER

So it came to pass that the first Russian ruler to occupy Rastrelli's baroque masterpiece was the doomed Peter III. In the six months of his reign Peter offered formal deference to his predecessor and hosted the ceremonial

FIGURE 2.01 Joseph Charlemagne. *View of the Winter Palace from the Neva River*. 1853. The State Hermitage Museum, St. Petersburg. Photograph by Pavel Demidov.

duties of winter and early spring such as the New Year's reception for foreign dignitaries and grandees and the blessing of the waters (of the Moika in this case) at Epiphany from the wooden palace on Nevskii. Like the deceased empress, Peter longed to occupy the fabulous palace, and he urged workers to ready it for Easter. Thus more stoves and dampers were ordered in January, plate glass and "marble tables with carved legs decorated with gold, below the specified price," in February, and in March officials hurried to clear the meadow outside the palace's southern façade of the construction debris that had accumulated there over the years.[63]

The announcement directing those interested in removing debris from the "public courtyards of Kruys, Olsuf'ev, Musin Pushkin and Saltykov," buildings that lined the meadow, to apply at the main Court Chancellery appeared in the *Sankt-Peterburgskie vedomosti* on March 19. But with Easter just around the corner, the new ruler grew impatient and, according to the courtier Andrei Bolotov, ordered the city's police to go door-to-door announcing to the city's poorest residents that they were welcome to come and take from the meadow free of charge whatever they could carry away. He recounted in later years that the great "Admiralty Meadow" was in 1762 "completely cluttered with innumerable shanties, huts, lean-tos, and tents, in which lived all the masters who built the Winter Palace, and where the materials were prepared and worked on. Moreover, there were whole mountains of wood chips, plaster debris, half-finished bricks, detritus, and every other kind of rubbish."[64] The emperor reportedly watched from one of the palace windows, chuckling to himself as city residents cleared the space of every stick, board, and broken brick within a matter of hours.[65]

In the morning of Saturday, April 6, 1762 members of the Holy Synod gathered at the Great Palace Church for a ceremony at which Archbishop Dmitri of Novgorod consecrated it as the Church of the Resurrection of the Lord.[66] At noon the emperor emerged in procession from the wooden palace on Nevskii Prospekt and proceeded over the next six hours toward the "newly constructed stone Winter Palace," enjoying a twenty-one-gun salute from both fortresses. The next day, Easter Sunday, the tsar received dignitaries of both sexes from midnight until six o'clock in the morning, walking them through the formal rooms on the parade floor of the palace. Then he led his guests into the palace church for matins. At the conclusion of those prayers he greeted each of the guests by hand before the Easter liturgy began. At the conclusion of divine services Peter returned to greet his newly arrived guest the Princess of Holstein, in whose company he dined with "106 people of both sexes who were admitted by ticket."[67] Italian musicians and singers entertained the diners and a canon salute underscored toasts to the monarch's health. If Peter's wife,

Catherine, or son, Paul, attended this Easter celebration the official description makes no mention of them.

The consecration of the palace church and the celebration of Easter required two pages of description in the *Sankt-Peterburgskie vedomosti*, but the second and final of Peter III's formal entertainments in the Winter Palace took more than twice as much space. This was the celebration of a peace treaty with Prussia on June 9. Peter's Holsteiner loyalties and Prussophile foreign policy were chief among the reasons for disaffection among a growing number of courtiers and guards officers, but he surrounded himself with over two hundred great nobles and members of the Preobrazhenskii Regiment, leading them through the parade halls and galleries to the palace church for a liturgy and prayers of thanksgiving. Following the services both Peter and his wife, Catherine, received greetings from city residents and clergy arrayed on the meadow before the palace, as well as musket volleys from regiments on parade there which Peter, himself, went down to command.

The meal following these civic and military formalities on what would one day be Palace Square took place in the great gallery on the parade floor of the palace, where Peter and Catherine received Frederick the Great and his wife. Ninety guests accompanied the monarchs at the head table while 440 other courtiers, officers, and foreign dignitaries were seated in other galleries. After music and toasts the imperial couple retreated to Peter's private quarters, where Catherine watched as her husband conferred military decorations on a number of his favored courtiers, beginning with his mistress, Elizabeth Vorontsov, who received the Order of St. Catherine. The celebrations continued on the next day, presided over again by Peter and Catherine and the Prussian monarchs, who again enjoyed a meal in the palace galleries with 90 at their table and 140 arrayed in other spaces. Following this meal the entire company moved to the windows of the antechamber to watch a fireworks extravaganza across the Neva that provided allegories of eternal love and friendship between Russia and Prussia. The evening concluded with an artillery salute and the singing of a choir.[68]

During his six-month reign Peter III conferred upon the beautiful new Winter Palace, and by extension upon its thousands of builders, the dignity that was due an edifice meant to house a European dynasty of the first rank. Upon the court architect who had labored for so many years to beautify St. Petersburg he conferred the Order of St. Anna and the rank of general major. In May Rastrelli received a gratuity of three thousand rubles.[69]

Peter III filled the building he had inherited with important foreigners, Russian noblemen and women, and with Guards officers whom he favored and almost certainly feared. He pioneered what was to be a century and a half of resplendent dinners and entertainments in the grandiose rooms. But the imperial court over which Peter struggled to rule was the political province of men who deeply distrusted him and of a woman who outwitted him. One week after the *Sankt-Peterburgskie vedomosti* published its account of the peace treaty celebrations, Catherine and her allies deposed the emperor, and within a few more months he was dead.

The new Winter Palace did not bring either Elizabeth or her immediate successor much luck. But for the thousands of brickmakers, timber cutters, carpenters, bricklayers, and craftsmen, the palace project held out the kind of desperate opportunity that people latched onto all over Europe in the eighteenth century. Sometimes slipping away from distant masters and sometimes bearing the humiliations of government service, builders of the Winter Palace took on poorly paid work with a silver lining: the possibility that they might start on the bottom rung of the court ladder and begin to make their way up. For many across Russia's Northwest it meant the possibility of earning seasonal pay and returning to the country. For others, it meant staying on in St. Petersburg and becoming urban people. Those people found themselves residing in a city increasingly defined by the imperial stage they helped to build.

3

A NEW CITY CENTER

Working people drawn to St. Petersburg by the court's great building projects found few accommodations when they arrived. They erected shelters on the city's many islands, within walking distance of their work sites. Peter the Great intended that most people would settle on Vasilevskii Island, but as George Munro has written, "the planned city is not always the city that results."[1] In fact, by 1720 the largest part of the St. Petersburg's population lived on the Admiralty side, crowding around the upper embankment on the south shore of the Neva.[2] This tug to the south—as if a refusal by Peter's people to accept any further inconveniences—proved to be permanent.[3] Steady population growth on this side of the river increased the value to the city's humble people of the open commons along the southern flank of the Admiralty moat and behind the imperial and noble palaces facing the Neva. At the same time the court's decision to establish its beachhead on the southern bank of the river imparted ceremonial significance to the same turf. As such the so-called Admiralty Meadow was the zone where court and city met. It was a more or less accidental process by which this space became Palace Square, the future center of monarchical display and, eventually, of civic life.

For the first five decades of the city's existence an expansive commons stretched out behind the Admiralty and extended east behind the riverfront palaces. The state of this open field varied with the seasons. It was an impassable bog in spring and fall, a snowy waste in the winter, and a dry expanse of dust clouds in the summer. This neglected space was attractive to the workmen and fortune seekers converging on the boomtown capital. Squatters threw up every manner of wooden shelter, eliciting periodic official orders to clear the space of all construction.[4]

In the wake of devastating fires in the late 1730s Empress Anna directed the new Commission on Construction to undertake the planning of streets and squares.[5] Tackling the untamed Admiralty Meadow this commission ordered the planting of trees along Great Meadow Street, which bordered the entire southern extremity of the esplanade from Anna's palace to the western end of the Admiralty. The commission called also for entrenching a canal along this boundary that would be protected by a railing and a latticework or border of trees.[6] Thus imperial prerogative began to encroach bit by bit on the urban commons.

ORDERING COURT SPACE

While Elizabeth made do with renovating her predecessor's winter home for the first decade of her reign, the expanding population of the city that supported this monarchy was digging in nearby, along the rivers and canals of the Admiralty quarter. The most densely built part of what was coming to be known as the Palace Embankment was east of the imperial winter home. Behind the waterfront homes of the great nobles arose a crowded quarter housing Russian and foreign workers, originally known as the German Settlement. The alley first called German Street (later Millionnaia) was a short lane extending from the monarch's winter home to Tsaritsyn Meadow.[7] By the 1740s this short stretch housed twice as many buildings as the much longer expanse of Nevskii Prospekt between the Admiralty and the Fontanka River. By Elizabeth's time the construction brigades had yielded to medics, chefs, commissars, merchants, brokers, and a smattering of higher officials: in other words, to the merchants and court employees who now tended to the ruler and her household.[8] At the same time, it was still quite inconvenient to access Admiralty Meadow from the south, since there was no bridge across the Moika River.[9]

From the very beginning of her reign the empress sought to exert control over the palace precincts verging on Millionaia and the meadow behind the Winter Palace, but her efforts met with repeated disappointment. Whereas Elizabeth and her courtiers could enjoy a stroll in the expanding Summer Garden along the Moika River, her more humble subjects were not admitted there, and they converged instead in the precincts that were steadily acquiring luster from the proximity of a glittering court.[10] The long expanse of the Admiralty Meadow persisted as a place for public festivals during Shrovetide and other seasons and in ordinary times attracted working people who converged in the neighborhood to frequent informal food shops, street vendors, and drinking establishments.[11] These were the activities that Elizabeth endeavored to regulate as she sought to discipline popular behavior in the palace precinct.

A decree from late 1742 required the major streets of the capital to be cleared of taverns and cook shops, all of which had to be removed to designated places and markets. People selling fruit as well as wineshops (*pogreby*) were to move off the streets and into courtyards. Elizabeth demanded that signboards be removed from the major streets. The laws testify to the limits of absolute monarchy in the face of persistent patterns of urban life, however. Ten years later Elizabeth issued a new decree reiterating all the terms of the 1742 law, indignantly recording the fact that "now there are on Millionaia Street, right across from the old Winter Palace and all the way to the Moika, taverns where just like before there is entry from the streets."[12] She demanded that the police broadcast the regulations and that the Senate enforce them precisely.

What sealed the fate of this future Palace Square was Elizabeth's eventual acquiescence in Rastrelli's scheme to turn the new imperial Winter Palace toward the city. As early as the 1730s, when Rastrelli father and son had worked on Anna Ioanovna's cobbled-together palace, they had created a ceremonial entrance facing the Admiralty, effectively turning the "front" of the palace away from the river. They had also put the southern flank of the palace to new use, as the entrances facing the expansive Admiralty Meadow provided access for the scores of honor attendants and serving people who now came and went.[13] Perhaps it had escaped their patron's notice but the imperial home was slowly being turned toward the growing city, and toward the open expanse on its southern face. The design that Elizabeth finally approved for her new Winter Palace made this move permanent.

This reorientation focused imperial attention on the section of the rough-and-tumble Admiralty Meadow that extended south from the palace façade to the triangular point formed by the intersection of the Moika River and Nevskii Prospekt. Rastrelli and Elizabeth seemed to agree that this space required intentional design, but apparently they failed to arrive at a meeting of the minds. To satisfy his patron Rastrelli drafted several variations of the idea for a "circular square," and each successive drawing simplified and opened up the vista facing the southern flank of the palace.[14] It appears that as his thinking evolved Rastrelli was coming to see the need for a great formal entrance to the palace from the south. While the Neva enfilade would house important ceremonial features of the palace, the architect was beginning to envision an edifice that faced a beautified square or park. Here he would position the empress's apartments as well as a magnificent palace church and theater.

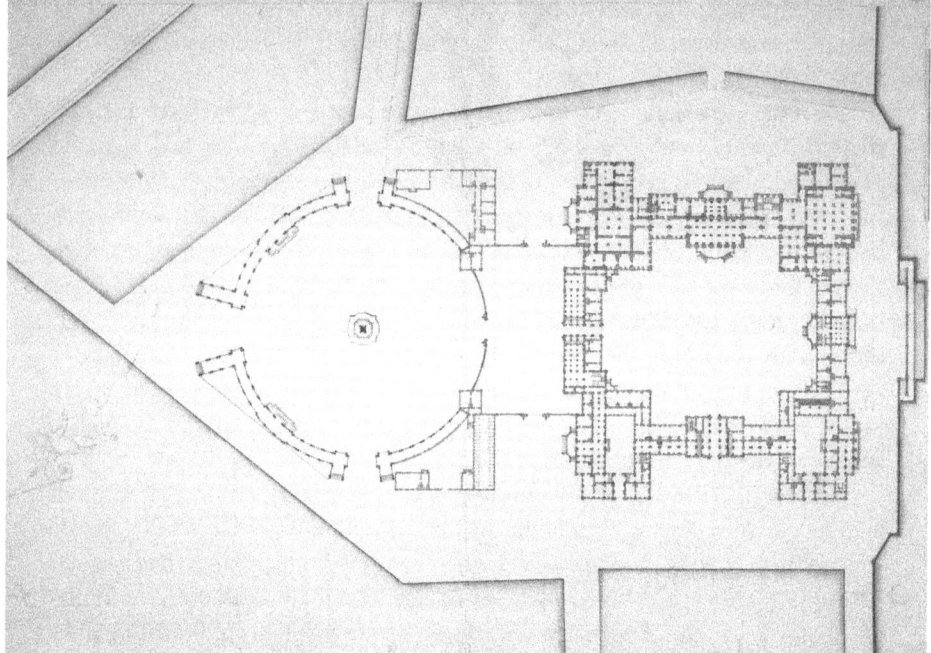

FIGURE 3.01   F. B. Rastrelli. Plan to expand the palace while preserving the third Winter Palace and the home of F. M. Apraksin. Variant B. 1753. The National Library of Poland.

Among the collection of Rastrelli's drawings and notes preserved in the National Library of Poland there is more than one plan for the square. One variant details instructions for razing the homes of "General-marshal Shepelev, Golovin and Krius," which stood on various parts of the projected plaza. In place of these structures, at the extremity of the triangle, the architect called for the erection of "servants' quarters, the Olsuf'ev Palace, the old Winter Palace, the wooden Winter Palace and the Neiman Palace," several of which would be moved from the Neva embankment where they were in the way of the new, expansive imperial edifice.[15] In another variant there are no substantial buildings apart from an amphitheater and small service structures squaring off the northern part of the circle, closest to the palace.[16]

After many revisions and much consideration the monarch granted Rastrelli permission to clear the meadow south of the palace, so that a great square could be created on the whole southern flank of the new building.[17] Although she conceded to the architect the liberty to start the building from scratch, to turn it toward the south, and to clear the expanse in front of it, Elizabeth still rejected the extensive system of courtyards and gardens

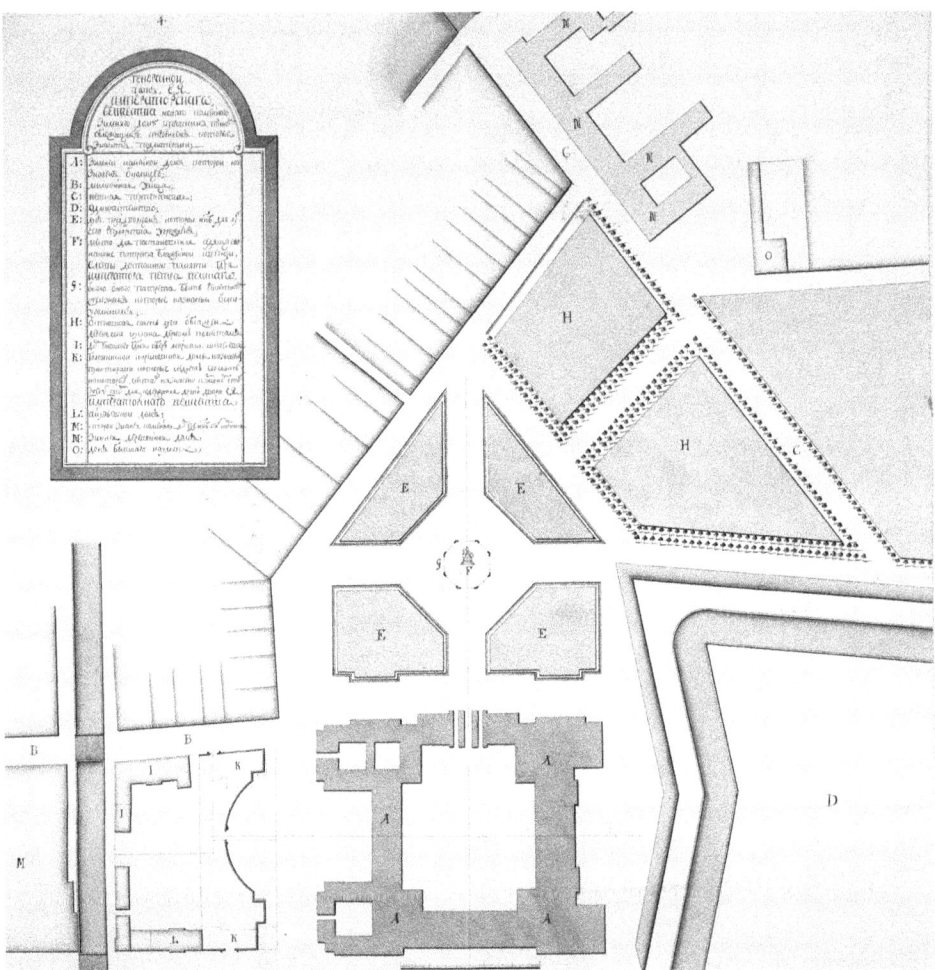

FIGURE 3.02 F. B. Rastrelli. General plan for palace square and surrounding buildings. Variant 1761–1762. The National Library of Poland.

envisioned by Rastrelli.[18] Nonetheless, between 1753 and 1755 Elizabeth did gradually embrace some elements of Rastrelli's vision of a transformed Admiralty Meadow. In particular she approved his idea of a great circular space opening up on the south flank of the palace, at the center of which would stand a monumental equestrian statue of Peter the Great, sculpted by Rastrelli's father.[19]

Rastrelli seems to have been motivated by his idea that this semicircular space should accommodate a multitude of people and offer an appropriate perspective from which to view the new palace's southern flank. He appears to have been the first to propose that the great imperial palace on the embankment should face the city that had arisen more or less spontaneously "behind" it. However, it is not altogether clear what kind of people Rastrelli thought might mingle in this space. One specific version of Palace Square that Elizabeth rejected in early 1754 called for a much larger plaza than currently exists, with its center approximately where the General Staff building stands today. In this version, the southern extremity of the plaza would have been bounded by a curved amphitheater, giving the ensemble of plaza and palace together the feel of an eighteenth-century country estate. As the architectural historian N. Veinert observed, in this arrangement the palace "would not have been so much a part of the city as the city would have become part of the Palace grounds, a great *cour d'honneur* along the lines of the Tsarskoe Selo Palace Park."[20]

Perhaps Elizabeth envisioned a more publicly oriented court space suitable for mounting displays of military and cultural spectacle to a wider group of people including city residents. If so, this was something St. Petersburg generally lacked in the first half of the century. Keenan chronicles the St. Petersburg–based court's gradual ascendance as the center of Russia's representational culture in this period, a process that required occasional convocations of urban subjects to share in and observe court spectacles. By mid-century the scale of court display was outstripping the spaces available along Nevskii Prospekt or at Trinity Square on the Petrograd side.[21] The river itself only accommodated military or court pageants when it was frozen.[22] Keenan observes that, although most of the public celebrations staged by the court marked events on the church calendar, in Elizabeth's time these were also taking on distinctly civic, and even military, garb.[23] It is possible that she sensed the need for a public plaza where larger displays could be staged year-round. At any rate, Elizabeth died before arriving at a conclusion about what to do with the meadow/square, and without giving final approval to any of Rastrelli's drawings.

Despite his patron's rejection of his ideas, Rastrelli's influence on the space was profound. The current Palace Square reflects his circular solution to the problem posed by the direction of the Moika River as it angles from the Winter Canal to Nevskii Prospekt, and later architects retained Rastrelli's circular shape. But most important, in his designs for the square, Rastrelli reoriented the palace itself, elevating the southern façade to primacy over the Neva and Admiralty flanks, and pointing the palace toward the most populous section of the city. He projected the great palace gate and a second-floor belvedere toward this space.

ENVISIONING A PALACE SQUARE

Although it fell to Elizabeth's successors to determine how they would use the square, she had fixed this space as one where ruler and ruled could regard each other at close, if regulated, range. Thirty years before the urban revolt that undid French absolutism, Russia's ruler had solidified her grip on the heart of her capital city. In the century that followed, the Romanovs faced no threat from the people of St. Petersburg, who could observe their comings and goings from the Winter Palace at surprisingly close quarters.

Even so, the actual shape of its architectural ensemble on the square emerged only slowly. Ideas about how to order this pivotal space gestated for several decades, and it may be that the indecision reflected subtle resistance. For one thing, the imperial court did not own all of the buildings on the meadow. It proved difficult to get the public to comply with Senate regulations. Further, rulers seemed to have trouble envisioning precisely what kind of uses they needed to make of the square. Russia's eighteenth-century empresses had few models for the kind of urban space that presented itself in the lee of their principal home.

During the course of her long and significant reign Catherine II (1762–1796) presided over many projects to beautify her capital city, but in the first decade and a half she was occupied with weighty military and domestic matters that delayed her urban reform efforts. Within a few years of taking power she launched a great project to transform Russia's legal and judicial system and shortly thereafter found herself enmeshed in a long war with the Ottoman Empire. In the midst of that war came an outbreak of plague in Moscow. The empress also undertook long sojourns to far-flung outposts of her empire. The most serious popular challenge of her reign also came in the early 1770s, as millions of trans-Volga peasants joined Emelian Pugachev's rebellion.

As a result, although she solicited projects of urban planning and beautification at the very beginning of her reign, Catherine did not allocate funds to fulfill them until the 1770s.[24] In 1764 she endorsed city designer Aleksei Kvasov's vision for the unfinished Palace Square, which retained Rastrelli's circular shape. Kvasov's plan required the removal of several buildings on the western side of the square, and here the court gradually was able to erect a series of new buildings for favored institutions and courtiers. In 1766 the Free Economic Society office was established at the intersection of Palace Square and Nevskii Prospekt. Meanwhile, the court very gradually acquired the properties along the Millionaia (eastern) side of Palace Square. By now this space sported several private houses, and the view from the palace took in the rear courtyards of homes facing the Moika River.[25] Over the course of Catherine's reign the court established its prerogative over the entire square, eventually acquiring all of the privately owned buildings and razing many of them. Catherine deployed this valuable resource, proximity to the Winter Palace, in a typically patrimonial way: she granted buildings to favored courtiers, institutions, and lovers. Neither she nor her counselors conceived of this plaza as a truly public space, so they resisted efforts to unify the whole with a coordinated architectural ensemble. For example, Elizabeth's temporary wooden winter palace stood crumbling in disrepair at the far end of the square's triangular terminus until 1767. In that year Catherine had the old place razed and gave the site to her police chief, N. I. Chicherin.[26]

After a decade of war, pestilence, and rebellion Catherine finally turned her attention to the Palace Square, directing the Academy of Arts to conduct a contest seeking designs for the space. The winner was Iurii Felten (Georg Veldton), Rastrelli's chief apprentice, who adapted his master's semicircular solution, proposing to build three matching buildings joined by curved gates to complete the shape, with a portal composed of a series of Doric columns.[27] Catherine had these edifices built and bestowed one of them upon Count Brius, then Petersburg's governor. Another she gave to her young favorite, Aide-de-camp Alexander Lanskoi.[28]

When Catherine imposed order and elegance on what had once been the neglected semi-rustic expanse "behind" the Neva palaces she was ordering her imperial capital and bestowing upon her august forebear's frontier city a true ceremonial center. As the Winter Palace turned to face the falcate plaza, the expanse lost its rustic character, but cabbies and other humble people still occupied the Palace Square and its periphery. The nineteenth-century city historian Mikhail Pyliaev chronicled the iron "warming stations"—round, open structures inside which people could gather about a stove—"all around" the Winter Palace, established by Catherinian decree.[29] The German painter Christian Geisler etched one of these structures at the end of the eighteenth century. In his picture, about a dozen men of various ranks, including cabbies, workmen, and officers, are crowded sociably around a small, smoking stove.[30] Catherine's solicitude for the hardworking cabbies (*izvozshchiki*) was especially appropriate, as they were increasingly the glue that held the sprawling city together.

In fact, the city over which Catherine began to reign in the middle of 1762 was growing at a breakneck pace. The Winter Palace and other imperial building projects had attracted thousands of people who wound up settling permanently in the city. Between 1750 and 1784 the population of the city more than doubled, from 95,000 to 192,000.[31] By the 1760s the lopsided preponderance of men in the city was well established, as they comprised

FIGURE 3.03   Christian Geisler. A warming station outside the Winter Palace, late eighteenth century. M. I. Pyliaev, *Staryi Peterburg* (1887), 167.

over 60 percent of all residents. The largest part of the population crowded into the three Admiralty districts closest to the Winter Palace, and although these central precincts housed the city's wealthiest nobles and merchants they were also home to a large number of servants, construction workers, and other laborers who often took lodgings in the basement of grand houses or the bottom floors of buildings under construction. As the population continued to expand (to 220,000 by 1800, and to 425,000 by 1825), working people settled in outlying districts closer to their places of employment where rents were more affordable.[32] Thus Petersburg's expanding population flocked especially to the south of the city center, but also to the Petrograd side and Vasilevksii Island.

The outlying regions of the city attracted less police scrutiny than the central zone, and this meant less regulation of behavior and also less attention to cleanliness and sanitation. Over the course of the eighteenth and nineteenth centuries Petersburg's neighborhoods grew more segregated by occupation and developed distinct traditions, often centered around one major church or square. In their rare leisure hours, working people gathered at such sites to celebrate holidays and enjoy each other's company, but on great dynastic and civic occasions or during the Shrovetide festivals associated with the week before Lent, and when otherwise bid by their sovereign, thousands of city people made their way to Palace Square. When they did so they found themselves in the lee of a building meant to overwhelm observers from all sides. The inordinate length of the straw-colored palace was better absorbed from the far bank of the Neva, but standing in its shadow also made an impression. What people saw in the eighteenth and nineteenth centuries was an extremely long but not very tall edifice of light yellow, with its rank upon rank of columns and architectural details painted white. Encircling the roof of the palace stood scores of stone statues.[33]

Sometimes people gathered at the abutting Admiralty side entrance just to watch the grandees who assembled there before entering the palace for court events. At such times the police were reportedly hard-pressed to impose order on the scene. Pyliaev maintains that on big court occasions the great carriages of noble guests entirely covered Palace Square, but the bedecked notables attempting to enter the palace at the west-facing entrance had to make their way through "crowds of people gathered in numerous groups all over the square to cast a glance at the arriving grandees. The police fulfilled their duties with the aid of blows from their batons," forcing the onlookers to make a path for the invited guests. It was not much easier for guests to make their way up the stairway inside the palace thanks to the "crowds of servants."[34]

How did Catherine use the Palace Square, which was continuously being refashioned during her reign? What did her use of it suggest about her notion of monarchy? The most memorable example comes from early in her reign, in a performance that blended court and public purposes in a spectacle of enlightenment and imperial monarchy.[35] This was the so-called carousel, a mock medieval tournament staged on Palace Square in 1766. After a year of preparation Catherine mounted this spectacle involving a number of court ladies (in chariots) and gentlemen (on horseback), formed into four separate teams or "quadrilles" representing four different civilizations: Slavs, Romans,

Indians, and Turks. The event took place twice in the summer of 1766, on June 16 and July 11. The master of ceremonies, Prince P. A. Golitsyn, oversaw construction on the Palace Square of a temporary amphitheater measuring 180 yards by 220 yards, to which court officials admitted people who had procured tickets.[36] He dispensed the tickets, "first to notable persons of both sexes, including all military and civil service ranks and all who were appropriately dressed."[37] These groups represented a remarkable range of social ranks, if the description is correct, because there was a vast and rarely transcended distance between the lowest civil service or military ranks and the great merchants and nobles of St. Petersburg. The attention to dress suggests that officials were interested not only in attracting orderly people of quality but also in creating an appealing backdrop for the spectacle. But masses of other people came to get a glimpse of the proceedings as well, and they lined the streets all around the Palace Square. The empress and her son, Paul, took their places in specially constructed loges facing each other across the course of the carousel.

What the spectators saw was a series of European-inspired contests for both men and women, including races and javelin throwing, and a procession of four different dances performed by courtiers in appropriate costumes, "which sprang from correct information about old and new history."[38] When the public festivities concluded, the performers marched to the Summer Palace, where Catherine conferred diamond-studded prizes upon winners of the various contests.

In choosing to host the spectacle outside the walls of her ceremonial residence, Catherine added to the luster of both the new Winter Palace and its emerging Palace Square. A broad array of official St. Petersburg was accommodated as spectators, seated in a temporary amphitheater that boasted six rising rows of seats on all four sides, the lowest rank of which started about eight feet above ground. From this vantage point they could watch a spectacle carried out on a path of about five yards wide. A quintessential court festivity, the grand carousel was nonetheless mounted in the heart of a populous capital city. Although it was unlikely that urban spectators could see much of the show from behind the towering amphitheater, they no doubt did witness the procession of the four different quadrilles from "the several places they were stationed at in different and opposite parts of the City," each preceded by a band playing music from "its" country.[39] If Catherine had not wanted the public looking on she could have staged this event at Tsarskoe Selo or Peterhof, but here in the city center, during the festive atmosphere of St. Petersburg's white nights, the monarch could enlist her stylish courtiers in a playful performance of Russia's European elegance at least partially witnessed by the city's working people. Catherine gave those crowding onto the verge a taste of enlightenment, staged at least partly for their benefit. From this show the people of her capital city might intuit something about history, about modern orchestral music, about refined amusements, and about the proper way to behave as a backdrop for their monarch's court.

THE NEVA FAÇADE

Even as Catherine experimented with the public purposes to which Palace Square might be put, she also extended traditional use of its other flanks, including those facing the Admiralty and the Neva. Petersburg had not abandoned its maritime character, and in the warm months people could line the banks of all three islands facing the Great Neva to watch cannon displays and fireworks emanating from the Peter and Paul Fortress or the Admiralty. There was no permanent Palace Bridge until the early twentieth century, but people could cross in ferries or small vessels as well as via seasonal pontoon bridges. In the winter the river froze solid, making it by far the most convenient season for moving around the water-laced city. Not only did a regular ice-road open up across the Neva at the Palace Embankment, but the river also became a playground for city people who came to take advantage of ice slides and other amusements often erected at court expense. It is tempting to imagine the Winter Palace's residents and guests gazing out the windows of the building's ceremonial galleries—in this case being themselves the cordoned-off spectators at displays of popular festivity.

By far the most famous public use of the western and then the Neva side of the palace in monarchical times was the annual Epiphany ceremony of Blessing the Waters. This rite was the most plastic of all the imperial ceremonies, changing significantly from its origins in sixteenth-century Moscow through the middle of the nineteenth century. On this feast day commemorating the baptism of Christ, January 6, it was an ancient custom for Orthodox priests to process with the parishioners out of the church following divine services to a river or lake where they pronounced a blessing on the waters. Following the conclusion of the prayers the people gathered vials of the blessed water to take home with them. Moscow tsars observed this ritual publically at least from the time of Ivan the Terrible.[40] In the sixteenth century this was already a partly public ceremony, some of which took place outside the Kremlin walls on the frozen Moscow River and included the city's people as minor players. The central blessing took place where a small hole in the ice had been decorated, and this spot was known as the "Jordan"—that is, the Jordan River. Over time the ceremony came to underscore not the humility but the power of the ruler.[41]

The famously pious Tsar Alexei innovated, adding hundreds of musketeers to the parade route.[42] According to Paul Bushkovitch, Peter the Great had instituted a public Epiphany ceremony in St. Petersburg by 1715.[43]

All of Russia's St. Petersburg monarchs continued the Blessing of the Waters, the classic church-court-public ceremony, which was connected spatially to the monarch's own household. The *Sankt-Peterburgskie vedomosti* reported that Elizabeth celebrated the Blessing of the Waters, "in the usual fashion" in January 1756, with churchmen processing from the newly completed temporary palace to the nearby banks of the Moika River, where detachments of guards and garrison regiments lined up for the annual blessing of their flags and standards. From the Peter and Paul Fortress and the Admiralty volleys rang out, and troops fired three rounds of blanks.[44] On the only Epiphany of his brief reign, Peter III copied his predecessor's ceremony but added to it the masculine element of personally inspecting the troops drawn up opposite the temporary palace. Again the Blessing of the Waters proceeded in the Moika River, with troops lining both banks.[45]

When Catherine first occupied the new Winter Palace she conducted the Blessing of the Waters in the Admiralty Canal, which then separated the Winter Palace from its neighbor to the west. The procession of the cross circulated from the Great Palace Church, through all of the family quarters of the palace, out onto the Palace Square, and to prepared spots near the Admiralty-side court entrance.[46] The ceremony continued this way throughout her reign, but she did not always attend the outside portion, from which extremely cold weather tended to exempt women.[47]

Catherine's son, Paul, conducted the ceremony in the same spot but added formal military reviews, which he conducted personally, to the Blessing of the Waters. Paul required his wife and older children to join him at the Admiralty moat, weather permitting, underscoring that the soldier was also a father.[48] Paul's son, Alexander, maintained the military review but moved the ceremony to the Neva side of the palace, which opened it to the participation of a much larger number of city people. Henceforth spectators assembled on the ice or observed from Vasilevskii Island or the Petrograd side.

Alexander had the court and St. Petersburg military units assemble on the Palace Embankment just outside the Hermitage dining room. After the ceremony on the ice and review of troops, the emperor provided a palace breakfast including vodka and wine for all of the officers who had been involved in the frigid solemnities.[49] Although it increasingly became a public ceremony, in the early nineteenth century the Blessing of the Waters was still on the list of important court ceremonies that the entire foreign diplomatic corps was compelled to attend. It was in his capacity as the US Minister Plenipotentiary to Russia from 1809 to 1814 that John Quincy Adams recorded his impressions of the Jordan Ceremony, which he reluctantly attended in January 1812. Nursing unhappy memories of the long, bone-chilling proceedings from previous years he had been pleased when the 1812 observance was called off because of extreme cold. When he visited the Winter Palace in honor of the empress's birthday on January 25 (N.S.), he was dismayed to discover that instead of a birthday party the court would proceed with "the most unpleasant and dangerous part" of the Blessing of the Waters, "which I had flattered myself we should escape this year."[50]

The diplomatic corps observed the procession of the troops along the embankment from the galleries on the parade floor of the Neva enfilade. Alexander, himself, was outside reviewing the troops throughout the day. Although the temperature was only about ten degrees Fahrenheit, when the emperor's wife and mother appeared bundled in furs it was necessary to follow them out onto the balcony, "bare-headed, without pelisse, with silk stockings and thin shoes."[51] The women urged the inadequately dressed diplomats to return to the vestibule, which was also none too warm. Only the stoutest of courtiers stuck it out for the entire hour of the military procession, but Adams "thought my privilege as a republican would be an apology for me."[52]

AN EMERGING PUBLIC SPACE

The narrowness of the space in front of the Admiralty façade and the seasonality of the Neva flank meant that the Winter Palace was most easily approached from the south. Palace Square continued to take shape as a planned imperial space from the later years of Catherine's reign onward. Nonetheless, the square remained openly accessible from all sides except the palace itself, a hub of commercial and administrative life, and a place often traversed on foot or by cab. With the barracks of imperial guards units ringed around this section of town, the Palace Square was not a place for rowdiness. When gathering to witness great ceremonies or court events, the crowd would have noticed a significant police and military presence. Russian subjects specifically lacked freedom of assembly, and groups of people hoping to gather for some organized purpose needed to procure permission from the police, which was rarely granted. Nonetheless, city people did not cede the space entirely to the court and to officialdom as they took their walks or socialized on the expanse. And on one notable occasion people with a grievance appropriated the square to speak "directly" with their sovereign.

This took place in the late summer of 1787. A group of some four thousand peasants working for a contractor named Dolgov to install new granite embankments along the Fontanka River and the Catherine Canal walked off the job protesting low pay and poor treatment. The trouble simmered for several weeks as officials struggled to return the peasants to their work and grew sharper when two delegates were arrested after trekking out to Tsarskoe Selo hoping to see the empress. When the workers learned that the empress had returned to the Winter Palace from a long sojourn they determined to take their case to her there. On August 7, 1787, they chose four hundred from their number to march to Palace Square and request a meeting with Catherine herself. The workmen were orderly on the square all morning, trying to catch the monarch's attention through the windows of the palace. Each time they spied a woman in the imperial apartments they "bowed low and waved their petition."[53] As Catherine noted in a decree issued the following day: "We Ourselves saw workers who had abandoned their work on the Fontanka River and the Catherine Canal gathering on the square to submit a request having to do with their contractors."[54] She did not deign to receive the workers, and ultimately guards dispersed them by arresting seventeen of their number. In the legal proceedings that followed, Catherine intervened to have the seventeen released promptly and eventually compelled Dolgov to meet their demands. Still, she blamed the police for the unlawful demonstration and reasserted that officials must prevent such gatherings in the future.[55] The workers and others watching them may have been gratified by the results of their daring demonstration, while at the same time concluding that it was too dangerous to repeat. What is most striking about this encounter, though, was the porousness of the interface between the empress of all the Russias and her most humble subjects: they took the measure of each other through the palace windows in the heart of the capital city. Two years before the outbreak of the French Revolution, monarchy was no abstraction to the seasonal workmen of St. Petersburg. For her part, watching her subjects through the window, the monarch intuited how to defuse the situation.

This urban center offered Catherine a new kind of stage, and late in her reign she deployed it in a significantly new way when she summoned the people to join her in celebrating military victory over the Swedes. Navigating the politics of female rule, Catherine did not deploy Palace Square for military displays.[56] In the nineteenth century the ensemble of palace façade and Palace Square mounted prodigies of military power and commemorated Russia's victories, but Catherine's celebration of military success gestured more toward national joy than martial strength. Upon the victorious conclusion of the Swedish War in 1792 the empress decreed the construction of two great platforms in the midst of the square. These bore mountains of food as well as internal pipes through which red and white wine flowed. The city's people were summoned, at her signal the fountains flowed, and the common folk helped themselves to the meats, fruits, and vegetables provided by a sovereign presenting herself to them as grateful, generous, and triumphant.[57] Here the sovereign performed for the people directly, rather than offering them back-row seats at a spectacle designed for courtiers and foreigners. Drawing the people into celebration of imperial military victory she prefigured the use to which her son and grandsons would put this malleable space.

How did the people of St. Petersburg experience Palace Square in the second half of the eighteenth century? Many of them must have experienced the imperial encroachments as loss. The commons that at one time offered free accommodation for impromptu homesteads fell under the gaze of police and guards. As has happened to so many poor people across time and space, the urge of the wealthy to "clean up" meant demolition and removal. Generally speaking, the poor workers, artisans, and servants who continued to live in the center of the city moved off the square and Millionaia and into basements elsewhere in the district.

The life of city people did manage to cause some friction for the police who tried to carry out imperial orders. Wine sellers and tavern keepers resisted removing their signs from public streets, and disgruntled workmen approached the walls of the palace caps in hand. Cabbies and soldiers clustered around warming fires, and the curious thronged the Palace Square during court events in order to catch a glimpse of how the other half lived. The authorities let some of this go. The square was a place of give-and-take, even if the contenders were far from equal.

By the end of the century, however, St. Petersburg's residents had on a few occasions witnessed more festive interaction between monarch and subjects. Court officials did not curtail traditional celebration of Shrovetide at the Palace Square, with the construction of show booths and days of revelry. Every now and then the sovereign extended hospitality to the city's people directly, whether performing strange feats of historical drama or proffering food and drink. On such occasions the humble people of Russia's imperial capital might have felt fortunate to work and live in the neighborhood of such a splendid stage.

4
STAGING MONARCHY

The outer facades of the Winter Palace were a transparently public stage, but the palace's baroque *interior* was full of potential as a space in which the imperial family could encounter and be encountered by selected groups of subjects. In the century and a half during which it was the formal residence of the Russian imperial family, St. Petersburg's Winter Palace was not only a place in which the ruler's family lived. The palace was also a peerless platform on which to transmit messages of power that were attractive rather than punitive. The classic encounter inside the palace was the performance and auditing of a gracious display of wealth, power, and taste by people of various stations and ranks in an atmosphere of cordial formality. The auditors were disciplined by their experience, through myriad requirements of dress and deportment, but the discipline was meant to be uplifting—edification by elegant example.

These were court displays rather than public displays. The Russian Imperial Court expanded in every way over the course of the eighteenth century, and with the move into the Winter Palace both the magnificence of the monarchical performance and the supporting cast grew to unprecedented levels. The number of people employed by the Court grew over the course of the century from around 350 to almost 3,000. By one careful calculus the expenses of Peter the Great's court had amounted to sixty-one thousand rubles annually. During Catherine's reign, that figure rose to over one million rubles. All of this seemed necessary to monarchs who perceived that it was only "through the wealth and luxury" of their imperial court that they could "suitably represent their country to the outside world."[1]

Many of the people on the imperial court payroll were honor attendants: members of the nobility who were housed in the Winter Palace or other court buildings and who personally "attended" the monarch. In this sense the attendants did not perform actual work such as caring for clothes or person but simply enhanced and emphasized the ruler's elegance by forming a carefully groomed circle around her. The livery of uniformed room attendants was also part of the show.[2] Beauty and good taste were deemed inherently valuable, and displaying them to powerful Russian lords and important foreign representatives was the principal purpose of the imperial court and the Winter Palace.

It follows, then, that over the course of Catherine's reign, foreigners and Russian grandees dominated the ranks of palace guests. However, two groups who demonstrated the widening circle to which the Russian court displayed monarchy in the late eighteenth century were the city's leading merchants and its most talented craftsmen. These two expanding groups of St. Petersburg residents crossed the palace-city boundary with some regularity. Through their eyes we may glimpse one image of Russia that Catherine sought to project to and on behalf of her subjects: a state that valued commerce and a court that patronized art and craft. We also catch a glimpse of how merchants and artisans reacted to her scenario.

MERCHANTS IN THE PALACE

The palace occasions most widely commented on at the height of monarchy were "public" masquerade balls held in the Winter Palace on or near New Year's Day. These events, and a few other balls held during the fall and winter months, were designated as "public," meaning that qualifying people, including lesser nobles and greater merchants, could pick up free tickets at the Court Office and attend. The relatively small number of so-called public masquerades stood in contrast to the much larger number of formal court balls, dinners, receptions, church services, and family celebrations that ranking courtiers were obliged to attend regularly.[3] The public New Year's masquerades at which eighteenth-century guests donned fancy costumes and court-issued masks were the largest events held in the Winter Palace, and the number of people admitted to them steadily expanded between the reigns of Catherine II and her grandson Nicholas I.[4]

In the memoir literature the balls are often described as "all-estate," and foreign observers characterize the monarch as moving about among a throng of "commoners."[5] However, the record preserved in court journals and the *Sankt-Peterburgskie vedomosti* clearly indicates that the two categories of people invited to attend were the nobility and the merchantry, along with their wives and grown children. While this guest list may not strike modern observers as overly democratic, it did represent an extension of the monarch's hospitality many notches down the social ladder of capital residents from the usual palace guest list, which typically limited itself to ladies and gentlemen of the top four—or "court"—ranks on the official Table of Ranks and foreign dignitaries.[6] There were thousands of people holding the formal rank of *dvorianin* (noble), who were often cash-strapped and possibly actually employed in government service, living primarily from their civil service salaries. Although such people occupied a privileged stratum of Russian society, they were by no means regular guests of the monarch's court.[7]

Many memoirists were struck by the presence of common folk at these New Year's balls, and since the records indicate that only nobles and notable merchants were invited, this raises the question as to whether merchants of the lower guilds or the even lowlier townsmen (*meshchane*) attended. In the 1770s Catherine clarified the privileges and obligations of each of the three merchant guilds and greatly reduced the number of people occupying the lowest of them. While the number of all registered merchants in the empire declined from 214,000 in 1762 to 24,470 in 1775, all were now exempted from compulsory service and payment of the poll tax. The first two guilds were also spared corporal punishment, could purchase exemption from military service, ride in carriages, wear swords, and be received at court.[8] The very wealthiest—or first guild—merchants were almost indistinguishable from the noble grandees, but even those of smaller fortunes occupying the second and third merchant guilds benefited from privileges and rank superior to that of townsmen and other St. Petersburg residents.[9]

It is not clear that the merchants attending New Year's masquerades included those of the lowest guild. In 1777, for example, all noblemen and notable merchants (*znatoe kupechestvo*) were invited with their families. It seems unlikely that third guild merchants, those not holding the right to wear swords, were invited to the public balls during Catherine's reign, particularly after 1778 when for the first time the wearing of "swords, daggers or other weapons" was expressly required according to her New Year's masquerade announcement, probably as a means to help guards identify who was to be admitted.[10]

If it seems unlikely that third guild merchants were invited it is even more certain that members of the urban public classified as townsmen were not invited, as the court journal mentions rooms assigned only to nobles and merchants. Nonetheless, foreign memoirists often mention encountering city residents of various ranks. English observer William Coxe recorded in the late eighteenth century that there was a special hall set aside for the dancing pleasure of those not admitted to court, people he labeled "burghers and so on." One recent Russian work translates Coxe's "burghers" as "*meshchane*," and several scholars conclude that townsmen and lower guild merchants were in attendance at the biggest masquerades.[11]

G. N. Komelova suggests a reasonable resolution to this conundrum: townsmen were not invited but they often managed to attend anyway. The Winter Palace balls were massive and attractive events, city people were naturally curious about what the inside of the Winter Palace looked like, and those determined to get inside during one of the New Year's or other public masquerades could often do so. Komelova points out that each eighteenth-century press announcement inviting people to procure a ticket repeated apparently dire warnings about how those who were *not* eligible to attend—such as "gentlemen servants," "teachers," "those not holding officer rank," and "anyone forbidden the right to enter"—would be fined and escorted out under guard. The need to repeat this litany in each announcement suggests that people kept slipping through the net.[12] Although one had to present oneself at the door without a mask, everyone dressed in a costume of some kind and soon donned a court-issued mask. After that the crowded gaiety of the massive event allowed discreet interlopers to enjoy the evening, and memoirists attest that it was not difficult to move between the various rooms designated for people of different ranks.

The one requirement was to possess a ticket issued from the Court Office, but these, too, seemed to circulate somewhat freely in the city. Memoirist Giovanni Cazanova recorded that in December 1764 the owner of a small hotel at which he was staying encouraged him to attend the Winter Palace ball that evening. When Cazanova protested that he had not been invited, the hotelier produced a ticket and told him that with six thousand people there he would not have any trouble getting in. So Cazanova, "wearing a domino," mounted the Winter Palace steps and took in the splendid surroundings, the tasty snacks, and the shocking proximity of the empress.[13] Whatever the precise social composition of those attending the New Year's galas at the palace, it is clear that their numbers grew over time, reaching gargantuan proportions during the public-oriented reign of Nicholas I.

TABLE 2. Number of Guests Attending New Year's Masquerades at the Winter Palace

Year	Nobles	Merchants	Total
1755			767
1777	2,806	309	3,115
1778	2,525	390	2,915

1779	2,950	460	3,410
1781	2,605	445	3,050
1803	7,912	2,416	10,328
1810			15,270
1812	10,296	2,954	13,250
1817	14,216	3,113	17,329
1830			22,000
1832			22,364
1839			30,000

SOURCE: 1777–1817, *KfTsZh* entries for early January of each year; 1832: "Imperator Nikolai Pavlovich v ego pis'makh k Kniaziu Paskevich," *Russkii arkhiv,* no. 1 (Jan. 1897) 6; I. I. Pushkarev, *Opisanie Sanktpeterburga i uezdnykh gorodov S. Peterburgskoi gubernii,* vol. 3 (St. Petersburg: 1839–41), 134.
NOTE: The figure for 1839 refers to the number of tickets distributed.

Ever since Elizabeth's 1755 ball, the last held before the demolition of the old winter palace, guests had been summoned to the public masquerade ball (*publichnyi maskerad*) by public written notice published in the *Sankt-Peter-burgskie vedomosti* two days before the event. They presented themselves at the Court Office near the Admiralty entrance to the palace in order to request tickets. Originally potential guests requested tickets in writing, specifying the number of tickets required, so that officials could prepare for the expected number of guests. Those who took tickets but did not appear were threatened with a fine.[14] The tradition of requiring tickets procured in advance took root, but there was no reference to fines for nonappearance in later years; in fact, available data indicates that in Catherine's time there was generally about a 37–40 percent attendance rate among nobles who picked up tickets, and a slightly lower percentage among merchants. During the reigns of her grandsons Alexander and Nicholas a higher proportion of those who procured tickets seemed actually to show up.

Attendees did not have to pay, but they did need to dress appropriately.[15] Security concerns induced the court officials to provide guests with masks, rather than permitting them to bring their own, and this practice also spared guests the cost of procuring masks. Arriving a few hours before the masquerade commenced, guests were ushered into halls appointed for the donning of masks, and to await the arrival of their imperial hosts before processing into their designated ballrooms. The main pastimes of the evening included dancing and card playing. The sovereign greeted guests and sometimes sat for a round of cards with the guards before an early departure for supper with a more select group in her private quarters. The masquerade then proceeded in her absence into the wee hours of the morning.

Catherine built on her predecessor's example, but she had her own ideas about how to conduct this great "public" fête. Typical was the January 2, 1779, event, to which all nobles, as well as Russian and foreign merchants, were welcomed beginning at five in the afternoon. Palace servants ushered nobles and merchants into separate suites of rooms on the main floor. In Catherine's time, the merchants and city people occupied the Neva side galleries and the northwest block, which housed Rinaldi's oval-shaped Apollon Hall and several antechambers. Nobles assembled in a suite of rooms along the eastern flank, between the two principal stairways, which was closer to Catherine's private quarters and which looked out on the interior courtyard.[16] In their appointed spots the two groups of guests donned masks. Those in Roman dress were bid to enter the Jewel Room for the opening Roman quadrille. Music commenced in all the rooms at half past six, and at seven o'clock the empress opened the dancing. Somewhat later Catherine's heir, Paul, and his wife, Maria Fedorovna, appeared, and they tarried until half past nine. Catherine deigned to greet the merchants and the nobles in their respective halls as she proceeded to the Cavaliers' Hall, where she sat down to play cards with the officers.[17] She retired at nine o'clock, eschewing even the dinner for fifty select guests. The rank-and-file guests continued their revelry until two in the morning.

These public galas transpired without recorded security procedures, but guards posted to the Winter Palace provided a deterrent to misbehavior. Subversion did occur at the New Year's masquerade in 1774, the height of the Pugachev rebellion. Someone who described himself as "an honest man" left behind a placard of some sort, alleging that Catherine's government was corrupt. Palace authorities endeavored without success to identify the miscreant, and failing to do so had the placard burned in front of the Senate a few days later. For some time thereafter access to the palace was restricted to those holding the rank of major or its civil equivalent.[18] The public destruction of the offending paper implies that the incident had achieved considerable publicity in the aftermath of the gala.

Catherine did not host a public New Year's ball every year, but there were very few years in which she did not hold any public masquerade at the Winter Palace for nobles and merchants (on two or three occasions during January and February). The pattern for these events followed the New Year's dances. In 1780, for example, she held masquerades on February 16, 21, and 27, with attendees numbering between thirty-five and forty-seven hundred, of which merchants and their family members comprised between four and six hundred. Catherine's successors continued the New Year's masquerades, although there were years in which mourning periods, wars, or other overwhelming national events prevented the masquerades from occurring. Each monarch put his stamp on this venerable tradition.[19]

Out-of-town merchants also gained entry to Catherine's palace, not as masquerade guests but in connection with their business. The young grain merchant Ivan Tolchenov recalled being summoned to the Winter Palace in 1775, concerning the price of rye in the capital. The patriotic young scion of his family firm, Tolchenov had arrived from Moscow in early June to meet the barges hauling his cargo to St. Petersburg. He recorded in his diary that on June 8, 1775, he and other merchants were summoned to police headquarters, "where they endeavored to persuade us to sell our rye flour for no more than 3.50 rubles a sack. But all the traders gave their final price as 3.80."[20] Eight days later Tolchenov noted that, "along with the other merchants I was called on the same matter to the Winter Palace, where, in the absence of the court, Military Governor General-Fieldmarshal Prince Aleksandr Golitsyn was residing, and he too tried to persuade us to reduce the price on rye flour; however, everyone refused because of the lack of any profit."[21] This was a case in which the imposing grandeur of the palace, deployed we might imagine in hopes of weakening the merchants' resolve, failed to do so. David Ransel considers this 1775 incident Ivan Tolchenov's "graduation day, when at age twenty he stood together with his fellow merchants in the Winter Palace and rejected the entreaties of the leading tsarist military official."[22]

It is noteworthy that Tolchenov records his visit to the Winter Palace in the course of doing business rather matter-of-factly, suggesting that at least in broad daylight the surroundings were not bewitching enough to dim his business sense. At the same time, this little story, preserved for posterity in a diary, underscores the fact that even during Catherine's reign the Winter Palace was taking on a civic life of its own, in which officials made use of it for state purposes in the absence of the monarch, and tsarist subjects came and went in the course of conducting their personal affairs.

Catherine also regularly hosted provincial deputations in the Winter Palace, according to a practiced formula. Typical was one such event in January 1778, when the Fieldmarshals' Hall was the setting in which she received two groups of deputies chosen by their localities (*namestnichestva*) in Pskov and Iaroslavl Provinces.[23] The deputies assembled at noon and at one o'clock the empress appeared and conversed with them before inviting them to dine with her. The following year she likewise received a deputation from Vladimir Province, the court journal noting that the visitors were joined at table by the honor attendants of the day. In 1780 there was a flurry of such receptions in January and February. When she received representatives from Nizhni Novgorod, Kursk, and Kaluga in late January, she gave each of them her hand. The dinner to which they were invited was intimate, just twenty-seven people including the honor attendants du jour. Within a few weeks of that event Catherine also received deputies from Tambov Province and others from Bukhara. That fall, her visitors included deputies from Vologda. The next year's social season witnessed receptions for delegations from Iaroslavl, Pskov, Tula, and Simbirsk. This pattern continued throughout Catherine's reign. She hosted the Kirghiz khan at the palace in January 1790 and Urals elders in February of the same year.[24] However arduous the long journey to the imperial capital at the height of winter (when travel in Russia was generally the easiest, if not the most comfortable), in the absence of recorded memories we are left to imagine the impact of this culminating moment, when a small group of provincial men dined in the empress's company deep in the heart of her urban palace. Catherine's famous charm could only have been amplified by these surroundings, which she knew how to use to advantage. Here she conveyed graciousness, wealth, dignified condescension, and public spiritedness, even as the setting conveyed the solidity of her imperial project. Certainly some impressions of this place found their way back to the provinces when the delegates returned home.

ARTISANS IN THE PALACE

If city merchants and provincial elders were chief among the non-courtier subjects admitted to the Winter Palace in Catherine's time, architects, artists, skilled craftsmen, and their helpers constituted another layer of habitué in a palace that was always under expansion, remodeling, and redecoration. While many of the chief architects and cabinetmakers were of foreign birth, the majority of men who carried out the decorating, and many of their directors, were Russian subjects. Those who made the Winter Palace the beautiful building it is crossed the boundary between palace and city on a regular basis, assisting in mounting the monarchical scenario while also consuming it. Clifford Geertz bequeathed to us the image of a "theater state," in which the monarch's presentation is manifested not only to the invited audience but also to the myriad members of the "supporting cast [and] stage crew."[25] Those who build the stage also imbibe the essence of the performance. Since the interior of the building over which Catherine became a widowed mistress in 1762 was only partially furnished, and many of its primary rooms were not only empty but also unpainted, hundreds of specialists in the decorative arts were soon drawn into its circle.

Even if she had not set out to recast the Winter Palace from the epitome of the baroque to an exemplar of neoclassicism she would have presided over the outfitting of its interiors. As it happened, one of Catherine's first acts was to grant the sixty-two-year-old Rastrelli a yearlong leave of absence, ostensibly on account of illness, and a grant of five thousand rubles.[26] After a sojourn in Germany and Italy, Rastrelli saw dismissal coming and secured a post in Courland from his old patron Count Biron.[27] The Senate subsequently granted the long-serving court architect an annual pension of one thousand rubles.[28] There are various theories surrounding Catherine's dismissal of Rastrelli: the architect's poor health and old age; his reluctance to work under the newly appointed head of the Commission on Construction, I. I. Betskoi; or his overly close connections to the dispatched Peter III. Soviet scholar A. F. Krashennikov speculated that the reigning baroque style required too many skilled bricklayers, carvers, and gilders to support the palace building boom of the late eighteenth century, and that growing peasant opposition to serfdom as well as expanding enlightenment undermined an architectural style so strongly associated with absolutism.[29] One thing that is beyond speculation is that Catherine preferred a clean and simple classicism to the exuberant baroque of which Rastrelli was reigning master.

Catherine was gracious to the old architect. He returned to Russia two more times, the first time in late 1763 to receive his confirmation as general major and his elevation to the Order of St. Anna, both granted him by Peter III. Catherine's adviser N. I. Panin gave him six post-horses for his return trip to Courland. A few years later Catherine dispatched Panin to visit Rastrelli in Jelgava, where she conveyed a grant of twelve thousand rubles, probably so that he could make a bequest to his children. In the fall of 1770 Rastrelli returned a final time to St. Petersburg, the city that bore his imprint. He was admitted to the Imperial Academy of Arts a few months before his death in the city on April 29, 1771.[30]

Before his dismissal Rastrelli had only completed the interiors of the Great and Small Palace Churches, the great parade staircase, and the private suites assigned to Peter, Paul, and Catherine, stretching across the parade floor's southern flank. These had been mostly completed, although in some the parquet floors had not yet been installed.[31] The formal rooms along the Neva had been hurriedly decked out in advance of the peace celebrations with the Prussian king by bringing in items from the wooden palace on Nevskii Prospekt. Otherwise none of the interiors were complete. Some of the remaining construction workers still occupied the ground floor, which also housed the kitchens, storage rooms, and offices.[32]

Catherine did not immediately elevate any single architect to the lofty perch vacated by Rastrelli. Her construction chief Betskoi parceled out commissions to several different men, include Vallin de la Mothe, Antonio Rinaldi, and Rastrelli's chief apprentice, Felten, while frequently imposing his own ideas on their designs. In the first years of her reign De la Mothe led most of the palace building projects, the first of which was the palace theater, or Opera House, planned but not undertaken by Rastrelli. While Catherine spent nearly a year in Moscow in connection with her coronation, De la Mothe also set to work relocating Catherine's private quarters toward the southeastern corpus of the palace, outfitting them with classical furnishings. The location of a suite of formal reception halls, including a throne room, was also in flux. Betskoi assigned De la Mothe to rush the establishment of this formal suite closer to Catherine's new quarters and the Great Palace Church.[33] A more enduring design decision from this period included rooms for the ladies-in-waiting on the top floor of the palace. A suite of rooms directly beneath Catherine's on the ground floor housed her informal consort, Grigorii Orlov. Not far away they positioned an expansive *banya*, or sauna, just beneath the altar of the great church above, a decision viewed by the pious as bordering on blasphemy.[34]

The other great building project at the Winter Palace in the early years of Catherine's reign was the first of the auxiliary edifices that would comprise the complex known as the Hermitage. Rastrelli himself had left some general plans for the site directly to the east of the palace, which called for razing a few of the surviving homes and erecting stables, a riding hall (*manezh*), and kitchens. While she was in Moscow for her coronation Catherine conferred with Felten, and he returned to St. Petersburg armed with plans to add a "hanging," or second-story, garden to the ensemble. Of the buildings created between 1764 and 1766, today only the hanging garden remains, the riverfront stables having been judged incongruous with the palace environs and torn down in 1777.[35] Meanwhile, Felten oversaw the construction of the hanging garden, which formed the long center of a narrow, new building that extended from the river embankment all along the eastern façade of the palace. By 1765 Felten was at work on the southern pavilion of this building, the section that originally attracted the title "Ermitazh." The next year he began a northern pavilion. Eventually Catherine decided also to construct long picture galleries along the sides of the garden itself, connecting the northern and southern pavilions. By 1767 the building today known as the Small Hermitage was completed, housing three of Catherine's favorite things: an indoor garden, her fledgling art collection, and Grigorii Orlov, who occupied rooms in the southern pavilion, connected to the private quarters of the Winter Palace by a flying bridge.[36]

The pace of work during the 1760s allowed the supervising architects to produce only sketches for their master workmen, who consequently played a significant role in the shape of the final product.[37] Even at this early date Catherine and her court officials were striving to build up native crafts by a variety of means. As apprentices and assistants, Russian workmen were part of every contract let by the Construction Commission. For example, Russian masters Efim Ivanovich Bel'skii and D. Pozdniakov assisted the Italian Antonio Perezinotti in painting the ceiling of Catherine's formal bedchamber. Bel'skii and his two brothers were well known by the 1760s and enjoyed important imperial commissions throughout St. Petersburg. As children they had been enrolled in a training program overseen by the Construction Chancellery. In time they were elected to the Academy of Arts and were eventually granted the tax-exempt status of master painter. Early Russian sculptors whose work also graced the palace were F. G. Gordeev and M. I. Kozlovskii. The carpet in Catherine's bedchamber was manufactured in Iaroslavl to a design by De la Mothe.[38]

Catherine greatly expanded the court's practice of paying to train young people whose talent came to its attention. Her officials were especially keen to identify talent among those who belonged to one of the fiscal categories under state tutelage. The Court Office summoned boys living on state or crown lands who seemed to be likely prospects for training in the skilled trades or court service when they were as young as six years of age. Parents of such children received a stipend of thirty rubles per year for each boy so identified, but generally both parents and children were bound people who had no say in the matter of the boys' training and future career.[39] Orphans, who by the eighteenth century were effectively wards of the state, provided another source of hereditary palace artisans. A third group included the sons of soldiers, taken on for kitchen or other work. If officials noticed artistic talent among any of these youngsters, it was possible that the court officials would take them into one of the palace's specialized "commands" or assign them to independent masters for training. Young men who followed this path remained on the fiscal rolls throughout their lives and provided a cadre of talented workers available for palace projects. The serfs among them generally received their compensation in room and board rather than in wages. For eighty years carpenters, joiners, smiths, security guards, and firemen lived with their families in the so-called Masters' Court next to the palace, enclosed by the old Shepelev Palace, home of the Court Ober-Hofmarshal, and the imperial stables.[40]

As Catherine's building boom went on, however, the public rolls could not support the demand for talent. So the imperial court expanded the scope of private ateliers with whom it contracted. To encourage native talent beyond the fiscal ranks, Catherine imposed import taxes on furniture in 1765. Within a year the French chargé d'affaires observed that Russians were learning very quickly how to create beautiful furniture on their own, and there appears to have been a marked decline in the import of French furniture after 1770.[41] This was the same year that Catherine granted artisans the right to live in a privileged residential area adjacent to the Winter Palace, on Millionaia Street and the Moika Canal. She further strengthened the social and economic status of craftsmen with the Artisan Regulation, a corollary of the Municipal Charter of 1785, which sought to strengthen Russian crafts by enabling masters to create guilds, elevating the status of artisans employed at the Winter Palace and elsewhere.[42]

Most of the furniture and decoration of the Winter Palace whose origins can be confirmed date from the period when the palace interior was reconstructed after the devastating fire of 1837. We have some idea of what the furnishings looked like before the fire, because craftsmen created some of the restored decorations according to surviving designs. Nonetheless, the fire complicates efforts to attribute individual pieces to their creators. Adding to the difficulty of identifying craftsmen who produced the original furnishings of the palace in the 1760s and 1770s is the Russian tradition of not marking one's work. The very humble status of most native workmen also hinders our knowing much about them. By default, therefore, the work produced by foreigners is better known.[43] What is clear, however, is that over the course of Catherine's reign the furnishing of the Winter Palace expanded the ranks and skills of St. Petersburg craftsmen.

By the 1780s there were a number of well-known Russian masters and even several shops owned by Russians or Russified foreigners of long residence in the city. Master craftsmen who operated or labored in private workshops in the capital were a special caste in the late eighteenth and early nineteenth centuries. By virtue of the need to earn a living by working with their hands they were what the age considered "dependent" people, meaning they depended upon employment by others. In a period when, even in Russia, the language of "independence" and "sovereignty" took wing, dependency of this kind imparted inferiority. But men who acquired particular skill in crafts appreciated by the wealthy did possess something valuable and rare in which they could trade—and through which, at least to some degree, they obtained influence over people of superior social status. A few highly placed people themselves undertook informal apprenticeship in woodworking, as did St. Petersburg's Lt. Governor-General Prokofi Vasilievich Meshcherskii, who was a painter, sculptor, and amateur cabinetmaker said to be the first to use Karelian birch in furniture making.[44] In Catherine's time the symbiotic relationship between lovers and producers of beautiful objects was on full display at the Winter Palace.

The chief example of a successful local craftsman with imperial commissions is cabinetmaker Christian Meyer, who despite his foreign-sounding name was the scion of a German family that had immigrated to Russia several generations earlier. In the 1780s Meyer placed several pieces in the Winter Palace, including corner cupboards decorated with marquetry and eighteen display cabinets with mahogany veneer and gilt bronze ornaments. In 1789 Meyer delivered thirty more glass-fronted cabinets for Catherine's private apartments, designed to house her collections of precious minerals and other treasures. While much about Meyer is obscure, the volume of furnishings his workshop supplied to the Winter Palace alone in the 1780s and 1790s indicates that it was one of the busiest workshops in the city. Surely Meyer's staff grew intimately familiar with a building into which they installed sixty-four bookcases (1793) and thirty-five more, two years later, along with sideboards for window niches.[45]

Nothing better exemplifies the esteem in which imperial patrons of Russian craftsmanship held artisans than the efforts made by Catherine's daughter-in-law to provide her sons with instruction in woodworking and to master various crafts herself. The future Empress Maria Fedorovna fell in love with European furniture on her incognito visit with her husband to France, Holland, Switzerland, and Germany in 1782. She returned to Russia laden down with purchases and soon installed them, along with many others made in Russia, at Pavlovsk Palace. She, herself, was a craftswoman. Besides painting on wood and glass, she was a turner, who produced "twelve ivory columns which I turned on the lathe" for a table produced in the 1790s.[46] She also had her sons Alexander and Constantine try their hand at furniture making. The boys' proud grandmother noted in a letter to Baron Grimm in 1784 that, "as for master Alexander and master Constantine, who like to try their hand at any trade, they have finished their carpentry course with Mr. Meyer."[47]

Another important workshop belonged to the Würtemberg immigrant Heinrich Gambs, who first arrived in Russia as an assistant to the famous Moravian cabinetmaker David Roentgen in the 1780s or 1790s.[48] Although Roentgen came and went, Gambs settled down in St. Petersburg, and his sons can be considered native master craftsmen whose expansive workshop engaged scores of St. Petersburg cabinetmakers and bronze smiths in outfitting the Winter Palace. Taking on an Austrian partner, Gambs first opened a workshop near the Kalinkin Bridge and, imitating his master's strategy, ingratiated himself to his countrywoman Maria Fedorovna. In October 1795 Gambs opened a large workshop on Nevskii Prospekt, which was supported by his first imperial commission to furnish Grand Duke Alexander's new palace at Tsarskoe Selo and to refurbish the old Roentgen pieces in the Winter Palace.

By the 1790s Gambs presided over a thoroughly Russian-style workshop. Here there was considerably more freedom than in western Europe for craftsmen to engage in a variety of specialties due to the looser guild restrictions. Antoine Chenevière considers this "flexible organization" the primary explanation for the "high technical standards attained by Russian workshops after thirty years of constant progress."[49] Thus a gifted cabinetmaker might also try his hand at producing bronzes or clocks. In Gambs's workshop there were different sections that produced veneers, brass motifs, gilding, and mechanical devices. Catherine's successors continued to do business with atelier Gambs, which provided a substantial amount of furniture for many imperial palaces including a quantity that is still part of the Hermitage collection today. In 1810 Alexander made him court cabinetmaker, launching Gambs and his young sons Peter and Edward on decades of palace furnishing that spanned the restoration work following the 1837 fire. As late as the 1850s Peter Gambs was attracting commissions from the wife of Nicholas I and for decorating the New Hermitage.[50]

Although it is difficult to know how many Russian craftsmen and assistants frequented the Winter Palace in these years of unbridled decoration and expansion, it is safe to assume that scores of them came and went as employees of the city's expanding network of fine ateliers. Just as the building of the palace in the 1750s had provided work for armies of bricklayers and carpenters, in the years of Catherine's reign the palace employed either directly or indirectly cadres of young men who became the unacknowledged founders of a distinctive Russian style of furniture, which to this day attracts enormous prices from collectors eager to own the unsigned pieces created in St. Petersburg at the end of the eighteenth century. Chenevière argues persuasively that, while many Russian aristocrats imported quantities of French and English furniture in the late eighteenth century, the imperial court did not: "The reason why comparatively small amounts were spent on furniture, as opposed to the large sums spent on porcelain and other works of art, was simply that furniture could be obtained in Russia itself."[51] As early as the 1780s imported furniture was taking a backseat in the imperial palaces to pieces crafted in St. Petersburg.

When the renowned German geographer Johann Georgi published his survey of Russia during the reign of Catherine, he described an artisanal system that was considerably less regulated and regimented than what he was accustomed to in western Europe. Before Catherine's charter to the towns and its accompanying artisanal regulations in 1785, Georgi understood that foreign artisans in Russia had been organized by shops, each with elders, submasters, and apprentices with well-defined roles. However, "Rossiiski" artisans, meaning those who were subjects of the tsarina, were often young men of foreign birth who were registered in their twenties as belonging to a shop if they so chose, without any kind of examination. These young men were not restricted to just one craft but could undertake a new one and dispense with the old as they wished or could, indeed, practice several at once.[52] Georgi described the increased orderliness imposed by new regulations in the mid-1780s. However, Georgi still found that in practice there was little to prevent a craftsman from taking on work outside his shop or trying his hand at a craft in which he was not registered. The freedom of the Russian practice allowed Russian craftsmen to experiment in or even to master two or more trades, something no French or German artisan would have been able to do in the late eighteenth century.

According to Georgi by the beginning of the 1790s the guild of Russian cabinetmakers in St. Petersburg included 124 master craftsmen, 285 journeymen, and 175 apprentices, while the guild of foreign cabinetmakers in the city included 90 men. Other Russian skilled craftsmen registered in St. Petersburg shops included 85 master glaziers, 86 submasters, and 70 apprentices as well as 23 master and 19 submaster wallpaper hangers. For each of the last two trades the number of registered foreigners was much smaller (14 and 4, respectively).[53] Georgi concluded that there was much to envy in the position of St. Petersburg's skilled artisans:

> As everywhere, it is now the same here, that several of the crafts and arts have attracted more people, and now these provide a very slim profit; but in general one can say that because of the vastness of the country, the magnificence of the court, the flowering of trade, the wealth, the prevailing luxury, and above all the effort to supersede other provinces in matters of taste, St. Petersburg artisans have become richer, and are living better and rather more pleasant lives than artisans in many other capitals.[54]

Besides the young men being attracted to learn decorative arts from various fiscal and private ranks late in the century, there were also many serfs who had been trained on the estates of large landowners such as Count Stroganov who found their way to the capital during the palace-building frenzy. There was another source of skilled native tradesmen in the Okhta shipyard workers who were descended from those brought in by Peter the Great. At the turn of the nineteenth century this company included joiners, carpenters, and gilders who supplied furniture to Maria Fedorovna. Chenevière concludes that over the course of the years during which Catherine expanded and furnished the Winter Palace, these various strands of native talent merged to form an anonymous cadre of skilled Russian craftsmen who must be considered the creators of "the new national furniture trade."[55]

Personifying these various strands was the career of Okhta craftsman Ivan Iosifovich Bauman, who had arrived in Russia as a young man at the end of the eighteenth century. Bauman became known for woodcarving, for creating birchwood furniture, and also for bronze work. He was also the co-inventor of a mechanical saw. Bauman attracted several noble and imperial commissions before being appointed supplier to the court in the 1820s, which included an order for a suite of chairs and settees after designs by the court architect Carlo Rossi that still graces the Winter Palace today.[56] By 1824 Bauman had his own furniture shop in the Admiralty district, a bronze fabricating studio (or "factory"), and by the 1830s also a leather-painting shop.[57]

It was also in Catherine's time that the court invested extravagantly in the expansion of stonecutting and the national decorative stone technique that came to be known as "the Russian mosaic." Entrusting this effort to Count Stroganov in his capacity as president of the Academy of Arts (not to mention as a palace builder and decorator of the first order, himself), Catherine's government presided over the discovery of many new stone deposits in the Urals Mountains and beyond. The beautiful objects made from native Russian stone such as jasper, Amazonite, aventurine, porphyry, rhodonite, lazurite, and malachite between the 1760s and the 1860s represented a uniquely Russian art form, blending technical advances in excavating and mining, mechanical advances in stonecutting machinery, and profound artistry nurtured in several generations of artisanal families trained at government expense in St. Petersburg's Academy of Arts.

Russian decorative stonework originated in a factory at Pavlovsk, in the St. Petersburg suburbs, in the first half of the eighteenth century. As early as 1765, however, officials recognized that they could overcome the distance that lay between the trans-Urals quarries and the Pavlovsk factory by establishing a new factory at Ekaterinburg. Russian artisanal families Nalimov and Kokovin rose to the pinnacle of Ekaterinburg artistry, perfecting the craft of mosaic stone decoration, particularly in malachite. Stroganov saw to it that the sons of these families could study in St. Petersburg on scholarships. His favored architect (and most likely illegitimate, serf-born son), Andrei Voronikhin, who built Kazan Cathedral and had important commissions redecorating the Winter Palace after the fire, designed pieces for these stonemasons to create— projects that sometimes extended across a decade or more. The magnificent jasper columns, malachite tables, porphyry bowls, and other stone objects that began to grace the Winter Palace in the 1780s and that comprised much of the reconstruction after the fire were the purest examples of the collaboration between imperial wealth and Russian craft. Only Catherine and her court could assume the expense involved in distant mining expeditions that bore no guarantee of success or the transporting of enormous stone slabs across thousands of miles. As the mineral wealth of Siberia found its way west, it was Russia's largely unnamed, innovative stoneworkers who created internationally celebrated monumental works of art. The third of the imperial stoneworks, at Kolyvan, produced a five-foot-by-three-foot porphyry bowl that earned first prize at the Great Exhibition in London in 1851, the citation stating: "We do not think that objects which are so difficult to produce and are so well finished have been made since Greek and Roman times."[58]

Catherine never stopped expanding and remodeling her palace on the Neva. When the Italian architect Giacomo Quarenghi arrived in St. Petersburg in 1779, Catherine found her Rastrelli. Within a few years Quarenghi acquired the title of court architect, and he went on to build the Alexander Palace at Tsarskoye Selo and the Hermitage Theater adjoining the palace complex along the embankment. Inside the Winter Palace he left his mark particularly in the design and construction of St. George's Hall. Originally conceived of as "Marble Hall," this space was to serve as a magnificent throne room lined with giant marble columns and other stonework created by Russian sculptors of humble birth: Fedor Gordeev, Ivan Martos, Mikhail Kozlovskii, and eighteenth-century Russia's greatest sculptor, Fedot Shubin.[59] By the end of her reign Catherine and her architects had successfully expanded the pool of native talent from which members of the court and other wealthy patrons could draw. Russian artisans were the master decorators of the stage from which their rulers projected the drama of imperial power and wealth.

In addition to supporting native crafts Catherine also shared with monarchs of her time a passion for acquiring artistic masterpieces from all over Europe. Over the course of her long reign she amassed an enormous collection of paintings and drawings by sending her own agents into the competitive fray at European auctions.[60] Not long into her reign she conceived the idea of displaying her treasures in a specially built space on the palace grounds. Consequently Catherine eventually erected not one but two "hermitages" (supposedly private retreats) adjacent to the Winter Palace, with galleries for displaying paintings to her intimate circle.[61] In 1770, even before the original "Small Hermitage" was completed, Catherine understood that she would not be able to gather her entire art collection there, and in the late 1780s she commissioned Quarenghi to erect a second building, the Large Hermitage, situated to the east of its predecessor along the river. This edifice included a wing extending south along the Winter Canal that housed "the Raphael Loggias," a replica of the Renaissance gallery in the Vatican Palace.

Catherine deployed her palace, as her predecessors had, to exhibit the glory of her monarchy to the imperial court. It was thus to her friends and foreign dignitaries that her art collection was mainly displayed. She held informal dinners in the Hermitage buildings for select guests, and while the court was in residence at the palace only Catherine and her associates had access to the picture galleries. When she was away, however, a "somewhat more democratic" clientele gained access, on an individual basis, including painters, students, the gentry, and the educated public.[62] One memoirist recalled that students at the Smolnyi Institute for Noble Girls toured the picture galleries in the spring of 1773.[63]

PUBLIC LIFE AND PRIVATE LIFE IN CATHERINE'S WINTER PALACE

While the Winter Palace was regularly the setting of imperial government, which Catherine and her successors conducted from their palace offices, one extraordinary moment of public representation took place there in February 1768. Catherine reconvened the Legislative Commission she had originally summoned to Moscow the previous summer to hear and consider her own extensive "instructions" on Russian law and to offer their own recommendations for changes in the empire's legal code. At its height the commission was comprised of "165 delegates from the nobility, 208 from the towns, 28 from governmental institutions, 42 from the *odnodvortsy*, 45 from the Cossacks, 29 from the state peasants, and 54 from the non-Russian peoples of Siberia, the North, and the Volga region."[64] Delegates received a modest stipend from the frugal empress, but it did not always cover the expenses of those who traveled great distances and it was paid irregularly. The inconveniences of attending particularly for those of humbler station were such that one scholar estimates as many as 170 delegates may have taken advantage of the right to turn their credentials over to someone else. When the assembly met in Moscow a few of the St. Petersburg delegates did not attend any sessions, and the reverse occurred when the body moved to the northern capital. We do not know the reason but in mid-December 1767 Catherine abruptly ordered the presiding marshal A. I. Bibikov to adjourn the meetings and ordered the delegates to reconvene at the Winter Palace in St. Petersburg on February 18, 1768.[65]

When the delegates from across the empire reconvened in the Great Gallery of the Winter Palace in midwinter Catherine continued to publicize the commission's work by inviting important guests to view the proceedings from a specially prepared spectators' balcony that adjoined her own private viewing station. In August the English ambassador Charles Cathcart accepted an invitation to observe the proceedings from this spectators' gallery, "over the room where the assembly was held and separated from it by casements."[66] Gazing down at the gallery through a window Cathcart concluded that the room did not in either "extent or magnificence ... fall short of Inigo Jones's idea for Whitehall, with which it also corresponded in the happy circumstance of being situated on a very noble river."[67] The Englishman recalled the arrangement of the space with the throne itself standing at one end of the hall, on the left side of which stood a "table of State." The imperial officials overseeing proceedings had chairs near this end of the room. At the other end "both sides have benches as in the House of Commons," and the room seemed stuffed with people busily engaged in separate conversations.[68] Like other English observers of Russian court events, Cathcart was struck by the exotic diversity of representatives from "the different corners of this immense Empire whose different names and dresses it would be too long to describe in a dispatch," as well as by the attentive deportment of so many rustics.[69]

Most residents of St. Petersburg had no such access to the proceedings, but they would have had some access to information about the commission's meeting dates and general work, which was posted at police stations and printed in newspapers. Important people could procure tickets from the procurator-general's office to view proceedings from the spectators' galleries. What either the Russian public or the humble participants in the commission took away from their experience we do not know, but the Legislative Commission was a brief, extraordinary interlude of civic theater on monarchy's grandest stage.[70] Citing the outbreak of war with Turkey Catherine closed the commission in December 1768, although she may have been grateful for an excuse to end her frustrating experiment in popular representation.

Despite this civic interlude the principal function of the Winter Palace was to house the monarch and her family. Nothing indicates the dual nature of being a monarch as clearly as the challenges involved in conducting private life privately inside a building that housed so many supporting players and court spectators. As an eighteenth-century monarch Catherine was still free from the next century's pressure to manifest familial piety and domestic order. Still, she tried to be discreet inside her palace. Living as a widowed woman and "serial monogamist," Catherine's practices revealed to her immediate household that the empress did not embrace a conventional domestic morality.

For example, when she was falling in love with Grigorii Potemkin, the man she would refer to as "my spouse," it was Aleksei Orlov who confronted her early in 1774 as to whether the prince had replaced his brother in her affections. When she admitted as much Orlov conceded that this was generally known, along with the fact that they had been meeting in the first-floor bathhouse, "because for about four days we have seen a light in the window rather later than usual."[71] Even once Potemkin was ensconced in his own suite just downstairs from Catherine's, however, she complained that it was not always possible to meet him. Sending him a note from one floor to the next she wrote on one occasion: "My little darling, hello! I could not visit you as usual, because our premises are stuffed with every kind of living creature, just roaming around."[72] The empress of all the Russias was apparently unwilling to parade her private life openly before the "creatures" occupying the palace corridors, even though she did not make strenuous efforts to display traditional family life for her palace household.

When Catherine died in November 1796 after thirty-four years on the throne she left to mourn her passing a much-expanded court. Inside the palace, somber members of the Guards regiments stood watch in the audience chamber outside the palace church and her ladies wept in corners. As the denizens of the Winter Palace grieved, stood watch, and worried about the reign to come, in the Palace Square thousands of St. Petersburg's people quietly assembled. This was the first time that the urban public assembled to honor a fallen monarch in the place that Catherine herself had done so much to beautify. The French portraitist Elisabeth Vigée Le Brun remembered being struck with initial anxiety at the sight of "the immense mob" that assembled on the day of Catherine's death in the Palace Square, but she soon concluded she had nothing to fear since "all those people were so quiet." She continued, "the next morning the populace gathered again at the same place, giving vent to its grief under Catherine's windows in heartrending cries. Old men and young, as well as children, called to their 'matusha,' and between their sobs lamented that they had lost everything."[73] As the prima donna played her final scene on the great stage, shadowy figures from a far-flung audience were drawn to the stage's apron. Here, for a moment, the audience became bit players in an unscripted scene of public mourning.[74] The performance was not official. Rather, it prefigured the civic significance of Palace Square for the publicly oriented urban monarchy that took shape in the approaching century.

Catherine's successor was her son, Paul, born forty-two years earlier during her unhappy marriage to Peter III. Famously distant from his mother who openly preferred her oldest grandson, Alexander, Paul asserted the legitimacy of his own birth through symbolic actions connected to his mother's funeral. Apparently with some reluctance Paul presided over a suitably grand lying in state for his mother. She lay in a "chamber of mourning," a dome-shaped temple, complete with columns and bronze eagle, temporarily installed in the Winter Palace Great Gallery. Here Catherine lay in an open casket, as courtiers and clergymen maintained a vigil around the clock. For the first time, members of the city's general public were admitted to view the dead sovereign, and they streamed past the bier to kiss her hand. Guards surveyed the common folk seeking admittance and reportedly excluded only "badly dressed peasants."[75]

Meanwhile Paul advanced his plan to hold a joint funeral for both his mother and his long dead father who had been buried thirty-four years earlier in a humble grave at the Alexander Nevskii Monastery in the southern part of the city. One thing Catherine had never been, of course, was a father, and fatherhood was destined to be one of the prevailing tropes of the nineteenth century's masculine monarchy. When Paul came to the throne he was the father of nine children. He was determined to honor the memory of his own ill-used father and to bury his parents together, which required disinterring Peter's body and conveying it in a stately procession first to the Winter Palace where it was placed beside Catherine's. Then, about a month after Catherine's death, she and her husband were conveyed per custom across the frozen Neva from the palace to the fortress, where they were entombed side by side. Many of Catherine's devoted courtiers, and many others such as the merchant Tolchenov, registered their disapproval of these events in diaries and memoirs composed, presumably, after Paul's demise.[76]

At the end of the eighteenth century the Winter Palace that had done so much to populate and center the city of St. Petersburg had become a showcase of fine arts and Russian craft. Here the great Catherine had presented herself as the peerless patron of native talent and champion of Russia's human resources. Her relationship with the city's premier cabinetmakers and bronze smiths admitted them to one of the intimate circles of the palace household. She had expanded the court circle to include the city's wealthy merchants, entertained regularly at galas and intimate suppers. At New Year's she gathered an even wider circle of city residents. Here she also received provincial delegations, bestowing the cachet of monarchical authority on the empire's distant reaches.

Whether on Palace Square or inside the public halls of the Winter Palace, Catherine presided over a grand stage for enacting public fêtes, showcasing renowned artworks, enacting the Enlightenment, entertaining commercial leaders, and patronizing native craft. Diarists considered their reception here worthy of note, but how most of the spectators perceived these displays of wealth, grandeur, and order we do not know. However, from their life stories it is clear that for those willing to play designated roles, the Winter Palace was a place of opportunity.

PART II

ENACTING URBAN MONARCHY

5

PALACE OF PATRIOTISM

Catherine the Great was Russia's last female ruler. Thereafter until the monarchy's collapse the Romanovs always produced an adult male capable of asserting himself as the legitimate sovereign of the Russian Empire. Catherine's own son, Paul, was the one partial exception to this rule—inheriting the throne as a healthy adult male but losing it, fewer than five years later, thanks to his lack of popularity among officers, courtiers, and possibly the British government. When conspirators removed him from the throne it was with the full consent of his own able-bodied twenty-four-year-old son Alexander, whose lifelong feelings of guilt for Paul's murder on the night he was deposed shaped his own reign. If the primary reason for the long duration of masculine rule after 1796 was the good health of male Romanovs and the fecundity of their foreign wives, it was also the case that the imperial nation over which this dynasty reigned in the nineteenth century lent itself to being represented by rulers who could style themselves as soldiers, fathers, and masters of the imperial household.

Part of the reason for this fundamental shift in the self-presentation of Russian monarchy at the beginning of the nineteenth century was particular to the fortunes of the Romanov dynasty itself. But a more profound pressure toward restyling their ruling scenario came from the course of historic events. The expanding audience to whom Catherine had manifested sovereign power still consisted primarily of foreign diplomats, ranking courtiers, and leading merchants. However, the revolution that broke out in France in summer 1789 was the distant herald of a new world in which lowly stagehands might themselves take the stage. Catherine did not grow overly alarmed about the French events until the middle of 1791, when she set aside funds to assist the

French monarchs and émigrés. It was her son, Paul, who first sent Russian troops to join an anti-French coalition in 1798, but even he did not have time to absorb fully the political impact of the French events before his brief reign ended in 1801.[1]

Europe's age of revolution, from 1789 to 1848, gradually imposed upon Russian monarchs an existential question: How could conservative absolute monarchy based largely on foreign models survive in an international atmosphere of spreading constitutionalism, tentative democratization, and expanding publicity? The shifting role of the Winter Palace in the life of St. Petersburg rather literally reveals the efforts of Paul, Alexander I, and Nicholas I to find an answer to this question. Each of these men innovated with traditional ceremonies and conventions, and each of them invented new traditions. Each embraced conservative reforms, seeing themselves as modern men in modern times. But their experiments, innovations, and reforms all aimed to refute the inevitability of revolution and democracy and to model a kind of monarchy appropriate for nineteenth-century Russia. At the apogee of autocracy Nicholas I pulled together at the Winter Palace the various strands of this new fabric: patriotism, familial order, and cultural uplift. He embodied and performed these modern, public values for an urban audience on St. Petersburg's central stage.[2]

Russia's nineteenth-century rulers began to put the Winter Palace and Palace Square to various patriotic uses during and after the Napoleonic Wars. As they did so, a new layer of significance attached itself to the center of the imperial capital, a city that was overwhelmingly male and young.[3] Contemporary statistician Karl German provides a breakdown of the population by sex for 1813, when the city's total population reached 317,730, of which 222,252 were male and 95,478 were female.[4] In addition, most of its people were newly arrived. Among the upper classes of more or less permanently settled families the ratio of the sexes was balanced, but among the city's main social groups, which included soldiers, sailors, apprentices, laborers, and servants, males predominated. Most of these young men had come to the city seeking work or opportunity or were posted there under military or labor obligation. As most of the work that men could easily attract upon arrival was temporary or seasonal, as wages seldom were adequate to support a family in the city, and as many of the workers retained obligations in their villages, they did not send for wives until they had acquired more permanent positions. Many of the fortune seekers were unmarried youths, undertaking training in crafts or in the arts. This social makeup presented challenges to the urban authorities responsible for law and order.

Soldiers were a ubiquitous presence in the capital city. German estimated that in 1789 217,000 people lived in St. Petersburg, "not counting the military," of which he concluded there were generally between 30,000 and 40,000. His fellow academician Heinrich Storch provided figures for the military portion of St. Petersburg's population in 1789 as comprising nearly 31,000 military men of all ranks, accompanied by 5,800 women, as well as 10,000 sailors, accompanied by 3,700 women, for a total military population in that year of just over 50,000 people. Nearly 20 percent of the city's population, then, was connected to the military, in a peacetime year. The only group that exceeded this group in size was the general category of servants.[5] The number of troops garrisoned in St. Petersburg fell somewhat when the country was at war.

TABLE 3. Population of St. Petersburg by Category, 1811 (Men and Women)

Category (*soslovie*)	Number
Clergy	1,896
Nobility	33,993
Military	47,273
Merchants (*kuptsy*)	14,083
Townsmen (*meshchanstvo)*	33,022
Servants	63,710
Other categories	154,004

SOURCE: Karl F. German, *Statisticheskaia izsledovaniia otnositel'no Rossiiskoi imperii*, pt. 1, *O Narodo-naselenii* (St. Petersburg: Imp. Ak. Nauk, 1819), 269.
NOTE: Women and minor dependents were classified according to the status of their husbands or fathers. "Other categories" would have included, primarily, members of the peasant *soslovie*, in the city as temporary or permanent workers, as well as *raznochintsy* assigned to private or state factories, to the Court itself, or working as independent contractors or laborers. Foreigners would have been another significant part of this category.

The Winter Palace and Palace Square reflected the city they anchored. Palace guards were a ubiquitous presence within and outside its walls, and their barracks and other posts dotted the palace neighborhood and embankment. As military men who had both the responsibility for protecting the life of their sovereign and the opportunity to end it, the officers and men of the Life Guards units, as they were formally known, figured importantly in the politics of Russian absolutism, particularly in the eighteenth century. No ruler preserved her or his claim to the throne without a convincing display of legitimacy to this inner circle of the palace household. The history of the Romanovs in this period makes it clear that their personal security was rooted in the personal and political bond they forged with these guards and not in the construction of fortified places inside the city. In fact, the Winter Palace itself—a building penetrated daily by scores if not hundreds of people and lived in by thousands—was fairly lightly guarded. Yet no monarch ever was deposed inside this building.[6] As we have seen, Catherine's practices in the palace included frequently sitting down to a hand of cards with her cavaliers in the guard room, and she included ranking officers at regular dinner parties where the number of men invariably far exceeded the number of women in attendance. She managed to present herself to guards officers simultaneously as their commander in chief and their charming patron.[7]

REASSERTING MASCULINE MONARCHY

Although Paul's short reign may fairly be judged a political failure, based on the fact that officers murdered him in 1801 at the fortified "castle" he had build a few blocks from the Winter Palace, he did succeed in reorienting Russia's ruling dynasty toward such conventionally masculine gestures as formal public military reviews and meticulous regimentation of a palace household presided over by its patriarch. While he implemented a foreign policy less bent on expansion than Catherine's, Paul asserted himself as the male head of the dynasty and ruler of the empire. He took steps to gain control over the finances of the imperial household by establishing the new Department of Appanages, and he decreed strict male primogeniture for his Romanov descendants, something none of the men who succeeded him saw fit to overturn.

Most telling was Paul's relationship to the armed forces of his empire. Paul's personal preferences ran to the Prussian military culture so beloved of his father, Peter III. On his own estate outside the capital at Gatchina, Paul had for all the long years as heir presided over a militarized household in which he took personal command of units for long hours of parade drill and in which he included his two oldest sons, Alexander and Constantine. When Paul came to power he was determined to end the laxity he perceived in the army as well as among Catherine's dissolute nobles. He intended to render the dynasty permanently and definitively male, military, meticulously disciplined, and personally dominated by an imposing monarch. His efforts extended to the traditionally privileged guards units, to whom he issued new uniforms along the Prussian style and detailed instructions concerning the spacing of men on parade. However much the status quo called for the attention of an energetic young reformer, Paul's manner as well as the impact of his new discipline soon proved fatally unpopular.[8]

It was during Paul's reign that military reviews on Palace Square became large and frequent. According to court insider Adam Czartoryski, soon after his ascension Paul assembled his special Gatchina units "in battle array on the great square of the Winter Palace in the midst of a timid crowd astounded at the sight of soldiers entirely different from those it had been accustomed to see."[9] As early as 1796 Paul built an "Exercisehaus" for storing military equipment on a recently cleared site just across from the eastern flank of the palace on Millionaia Street. He staged these martial performances not only on special occasions including New Year's Day and Epiphany but also every day that he was in the city, when he reviewed Guards regiments during a *wachtparad*, or changing of the guard.[10] Clearly Paul had in mind an urban audience beyond the court.

Apart from his public uses of Palace Square, however, Paul had little affection for the palace on the Neva, associated so strongly with his mother. The most festive events of Paul's reign took place at his preferred estate in Gatchina. Here he and his wife presided with meticulous etiquette over a court that included elder soldier-sons, many daughters, and a succession of favorites. Paul's efforts to cut traditional court elites down to size extended also to his own family, and by the turn of the new century both Maria Fedorovna and her eldest son, Alexander, had reason to feel that the emperor's displeasure toward them was mounting.[11] For his part, Paul had commissioned a new urban "castle" a few blocks away from the Winter Palace, on the site of the razed Summer Palace. Named for the soldier-Archangel Michael, this red brick fortress was surrounded by a moat complete with three drawbridges. Having eschewed New Year's balls for St. Petersburg's nobles and merchants, the emperor did open this new home to courtiers at a masquerade and an opera, when he moved in on February 1, 1801. Paul had delayed his return to the city for the winter season that year by several weeks in order to settle himself and his family in the completed new palace, but he was so impatient to do so that the plaster on the walls was still dripping. Unfortunately for Paul, his fortified castle could not protect him from his chief officials who had become alarmed over Paul's precipitant rupture with Great Britain in favor of Napoleonic France. It was in his bedchamber at the Michael Castle that Paul met his death on March 11, 1801.

On the night of their father's death, Alexander and Constantine were present in the Michael Castle, where the suspicious Paul had required them to move, along with the rest of the family. On the following day the new ruler returned to the Winter Palace. Although courtiers and many others greeted

Alexander's accession to the throne with relief, the twenty-four-year-old monarch did, in fact, exhibit traits of his father. While he was inclined to rule more in the style of gracious enlightenment than military rigidity, Alexander fully embraced the persona of military commander that he had been trained to recognize as the primary role of an emperor. Paul had conferred military positions on both of his elder sons, and during the period of his father's reign Alexander was appointed as colonel of the Semenovskii Regiment, First Military Governor of St. Petersburg, Inspector of Cavalry and Infantry in St. Petersburg and Finland, and president of the military department of the Senate.[12] He savored military parade and uniform, although his father's endless appetite for repeated drill exhausted even him. Thus in spite of the remarkably liberal ideas that animated Alexander in the late 1790s, including the need for a written constitution and an end to serfdom, he had imbibed his father's conception that the role of ruler was necessarily male and specifically military. He did not conduct the *wachtparad* on the Palace Square every day, but he retained the use of this central plaza to demonstrate the glory of Russian arms. Massive parades displaying thousands of Russian troops had the power not only to impress foreigners but also to display for St. Petersburg's public the bond between the emperor and his army.

Thus Alexander built upon Paul's martial and masculine reorientation of the monarchy even as he restored gaiety and graciousness to the role. On one notable public occasion early in his reign Alexander drew the entire city to the Palace Embankment for an all-day celebration of St. Petersburg's centenary. It was the city's military units that played the leading role in these festivities. On May 16, 1803, rank upon rank of military units arrayed themselves all along the great open expanse that stretched from Palace Square along the Admiralty Boulevard and toward St. Isaac's Church.[13] The units included the Life Guards, infantry and cavalry units from the city, and military and naval cadets.

Meanwhile, at nine o'clock in the morning members of the imperial court assembled in the Hermitage, including male and female courtiers from the top four ranks, foreign ambassadors, notable merchants, and members of the Holy Synod as well as prominent clergymen. Led by the emperor and the imperial family, all of these dignitaries processed down the Hermitage stairway to specially decorated carriages, which conveyed the whole parade to the doors of St. Isaac's by eleven o'clock. There they observed the great military parade and attended services inside the church.

Later in the day Alexander received leading representatives of St. Petersburg's merchants in the Winter Palace. The emperor presented them with a specially commissioned gold plate that commemorated the city's founding. In the evening the celebration continued with the illumination of the city and a concert of "church music" played outside at the Michael Garden between eleven and midnight, which was attended by the imperial family. The generally restrained court journal noted that at nighttime "crowds lined up and completely filled the garden at the Michael Castle and the banks of the Neva from the Winter Palace to the Liteinyi Bridge. An innumerable number of all ranks of the people manifested cheerfulness and hearts full of good wishes for their sovereigns."[14]

With this gesture Alexander conveyed a subtle but important shift in the ruler's understanding of the bond between monarch and subject. At Catherine's great Palace Square fête in the 1760s her courtiers played consummately orchestrated roles for a public summoned to stand quietly at a regulated distance, from which it was assumed they might nonetheless be edified. Her grandson and his officers presided now over an equally formal but much larger and more martial display of soldiers, men drawn from the ranks of the common folk. Their disciplined ranks stretched out from the imperial palace in all directions, tangibly linking ruler and people. The intermediaries in this display were loyal officers, received often at the palace itself, who took up their position between the lower ranks and their commander in chief. A great number of St. Petersburg's inhabitants were drawn to this irresistible festival linking city, soldiers, and emperor.

Early in Alexander's reign there was also time for restoring the court events at the Winter Palace that Paul had eschewed. As though freed from prison, the city's great merchants and nobles thronged in unprecedented numbers to the New Year's masquerades that Alexander and his wife, Elizabeth Alekseevna, resumed in the Winter Palace. For example, in 1803 almost eight thousand nobles attended the Palace New Year's ball, a figure that represented nearly 60 percent of all nobles registered as living in the city. The nearly twenty-five hundred merchants who joined them comprised the great majority of those eligible to attend from the first guild and foreign merchants.[15] Thus Alexander extended the firsthand display of hospitality and imperial charisma to the entire mercantile elite of his capital city.

The charming young imperial couple seemed to relish the party they hosted at New Year's in 1803. On January 1 at half past six in the evening the guests who had been summoned by an announcement on December 26 began to arrive at the palace. Surrendering their tickets they proceeded up the great staircase, merchants proceeding to the Antechamber and nobles taking their place in the relatively new St. George's Hall.[16] The court officials distributed masks to all of these guests, and the process of donning them took until nine o'clock. At that hour the music commenced in each of the rooms, and eventually the imperial couple, accompanied by the dowager empress, her relatives, and Constantine, circulated among them. After playing cards for a little while, the imperial family departed for a ticketed dinner for 250 grandees in the Hermitage theater. Departing from the practice of Catherine's later years, Alexander and Elizabeth returned to the masquerade after dinner and remained among their guests until two in the morning. Thereafter the festivities continued in their absence for two more hours.

In Alexander's time the court journal began recording the persons receiving the first and the last of the thousands of masks distributed, as a mark of particular distinction. This was another way of extending courtesy to merchants and officers. On this occasion it was "St. Petersburg merchant Vasilii Ivanov" who received the first mask. The last was distributed to Lieutenant Klaver, "of the Palace quarters of the retired guards."[17] The economic and military leaders of Russia's capital city had reason to see themselves as duly appreciated by their sovereign and even enlisted as bit players in courtly and military performances of monarchical power.

COMMEMORATING 1812 IN ST. PETERSBURG

If the parade ground had acquired symbolic power by the first years of Alexander's reign, it was the battlegrounds of the Napoleonic wars that defined his reign. Readers of the *Sankt-Peterburgskie vedomosti* could follow diplomatic and military events from 1805 onward, but nothing prepared the Russian public for the unprecedented upheaval of the 1812 invasion by the Grande Armée of France. Napoleon's famous strategic decision to drive his army toward the old capital meant disaster for the residents of Moscow, Smolensk, and many other towns along the invasion and retreat routes. Crucially, it also meant that the social and economic life of St. Petersburg was hardly disturbed during the fateful months between June and December 1812. The number of troops in the garrisons declined, and successive waves of recruits were called up from all parts of the empire. But the court journals as well as the newspaper confirm that life in the capital simply went on. The journals indicate the dearth of parties and dinners but do not reveal the cause. The back pages of the *Sankt-Peterburgskie vedomosti* reveal that important residents continued to come and go, that wealthy nobles and factories still solicited laborers and supplies, and that the emperor continued to bestow honors on military officers. Alexander tarried in the city between mid-July, when the commander of the Russian forces, Marshal Barclay de Tolly, managed to dissuade him from riding with the retreating army, until foreign troops were expelled from the country at the end of December, when the emperor resolved to pursue the remnants of Napoleon's force all the way to Paris.

After the crucible of 1812–1814 Alexander returned to Russia a changed man. He had undergone a religious awakening in the course of 1812, and his quasi-protestant pietism now infused not only his personal life but also his foreign and governing policies. He saw himself now as the servant-leader of a sacred nation, and his efforts at commemoration focused particularly on the sacrifice of soldiers and citizens of Moscow. Residents welcomed him there in 1817 as he laid the cornerstone of a church to be built in memory of the dead.[18] Remembering the war in St. Petersburg proved somewhat more problematic. As the country's capital city and home of its ruling dynasty, St. Petersburg required some kind of monument to the country's costly victory over the invader. However, visitors to such a memorial would be reminded that St. Petersburg and its citizens had suffered nothing like the trauma of Smolensk and Moscow and so many smaller towns and villages. Thus the capital had to commemorate not its own sacrifice but that of the nation for which it purportedly stood. The emperor's first gesture in the North was toward troops returning to the capital from Europe. He commissioned Quarenghi to design a triumphal arch on the Narva highway southwest of the city, through which returning troops would pass. By its nature, however, this monument was meant to be temporary.[19]

When Alexander turned his attention to creating a more permanent monument he focused on Palace Square. Like his predecessors, he had not resisted putting his own mark on this most conspicuous plaza. Only a few years into his reign he had tackled the Winter Palace's aging neighbor to the west, assigning A. D. Zakharov to redesign the Petrine Admiralty and wharves. This project stretched across seventeen years and fundamentally altered the western edge of Palace Square. The century-old moat was filled in and the great corner bastions removed.[20] As the wharves were relocated and their canals filled in, it became possible to erect a row of stylish buildings between the Admiralty and the river. The easier access now opened up along the western flank of the palace between the Neva and Nevskii Prospekt presaged the eventual construction of Palace Bridge. It was not until several years after the war that the Admiralty project was finally completed. When gardeners planted a boulevard of trees along the edge of the park surrounding the Admiralty's southern façade, they revealed a long and picturesque public garden between Palace Square and Senate Square. On this long three-quarter-mile expanse, including both squares, Russia's monarchs would henceforth be able to assemble as many as one hundred thousand troops on parade, all visible from the balcony of the palace overlooking Palace Square.[21]

FIGURE 5.01   Eduard Hau. The Military Gallery of 1812 in the Winter Palace. 1862. The State
Hermitage Museum, St. Petersburg. Photograph by Pavel Demidov.

In 1819 Alexander turned renewed attention to Palace Square. What animated the emperor now was resolving once and for all the more or less improvised jumble of buildings across the square from the palace into a harmonious ensemble to complete a space that had acquired so much ceremonial significance. It was here that Alexander created his chief monument to the national victory of 1812. On March 16, 1819, he named Carlo Rossi to head the project. Eventually the Senate allocated over one million rubles to acquire the old houses of Brius and Lanskoi, which Rossi incorporated into the fantastically long General Staff building that now definitively closed off the southern border of Palace Square. In the center of the expansive edifice Rossi placed a permanent triumphal arch dedicated to the warriors of 1812, which gave access to Bol'shaia Morskaia Street. Atop the arch Rossi placed a sculptural ensemble including the winged chariot of Nike, goddess of victory, pulled by six horses.[22]

The years between 1818 and 1820 brought Alexander's conservative patriotism, religious idealism, and nostalgia for the campaign days into decisive conflict with what remained of his reformist instincts. These years saw an intensifying wave of revolution and political assassination in Europe, to which the continent's leading powers responded at the Conferences of Aix-la-Chapelle (1818) and Troppau (1820). According to Alexander's biographer, these were also the years during which his sporadic contemplation of abdication bubbled to the surface.[23] At the beginning of 1819 his beloved sister Catherine died unexpectedly. Not long afterward his sister-in-law recalled the emperor musing aloud at a family dinner about stepping down from the throne.[24] In the midst of this melancholy Alexander enlisted the British society painter George Dawe to produce a series of portraits of Russian generals who had participated in the campaign of 1812. The emperor had first encountered Dawe, who enjoyed the patronage of English aristocrats, at the Aix-la-Chapelle conference. On the promise of "a generous compensation for his labor," Dawe accepted the emperor's invitation to come to Russia and paint Alexander's generals.[25]

Dawe traveled to St. Petersburg in 1819 and received permission to set up his studio in the old Shepelev Palace, which adjoined the Winter Palace and Small Hermitage.[26] Over the course of several years Dawe painted or oversaw the production of 332 portraits of Russian generals, a project that extended beyond Alexander's death. Dawe's accommodations in the Shepelev Palace were extraordinary. A contemporary painting depicts his huge workshop, which opened into the Raphael Loge of the Large Hermitage.[27]

While his imperial commission made Dawe one of the city's wealthiest and most fashionable portraitists, the emperor's choice of a foreigner to oversee such a profoundly patriotic commission attracted veiled criticism. One critic was the prominent editor of the journal *Otechestvennye zapiski* (Notes of the fatherland), Pavel Svinin, who demurred from the widespread praise of Dawe's rapidly executed portraits. Svinin found Dawe's pictures excessively dark, thanks to his use of "asphaltum." More generally, Svinin opined that the tendency to seek portraitists abroad continued to arrest the development of native Russian talent.[28] It was at precisely this time, during the 1820s, that a group of well-connected art lovers established the Obshchestvo Pooshchreniia Khudozhnikov (Society for the encouragement of artists), a group that worked to subsidize foreign study for worthy prospects, to procure the emancipation of serf artists, and to promote broader interest in art by means of graphic arts and lithography.[29]

In fact, Dawe employed—and took credit for the work of—a number of young Russian painters, engravers, and lithographers, both enserfed and free, in order to fulfill the imperial commission and to capitalize on many private commissions that came his way as a result of it. The most prominent of those employed to work on the 1812 portraits was Alexander Poliakov, of Kostroma Province. A serf belonging to the estate of General Kornilov, Poliakov studied painting in St. Petersburg, very likely on a government stipend, and attracted Dawe's attention because of his talent. A significant number of the generals Alexander wanted to see represented in the gallery were either deceased or serving far away from the capital. Dawe hired Poliakov and a free painter named Vasilii Golike to produce original portraits from pictures sent in by those who could not sit in person. When Poliakov and Golike finished their copies Dawe is said to have applied a few brush strokes and then collected the full pay for each of "his" pictures. Whereas Golike received a salary for his work on the project, Poliakov received only room and board. He lived in the palace while he completed the assignment receiving food and a clothing allowance. Dozens of Poliakov's paintings hang to this day in the upper rows of the Military Gallery, and some authorities believe that his impact on the exhibit extends considerably further, as he corrected many of the darkened portraits produced directly by Dawe.[30]

In his own day Poliakov's case stirred patriotic indignation in high places, as it continued to do among Soviet and post-Soviet commentators. One of the founders of the Society for the Encouragement of Artists was State-Secretary Peter Andreevich Kikin, a retired general whose own likeness hangs in the gallery. With first-hand knowledge of Poliakov's role in the production of these paintings, Kikin worked persistently to procure the serf artist's freedom. Eventually the society was able to pay Kornilov an acceptable redemption price, and at length, Poliakov received official confirmation of his emancipation—many years after the death of Emperor Alexander and only a few years before Poliakov's own death in 1835 at the age of thirty-one. The society paid for his funeral.[31]

Alexander's friend Alexander Mikhailovskii-Danilevskii reminisced that in the final years of his reign the emperor often wandered into the gallery where Dawe was painting, to observe his work, but he did not himself sit for a portrait, suggesting that he would leave such a commission to posterity.[32] It is not clear what Alexander planned to do with this enormous collection of portraits, but he may have made his plans known to his younger brother and heir before his death in 1825.[33]

While Alexander nursed a tender affection for the "companions" of the campaign years and honored the officers who had lost their lives, by 1818 there was evidence that this sentiment was not altogether mutual. The persistent difficulties of life in the Russian army, which entailed a twenty-five-year hitch for enlisted men, and the tightening discipline imposed on officers by the head of the War Department Aleksei Arakcheev produced mutinous stirrings in the unit closest to Alexander's heart, the Semenovskii Regiment. When he learned of a mutiny in this unit while he was at the Conference of Troppau in 1820 the emperor had to face the unwelcome truth that the bacillus of rebellion had found its way even to Russia. The ensuing punishments only reinforced unrest among young officers and the lower ranks as well. Although Alexander did not grasp the extent of sedition among officers, it subsequently became clear that scores of them were drifting toward a succession of secret societies that eventually produced the Decembrist Rebellion of 1825.

When the childless Alexander died far from the capital in November 1825, there followed a confused month during which his two younger brothers appeared to be sparring over who would not accept the crown.[34] Within the imperial family it seemed to be widely understood that Alexander had bequeathed the throne not to his next oldest brother, Constantine, but to Nicholas, the second oldest. From Warsaw, where he served as military governor and lived with his Polish wife, Constantine made no move to return to St. Petersburg, but scores of elite officers in units of the guards had been conspiring to make a move upon Alexander's death in hopes of imposing a constitution upon his heir. The one-day drama played out on December 14, the first day of Nicholas's reign, and culminated in the new emperor reluctantly ordering loyal artillery units to fire upon units that had stood on Senate Square since morning denying Nicholas the oath of loyalty.

Nicholas had ridden out from the palace late in the day to confront the rebels, accompanied by ranks of loyal troops as he moved down Admiralty Boulevard. He was anxious for the safety of his family and ordered extra guards to be posted at palace entrances, although it was many months before he could be certain of which units harbored plotters. Eyewitnesses report that Palace Square itself was covered with all sorts of people during the tense hours of confrontation a few blocks away, including generals and other officers not connected to the secret plot or attempting to disguise their connections. Colonel A. M. Bulatov, a close acquaintance of the conspirators who was later arrested but not convicted, recalled that during the showdown in front of the Senate building, "I walked around on Palace Square, met a fair number of acquaintances and saw several generals, to whom I bowed and went peacefully on my way."[35] He bumped into "about ten soldiers of the Life Guards, one of whom I knew, and he urged me to turn back"—that is, to remain loyal to Nicholas.[36] On this day of perilous disorder the palace precincts apparently remained the preserve of those who supported the monarchy, separated if only by a few blocks from the proponents of revolution. Some of those subsequently interrogated reported that, as conspirators were passing by the Winter Palace on their way to Senate Square, they spotted loyal units inside the palace courtyard and recognized that these were "not with us."[37] Later that night, as the arrests began, most of the officers brought in for questioning made their first appearance before Nicholas himself inside the Winter Palace, before being dispatched to the Peter and Paul Fortress.

In the coming months the investigation commission, with offices at the palace that were often visited by the emperor, unearthed the extent of the conspiracy among officers high and low, both in the capital and in the South.[38] One of the most disturbing pieces of information investigators received concerned a purported plot to attack Alexander personally, and perhaps other members of his family, during a ball in the White Hall (the Great Gallery) in the spring of 1824.[39]

More alarming was evidence that in the days immediately preceding December 14, some conspirators had even considered seizing Nicholas and his family inside the palace. Some had referred to the Swedish Revolution of 1809, in which Gustavus IV had been arrested but not executed, although the Swedish reference would also have brought to mind the 1792 fate of Gustavus III, who had been murdered by frustrated nobles at a masquerade ball in his palace. Some gave testimony implicating Decembrists Konstantin Ryleev and Alexander Bestuzhev in a conversation about how to arrest the imperial family. When Ryleev asked someone to bring him a map of the Winter Palace, Bestuzhev purportedly "answered with a laugh: 'the emperor's family is not a needle, and it won't be hiding when you come to arrest them.'"[40] According to one report, A. P. Arbuzov suggested to Ryleev that nothing would be easier than to kill the emperor by rousing a violent mob from the city's taverns, seizing "banners from some church or other," and leading a crowd bent on pillage to charge into the palace; but in the end the conspirators settled on the idea of holding the family under guard until a tribunal could decide its fate.[41]

This prospect must have worked strongly on the imagination of Nicholas, to whom the Winter Palace was at once a beloved family home, the center of his government, and the very symbol of the bond uniting emperor, army, and people. Thus, in the wake of the Decembrist Rebellion, Nicholas's portrayal of patriotic monarchy was oriented more toward the rank-and-file troops than toward the unreliable elite. Nicholas and his minister of education, Sergei Uvarov, came to enunciate a new governing formula defined by "orthodoxy, autocracy, nationality," or "official nationality [*narodnost'*]," for short.[42] The publicists of this doctrine made the case that the special bond between ruler and ruled was rooted in the Russian people's ancient acceptance of the foreign rulers who were Nicholas's ancestors. Thus Russians, along with other peoples of the empire, were construed as valuing loyalty and obedience to the emperor above all. It was to these worthy folk, therefore, that the ceremonial display of monarchy should be primarily displayed.[43]

THE VETERANS' PALACE

Nicholas I was a far less conflicted character than his older brother, and he possessed an uncomplicated patriotism that was manifested throughout his reign in a more expansive public commemoration of the Fatherland War. Nicholas countered continuing exhibitions of rebellion abroad and disobedience at home with manifold monumental and sentimental reminders of the pivotal years when the sacred bond between a fatherlike emperor and his devoted soldier-sons had rescued Russia from its unholy invader. It was Nicholas who launched the cult of 1812 and made Alexander the cult's central figure, but as time went on Nicholas adjusted the memory of Alexander's army to emphasize the common soldiers over the increasingly tainted officers.

Nicholas's first move to sanctify the memory of 1812 took place inside the Winter Palace. In 1826 he commissioned Rossi to construct a new gallery out of several small chambers adjacent to the throne room of St. George's Hall, for the display of Dawe's portraits.[44] Rossi worked on the project between June and November, and the gallery was ready for its dedication by December 25, 1826, the anniversary of the day in 1812 that Emperor Alexander had designated for marking victory over Napleon's forces. The ceremony of consecration for this Military Gallery commenced with divine services in the palace church, attended by the entire imperial family and the surviving officers

FIGURE 5.02   Vassily Sadovnikov. *View of Palace Square and the General Staff Building*. 1847. The State Hermitage Museum, St. Petersburg. Photograph by Vladimir Terebenin.

of the 1812–1814 campaigns. Later, detachments from cavalry and infantry units marched past the paintings, which included full-length portraits of M. I. Kutuzov, M. A. Barclay de Tolly, and the late emperor.[45]

Thereafter, Nicholas made December 25 a day for annual commemoration of Russia's salvation at the hands of its armed forces. Every year on that date he invited all veterans who had received medals for service in the 1812 campaign or the taking of Paris in 1814 to a special commemorative ceremony in the Winter Palace, which included a service of prayers and a "parade." In 1827 veterans of all the relevant infantry, cavalry, and artillery battalions, which included all of the elite units of the Life Guards, lined up in the major Neva-side halls of the palace on December 25, and the military newspaper *Russkii invalid* (Russian veteran) provided a detailed list of participating units and commanding officers a few days later.[46] By 1832 the ceremony had grown more elaborate. Now the day began with solemn liturgy in the Great Palace Church, attended by the emperor, empress, and heir as well as all leading courtiers and officials. Following the service the aged veterans of the 1812 and 1814 units assembled in the palace's great halls. Now it was the newly created honorary unit of Palace Grenadiers who were privileged to assemble in the Military Gallery, while other units filled up the great staterooms. The emperor's youngest brother, Michael Pavlovich, served as parade marshal. Following prayers Nicholas and his wife proceeded to the Military Gallery, where they were toasted with wishes for a long life.[47]

In the 1840s Nicholas undertook a strategy to extend the impact of his portrait gallery beyond the palace walls. In one of the first Russian examples of using fine art prints to promote both patriotism and monarchy, he assigned Borodino veteran and historian Lt. General Alexander Mikhailovskii-Danilevskii to oversee publication of an album of lithographic reproductions of Dawe's portraits. This six-volume work offered a collection of over two hundred portraits, drawn by the artist I. A. Kliukvin from Dawe's originals, with brief biographies of the generals. It appeared in print between 1845 and 1849. In his introduction Mikhailovskii-Danilevskii informed readers that Nicholas was making this set of lithographs available in order to publicize the Military Gallery, which he intended "to be cherished by the whole Russian Empire."[48] Entitled "Emperor Alexander I and His Companions in 1812, 1813, 1814 and 1815: The Military Gallery of the Winter Palace," the book was underwritten by a list of prominent figures and made available to wealthy purchasers on a subscription basis.

It is worth noting that this foray into publicizing the imperial residence corresponded in time to the initiation of publicized royal photography in Victoria's Britain, where the first royal photographs were taken in 1842 and first publically displayed in 1857.[49] Nicholas refrained from being photographed personally, aligning himself with those who believed that mass-produced images of the sovereign would do more to undermine the mystique of monarchy than to augment it. But he was interested in publicizing images of Winter Palace interiors, at least under the controlled circumstances of expensive fine art reproduction and in the service of the cult of 1812.

An even more dramatic confirmation of Nicholas's veneration of the monarch-soldier bond came in 1827 when he created a new honor unit of palace guards, the Company of Palace Grenadiers. Although the Decembrist Rebellion had ended in ignominious failure, it colored the new emperor's understanding of his relationship to the army. As interrogators uncovered the low-grade fever of rebellion that had infected even the army of Europe's most pious and conservative monarchy, Nicholas concluded that the spirit of revolution was limited to a relatively small number of aristocratic officers whom he consigned to Siberian exile. At the same time Nicholas and his loyal officers also came to the conclusion that rank-and-file troops, the proverbial simple peasants who constituted the mass of Russia's armed forces, remained fundamentally loyal to their sovereign.

It was to such men, particularly to the heroic veterans of the Napoleonic campaign, that Nicholas now turned in order to shore up the personal security of the imperial family inside its own palace. In the lower ranks of the Life Guards units that had survived the Battle of Borodino and other key battles of the 1812–1813 campaigns, Nicholas found true representatives of the imperial nation he had been called to rule. These men became the core of a special palace company that lasted until the collapse of the monarchy in 1917. The Palace Grenadiers are testimony to a kind of monarchical populism that Nicholas embraced, in which he and other members of his family cherished the notion that Russia's pious, patriotic commoners continued to revere their emperor in dutiful obedience despite the corruption of Russia's Frenchified elite. It was inside the Winter Palace household that many personal encounters between imperial family members and obedient subjects convinced the rulers that they were beloved by their subordinates. The Palace Grenadiers were bearded and dramatically uniformed exemplars of this reassuring devotion.[50]

Although many of those who had campaigned in the heroic years had by 1827 completed their twenty years of service and dispersed to all corners of the empire, Nicholas ordered that those veterans of 1812 still in the ranks be assembled into his special unit.[51] Most of those who joined at first were older soldiers in their last years of service before retirement. As late as the 1830s soldiers who had been part of the glorious years were still being accepted from other units into the Palace Grenadiers. The men in this unit undertook the chief ceremonial duties of guarding the monarch and his residences throughout his life and conveying his remains to the Peter and Paul Fortress upon his death. Nicholas took great care with the Grenadiers, commissioning special uniforms for formal and other occasions and spelling out in precise detail the order of march when the company processed from the Winter Palace to Palace Square. He decreed that the unit's flag would always fly at the entrance to the palace and inside its rooms.[52] Many of those who served in this unit were housed inside the palace with their families, and others were quartered privately around the city before the court purchased the former French embassy and built the company its own barracks. The Ministry of the Imperial Court took special interest in the fate of these men's families and provided monetary gifts to them on special occasions. Service in the Grenadiers was both an honor and a boon to soldiers who undertook it.

A handful of biographical sketches indicate the road soldiers traveled to the heart of Nicholas's palace. Grenadier First Class Gavril Zaitsev was a peasant from Penza Province, recruited in 1808. He was attached to the Grenadier Regiment of the prince of Prussia in 1809 and served there until being transferred to the Semenovskii Guards in 1821. During 1812 Zaitsev fought in the major battles of Borodino, Tarutino, and Viazma; in 1813 he served at Bauzen, Dresden, Kholm, and Leipzig and continued campaigning through France and at Paris in 1814. He served in the Russo-Turkish War of 1828–1829 and received the Order of St. George for exceptional bravery in that conflict. In January 1833 Zaitsev was received into the Company of Palace Grenadiers where he served for five years before being retired from service in 1838. Grenadier Efim Gadun was first recruited into the emperor's army in 1811 and served in the Arzamass Dragoons, the Ekaterinoslav Cuirassiers, and the Cavalier Guards. Gadun saw service against Napoleon's forces in October and November 1812. He served in Europe and fought at Paris in 1814. Gadun retired from service in 1832, but he was named to the Company of Palace Grenadiers the next year. Like Zaitsev he served for five years at the palace before retiring from the service for good. Gerasim Ovsiannikov of Tambov joined the Kostroma Regiment in 1809, saw action in 1812 against the Austrians at Gorodichno, and served in the regiment until 1834 when he was transferred to the Izmailovskii Guards for one *day* before being named to the Palace Grenadiers.

The most public of Nicholas's commemorative projects, however, was the creation and installation of the Alexander Column in the center of Palace Square. Richard Wortman has demonstrated that the imperial family nurtured a particularly tender attitude toward Alexander I, and Nicholas, to whom the late emperor had been more a substitute father than an older brother, made Alexander the center of the 1812 cult he so assiduously developed. As the Palace Square was at last "finished," the senior Rastrelli's chunky monument to Peter the Great long since forgotten, and soon after completion of the Military Gallery, Nicholas conceived the idea of focusing this central plaza on the memory of 1812 and its heroic leader.[53] The prolonged project of erecting this remarkable monument provided the capital's residents with a series of public spectacles between 1830 and 1834.

In late 1829 the emperor approved a design by Auguste Montferrand, the architect who at the time was building St. Isaac's Cathedral. By November 1830 workers had begun preparing the site in the center of the square, which entailed sinking over a thousand pine piles into a foundation pit four meters deep. Atop the piles workers set a foundation of twelve granite blocks. The granite for both the pedestal and the column came from a quarry in the Gulf of Finland where between three hundred and four hundred serfs deployed iron crowbars and sledgehammers for two years to wrest the granite from its mountain.[54] The massive stone that formed the pedestal and base of the column arrived on a specially constructed vessel in early November 1831 and docked at the landing stage that then existed between the Admiralty and the Winter Palace. For eight days men labored to haul stones weighing over one thousand tons from the river to the center of the square. A twenty-year-old foreman named Vasily Yakovlev supervised the work of dressing the stone and setting up the pedestal.

Several months later, in July 1832, a vessel docked in the city carrying the monolith from which the column itself would be created. Workers spent twelve days dragging it to the square on a sledge with the help of winches. The gigantic stone lay in the Palace Square for nearly two months as stonecutters and polishers prepared it and as engineers completed massive scaffolding that would be used to erect it. Finally the anticipated day of erecting the column arrived, the feast of St. Alexander Nevskii, August 30, 1832.

The imperial family engaged the entire city beginning with a liturgy at Kazan Cathedral, a church procession to Alexander Nevskii Monastery, and return to the Winter Palace. Crowds had begun to gather at Palace Square in the morning, hailing from near and far, including visitors from "Moscow, Riga, Revel, and even from England, in order to witness this one of a kind solemnity."[55] All observers were struck by the unprecedentedly large crowd, which Montferrand estimated at ten thousand. The *Sankt-Peterburgskie vedomosti* breathlessly reported in its lead story a few days later that observers occupied galleries near the scaffolding and the whole expanse of Palace Square, peered out of windows on all sides, and covered the rooftops of the palace, the General Staff building, and the Admiralty. The weather was reportedly splendid in the extreme.

The imperial family, court dignitaries, and foreign emissaries occupied booths specially constructed by Montferrand near the scaffolding. Special guests also included representatives from the Academies of Arts and Sciences along with professors and foreign artists. After a short prayer, at two o'clock sixty capstans began slowly to move. The paper reported that all were silent as they watched with fear and hope. It took nearly two hours to raise the massive column, but when it finally stood upright the massive crowd erupted in joyful cheers. All around people congratulated Nicholas whose only thought, the paper reported, was to honor the memory of his beloved brother, the savior of Russia. To the famous statue of Peter the Great St. Petersburg now added an impressive monument to the man Nicholas presented as its second hero.

While some memoirists claimed that people enjoyed placing bets with each other about when the column would fall, and in which direction, the spectacle favorably impressed the government clerk I. V. Roskovshenko who wondered in a letter to his family in Ukraine how to describe the brilliant procession of the emperor's family, the entire court, and the foreign emissaries.[56] Much less could he find the words to describe the size of the crowd, "which, without exaggeration numbered over 100,000; roofs, windows, in a word, everyplace possible was completely jammed with people," who watched for two hours as the column was erected.[57] The work of polishing, of erecting the statue at the column's top, and placing the bas-reliefs on the pedestal consumed two more years.

The formal dedication of the Alexander Column took place on August 30, 1834. It was a suitably warm summer day when members of the court assembled all the elements of Nicholas's 1812 cult before a massive crowd of St. Petersburg spectators. On this occasion engineers were replaced by troops and veterans, among whom the Palace Grenadiers arrayed in newly designed uniforms held pride of place. Over a hundred of them assembled that morning in St. George's Hall, as the company flag was retrieved from its station in the Military Gallery. To the beating of drums the Grendaiers proceeded down the southern stairway and lined up at the palace gate to await the signal for them to enter the square. At eleven o'clock the company took up positions along the palace façade, executing a careful drill, and holding their position as clerics offered prayers from the balcony above them. Throughout the proceedings the Grenadiers' flag fluttered from the balcony. Before the general military review began, the Grenadiers assumed posts guarding all four sides of the monument itself and remained in these positions throughout the parade.[58] The military review took full advantage of the parade ground now extending from Palace Square to Senate Square. Some 120,000 troops filled this space.

How did the people of St. Petersburg react to this spectacle and to the more general expansion of patriotic imagery that reached its zenith during the reign of Nicholas I? One pamphleteer believed that the crowd of city people observing the parade was there to honor the memory of Alexander, which they associated with kindness and Russian glory. For the aging Grenadiers now living under Nicholas's roof and the veterans honored each December in his palace, it seems likely that commitment to monarchy ran deep. One comment on the proceedings came from the former serf painter and now Academician Vasily Raev. Later that year he completed his "Dedication of the Alexander Column," which depicts the great space between the palace and the Senate filled to the vanishing point with rigid squares of faceless troops, arranged in geometric perfection. Grigory Kaganov concluded that what motivated Raev was a "secret feeling of powerlessness and lostness, almost of terror, before this incredible yet humanly created space" and, further, that "to the ordinary person it was terrifying to look into this architecturally ordered steppe."[59]

Naturally we cannot know how many other people reacted this way. Kaganov notes that most of the other paintings of this event assumed a less daunting perspective, taking in the spectacle from a more human point of view. Vasily Sadovnikov's series of paintings of Palace Square and the Winter Palace also convey the formality of the interchange between monarch and city people, but they impart a sense that people have come out to see a pleasant spectacle. His 1839 *View of the Winter Palace from the Admiralty* shows spectators grouped at a respectful distance from palace troops on the Admiralty side of the building during the changing of the guard, but the variety of city types as well as an eager child tugging at his father's hand conveys a civic cheerfulness as residents and visitors enjoy the sights of their national capital.

When the troops had dispersed, city people were able to close in on the great column and peer up at the sculpture at its apex: Alexander as an avenging angel, crushing a serpent.[60] Did they contemplate, as subsequent commentators invariably do, the monument's references to Roman grandeur? Did they imbibe the classical order of the finally completed architectural ensemble at the heart of their capital city? Were they daunted by the imposing display of government power? Did the city's newest monument, which had been standing in its place already for two years while the finishing touches were administered, stir patriotic sentiments in their hearts? It is not unreasonable to suppose that many nursed such feelings, which tend to be stronger in a crowd. But as the military occupation of Palace Square ebbed on the evening of August 30, 1834, city residents gradually reclaimed the space: socializing, discussing the day's events, going about their duties in what remained of the day. Only part of the square fell under the watchful gaze of the Palace Grenadiers who now manned the sentry box erected near the column because their post faced the palace itself. Behind it, in the lee of the palace, city life went on.

6

THE PALACE HOUSEHOLD AND ITS MASTER

From Victorian Britain to Romanov Russia, monarchy survived by adaptation. At the proverbial apogee of autocracy the Romanovs confronted the forces of demystification that other European rulers also faced in that era: a growing public sphere, the proliferation of print media, the expansion of a scientific worldview, secularization, and the challenge of representing increasingly complex and articulate societies.[1] In Russia the pressure for political modernization in the form of expanded participation and constitutional change intensified these pressures. The Russian monarchy was buffeted by elite rebellion in 1825, by dissatisfaction over serf emancipation in the 1860s, and political assassination in 1881. Despite these pressures Russian monarchs preserved their governing absolutism and extended their national and imperial significance throughout the nineteenth century. Catherine's grandsons Alexander I and, especially, Nicholas I positioned Russia as the leading defender of monarchical government and the Old Regime, seeking ways to modernize and preserve an institution weakened by peasant rebellion, dynastic confusion, palace coups, and constitutional challenges.

Extending the patriotic cult of 1812 was a mark of continuity with the reign of his older brother, but Nicholas departed from his brother's model by emphasizing his personal role as head of an orderly household. One of the most prevalent motifs of Nicholas's reign was the domestic tranquility and marital harmony of his own family. The point of his domestic display—offered to residents, servants, and visitors on the Winter Palace stage—was not to indicate that the emperor's family was just like theirs but, rather, to demonstrate the qualities of a well-ordered household. Other men, Nicholas seemed to be saying, bore responsibilities as masters of households large or small, and they could learn from him.[2]

It is one of the features of monarchy that it emanates outward from one family and one household, but for a long time European monarchs seemed at pains to disguise this fact. In the aftermath of the French Revolution and the execution of Louis XVI, however, whatever constitutional limits they were forced to accept or managed to resist, Europe's monarchs increasingly stressed their organic connection to their more humble subjects. They emphasized national or imperial bonds, which they represented as familial. Simon Schama has suggested that throughout Europe the image of a royal "family" emerged only late in the eighteenth century, receiving its full development in the nineteenth century and beyond. Contrasting portraits of Louis XIV and Queen Victoria, Schama observed that reigning dynasties gradually changed "from a clan of deities to a domestic parlor group." In Russia it was Nicholas I who took the first steps in a transition, expanded upon by his successors, in which they "replaced dynastic totems with family interiors, presenting themselves as devoted fathers and doting wives, rather than mounted warriors or judges."[3] Nicholas advanced what he believed to be the enduring rectitude of the Romanov dynasty by portraying that dynasty as a family.[4]

Alexander I did not bequeath his younger brother an entirely satisfactory familial model. His domestic arrangements appeared orderly but strained and represented a midpoint between those of his libertine grandmother and his straight-laced younger brother. Alexander's immediate family circle consisted of his widowed mother, the dowager empress, Maria Fedorovna, and his wife, the retiring Elizabeth Alekseevna, whose two daughters died in early childhood. This household was a staid adult affair. Elizabeth never presided as mistress over her own home, as her mother-in-law outlived her. The emperor and empress deferred to the dowager, who often presided over dinners for various dignitaries. Family gatherings invariably took place in Maria Fedorovna's quarters. Inside the household the discreet marital infidelity of the imperial couple was well known.[5]

DISPLAYING A MODEL FAMILY

Nicholas was a much more happily married father of seven, but in his efforts to project the role of household master he was constrained by the limits of the media available for mass communication in his time.[6] On the eve of the publicity explosion that photography, mass circulation print, and electronic communication would bring, Nicholas hit upon the practice of exploiting more fully than any of his predecessors or successors the great stage of St. Petersburg's Winter Palace itself. The palace was a medium in which he could cast himself as paterfamilias while preserving crucial elements of the mystery of monarchy. Here Nicholas transformed the elegant and aloof eighteenth-century imperial court into a modern, if vast, household anchored by a harmonious and dutiful family. Accordingly, he expanded all of the existing public uses of the palace, such as the New Year's balls, while adding new celebrations such as the December 25 military memorial and the practice of inviting multitudes of the very humble to attend Easter services in the Great Palace Church. Tens of thousands of St. Petersburg's people visited the Winter Palace every year of Nicholas's reign, and to a far greater degree than anyone else who was ever master of the palace household Nicholas turned the Winter Palace inside out. He loved the building he affectionately called "Zimnii" more than any other Romanov who lived there. For Nicholas the line between his family life and his imperial duties was blurred, and when he and his family resided in the Winter Palace they were rarely offstage.

The stage itself was the scene of constant remodeling and redecoration as successive and overlapping generations inhabited the palace. A building whose numerous rooms had at first gone largely unclaimed gradually filled up with children, with married daughters and their spouses, and with the heir's family. More often than not, newly ascended rulers continued to inhabit the same quarters they had occupied in their youth, although they generally installed more elaborate décor. Thus the monarch's private quarters moved around over time. Catherine and later Paul had lived where Peter III first established himself, in the southeast section, overlooking the meadow-square. After Paul's death his widow, Maria Fedorovna, maintained her own establishment on the southern enfilade. Alexander and Elizabeth occupied his childhood quarters in the Admiralty-side block. Henceforth successive monarchs all resided in more or less this section of the palace, which offered a water view away from busy Palace Square.[7]

Nicholas and his wife, Alexandra Fedorovna, gradually became the doting parents of seven boys and girls, but they did not occupy the quarters or the office of his venerated older brother, leaving the office undisturbed as a family shrine for many years. Instead, the imperial couple remodeled an extensive suite nearby, with windows looking out on the Neva to the north and the Admiralty to the west. The emperor's official study occupied the second floor of this block. It seems that Nicholas usually eschewed this grand riverfront chamber in favor of a Spartan office in the corner of the first floor facing Palace Square in which he often slept on a camp bed, and where he endured his final illness and died in 1855.[8] It is said that passersby could sometimes observe the figure of Nicholas working by lamplight in his ground floor office well into the evening.[9]

Nicholas and Alexandra Fedorovna seem to have enjoyed the life they created in the Winter Palace as much as any of the monarchs who lived there. The happy domesticity they modeled apparently was not just an act.[10] Nonetheless, while domestic harmony may have been Nicholas and Alexandra Fedorovna's natural inclination, its presentation on the palace stage was carefully planned. It was no simple matter to mount a convincing display of authentic family intimacy to an audience of strangers—particularly to subordinate strangers. One approach was to invite select observers to private performances of presumably everyday domestic life.

Intimate guests as well as servants witnessed a daily routine in which the empress received her children and grandchildren around the tea urn each morning. Even the littlest ones were required to stop their activities and traverse "many corridors, halls and stairways" in order to visit their grandmother. At ten in the morning Nicholas joined his wife for tea ceremoniously prepared by a lady-in-waiting and poured by Alexandra Fedorovna herself. The family teamwork often continued throughout the day, as government ministers who had reported to the monarch in his office were frequently invited to share a "home-style meal [*domashniuiu trapezy*]" in the empress's quarters afterward. Nicholas did not attend these dinners.[11]

The emperor also opened the doors of his palace church on Easter, beginning just a few months after ascending the throne. We have an account from Charlotte Disbrowe, the daughter of an English diplomat, who was struck by the novelty of Easter services in the palace church in 1826. Arriving with her husband at the palace church "in full puff," she had the "exquisite satisfaction of seeing Nicholas I slobber some hundreds of old and young, tall and short, thin and thick, ugly and handsome dutiful servants of the male kind." Lady Disbrowe reported that, in the course of nearly three hours, the emperor kissed some seven hundred subjects. "It really was a most extraordinary spectacle to see these people come up to him in regular files, or rather strings, to receive the accolade; and how thoroughly his Imperial Majesty rubbed and wiped and rubbed his mouth again."[12] Disbrowe was struck that the guests included cabbies and doorkeepers.

Nicholas also extended his predecessors' custom of receiving representative delegations of merchants to a new cadre of industrialists. An example was an occasion in May 1833 when Tsar Nicholas I invited five hundred people to dinner at the Winter Palace in connection with an exhibition of Russian manufactured goods.[13] Those invited included noble factory owners as well as first and second guild merchants, some of whom were seated at the emperor's table. Recording the occasion later, Moscow merchant Ivan Rybnikov recalled that each of the guests had received tickets to the event inviting them to dine at "the Winter Palace of His Imperial Highness."[14] The reception included vodka and *zakuski* in the Concert Hall followed by dinner in St. George's Hall. Rybnikov was impressed to witness the empress and emperor "hand in hand," the heir, the tsar's two daughters, and his younger brother, Michael, as they led guests into dinner. He reported that during the meal Nicholas engaged the manufacturers in a conversation about tariff policy.

If the tsar hoped that occasions such as this one might disseminate the customs of his household far and wide he would have been gratified by the actions Rybnikov took when he returned to Moscow. According to a relative who submitted his story to the popular journal *Russkaia starina* (Old times in Russia) five decades later, upon his return from Petersburg, Rybnikov "did not delay in sharing with all of his children not then residing in Moscow the impressions this dinner in the presence of the tsar's family made on a Moscow merchant, . . . and the meeting by which the Emperor Nikolai had honored him was described and disseminated in writing and among the merchants."[15] Rybnikov's descendants obviously preserved the story, which came down to this woman through Rybnikov's son. It is not surprising that a family would preserve a record of such a noteworthy event, but it is interesting that the tale as recounted included the emperor and his wife holding hands and accompanied by their children. By receiving this merchant paterfamilias in the Winter Palace, Nicholas had managed to convey both the wealth and grandeur of his dynasty and the essential humanity of his exemplary family. In so doing he apparently solidified a monarchical bond that persisted through three generations of Rybnikovs.

Another approach to disseminating the image of Nicholas's well-mastered household was to invite a representative circle of witnesses to family ceremonies of dynastic significance, which would then be described meticulously in the St. Petersburg press. On such occasions Nicholas made use of the Winter Palace in all its glory, welcoming sometimes thousands of city residents into his home. Family occasions such as name days, ceremonies for the religious conversion of imperial fiancées, and the newly minted "majority ceremony" conducted on the future Alexander II's sixteenth birthday, all took place in the palace church before large numbers of invited guests from many ranks of society, including merchants and lower civil servants.[16] The *Sankt-Peterburgskie vedomosti* along with the more popularly oriented *Severnaia pchela* (Northern bee) always carefully reported the cast of characters representing the imperial household, and these reports make it clear that such events were command performances of the entire extended family. Family members, following the emperor and empress, dressed in court garb mandated in meticulous detail, processed from the family quarters to the church, traversing most of the building's first floor, greeting members of different social ranks as they moved through the various parade halls. Olga Nikolaevna recalled holding her father's hand during greetings that went on "for countless hours. We were completely worn out by the time it was over."[17] Clearly, whatever the specific ceremonial occasion, most on display was the marital harmony, beauty, health, obedience, and piety of the empire's leading family.

By far the most exuberant of Nicholas's fêtes at the Winter Palace were the public New Year's balls, an inherited tradition that he deployed in the theater of domestic monarchy. These events grew to unprecedented size in the 1830s when as many as thirty thousand attended. Memoirists from Nicholas's era insisted that a much broader range of city residents attended his New Year's masquerades than had done so in earlier times. According to mid-century chronicler of city life and devoted monarchist Ivan Pushkarev, the public New Year's masquerade, unlike other court events, came to be understood as a "national [obshchenarodov] palace holiday," which attracted "almost every inhabitant of the capital."[18]

According to Pushkarev, for several days in advance of the event the Court Office distributed tickets "to whomever wished to receive them, without any impediment [bezprepiatstvenno]," because "the richness of the tsarist furnishings, the music of the Guards regiments and just the entertainment of the people, itself, commanded the attention of the visitors."[19] He stressed that the number and variety of people receiving the thirty thousand tickets had no parallel in the life of the city or the palace, as it included "a mass of merchants, shopkeepers with flowing beards, long caftans and round hats, their wives and daughters in wool and brocade dresses, in diamonds and pearls. Among them are Georgians, Cherkessians, Tatars, in their national dress," as well as military officers and foreign diplomats "in holiday clothes."[20] Pushkarev's description suggests that merchants of the lower guilds were now being admitted to the New Year's masquerade.

Beginning at eight o'clock in the evening all the great rooms of the palace were thrown open for this occasion, and in time the entire imperial family appeared in each room. The sovereign greeted people, chatting with some of them. The guests enjoyed tea, beer and zakuski, all the while "maintaining perfect order without the presence of police."[21] The guests' tranquility at these massive New Year's balls became legendary, and Peter Bartenev, publisher of the popular historical journal Russkii arkhiv (Russian archive) in the second half of the nineteenth century, repeated this assertion while introducing a letter from Nicholas to Prince Paskevich. In the 1832 letter the emperor commented upon the peaceful good manners of the 22,364 people who had just attended his palace masquerade, which he found remarkable "in the context of the international situation and how things are going in the world."[22]

One sixteen-year-old merchant's daughter left an account in her diary of the New Year's ball in 1831. Juliana Polilova well remembered the first of January that year, when among the visitors to her wealthy parents' St. Petersburg home were some elders of the St. Petersburg stock exchange who handed her father an envelope containing tickets to the Winter Palace public masquerade announced for January 4. Her father explained that "tickets from the Palace are distributed to the merchants through the stock market committee."[23] The elder Polilov here suggests the route through which members of various St. Petersburg communities, including non-Russian subjects of the empire, were invited to participate in the event, as "elders" of the various groups distributed tickets to trustworthy individuals, for whose behavior they were ultimately responsible.

Juliana's mother and a dressmaker helped the eager young lady prepare a shepherdess costume, *sans* mask, and on the appointed day she and her father made their way across the frozen Neva in a sleigh, shedding their outer garments before entering the palace. Their coachman remained outside, minding the sleigh and guarding the cloaks while they were at the ball. They ascended the great staircase in a throng of people, Juliana clutching her father's hand so as not to become separated from him. She was dazzled by the brilliance of the lighting and the uniformed court Araps standing guard along the stairs.[24] At the top they handed in their tickets and were ushered further into the formal rooms of the building's parade floor.

Each great hall through which they passed was flanked by mirrors, and in each hall there were musicians playing. There were soldiers and civilians in great numbers. Some of the guests wore costumes and others were simply in evening clothes. Everyone stood about chatting and tasting the treats passed around by servants. A handsome young officer asked Juliana to dance and became her partner for the evening. The highlight of the whole event came when "a rather tall man dressed in a domino and a mask, accompanied by another, shorter, man moved among the dancers engaging them in conversation. Even the girls were speaking with this tall fellow, laughing and joking with him."[25] The mysterious stranger made his way to her and asked whether she was bored. Juliana laughed incredulously and proclaimed her delight at the proceedings. The stranger took her chin in his hand and, complimenting her, asked whose daughter she was. Sensing that at the palace one should not dissemble, she told the stranger her father's name and then asked who he was. This caused him to chuckle as he moved on to speak with

FIGURE 6.01   Constantine Ukhtomsky. *The Arab Hall or Large Dining Room in the Winter Palace* (with a uniformed Court Arap). 1860s. The State Hermitage Museum, St. Petersburg. Photograph by Pavel Demidov.

others. Of course, our heroine learned soon enough that she had been speaking with the emperor himself. Juliana's escort assured her that her naïveté would only delight the sovereign, "who loves a masquerade and is always satisfied when he is truly not recognized. I assure you that he will tell the empress this story and remember you for a long time."[26]

This little story is a window into one of the mechanisms by which monarchy, at this proverbial apogee of autocracy, actually functioned. Deploying this grand stage Nicholas performed as master of the palace household, and his costumed guests reveled in their supporting roles even as they witnessed the spectacle. Ruler and subject together produced the monarchical scenario. When he spoke to young women as he did on this occasion we may suspect that he created monarchists for life. Indeed, Juliana reported that "the entire conversation with the sovereign is imprinted in my memory with burning letters," but what added to the effect of this event was that she not only recounted the story but also recorded the transcendent moment in her diary. There the anecdote became part of the family lore of the Polilov-Sievertsevs, appearing sixty years later in the memoir of a nephew she never met. Via this story a little glimmer of the Winter Palace traveled all the way to Siberia, where Juliana moved with her husband. Oral tradition, family stories, and anecdotes situated inside the Winter Palace were important media for the transmission of the monarchical idea, magnifying the effect of the emperor's personal charisma as few other media of the mid-nineteenth century could do.

A wider swath of the city population rubbed up against the monarchical stage at outdoor ceremonies on the square and the Neva embankment. The most festive moment on Palace Square came each year in the Maslenitsa (the so-called Butter Week) before Lent began. I. V. Roskovshenko wrote home that he was especially impressed by the *balagany*, or show booths, at least ten of which stood spread out around the square, extending toward the Admiralty, erected from planks and complete with columns and cupolas.[27] "Booth is an inadequate word to describe these huge castles.... Their grandeur gives the impression of a Khar'kov theater."[28] Music emanated from every quarter, performed by notable artists. Roskovshenko marveled at the thousands of people who gathered in the square and along Millionaia Street, as well as those who strolled along the boulevards and skied on the Neva banks. The celebration concluded with "theater twice a day. By that time people were not so much merrymaking as overcome by merrymaking."[29] No doubt Nicholas would have been pleased that Roskovshenko also noted in his letter the centennial of the First Cadet Corps, which was being marked with huge fireworks. "They say these cost 30,000 rubles," Roskovshenko wrote, "but I don't know if that's true."[30]

Nicholas also perpetuated the Neva-side spectacle of the Blessing of the Waters, which by the middle of the nineteenth century had become a much-attended ceremony more oriented toward the city's public than toward the imperial court. One English observer described the scene in the 1850s, with characteristic condescension. John Morell wrote that the tsar and all of his family, along with members of his court, processed out of the palace upon signal from a cannon volley, proceeding to a "magnificent octagon temple" situated on the frozen surface of the river. "Whilst the Procession proceeds towards the temple the crowd rushes in disorder, and soon the banks of the Neva, and the Neva itself, are lost to view, covered with the dense mass."[31] The crowd grew silent during the ceremony, as the archbishop plunged a cross into a hole carved in the ice in the center of the "temple." The emperor tasted the water from a golden cup before returning to his palace with the courtiers. "From this moment the people have the coast clear; they precipitate themselves with frenzy towards the temple, carrying pitchers to be filled with the holy water. It is a struggle, a tumultuous crowding, a pêle-mêle which it is impossible to describe. Some individuals even plunge into the river; mothers bathe their children in it."[32]

Morell's impression suggests a variety of motives for the popular enthusiasm elicited by the ceremony. Many saw the rite as a way to attract and extend a divine blessing on their homes and families. Others took advantage of the opportunity to view the monarchical family and members of court at close range. For others the opportunities were primarily festive—to see or be seen, to meet friends, to have a pleasant outing with their children, to be part of the life of their city. For example, in 1831 Polilova recorded in her diary that on Epiphany she had been greatly distressed that her parents did not allow her to attend the ceremony on the Neva owing to the great cold, because she had hoped to see her sweetheart there.[33]

OBSERVING THE DRAMA FROM BELOW

Apart from the Blessing of the Waters and the Shrovetide festival, what points of contact existed between the expanding population of St. Petersburg's poor working people and the master of the imperial household? The ranks and categories of police proliferated during Nicholas's reign, exerting dissuasive power over those inclined toward disorder or protest. But was Nicholas able also to convey an attractive image of Russian monarchy to the city's lower classes? Here we have few firsthand accounts, and it is all but impossible to imagine a lettered workman confiding critical sentiments about the emperor to some surviving diary. However, one concrete connection between city people and the monarchy were the servants and low-level employees of the Winter Palace. Palace employees often had relatives in the city, and some city people gained access to the palace through court employment or artisanal training. Some impression of the imperial household must have seeped through this seam, although we have virtually no information about what it was. What we can do is describe the points of contact that existed between the palace and the city's working people.

For Nicholas, commanding the imperial household meant not only that he was a husband and father but also that he was the aristocratic master of a large staff of servants, artisans, and employees. In this role he bore a responsibility for the proper training and monitoring of all in his care, and he believed his stewardship could serve as a model for lesser men and their own households throughout the city. Most palace servants and many other court employees lived inside the Winter Palace, but many threads bound them to the wider St. Petersburg working class, and they regularly crossed the boundary between palace and city. Palace residents maintained contacts with relatives and friends throughout the city and had their children baptized in neighborhood churches.

Widows of palace servants remained in the city, often on small pensions after the death of their husbands, and occasionally a male servant outlived his term of obligation and retired to some corner on the Petrograd Side. Official and personal errands regularly carried servants outside the palace, as deliveries and repairs brought city people in.

The capital city Nicholas inherited in 1825 held nearly twice as many people as it had a quarter century earlier, its population rising from 220,200 to 424,700 in that period.[34] Soviet demographers concluded that this rapid expansion of the city's population rested entirely on newcomers, as the city's death rate actually exceeded its birth rate between 1764 and 1860.[35] Seasonal workers from rural areas as well as the city's transient students, soldiers, and sailors flooded into the capital in growing numbers for a few months or a few years at a time. Among peasants, those newly arrived were likely to be seasonal migrants, temporarily released by their masters to work for wages partly returned to the serfs' owners. During the first half of the nineteenth century some of these people would have found employment in the city's blossoming textile and metalworking industries. Among those who had by hook or by crook established long-term residence, some found their way into palace service.

The working classes of the city were still overwhelmingly male.[36] In 1837 there were no females at all among the more than sixteen thousand people listed as holding temporary status as registered craftsmen.[37] If we add the temporary craftsmen to the ranks of migrant peasants and soldiers, well over half of the city's residents were newly arrived, were living in an all-male environment, and probably considered themselves initially as temporary. It is also clear that most of the city's inhabitants were young. Data from the city's first census in 1864 found that over half the population was under the age of thirty. The greatest gender disparity among age cohorts was among this age group.[38]

So St. Petersburg during the reign of Nicholas I was largely a city of unattached young men and boys who had come to the city as soldiers, sailors, apprentices, laborers, or house servants. While the army and navy had well-established means for imposing order on the waves of young men passing through their ranks, city authorities struggled to control the potentially volatile population that pressed into St. Petersburg in such numbers in the first half of the nineteenth century. This was the audience to which Nicholas sought to display a model of family harmony, temperance, duty, and piety, and there is reason to believe that he failed to understand the extent to which the scenario of a household patriarch was irrelevant to most of the city's inhabitants.[39] To those who became members of his household, however, Nicholas took considerable pains to model the values he associated with Russian monarchy.

Until the early nineteenth century it was possible to enter palace service as a freely hired worker not registered on the fiscal rolls. The freely hired came from city groups free to exchange their labor for room, board, and modest pay—such as townsmen, clergy, and lower ranks of the civil service. One such worker was Ivan L'vov, the son of a former parish clerk from the Vyborg Side who first entered court service in 1793 as a cook's apprentice. Thence he ascended the career ladder, becoming a cook in 1797 and a chef in 1806, a position commanding remuneration of 350 rubles per year.[40] There were many advantages to a position in the court, however humble. Besides the room and board there was free medical care, a reasonable expectation that one's sons would find court positions, and the possibility of a pension. Moreover, in 1765 Catherine excluded liveried servants at her court from corporal punishment.[41]

Early in his reign, however, Nicholas made a move to restrict all court positions to the children of those already in court employment. This measure had the dual purpose of filling sensitive positions with individuals who were familiar with court routine and expectations while also assuring loyal servants that they could hand down court employment to their children.[42] Nicholas's reign was the high-water mark of what Igor Zimin has called the "caste-like" quality of court service. As one of the most important divisions of the imperial court, the Winter Palace also came to be a place of inherited positions. Officials there clearly preferred to fill their staff with young people who had grown up acculturated to the rituals of the imperial household including, above all, the obligation to maintain propriety and scrupulous confidentiality about all that went on inside its walls.[43] Thus humble palace workers could reasonably hope that their sons would find lifelong employment in the service of the emperor. Even the daughter of a palace servant might be employed, particularly if her father died before her marriage as was, for example, the case of Afim'ia Andreeva, the granddaughter of a deceased worker, who was taken into service as a kitchen aide in 1810 and remained in that position until her death sometime after 1844.[44] Andreeva was especially fortunate, as the only palace jobs regularly open to females were laundress and kitchen assistant.

While employment at the Winter Palace came to be formally restricted to the children of court employees, it was not exclusively hereditary among Winter Palace servants. Many of the young people taken on at the palace in Nicholas's time were the sons of clerks (*chinovniki*) from various court offices who themselves had never worked at the palace or in close proximity of the imperial family. For example, Mikhail Ageev was the son of a lower-level chinovnik who received appointment at the entry level of "worker" in 1832 and was promoted to fireplace stoker in 1834. Four years later he was posted to the rooms of the grand duchesses, and he became a footman in 1843.[45] Others were transferred directly from the military to palace positions, apparently drawing military pensions as they did so. It was possible for talented boys to enter the Winter Palace and receive training as singers, as did Afonasii Alferov, the son of a fourteenth-class chinovnik. Alferov came in as a young singer in 1832, earning a salary and his own fourteenth-class rank in 1838.[46] Another route to palace service was open to those who would inform for the Third Section—that is, for the emperor's security services.[47] These examples attest that in the 1830s and 1840s, many hereditary court employees were, in fact, the first in their families to work inside the Winter Palace. These young men were city people, presumably with a network of friends and family outside the palace gates.

Although rural people were not admitted directly to permanent service at the Winter Palace in Nicholas's time, the Office of the Court had long-standing contracts with the elders of certain villages, primarily in St. Petersburg and Iaroslavl Provinces, to provide temporary labor. Such was the case with arrangements to cut wood for the Winter Palace each winter. Country people in the vicinity of the capital benefited from the court's appetite for labor just as their urban counterparts did. Their elders negotiated contracts with the Office of the Court and became accustomed to a level of remuneration not available in the hinterland, or even in Moscow.[48]

Once employed, the cadre of serving people working at the Winter Palace was itself a stratified society in which a servant manifesting long-term loyalty and compliance might achieve impressive upward mobility. Occupying the lowest rank were the temporarily contracted unskilled peasants, whose food was supplied by their own elder or work gang (artel') leader.[49] Next was the larger number of permanent servants employed directly by the palace. These included hosts of kitchen workers. Positions in the Winter Palace main kitchen included personal chef (mundkoch), chef, cook, cooks' apprentice, baking master, bread maker, frying master, baker, linen keeper, and kitchen aide.[50] Wine stewards (mundshenks) and table decorators (tafeldekkars) constituted an elite who might enter the Table of Ranks and advance through the twelfth rank after many years of exemplary service.[51] A very high-ranking member of the kitchen staff was the maître d'hotel. One of the men holding this position was Nikolai Semenov, who had entered the service of Empress Maria Fedorovna in 1780. Semenov became a cook's apprentice in 1786, a cook in 1791, a chef in 1795, and a mundkokh (personal chef) in 1799. Semenov was named maître d'hotel with the title of kamer-fur'er, or sixth class, in 1816. He apparently served in that capacity until his death in 1821.[52]

Outside the kitchen ranks, permanent workers included fireplace stokers, silver cleaners, scribes, barbers, hairdressers, wardrobe assistants, and footmen.

For many of these positions there were apprentices or assistants. Valets could ascend to the twelfth rank and were personally close to the emperor or members of his family. Despite a mix of German and Russian job titles, most of those employed in the nineteenth century were Russians, although chefs tended to be French and German. By the 1830s the German titles had largely been replaced by Russian ones on the list of lower-level palace personnel, but some remained, including all of the supervisory positions such as *hof-fur'er* and *kamer-fur'er*.

The stratification of servants is also manifest in what can be gleaned about those receiving pensions upon release from service. Servants of any rank, including those in such humble stations as barbers, stokers, or cook's apprentices, might be rewarded with occasional monetary rewards for special merit, and they received modest pensions for long service. Some of those who did not receive pensions were granted the relatively large sum of three hundred rubles in their last year of palace service. This also appears to have applied to the widows and children of deceased servants, as in the case of the widow and five children of the footman Pavel Afanasev, who received a pension upon his death in 1834.[53] It also happened that servants particularly close to particular members of the imperial family received monetary gifts when their patron died. These parting gifts generally went to survivors or retirees who would be moving out of the palace; presumably many servants died in service, their children already established in the palace household. The sons of lower-ranking servants who did not receive palace appointments could hope to receive a recommendation from palace officials, on impressive imperial court letterhead.[54]

The mid-level palace managers charged with overseeing the staff and its work included the *kamer-fur'er*, an official who could achieve a maximum civil service rank of sixth. *Kamer-fur'ers* oversaw the day-to-day management of the palace, acting as stage managers who kept meticulous records of all formal events and ceremonies. The *hof-fur'er*, who could earn ninth class after ten years of exemplary service with no further right of promotion, oversaw palace servants directly.[55]

Perhaps the most meaningful distinction within the palace staff, however, was between those who served the family and its guests directly and those who worked entirely behind the scenes. All servants who appeared on the parade floor of the palace wore uniforms meticulously designed and mandated by their rulers according to the changing tastes of court ceremonial. The livery of palace servants made them costumed characters on the imperial stage. In the eighteenth century even peasant nursemaids had been required to dress up for formal occasions, but this practice was later abandoned. Nicholas recalled a scene from his childhood that seemed unnatural to him:

FIGURE 6.02   Charles Bachelier. *View of St. George's Throne Hall in the Winter Palace* (after a drawing by V.S. Sadovnikov). 1858. The State Hermitage Museum, St. Petersburg. Photograph by Vladimir Terebenin.

For the christening services all the women had to wear gowns with hoops and bodices, even the nurse: imagine the spectacle of a rough Russian peasant woman from the outskirts of St Petersburg decked out in hoops and hairpieces, powdered, painted and laced to the point of suffocation! Nevertheless, it was deemed necessary. It was only my father who, on the birth of Mikhail, liberated the unfortunate creatures from this ridiculous torture.[56]

If Nicholas thought it absurd to costume peasant nursemaids, both he and his older brother, Constantine, robustly promoted the refinement and deployment of livery for serving men. Their footmen and coachmen bore the impressive palace livery into the streets of the city as they rushed about town on countless errands.

By far the largest number of Winter Palace servants and artisans whether permanent or temporary employees were single men and boys who resided on the premises. They lived in the groundfloor barracks eating meals they prepared themselves in an assigned kitchen. Temporary contract workers were also often housed in the palace and assigned use of their own kitchen. When in 1859 Winter Palace authorities undertook an inventory of "public property located on the premises occupied by unmarried floor polishers, lower ranks of the artisans' company, lower ranks of the servants' command, and Putilov peasants," among the items listed were over 150 beds, bedding, kitchen equipment, and one clock.[57] As the palace and court staff continued to grow, some unmarried servants and employees eventually were housed in a new residence for court employees located on Gagarin Street.[58] Married servants could also be accommodated in the palace with their wives, but by Nicholas's time male palace servants who married received housing allowances, allowing (or forcing) them to move out of the palace and into the city.

What most palace servants did not get much of before emancipation in 1861 was cash. Some categories of the staff always received money, including the court Araps. However, it was not until the 1880s that all palace employees received their pay in cash. When footmen were put on the cash rolls in 1881, those serving in the emperor's quarters earned 200 rubles per year while his valets received salaries of 144 rubles.[59] These employees still received room and board as part of their employment.

Like his predecessors as well as many great aristocrats, Nicholas understood his duty as master of the household to include training young people who showed aptitude in the arts and crafts. Characteristically, he applied himself energetically to putting this training on a regular and organized footing, and he expanded the Winter Palace training program considerably. From the very beginning of his reign Nicholas I directed Winter Palace administrators to organize a series of schools for the children of servants as well as a small number of newcomers who might be taken onto the palace staff. In 1826 Nicholas directed the palace quartermaster (*hof-intendant*) to set up a school for prospective artisans. These boys trained from age six to sixteen, hoping to be assigned thereafter to an apprenticeship in one of the palace artisanal companies or to be sent to a special arts academy. Those who proved unskilled could eventually be assigned to the Court Office as clerks and scribes, while those displaying even less aptitude were assigned to be workers in the gardens or palaces of the court.[60]

In 1839 Nicholas added a school for the children of palace servants not attached to the artisans' companies. Boys enrolling in this school were expected to emerge as liveried servants assigned to serve for a specified period of time. Nicholas tinkered with the training system throughout his reign and by 1852 the schooling for palace artisans and servants received its final, carefully articulated structure. The School for Court Masters and Servants would enroll eighty people from the fiscal ranks. Twenty slots would prepare boys as waiters and footmen and sixty would prepare boys in the crafts of goldsmith, coppersmith, joiner, blacksmith, metalworker, turner, or carver.[61] Aspiring artisans would study basic geometry and receive practical training for one of the palace trades. Aspiring liveried servants would study German, "in case they need to explain something in that language," while acquiring the necessary "dexterity and deftness" needed for palace service. "Although they would be able to exercise their rights upon graduation from such schools," the statute stated, "in view of their education at public expense, they will serve the court until they reach the age of 45, after which they are free to do as they wish."[62]

These schools provided a point of contact between children of palace servants and city children because the school was permitted to enroll up to fifty day students from "other ranks" outside the court system, or even more if demand for trained craftsmen increased. The provision for outsiders seems meant in particular to attract to palace service the children of free artisans, who comprised about 5 percent of the city's population.[63] It was also possible for people discharged from service elsewhere to enter the school if they could supply sufficient evidence that they had been honorably released. Thus, on the eve of emancipation, the Winter Palace was making room for newcomers. At the same time the school statutes make it clear that admission to this school and its privileges was not automatic for all palace servants' children. Specifically excluded were children of masters serving on contract or of *chinovniki* in the Court Office.

While most servants' children completing the course could expect to be appointed somewhere in the palace or in the Ministry of the Court, there was more mobility for the sons of craftsmen. Those masters' sons successfully completing the course were to be appointed as submasters in the appropriate company when a vacancy occurred, with the most able being assigned to the palace. If there was no vacancy at the court for a graduate he was free to work for an independent craftsman, who would pay his salary, but he must be prepared to return to the court when summoned. Those lacking sufficient skill to earn the master status but possessing good reading and writing abilities might be listed as scribes in the Chancellery Office for a term of twenty-five years, with the possibility of attaining rank fourteen after at least ten years of exemplary service there.

In 1854 a girls' section of the employees' school opened. There were twenty places for fiscal students and twenty for private. Upon graduation girls received assignments to work as laundresses in one of the palaces. Those who were especially able might receive appointment as an assistant linen matron

(*kasteliansha*) or even as a teacher at the school. All the female students had
the right to earn money from the sale of their own handwork during their
school years.[64]

Thus there were several points of contact between people who worked
and lived inside the Winter Palace and the broader working population of
the city. The desirability of these positions induced ambitious parents to seek
to enroll their children in palace schools. Conversely, talented sons of palace
employees who received training there were sometimes released into the city
to seek employment on their own. Daughters of palace servants left palace
employment when they married, receiving modest monetary gifts from the
court. It was also possible to be dismissed from palace service if one were
suspected of being a thief.[65]

Before emancipation, palace servants on the court staff were required to
serve up to the age of forty-five.[66] Certain groups were obligated for shorter
periods, but most of those dismissed from the palace were probably elderly
or in poor health. Upon retirement or upon the death of one's husband, many
servants or spouses of servants were "given their passports"—that is, sent
away from the palace, with or without pensions, to make their own way either
in the city or in the countryside.[67] People sent out from the palace were not
free to enter a taxpaying soslovie category without special permission. They,
but not their children, would continue exempt from the soul tax but would
also be forbidden to engage in most kinds of remunerative employment. By
mid-century such people had grown numerous, posing a potential problem to
good order in the city. In 1846 Minister of the Imperial Court M. P. Volkonskii
estimated, with alarm, that there might be as many as eighteen hundred
people dismissed from palace service, or their children, living and working in
St. Petersburg and Moscow combined.[68]

We know little about how such people lived, although the documents hint
that the majority preferred to stay in St. Petersburg, the only home most of
them had ever known. The cost of living in the city sometimes prevented this,
and retired servants who had village connections sometimes left the city. Still,
the fact that servants who had outlived their terms of service as well as widows
of deceased servants were expected to find living arrangements in the great
and expensive city on little or no income, suggests that many such people had
some kind of family ties beyond the palace gates.

One other clue to the family and social connections between palace
employees and city folk is the number of recorded cases in which palace
servants asked city residents to stand as godparents to their children. Court
archives contain twenty-one baptism certificates for children born to palace
employees or servants in 1835 and 1836. Of the twenty-one baptisms it appears

that in ten cases the godparents were not fellow court employees. For example, the child of a court sexton was sponsored by the deacon of a St. Petersburg church and a priest's daughter. A St. Petersburg townsman and the daughter of another townsman stood godparents to a court artist.[69] *Meshchane* also served as godparents for the child of a palace linen keeper and a stoker. One court apothecary's apprentice who held the fourteenth rank had a St. Petersburg third guild merchant and the wife of a local townsman as godparents to his child.[70] While this little file attests to Nicholas's meticulous recordkeeping, it also reveals the extent to which the world of the court and the palace intersected with the middle ranks of St. Petersburg's working population.

Kinship and social connections between servants and city people and the verifiable exodus of skilled workers from the palace to the city point to the fact that there was some knowledge of conditions inside the palace household among St. Petersburg's working class, as well as the reverse. It was not only the upper crust of memoir-writing courtiers, famous foreigners, and privileged Russians who conveyed impressions of Nicholas's household to their counterparts. We can be confident that working-class people did so as well, but because none of these impressions found their way into print we do not know how many of the impressions were positive and how many were the reverse. Julie Buckler advances the thesis that in nineteenth-century St. Petersburg the "cultural middle" predominated, while the binary system of palace and slum so often evoked existed more in the minds of the city's interpreters than in the historical record. This milieu of laboring people of modest income included monarchy's countless stagehands. Moreover, the Winter Palace was also another kind of middle place, one where "palace and slum" encountered one another face-to-face.[71]

THE PALACE HOUSEHOLD AND THE TRIALS OF URBAN LIFE

The early 1830s presented Nicholas and St. Petersburg with a series of extraordinary crises. In November 1830 rebellion broke out in Poland enflamed by several years of Nicholas's increasingly repressive policies and inspired by the summer's revolutionary events in Paris. Despite the deployment of thousands of troops the imperial government did not reestablish control in Poland until late 1831. At about the same time cities in the southern part of the country were gripped by Europe's first modern encounter with what was then known as Asiatic cholera.[72] In June 1831, just as readers of the *Sankt-Peterburgskie vedomosti* learned that the disease had arrived in their city, Nicholas received word that his brother Constantine, governor-general of

Poland, had succumbed to the illness in Warsaw. General Dibich, commander of Russian forces in Poland, had also died of cholera two weeks earlier.

St. Petersburg newspapers reported the first confirmed case of cholera in the city on June 18, 1831, and soon began to tally new cases and deaths as they had been doing for other Russian cities all year. The death toll rose steadily, reaching nearly five thousand by the end of September.[73] In the face of this danger, palace authorities implemented a prepared plan on June 26. In an effort to limit the number of people entering the palace, Grenadiers who lived on the premises with their families were ordered to leave the palace for the duration of the epidemic. Those Grenadiers on duty were now commanded to stay at their posts for two months and to report to superiors if they felt sick so they could be dispatched to a private cholera hospital. The Grenadiers were armed to prevent entry of infected people into the palace. In the end, five Grenadiers became infected and three died.[74]

City officials mishandled the situation, forcing families to yield their sick relatives to hated cholera hospitals. Mistrust took hold and resistance to official policies grew quickly. In working-class sections of the city, especially on Vasilevskii Island and the Haymarket, groups of people attacked cholera wagons that were carrying away the afflicted and stormed the hospitals.[75] The culmination of this unrest came on June 22 in the Haymarket district several blocks from the Winter Palace. Throughout the day crowds grew, milling about and finally invading the cholera hospital, attacking and killing a German doctor and chasing police from the neighborhood. Nicholas had already understood that elite rebellion was possible in his capital, but up to this point he had had reason to believe that popular revolt could occur only when people's affection for their monarchs fatally declined.[76]

Nicholas and his family had retreated to suburban Peterhof as they generally did in June. Several sources repeat the story of his reaction to news of the cholera riot. When he heard of the disturbances from Count Benkendorf, Nicholas left the quarantined suburb for the city. By the time he arrived at the Haymarket, without military guard, a crowd of five thousand people had assembled. According to various accounts the emperor arrived in their midst, stood up in his carriage, ordered the people onto their knees and made the sign of the cross over them. He chastised the people for their disobedience to his laws and exhorted them to ask God's forgiveness for the murder they had committed. He addressed those in the crowd who were "peaceful men, fathers of families," proclaiming his confidence in them and in their ability to "enlighten the ignorant." Most tellingly, the tsar is reported to have shouted to the assembled crowd the question: "Are you Russians? You are behaving as though you were French or Polish!"[77]

The legend of Nicholas's positive intervention led some to conclude that the emperor's courageous appearance stilled the crowd and even turned the tide of the disease. McGrew concedes that this view was not entirely baseless but concludes that what was probably most effective was the government's prompt reversal of key cholera policies. Within a few days St. Petersburg authorities, over medical objections, relaxed the most onerous sanitary regulations. Moreover, whereas rioters in other cities had been dealt with harshly, there were no police investigations into the events in the capital and no extensive recriminations. There seems to have been a decision made in high places to do what was necessary to calm public passions in the capital city.

The St. Petersburg cholera riot of 1831 made it clear to Nicholas that people living within walking distance of his Winter Palace were capable of antigovernment violence. His response to his urban subjects in following years revealed much about his analysis of the problem. He continued to believe that such rebellion was fundamentally un-Russian, just as it was undoubtedly un-Orthodox. Consequently he devoted considerable energy to enacting "nationality, orthodoxy, and autocracy" to the urban public. In ordering and publicizing his household Nicholas strove to inspire St. Petersburg's male residents to fulfill their own roles as "fathers of families." Either Nicholas did not understand how small a number of the capital's working-class men fell into that category or he exaggerated the influence such men could exert over their neighbors. Perhaps more fruitfully, he enlisted all St. Petersburg residents in monarchical enactments of piety and patriotism, such as erecting and dedicating the Alexander Column. The Winter Palace and its public Palace Square now became the foremost stage for performances aimed at binding St. Petersburg inhabitants more closely to the monarchy, especially during the 1830s when the mood of the city's writers and intellectuals darkened perceptibly.[78]

One last disaster shook the imperial family in the 1830s, but for Nicholas it confirmed that efforts to shore up his bond with St. Petersburg's people had borne fruit. On the evening of December 17, 1837, the Winter Palace caught fire, drawing the whole city into a domestic tragedy with public significance. Notified that smoke was filling the building the emperor abruptly departed from the opera, leaving his wife without an explanation for his departure. After rescuing his sleeping children from danger and sending them off to the Anichkov Palace on Nevskii Prospekt, Nicholas took command of troops and fire brigades that converged on the scene. Fire crews from both the palace and the city of St. Petersburg battled the blaze in its early hours, assisted by members of the Guards regiments and other troops. Thousands of palace residents managed to escape the flames, although all would now be homeless for nearly eighteen months. By the end of that night crews had prevented the fire from spreading to the adjoining Hermitage, which became Nicholas's priority once he understood that the palace itself would be a total loss. The fire demolished the entire interior of the palace but left standing the stucco-covered brick outer walls, as high as the first floor.[79] The ruin smoldered for three days.

Thirteen people were reported to have died fighting the fire.[80] Not only were the imperial couple and their seven children displaced, but so were the nearly thirty-five hundred other people who lived in the Winter Palace, most of whom were servants. Count A. F. Orlov wrote to a friend that the empress, upon learning what was happening at home, hurried to the scene consumed with worry that someone would be forgotten in the vast building. She rested only when she knew that everyone had been rescued, concerned about the fate of "those old servants and honest poor people who had served in this huge building, living under this roof through the course of three reigns."[81]

As urban fire crews entered the palace and as thousands of servants, employees, and attendants fled, the porousness of the boundary between the palace household and the city of St. Petersburg was manifest. Despite the existence of an urban fire brigade, fire was one of the most frequent and costly disasters to which the city's people were subjected, and when flames consumed the imperial palace it became clear that people of every station in life were equally subject to their terrible power. Not even a year before, one of the worst fires in the city's history had occurred on Palace Square itself, during Maslenitsa in one of the show booths.[82] In fact on the same night as the palace fire, many eyewitnesses reported that Nicholas learned of a large fire also burning in the working-class neighborhood on Vasilevskii Island. He ordered his nineteen-year-old son, Alexander, to leave the palace and attend personally to that blaze.[83]

The palace had a two-hundred-man fire company of its own as well as a system of reservoirs and pumps. But on that frigid night the pumps gave out after just ten minutes, perhaps because the firemen were inexperienced and perhaps because the equipment was not properly maintained.[84] Nicholas stayed at the palace all night, personally directing the efforts to determine the source of the blaze, to determine where manpower should be deployed, and to remove valuables from the building, which gradually filled with smoke for several hours before giving way to flames. Although an apothecary shop on the ground floor was suspected at first, the post-fire report indicated that the trouble started in the new Field Marshals' Hall and Peter the Great Throne Room, constructed in 1833–1834. A stove vent near the ceiling of the partition between the two rooms had not been enclosed in brick, and when this finally started a fire in December 1837 it spread into the upper floor and garret, where the seventy-five-year-old trusses were made of dry wood.[85]

Before the night was over, several men lost their lives preventing the fire from spreading to the Hermitage. They tore away the flying bridge connecting the Small Hermitage to the palace, leaving only an iron beam suspended in mid-air. They perched there, attempting to spray water onto the eastern wall of the palace, but some of them fell. Thousands of troops eventually arrived, and it was they who labored through the night to rescue paintings, sconces, light furniture, mirrors, books, papers, and personal belongings, laying them in the snow at the base of the new Alexander Column. Troops were reportedly keen to salvage the clothing and other possessions of the building's most humble inhabitants. Several witnesses claimed that they exhibited such eagerness to save the emperor's finery that at one point Nicholas threw his opera glasses to wreck a heavy mirror that he could not dissuade them from trying to pry off the wall. Out on the square troops formed a perimeter around the growing mountain of treasure but no disorders occurred.

By all accounts a great crowd of city people gradually assembled all around the palace, having been summoned by a fire that could be seen throughout the city. Foreign memoirists maintained their conventional astonishment at the tranquility of the Russian crowd. With so many police and troops on hand it was a far from opportune moment to steal precious objects, although one silver coffee pot was later reported missing.[86] In the ensuing months of palace reconstruction these furnishings were stored in all of the buildings surrounding the square, including the Admiralty and the General Staff building.

Writing to Prince Paskevich a few weeks after the fire, Nicholas revealed that he "felt sorry for the dear old Palace, it was a good one." Still, he hoped "with God's help to have one a year from now that's no worse." But what especially touched Nicholas was the reaction of the people. "One of the members of the nobility here wanted to give me twelve million rubles the other day, merchants as well, and even poor people. These feelings are even more precious to me than the Winter Palace. However, I will not accept anything, because the Russian Tsar has enough. Still, I will treasure the memory of these blessed efforts."[87]

The Winter Palace fire of 1837 entered the lore of Nicolaevan St. Petersburg. The *Sankt-Peterburgskie vedomosti* carried stories about the fire and reconstruction every week for several months. The often repeated themes in these reports were the heroic sacrifice of the firefighters and troops, the respectful masses who assembled silently to share the sovereign's distress, the priority the empress and her daughters placed on caring for displaced servants, and the stoic leadership of the emperor during the hours of greatest peril. Many observers believed they witnessed at firsthand mutual bonds of tenderness between the sovereign and the people. At any rate, these were certainly the sentiments that Nicholas and his censors expected to see reported in the press.

It was not easy for critical commentary to makes its way into the record, but there are hints that even the emperor himself weighed the possibility that the fire was a bad omen. Empress Alexandra wrote to her brother that her husband was worried for weeks that city people would think the same.[88] In order to overcome such sentiments Nicholas launched a spectacular reconstruction project, aiming to celebrate Easter 1839 in the palace. Under the general supervision of Minister of the Imperial Court Prince Volkonskii and General P. A. Kleinmichel, the restoration projected (to cost fifteen million rubles) got under way immediately. Once again the city's people found work and business as well as spectacle in a palace-building project. By some reports, up to ten thousand workers at a time were laboring on different parts of the project.[89] In demonstrating how to overcome disaster, the master of Russia's imperial household sought to exhibit energy, resolve, and mobilization of vast resources, as if such a performance might banish darker thoughts.

Chief architects V. P. Stasov and A. P. Briullov restored many of the formal halls to nearly the same form as before the fire, updating the décor along the way. In private quarters they made more changes, particularly in Alexandra Fedorovna's suite in the western enfilade. One of their most striking additions was the Malachite Hall, a sitting room that survives to this day, through which visitors entered the empress's quarters. Only a few of the spaces, notably the Jordan Staircase and the Great Palace Church, were restored to their Rastrelli originals.[90] Much of the furniture that visitors to the palace can see today was ordered from Petersburg ateliers during the reconstruction project, some reproduced to eighteenth-century designs and others displaying the tastes of Russia's mid-century. Everyone concerned, and foreign commentators as well, were struck that the ceremonial halls and staircases, as well as the church, were completed in time to celebrate Easter 1839. Enthusiastic official A. P. Bashutskii effused that "at the present moment the most important news in the contemporary life of Russia is the unprecedentedly rapid, splendid, and brilliant re-creation of the imperial residence in the northern capital."[91]

Nicholas orchestrated the great celebration of the imperial family's return to its home, deploying the arsenal of patriotic and household symbols he had assembled at the heart of the city. He mounted a series of ceremonies at the palace where he thanked Guards units, workmen, and city residents. He had a special medal struck for workers who participated in the reconstruction project; he decorated military men and architects; he provided for those widowed and orphaned in the blaze; and he directed the public and the court to join him in acknowledging divine providence.[92] Easter services in the palace church were the centerpiece of the drama. The emperor and his family, "surrounded by over 3,000 of his subjects," attended services there on the first day of Easter, after which they all "broke their fast in his palace."[93] To underscore the centrality of the Winter Palace to the life of the city, within a few years Nicholas decreed that no building in St. Petersburg could surpass it in height.[94] As the household and its master were reunited, Russia's autocrat meant for other fathers of families to be inspired by his enactment of monarchy as household mastery.

While it is hard to know what the city's working people made of such displays, it seemed to many observers that after the traumas of the 1830s there was a darkening of the city's mood. In the view of Grigory Kaganov, the artistic and literary renderings of the 1840s turned inward, and the city heretofore portrayed through its spacious public squares and broad prospects now appeared as a series of unconnected, enclosed interior courtyards, slums, and corners.[95] The next few decades seemed to bring a retreat from the ceremonious public spectacles mounted on open terrain, as people concentrated on meeting the individual challenges of life in the big city. This retreat, as it were, from the public square dominated by imperial monarchy allowed the growth of individual neighborhoods more human in scale. In these outlying districts of St. Petersburg a broader cross section of the city's diverse people had a chance to find their voice. When people returned to the public squares toward the century's end they were less willing simply to consume the monarchical spectacle.

7

PALACE OF CULTURE

The third great demonstration of Nicholas's conservative urban monarchy to be projected from the grounds of the Winter Palace was the public exhibition of Russia's imperial art collection in a New Hermitage erected specifically for that purpose. In February 1852 Nicholas christened the newest building in the Winter Palace complex, which was to house the Imperial Hermitage Museum of Fine Arts. Like his grandmother, Nicholas was a collector and lover of paintings and sculpture, probably surpassing her as a knowledgeable connoisseur. Whereas Catherine had deigned to open her Hermitage to intimates and courtiers and even to noble schoolgirls when she was not in town, Nicholas's decision to open a modern art museum adjacent to the Winter Palace and to welcome the St. Petersburg public to view the Romanov collection, on the emperor's terms, revealed the more public orientation of his monarchical performance.

The opening of the Imperial Hermitage was an inflexion point for Russian monarchy. While absolutism survived Nicholas by several decades, after his death it slowly lost its grip on the national imagination and even began to subside as the focal point of civic attention in St. Petersburg itself. As members of the city's cultured and educated elite found their voice, their leaders insinuated themselves into the court institutions and buildings created at monarchical expense. The creation of Nicholas's new museum was part of this gradual process. In his time, and even more so during the reign of his son Alexander II, a rapidly expanding cohort of art historians, artists, archaeologists, conservators, and educators began to oversee every aspect of museum operations, from maintenance to acquisition to preservation to education. The reign of the experts thus began in the monarchical context, when it was still tempered by deference to the imperial patron. As time went by, the experts acquired more clout. These scholars and their attentive students eventually became the true masters of the Imperial Hermitage and guardians of monarchy's tangible legacy.

The New Hermitage also proved to be a point of disciplined entry into the Winter Palace complex for the city's rank and file. Those inclined to visit the newly opened museum had to take on the manners and demeanor expected of them. They were restricted at first by complicated admission requirements—and perhaps unsure what to make of the objects they beheld. As time went by, the museum's professionals produced guidebooks to assist visitors and arranged displays so as to educate them about the chronological and geographical development of Western art.[1] Thus it was under the gaze of cultural pedagogues that thousands of the emperor's ordinary subjects took their first steps up the marble entryway and into the Russian monarch's meticulously staged temple of art.

NICHOLAS BUILDS A MUSEUM

Nicholas had more than one motive for building the New Hermitage, several of which he shared with his fellow monarchs. Europe's great royal art collections had gradually opened to the public, including the Dresden Museum of Art in 1744, the Vatican Museum in 1784, the Louvre by decree of France's revolutionary government in 1793, the Prado in Madrid in 1819, and the Berlin Altes Museum on its Museum Island in 1830.[2] All over Europe owners of royal collections embraced the opportunity to enlighten their subjects and to evince hospitality at the same time, but only in Russia did the ruler create a public art museum as an extension of his primary residence.[3]

The potential for public edification took on new significance in a more enlightened era, as it was used to justify the expense of expanding and maintaining royal collections. For his part, Nicholas had no doubt either that the cost of expanding and maintaining a world class art museum befit the greatest empire in Europe or that the Romanov collection could be a source of national pride. His disposition was essentially patriarchal. He saw himself as choosing to share that which he was under no compulsion to share but which would allow the people under his tutelage the possibility of cultural uplift.

Nicholas also perceived the possibility of more intentional propaganda both in the selection of objects for exhibition and in the manner of their display. The new museum was an extension of the palace stage perfectly suited to conveying historically rooted ideas about Russia's place in the world and monarchy's role in Russian history. From the start of his reign the emperor had subsidized archaeological investigations in the newly acquired southern regions of his empire. Archaeology spoke to fundamental questions of national identity, and Nicholas's patronage of excavations and acquisitions arose from his confidence that ancient objects would manifest Russia's place in the world. Thus the Imperial Archaeological Commission came into existence in the 1840s, in part to oversee the purchase of antique statues in Italy and in part to conduct excavations on Russian territory.[4] This commission held its meetings inside the Winter Palace. As researchers unearthed coins, metal objects, and other goods Nicholas grew determined to display the best of them inside a new museum. Archaeological displays comprised a significant portion and primary purpose of Nicholas's public museum and the new commission endured as a court institution and integral affiliate of the Imperial Hermitage.[5]

Another motive for commissioning a new museum was that he needed more room. Nicholas intended to keep collecting, and he made three substantial art purchases in the 1820s and 1830s.[6] He simply loved to visit his collection and wanted to see more of it on display. Nicholas never considered building this museum anywhere but adjacent to the Winter Palace, although by the 1830s other monarchs had begun to distance their public museums from the monarch's residence. Nicholas took the opposite approach, drawing into the new Ministry of the Imperial Court that he had created in the first year of his reign all of the things he cherished the most, including the Imperial Hermitage and the Imperial Archaeological Commission.[7]

All of these considerations made Nicholas eager to tour the most modern and celebrated art museums of the day, which were in Munich. There Leo von Klentz had designed the Glyptothek (for sculpture) and Pinakothek (for paintings) for King Ludwig I. The older Glyptothek housed the king's outstanding personal collection of antique marbles, which he had been amassing for twenty-five years. The Pinakothek opened in 1836, the largest museum in the world at the time, and displayed paintings belonging to the Wittelsbach dynasty. This museum and its famous architect attracted attention all over Europe.[8] Nicholas, half German by birth and married to the sister of Prussia's king, always felt at home in Germany, and he looked for an opportunity to visit the celebrated new museum.

The fire of 1837, with the dramatic rescue of the Hermitage from the flames and the outpouring of public sympathy for the displaced imperial family, finally solidified the emperor's resolve to commission a purpose-built art museum on the palace premises.[9] As court architect Vasilii Stasov oversaw the forced march reconstruction, Nicholas and Alexandra Fedorovna traveled to Munich in 1838 to tour Klentz's museums. Suitably impressed, the Russian ruler commissioned Klentz to design a New Hermitage for St. Petersburg, whose residents had demonstrated such touching solidarity with their master in the wake of the palace fire. Nicholas found a sympathetic figure in Klentz. A monarchist and art historian as well as a gifted designer, the German architect engaged his imperial patron in protracted considerations of how best to edify the gallery's future visitors. Ideally, they would come away from their visit with a firm grasp of the outline of art history while absorbing a positive impression of the wealth and good taste of their monarch.

The design process took nearly four years. The siting of this museum was a marvel in itself. Since he was determined to keep his collection within the palace complex, Nicholas agreed to raze the decrepit and crumbling hundred-year-old buildings of the so-called Masters' Court, the old Shepelev Palace on Millionaia, and the imperial stables and riding hall, which had been the subject of repeated plans for replacement or reconstruction. Not content to leave all the design decisions to his foreign (and often absent) architect, Nicholas appointed a local construction commission to vet and translate Klentz's ideas. Stasov supervised the first phase of the new edifice's construction, which began in 1842. After Stasov's death in 1848, N. E. Efimov took over and completed the museum building in 1851. Stasov's relations with the German architect were strained, but he was able to impose several improvements on the project. Stasov prevailed upon the construction commission to use better materials than the chief architect called for, such as iron for the balustrades as well as native stone, and thus better fitted the building for the city's severe winters. The commission deflected Klentz's insistence on sending sculptors from Munich. One great challenge was how to connect the new building to the Small and Large Hermitages, and it was apparently through the energetic pleadings of Stasov and Efimov that the Raphael Loggia and much of the Large Hermitage was preserved.[10]

If many of the artistic and construction decisions were contentious, the building's most famous feature, the main portico with its ten giant *atlantids* (male sculptures supporting the roof) produced more harmony. Klentz had this idea from 1840 on, although he had proposed red granite. The construction commission changed the design to gray, "the color of the cobblestones." The Russian sculptor A. I. Terebenev executed the colossal figures. Terebenev's assistant remembered that "150 master stone dressers, Russian peasants [*muzhiki*]" assisted in his workshop. Terebenev himself finished each of the faces. This work impressed Klentz, who wrote that "the beauty and delightful style of these sculptures, the purity and delicacy of the work, and the brilliance of the polishing leaves nothing to be desired. If the Egyptian pharaohs had produced their own monoliths these *atlantids* of the far north would prove no worse than those."[11] Overall the collaboration was fruitful and the completed

FIGURE 7.01   Vassily Sadovnikov. *View of the New Hermitage from Milliionnaia Street.* 1851. The State Hermitage Museum, St. Petersburg. Photograph by Pavel Demidov.

neoclassical masterpiece, outfitted with Klentz's signature skylights and other natural lighting, was the most modern art museum in Europe when it opened in 1852.

Klentz aspired to impart the essence of art history as understood by his contemporaries to museum visitors, and he decorated the New Hermitage to this end. The walls and staircase bore instructional bas reliefs, and the floor plan suggested that classical sculpture was the foundation of Western art. Where the Hermitage collection was lacking, Klentz filled in with the galleries' décor. One of his most intriguing designs was the room in which he set treasures from royal Scythian burial sites discovered in eastern Crimea and recently unearthed by archeologists. He gathered these ancient items together in an unusual gallery at the center of the ground floor called the Hall of Antiquities from the Cimmerian Bosporous. Here the interpretive collaboration between Klentz and his imperial patron cast Russia as a Eurasian empire rather than a Slavic nation. The Hall of Antiquities foregrounded the expansive imperial reach of his ancestors, in a picturesque gallery situated between the museum's Greco-Roman marbles and its collection of East Asian art.[12]

As was the case with all the construction and decorating projects in the history of the palace, erecting the New Hermitage was a boon to St. Petersburg businesses, sculptors, architects, and workmen. The state-owned Alexandrovsk Iron Foundry produced iron trusses for the roof. Other commissions went to state-owned Urals iron- and steelworks as well as to imperial stone-polishing factories in Ekaterinburg, Kolyvan, and Peterhof. Private St. Petersburg glass and mirror manufacturers along with the metalworking and mechanical concerns of Baird and Nobel also received contracts. Metal bas reliefs on the second floor employed the galvanization process of electroplating recently perfected in Russia by B. S. Jakobi.[13]

THE STAFF COMES ABOARD

As the building neared completion Ober-Hofmarshal of the Imperial Court Count A. P. Shuvalov and Hermitage administrators F. I. Labenskii and Ch. A. Bruni turned their attention to the organization and staffing of the museum, designating two primary departments in 1849. The first department supervised the museum's library as well as its collection of medals, money, rare stones, engravings, and precious objects. The second department oversaw paintings, original drawings, sculpture, ceramics, and works of bronze and ivory. This second section also, significantly, assumed oversight of valuable objects displayed in galleries of the Winter Palace itself, including Romanov family portraits and St. Petersburg scenes. The specialists who were now added to the museum staff included art historians, conservators, frame restorers, and educators. These men embraced the mission of preserving and studying the works under their care as well as instructing visitors about the pictures, statues, and objects they were viewing. Together they marshaled their forces for an assault on the bastions of artistic indifference, moving (if slowly) toward what M. B. Piotrovskii called "the permanent democratization of culture."[14]

With the establishment of the Imperial Hermitage, more of the specialists assigned to the collection were Russian subjects, gradually replacing the foreigners who had predominated in the days when the collection had no public function. Whereas just one of nine department directors appointed in Paul and Alexander I's times bore a Russian name, by mid-century five out of eight did.[15] The main subject matter of the Hermitage collection may have been foreign but the collection itself slowly came under the purview of native authorities. The museum's restoration school produced a cadre of young Russian art conservators including the painters A. F. Mitrokhin and F. Tabuntsov in the 1840s.[16] When the New Hermitage opened in 1852 it boasted a professional staff of twenty-nine men: two department chiefs, four curators, three assistant curators, two librarians, one assistant librarian, four conservators, one assistant conservator, two clerks, two correspondence supervisors, and eight soldiers. The biographical dictionary published by the State Museum of the Hermitage in 2004 lists thirty professional employees who might be considered the first-generation staff members of the Imperial Hermitage. Of these thirty, twenty-one were Russian subjects of various ethnicities.[17]

Besides the professionals, when the museum opened it was maintained by a staff of ninety serving people, including a *kamer-fur'er*, thirty-six lackeys, forty-four stokers, a doorman, and two medical officials.[18] These men were drawn from Winter Palace staff, and as was the case with palace service, employment at the Imperial Hermitage meant upward mobility. For example, Fedor Vasil'evich Varfolomeev began service at the Winter Palace when he was eighteen, first as a stoker in the rooms of Grand Duchess Ol'ga Nikolaevna, and then was transferred to the Hermitage as a lackey in 1855. After two years he was appointed to the emperor's quarters, where he served until 1873. Varfolomeev received the rank of chamber lackey in 1871 and in 1873 was transferred back to the Hermitage as *hof-fur'er*, ninth rank. He remained in this responsible position, receiving several medals from visiting foreign monarchs, until he retired due to illness in 1896.[19]

Likewise, Vasilii Iakovlevich Gintsenberg, the son of a theater employee, also first served at the Winter Palace, beginning as a cook's apprentice and proceeding up the ranks to chamber lackey by 1885. The following year, in the wake of another revision of the Hermitage staff, Gintsenberg became an assistant *hof-fur'er* at the museum, twelfth rank. Altogether he served the court for forty-seven years, twelve of them at the Hermitage, and his children received permission for him to be buried in his court uniform.[20] Senior noncommissioned officer Iuda Mytkin petitioned the minister of the court to be assigned to one of the imperial palaces, and he wound up serving at the Hermitage "as an employee hired with a salary and living quarters."[21]

Other people of humble origins found their way into the Hermitage through artistic talent. Ivan Sidorovovich Sidorov was one of four Kostroma peasant brothers who worked at the museum starting in the 1840s. Ivan was a cabinetmaker and also worked in conservation, duplicating pictures and crating them for transport. After thirty years of service Sidorov was granted the status of honorary citizen, later receiving a silver medal.[22]

One of the most vertiginous ascents was that of the son of a serf soldier from Kostroma province, Lavrentii Avksentievich Seriakov. He became a regimental singer when he was eight years old, later a member of the divisional choir, and finally a regimental musician. Seriakov was eventually transferred to an office job in St. Petersburg where he showed an aptitude for drawing and was assigned to the topography department. In the capital he began the independent study of woodcut engraving, and without any training he was able to exhibit his works in a bookstore and receive orders to produce illustrations for publication. Seriakov's work attracted the attention of V. F. Odoevskii, who introduced him to such luminaries of the contemporary art scene as F. A. Bruni and K. P. Briullov. His new patrons secured him a spot in classes at the Academy of Arts, still studying topography. Bruni wanted to enlist Seriakov to help him create a freestanding division of wood engraving, which was not a recognized craft in the academy, but this idea did not attract support. As time went on, however, Seriakov achieved fame and status as an engraver and printer, earned the status of academician, and was received abroad as a celebrated artist. Returning in glory from his travels, Seriakov received Alexander II's commission for a woodcut portrait in 1866 and was appointed "engraver to His Majesty." Thereafter Seriakov took up the post of assistant to F. I. Iordan, head of the department of drawings and engravings.[23]

If fine arts experts were the principal beneficiaries of the Imperial Hermitage in its early years, it was purportedly the St. Petersburg public for whom the new museum was intended. However, between its opening in 1852 and the death of Nicholas in late 1855 the museum occupied an awkward zone somewhere between the imperial court and the public. The Ministry of the Imperial Court arranged a grand opening of the newest building on the Palace Embankment on February 5, 1852. This gala was almost exclusively a court event and was not even mentioned in the *Sankt-Peterburgskie vedomosti*. The emperor hosted a spectacle in the Hermitage theater followed by supper within the halls of the New Hermitage for six hundred courtiers and dignitaries.

For the remaining years of Nicholas's reign, admission to the museum was regulated by the "Rules for the Administration of the Imperial Hermitage." Visits could now occur even when the emperor's family was in residence, almost every day of the year except Sundays and specified holidays. The museum would be closed to visitors each day between half past twelve and two in the afternoon so that the sovereign could visit the galleries in peace, which he did.[24] It was open to visitors between ten and one o'clock in the winter months and between eight and four o'clock during the summer, when the family was generally away. The 1853 "Rules" also provided guidelines for a special category of visitor, the Academy of Arts students who wished to copy one of the museum masterpieces. It was generally permissible to copy a painting where it hung, but with special permission a copyist could have a painting removed from its place and carried to the Copyists' Hall.

This was particularly necessary if a painting hung at a great height in one of the exhibition galleries. The lackey or footman on duty was to keep student painters under tight surveillance.[25]

The regulations reveal a lively tension between anxiety and invitation. There was concern about preserving the treasures from the stress and strain of crowds bearing the dirt of the streets into the Hermitage. Public visits also required the damaging heating of the galleries and raised concern about whether visitors from the lower classes would comport themselves appropriately. Those admitted had to inscribe their names in a guestbook under the gaze of a guard. The dress code specified that military personnel must appear in uniform and civilians were to wear frock coats "or other clothes appropriate to their rank or *soslovie*."[26]

However, the main control over admission came through the requirement to procure a (cost-free) ticket in advance at the Court Office, which was in a separate building on the Palace Embankment. This advance planning gave officials a chance to look over prospective visitors but surely discouraged casual or spontaneous outings to view the artworks. Above all, the ticket regime simply limited the number of people who could enter the museum in any one period of time. While many commentators have considered this an effort to keep away the hoi polloi, the "Rules" themselves suggest that the desire to hold down housekeeping costs also loomed large. At any rate, the number of tickets issued was strictly limited in the first year of operation.

TABLE 4. Number of Hermitage Admission Tickets Issued by the Court Office

Date	Number Available
April 14,1852	150
May 16, 1852	300
January 27, 1853	200
May 16, 1853	200
January 23, 1854	150

SOURCE: Figures extracted from documents reproduced in M. B. Piotrovskii, ed, *Istoriia Ermitazha. Kratkii ocherk; materialy i dokumenty,* "O vkhodnykh v Ermitazh billetakh" (Moscow: Izd. Iskusstvo, 2000), 214–218.

Fewer than six months after the opening, the chief curator of the museum, F. A. Zhil', lamented that in the period of time that three hundred tickets had been made available the number of people visiting had exceeded eight hundred: "the circulation of tickets is insufficient. There are not enough tickets!"²⁷ Particularly alarming, apparently, was the overly enthusiastic effort by members of the public to visit the Peter I Gallery, which housed jewels and imperial treasures. This led the authorities to create special tickets for this exhibit in 1854. By 1857 the Imperial Hermitage offered an annual pass admitting "only one person" to the Hermitage and the Peter I Gallery, and the color of this special ticket changed each year.²⁸

FROM NICHOLAS I TO ALEXANDER II

Nicholas's last years were consumed by war in Crimea and the Balkans, which commenced in 1853. Even without the profoundly demoralizing effect of military defeat and diplomatic isolation, by the 1850s Nicholas was a sterner and less optimistic version of the beneficent art connoisseur who had launched the museum project fifteen years earlier. Through his so-called Third Section the emperor cracked down on university students and literary circles that spread the first hints of brewing political discontent among the capital city's educated citizens. Combined with melancholy at home, the war prevented Nicholas from attending any further to the civic project of art edification.

Three years after the Imperial Hermitage opened, he contracted pneumonia and died suddenly, the loss of Russian forces at Eupatoria his final news of the war. Appropriately, this once energetic master of the Winter Palace household took his last breath on the camp bed he had often slept on in his unofficial first floor office overlooking Palace Square. His death was a subdued affair coming as it did in the midst of a major European war and while thousands of Russia troops were still serving far away from home. It was a depressing note on which to end a reign once devoted to the conservative reimagining and robust propagation of a modern Russian absolutism. Nicholas's practical accomplishments in government were not insignificant. He had presided over an impressive industrial expansion, a consolidation of the country's legal code, and a significant reform of the state peasantry. Still, what he had most hoped to do was to rekindle the flame of popular monarchism while quelling the spark of elite rebellion. In this his record was mixed.

At the end of Nicholas's reign there were no doubt many monarchists among residents of the capital city, not least among them the military veterans honored within his Winter Palace, the merchants' daughters who graced his New Year's masquerade balls, the businessmen who attracted palace contracts, many of the merrymakers who celebrated Maslenitsa on Palace Square or the Waters ceremony on the frozen Neva. Thousands of members of his own household also had reason to be grateful for the master's solicitude: servants and their families, boys launched in apprenticeships or sent to art schools, the sons of soldiers and clerks brought into the Winter Palace to ascend its orderly hierarchy. Absorbing the patriotism manifest in the cult of 1812 as well as the impressions of domestic harmony displayed on the palace main stage, the emperor's loyal subjects kept the flame of absolute monarchy burning at mid-century. Those less favorably disposed had been kept at bay for the time being.

It was Nicholas's last dramatic gesture that heralded a different era. The museum professionals he had welcomed backstage were the vanguard of monarchy's denouement. Perhaps it is better to say that as they went about the work of mounting exhibits and educating an often indifferent public the overseers of the Imperial Hermitage simply left monarchy behind. Never doubting that they worked for an imperial patron, they found nonetheless that he seldom interfered in the work they came to see as their own. As time went by, the experts became the true masters of the most publicly important wing of the great Winter Palace stage, and they even began to see the objects they displayed as a national patrimony. They saw themselves as missionaries of cultural uplift rather than as bit players in a performance of monarchical authority.

The new patron of the Imperial Hermitage and master of the monarchical household was Nicholas's oldest son, the comparatively liberal Alexander II, who ascended the throne committed to serf emancipation and broad social reforms and endowed with a respect for the professions. During his reign many of the empire's institutions were therefore submitted to the ministrations of experts, the Imperial Hermitage among them. Ceding responsibility to them, Alexander permitted a new conception of the place to take root: less a stage than a school, less the monarch's patrimony than the public's.

The cadres of art scholars who came to direct the museum's programs also contributed to Russians' slowly developing conception of public property. Ekaterina Pravilova has written suggestively about the nexus between the rise of experts in many areas of Russian life and the sense that certain kinds of valuable goods such as forests, minerals, monuments, art collections, and literary works belonged fundamentally to the empire and its people.[29] Administratively, the artworks of the Hermitage belonged to the Russian Imperial Court because they were furnishings of the Winter Palace, which was not in the "private" domain of the imperial family as Gatchina and Pavlovsk were. Although eighteenth-century rulers had clarified the distinction between the Romanovs' own lands (on which they paid taxes to the state treasury) and property of the court (which was a semi-public entity financed by the treasury), by the late nineteenth century the line between these two categories had blurred because of the absolute prerogative of the one person who headed both of them. Even murkier was the distinction between court property and "state" property. At the height of absolutism these were distinctions without much of a difference. Nicholas was able, for example, to sell several pieces from the Hermitage collection at his own discretion. Moreover, rulers transferred artworks from one palace to another without regard to these distinctions.[30]

Both despite and because of the ambiguous legal status of the Hermitage artworks, professionals who appreciated the collection wrote and taught about them in universal terms—citing the importance of certain painters and paintings, for example, as though they constituted something of value to all humankind. While this feeling gained more public traction when it came to Russian works such as icons, the overseers of the Hermitage collection conceived of a kind of good that could not be owned exclusively even by a monarch. They understood the works in the Imperial Hermitage to constitute a collection in and of themselves, which should be maintained as such. Consequently, Hermitage directors attempted to prevent pieces from being sold or transferred to other court locations. They also proved adept at appropriating works from other imperial palaces for display or preservation in the New Hermitage. By the turn of the twentieth century curators insisted that works be transferred to the Imperial Hermitage from neglected suburban palaces that were in some cases unheated.[31]

CULTIVATING A PUBLIC

If denizens of the art world were the most enthusiastic beneficiaries of wider access to the Imperial Hermitage, its official purpose was to promote public appreciation for the collections, and Alexander II was committed to advancing this project. However, attracting rank-and-file visitors proved challenging in the museum's first decades. In truth, it had been difficult to draw in even those cultured city residents who had been granted access to the Small and Large Hermitages since Alexander I's time. In those days visitors who procured tickets at the Court Office could tour four to eight at a time, under the direct supervision of a court lackey, but few of them did so.[32]

Even as Nicholas was making plans to erect a public museum, the German writer J. G. Kohl wrote in his 1838 guide to St. Petersburg that, although procuring a ticket to visit the palace's Hermitage collection was not difficult, few people took advantage of the opportunity: "There are in St. Petersburg a number of families of the educated classes who have never visited the Hermitage." Kohl also regretted that among those Russians and foreigners who did pass through its halls there was very little appreciation of what they were seeing. "For four thousand paintings reflecting half the natural world and mankind, a two hours' saunter. . . . For three rooms of statues, as many passing looks." He despaired that "the most admired objects here are beyond all doubt the crown jewels, and other valuables arranged in a separate cabinet with them."[33] If Kohl's characterization can be trusted it suggests that expanding art appreciation in the Russian capital might require more than a new building. This problem remained when Nicholas's son took the throne. What accounted for the paucity of visitors to the Imperial Hermitage and their apparent failure to appreciate what they were looking at?

It is interesting that Kohl thought Russian and foreign viewers of the masterpieces equally dilettantish. Certainly in the 1830s St. Petersburg remained a city whose population was preponderantly poor, male, young, and seasonal. Most of the city's residents lacked not only the leisure, manners, and wardrobe required to procure a Hermitage ticket but also the education that might have inspired an interest in doing so. Of the 470,000 people who called St. Petersburg home in 1840, the "public," the layer of residents enabled by wealth, education, and status to participate in the cultural life of the city, was not substantially larger than the number attending Nicholas's New Years' balls—perhaps 30,000, a total that included a number of foreigners.[34]

Katia Dianina has argued that what helped to dispose the Russian public to visit art museums was the flowering of a freer, more diverse press in general and the initiation of specialized art columns or art periodicals in particular. Russia's museum age got under way only at mid-century not only because its imperial art collection was not opened to the public until 1852 but also because there were so few periodical publications in which people discussed the fine arts. Dianina chronicles the exuberant flowering of art talk in the pages of general as well as specialized publications after 1850 and especially in the more liberal 1860s. The consumption of visual art, she suggests, rested on a simultaneous consumption of words about pictures.[35]

Another limiting factor may have been the foreignness of most of the paintings and sculptures in the Hermitage. When the museum first opened to the public it contained two halls of paintings by Russians, but those who wished to see Russian pictures were better served viewing private collections.[36] The journalist and playwright P. D. Boborykin recalled that "the public of the capital only began to visit [art] exhibits in the sixties, and art lovers with money began to buy pictures and commission portraits," a development he linked to the rise of the Wanderers, the painters of Russian life whose most prominent member was Il'ia Repin.[37] Eventually the demand for display of Russia's own artwork, much of it nurtured by imperial institutions, induced Alexander III to open the Imperial Russian Museum in the Michael Palace complex in the

1890s, at which time the Russian paintings that had occupied two sizeable halls in the Hermitage collection were moved there.[38] The Russian Museum generated a different ambiance when it opened, as the greater familiarity of the subject matter seemed more welcoming and invited more conversation among groups of visitors. Parents were keen to take children to a venue where they could impart information about their own history, and the surrounding gardens made for a pleasant outing.[39]

Efforts by Hermitage staff to render their collection more legible led to the 1859 guidebook by museum educator Andrei Somov. His *Kartiny Imperatorskago Ermitazha dlia posetitelei etoi gallerei* (Pictures of the Imperial Hermitage for visitors to this gallery) was the first such guide written with the public in mind.[40] Somov himself had turned to fine arts after a brief career teaching mathematics and physics, having studied drawing and the collections of foreign museums since his youth. He was an educator by calling, and for over a half century he worked in various capacities at the Academy of Sciences and the Academy of Arts and as a scholarly editor and publisher.[41] In 1886 Somov was named senior conservator of the picture galleries of the Hermitage, a post he retained until his death in 1909. One of his achievements in that role was to install a modern heating system.

Somov's guidebook proved to be a template for Russian museum manuals that persists to this day. Explaining his objectives in the prologue Somov wrote that he hoped not only to provide some information about the works in the collection "but also to acquaint the visitors with the history of painting and the main directions of this art." To that end he had arranged the pictures by national schools in chronological order, with a brief description of each painter. He briskly narrated the history of the Hermitage collection from its beginnings under Catherine through to the present when, he asserted, the Hermitage must be ranked among the world's leading art museums on account of "the grandeur and order that reign in this department of the Imperial Court, the easy access for artists and art lovers and the wealth of the collection."[42] He concluded by acknowledging that a comprehensive description of the works would run to many volumes, but in hopes of putting a handy reference work into the hands of visitors his brief description of major masterpieces encompassed only 176 pages, complete with index.

THE EXPERTS TAKE THE REINS

The reign of the experts commenced in earnest when Alexander II made scholar and writer Stepan Aleksandrovich Gedeonov the first director of the independent Imperial Hermitage Museum in 1863. Several of the dominant cultural interests of the age came together in Gedeonov, and during his fifteen-year directorship he imparted these concerns to the institution. His career in art began with his appointment to the Rome expedition of the Imperial Archaeological Commission in 1850, and by 1861 Gedeonov was overseeing the commission's work in Rome for the Academy of Arts. He made a name for himself by acquiring several significant collections of antique sculpture for the Hermitage, even carrying back to St. Petersburg the collection of the Marquis de Campana and installing it on the first floor of the New Hermitage. Gedeonov gained further renown when he acquired two Italian masterpieces, Leonardo da Vinci's *Madonna Litta* and Raphael's *Madonna Conestabile*.[43] He was also eventually appointed director of the Imperial Theaters, a position his father had held before him, a job that overlapped with his museum appointment for nine years.

As one of the country's leading establishment intellectuals Gedeonov was in the thick of the 1860s debates over the nature and historical position of the Russian nation, including the famous Norman controversy.[44] Conservative monarchism found its most articulate propagandist in Gedeonov. His patriotic scholarship rested on two convictions he shared with the reformist emperor. First, he affirmed that the "ancient" Russian monarchy was the natural and therefore best government for the modern Russian Empire. He believed Russian-style monarchy was a progressive force for all the peoples of the diverse empire, and that in Alexander II they had a sovereign both generous and wise. Gedeonov also shared his monarch's conviction that education was the main font of historical progress and that the empire's people needed more access to it. This was the rightful mission of the Imperial Hermitage as it turned toward a broader public. Russia belonged in its distinct way to the world of European culture, so its people could not fail to be edified by learning about the art and civilization of the classical period and early modern Europe. As visitors passed through the beautiful galleries, every part of the display could augment their understanding of the wider world to which Russia must make its own historic contribution.[45]

As the infrastructure for visitors took shape, the paucity of takers continued to frustrate Hermitage officials committed to the public mission, and Gedeonov tackled this problem in the first year of his tenure. He persuaded the minister of the Imperial Court to ease admission requirements. The hours of operations expanded somewhat, admitting the public daily from nine to five o'clock between February and September and from ten to four o'clock during the other months, except for July and August, when the museum would be closed for maintenance and repair.[46]

When these moves did not quickly attract more people Court Ober-Hofmarshal Shuvalov grew frustrated that "having granted easy access to the Imperial Museum to the public in the last half year" and having augmented the collection with notable masterpieces, published catalogues, and the like, granting the full right to visit the museum to "Petersburg residents," there had not been a swifter increase in the number of people visiting. This was the spur to address at long last the highly constricting "ticket regime," which increasingly attracted derision wherever it persisted throughout the city. A special commission considering how to increase public access to the museums of the Academy of Sciences had recently concluded that "requiring tickets to the museum is superfluous, because experience has shown that it is possible to overestimate the danger of any one-time confluence of visitors."[47] Hoping to broaden the public appeal of the uplifting Hermitage collection, the court finally overcame its anxiety about protecting the museum from the stress of excessive crowds. Shuvalov agreed to admit people without tickets "as is done in other European museums," and as of January 1866, admission to the museum no longer involved a prior trip to the Court Office.[48]

At the same time Gedeonov built up the institution's capacity for public instruction. He created an educational department with its own chief. He enlisted scholars and experts for special consultation, granting them the prestigious designation "attached to the Hermitage" in lieu of a salary. Into this category such luminaries as jeweler Karl Fabergé, Egyptologist V. S. Golenishchev, and art historian A. A. Trubnikov found their way. In addition to the professional museum staff the Imperial Hermitage now took on many employees charged with maintaining the public exhibition galleries. New regulations required the *hof-fur'er* to supervise the admission of visitors, the cleaning of the floors, furniture, and windows, and the maintenance of proper temperatures and ventilation. Altogether forty-five employees shared responsibility for keeping up the visitors' galleries.[49]

In the well-known Russian-language guide to St. Petersburg compiled by Vladimir Mikhnevich and published in 1874, the Imperial Hermitage held pride of place as the first entry in the "museum" category. Mikhnevich devoted six pages to chronicling the history of the collection from the days of Peter the Great, specifying in many cases the prices paid for foreign masterpieces. He detailed the architectural expansion of the Hermitage buildings but did not take particular notice of the decision to admit the general public during Nicholas's reign. His guide informed readers that they might visit daily between eleven and three o'clock, except in July and August. There was no charge for admission, and tickets could be procured either at the Court Office or at the door to the Hermitage itself, where visitors could also procure a catalogue. Mikhnevich informed art lovers that Emperor Alexander II had made available a published album of photographs of the important paintings, several of which were accompanied by descriptive notes. The rather breathless tone of this entry indicated to readers that what was most impressive about this art museum was the extraordinary wealth and rarified good taste that it represented and displayed.[50]

And so the Imperial Hermitage, appended to the Winter Palace, gained prestige as a space for art education and erudition. More and more threads tied the museum to St. Petersburg's thousands of students. Hermitage experts such as Somov were invited to lecture at both the Smol'nyi Institute and the Bestuzhev courses for women. Over time all of the academic branches of the Imperial Hermitage grew: the library, the numismatic collection, the art history division, and the restoration workshop. On the twenty-fifth anniversary of Alexander II's accession to the throne, Imperial Hermitage director Alexander Vasil'chikov proudly produced the first of many histories of the collection. A handsome volume with fourteen art plates, *Imperatorskii Ermitazh, 1855-1880* (The Imperial Hermitage, 1855–1880) offered wealthy art enthusiasts a full-throated celebration of the purported bond between ruler and subject that the Imperial Hermitage had forged.

The Imperial Hermitage could also impart good manners and self-control. While restrictions on access to the museum had eased, a certain kind of deportment was nonetheless expected. The directors and pedagogical staff of the Hermitage established practices for the public consumption of its treasures that have endured even down to the present. Visitors to the galleries learned by doing, as they still do: under the watchful gaze of trained guards the public learned to appear in respectable dress, to speak quietly, to manifest a certain hushed piety before the artworks, and not to touch anything. A new marker of respectability based on personal comportment took root among the museum-going public. If such an atmosphere put some people off, the number of visitors nonetheless expanded significantly. By the 1880s, 50,000 people visited the Imperial Hermitage annually; in 1914 the number had grown to 180,000.[51]

On the eve of the First World War the Imperial Hermitage had insinuated itself into the life of the city. It became a famous institution, described in guidebooks for foreigners and Russians alike, and astute visitors could traverse its galleries, instruction books in hand, imbibing the lessons so thoughtfully mapped out for them. On the other hand, as Klentz's great monument to art slid almost imperceptibly into the realm of public space, visitors brought their own purposes and agendas with them into its great halls. Vladimir Nabokov, for example, reminisced about seeking out secluded spaces to share with a sweetheart in the war winter of 1915, when he was sixteen years old:

> We haunted museums. They were drowsy and deserted on weekday mornings, and very warm.... There we would seek the quiet back rooms, the stopgap mythologies nobody looked at, the etchings, the medals, the paleographic items, the Story of Printing—poor things like that.... The Hermitage, St. Petersburg's Louvre, offered nice nooks, especially in a certain hall on the ground floor, among cabinets with scarabs, behind the sarcophagus of Nana, high priest of Ptah.[52]

Thus it was at mid-century that the palace-museum on the Neva began to build up the administrative and intellectual infrastructure that would within twenty years make the imperial art collection of the Romanovs accessible and legible to many layers of the urban public. The treasure spent to amass and then to exhibit this great store of artworks and antiquities had all been extracted from the taxpaying and laboring people of the Russian Empire. Mid-century monarchs deployed the collection in a gesture of edifying condescension that bespoke the public monarchy they aspired to present, particularly to the people of St. Petersburg. By the end of the nineteenth century the Hermitage attracted crowds to the monarchical stage on the Palace Embankment but the rulers themselves no longer controlled the drama's narrative. Even the expert intermediaries of the monarchy's treasures could not entirely ensure that their pupils made proper sense of the splendors they passed by. What museumgoers thought about the objects they viewed, how they socialized with one another as they visited, and whether they credited their rulers for the opportunity is impossible to know. What is clear is that they had crossed the boundary between city and palace on terms that were at least partly their own.

PART III

THE AUDIENCE TAKES THE STAGE

8

HEIRS

The Romanovs' Winter Palace became St. Petersburg's Winter Palace gradually. The moment at which it passed formally from one to the other came with the abdication of the last Russian tsar, Nicholas II, in 1917 and the Bolshevik seizure of the palace from the Provisional Government a few months later, but the Winter Palace had slipped into a quasi-public realm well before that. If we try to say just when that shift occurred we find a gradual process of monarchical retreat and urban advance that commenced in the reign of Alexander II (1855–1881) and culminated in October 1917.

Nicholas's son Alexander was the first ruler raised to believe that "the people's approval constituted an important moral basis of autocratic rule."[1] Nonetheless, the forces of change overtook him. Despite the significant achievements of his reign, which included emancipating Russia's millions of enserfed peasants, Alexander found himself hunted by autocracy's emboldened enemies on the streets of his capital and even in the halls of the Winter Palace. His assassination in 1881 did not prove to be the end of the monarchical drama but it was the climax—the event that changed the life of the Winter Palace more than any other before 1917. Feeling under attack from the city that monarchy had created, neither of Russia's last two emperors made the palace their primary residence.

As the monarchy itself became the target of those seeking constitutional modernization, the status of the Winter Palace came into question. Could a place so thoroughly associated with the monarchy be adapted to the new realities of popular rule? Ultimately the answer turned out to be yes. The palace and square were able to stage the drama of revolution and republican rule not only because the treasure and labor of the nation had created and sustained them for so long but also because the imperial complex at the heart of the city had become the symbolic center of St. Petersburg's civic life. In the second half of the nineteenth century the grandiose displays of military power on Palace Square gave way to spontaneous public convocations during times of national crisis or celebration. The palace before which the people gathered stood for the imperial nation, whether the tsar presented himself on the balcony or not.

The palace complex was not only a symbolic space, however. Larger and larger contingents of city people found their way into the Imperial Hermitage as employees or visitors. Others entered the palace itself to attend gatherings of various cultural societies. Even before monarchy ended, Russian monarchs essentially ceded the palace to the imperial court, whose institutions were dominated by St. Petersburg's cultural professionals. In this way the buildings on the Palace Embankment acquired both meanings and functions that survived the monarchy.

There were two parallel processes in the closing years of the nineteenth century: monarchy's forced retreat from the palace stage and, then, the assumption of leadership at the Winter Palace and Hermitage complex by St. Petersburg's increasingly self-confident cultural elite. Nicholas's son and grandson each endeavored to act the part of absolute monarch during four decades in which everything about the drama of Russian political life was shifting: the script, the stage, and above all the urban audience. As they did so, the city for which they mounted their scenario of monarchy seeped into the palace, with mixed motives.

MONARCHY'S CHANGING SCRIPT

When Alexander II assumed the throne amid a looming defeat on the Crimean Peninsula, he was the first in two hundred years to do so without any whiff of illegitimacy or fatal unpopularity. He inherited all the architecture for mounting an impressive display of absolute monarchy, but his embrace of absolutism was more ambiguous than his father's had been. Nicholas had imbued his autocratic monarchy with a romantic conception of the people. Without liberalizing government he had given the Russian monarchy a more public orientation. Alexander, on the other hand, was convinced he must not only embody a monarchy that represented the empire's people but he must also provide them with a more effective government. As the Crimean War culminated in crushing defeat, the paired questions of military reform and serf emancipation finally came to the fore. Nicholas had convened several commissions on the "peasant question" and had reformed the terms binding peasants who lived on state lands, but his son resolved to end a system that had been denounced at one time or another by each of his ancestors as far back as Catherine II. Armed with youth, confidence, and purpose the new ruler swiftly put into motion the process that resulted in a proclamation emancipating the serfs of private landlords in February 1861.

The complex emancipation legislation represented an unlovable compromise. The arrangement that forestalled civil war, revolution, and abject landlessness attracted little enthusiasm from either peasants or landowners who all believed that fundamental rights had been ignored. When people learned about the emancipation decree on the eve of Great Lent their reaction was subdued: it was hard to make out exactly what their ruler had in mind. The tsar's own attitude toward the legislation was also low-key. Government minister P. A. Valuev recalled that on the day the decree was made known in St. Petersburg, Alexander drove through streets lined by people who shouted "Hoorah!" but without excitement. "The government has managed to do almost everything that could be done to prepare for today's Manifesto this lackluster reception," Valuev wrote. "In the evening no one thought about illuminating the city."[2]

The Court Office officials did arrange a carefully staged ceremony one week later on Palace Square. A selected crowd of peasant artisans and factory workers was assembled there, and the emperor greeted them on his way to the weekly review of the Guards. Sovereign and subjects each offered brief speeches, and the assembled people presented their monarch with the traditional sign of hospitality, bread and salt.[3] It was a muted affair. Alexander's subsequent substantial reform projects also failed to attract civic enthusiasm at the palace or the square: there was little hooplah for the emancipation of state peasants and the reform of the judicial system, local government, and the armed forces. If there was a symbolic way to dramatize the liberalized absolutism that Alexander was embracing he did not find it. Perhaps the grand palace stage could not easily be adapted to such a purpose, but a deeper problem lay in the ambiguity of the play itself.

By the 1860s many of the elements of traditional rule that Alexander did retain were shifting their focus away from the imperial capital in favor of the old Slavic center, Moscow. The literary and political debates of the 1840s and 1850s had brought the long-running contest between Muscovite and Petersburg values into sharp focus. So-called Slavophiles such as Constantine Aksakov asserted that Moscow was Russia's true capital and Petersburg only the emperor's residence, "suggesting that in Russia, the presence of the ruler was not sufficient to establish the political center."[4] In the burgeoning press and literary circles there arose a challenge to St. Petersburg's primacy that steadily grew. Two major commemorations at which Alexander linked his own reign to Russia's history took place in Russia's old capital during 1862: the fiftieth anniversary of the rout of Napoleon and the millennial of the founding of ancient Rus'. Although Alexander loved "the emperor's city" in which he had been raised, and like his father continued to walk or ride unguarded in its streets and gardens until almost the end of his life, he could not entirely resist the embrace of the enthusiastic pan-Slavs who pointed to the reign of Moscow's tsars as proof of Russia's special place in the Slavic constellation.[5] His governing liberalization combined with such nationalistic gestures sent mixed messages and at times rendered Alexander's script illegible. At any rate, it was a script hard to play on the palace stage.

THE STAGE REDEPLOYED

If the script of monarchy was shifting at mid-century, so was the management of its principal stage. On the surface the palace routine went on much as it had during the reign of Nicholas. Alexander and Maria Aleksandrovna received dignitaries and others at the Winter Palace, albeit with less exuberance. While they continued to entertain at palace masquerades in the winter season, they changed the New Year's observance from the great "all-class" balls of Nicholas's time to brief receptions for foreign and native dignitaries and the St. Petersburg merchant elite. Typical was the reception announced in the *Sankt-Peterburgskie vedomosti* for New Year's Day 1871, when Russian dignitaries were to be received in the small throne room of the palace at eleven o'clock and foreigners at noon. The large crowd of ladies and gentlemen of "the ranks of urban citizens" was to assemble in the grandiose Heraldic Hall.[6] The St. Petersburg public was still welcomed into the palace but they witnessed a different kind of spectacle. Their brief daytime audience in this imposing gallery suggested a ruler more focused on efficiency than festivity.

While maintaining the main public ceremonial events inherited from his father, Alexander in fact presided over a rather different kind of household. At its heart was his unhappy marriage to the Hessian princess Maria Aleksandrovna. Together they became the parents of eight children, but the great tragedy of their lives came in 1865 when their eldest son and heir, Nicholas Aleksandrovich, died of meningitis at the age of twenty-one. His grieving mother withdrew almost completely from public life at this point and the new heir, Alexander Aleksandrovich, eventually married his elder brother's Danish fiancée. The emperor himself lost enthusiasm for his public role and sought comfort in private pleasures.

Always attracted to young women, in the immediate aftermath of his son's death Alexander began the main romance of his life with Catherine Dolgorukova, then a schoolgirl from the lesser nobility, not quite twenty years of age. Within a few years this affair was widely known not only inside the palace but within Petersburg society, and "Katia" was settled in her own residence where she eventually bore the emperor three children. This breech in propriety extended to the imperial household, including the womanizing of the emperor's son Alexei and the petty thievery of his nephew.[7] Such a palace household could hardly be held up as exemplary for those St. Petersburg residents who might still be watching. Nor could Alexander publicize this household as evidence of his personal mastery.

In fact the imperial family more and more was simply absent from St. Petersburg, spending time every summer at their new palace on the Crimean Peninsula, Livadia. Wortman concluded that all of this self-indulgence was "fatal to [the emperor's] image as transcendent monarch. . . . The ethos of self-sacrifice for the commonweal, which justified the tsar's monopoly of authority, now lost its persuasive power."[8] Queen Victoria and Tsar Nicholas I had each intuited that, in the age of publicity and democracy, only publicized virtue could keep the monarchy afloat, and they recognized that in the age of the people the virtue that counted was familial virtue.[9] Thus conventional propriety was more important to nineteenth-century courts than to eighteenth-century ones, and in the face of moral decay within, Russia's monarchy increasingly became a more unifying symbol for its critics than for its defenders.

Change took place "downstairs" as well as "upstairs." Emancipation had a significant impact on palace housekeeping, which became more expensive. The court had long provided only room and board for servants in the ranks of fiscal people, but beginning in 1859 it began transferring some palace employees to wage-earning status. The rising cost of servants inspired efforts to reduce the size of the permanent palace staff. Already in 1858 the court had abolished the Winter Palace fire command and specified the maximum number of servants to be hired in each of the other commands. As a result the total number of servants employed permanently at the Winter Palace fell to 294, although this effort to control the numbers was undermined by the additional provision that palace servants currently employed would be permitted to stay on as salaried employees after their specified terms ended. For the first time, officials recorded the precise number of days per month during which individuals would receive pay. In February 1868, for example, valets (*kamerdiners*) Semyon Zakharov, Petr Karpov, Mikhail Kostin, and Alexander Kuz'mich each worked for six to eight days at a daily rate of 3.50 rubles, while the waiter Ivan Ivanov earned 1.77 rubles for each of seventeen days.[10] In spite of these steps toward a contractual employment system, it was not until 1882 that Alexander III abolished the category (*soslovie*) of court employee (*pridvornosluzhitel'*) altogether and transitioned all palace workers to salaried positions.[11]

In lieu of a sizeable permanent palace staff, servants were employed and housed through a variety of contracts. Some joined specialized "companies" and "commands," and others were temporary workers, single men in work gangs who cooked for themselves in designated palace kitchens.[12] Palace records reveal new employment arrangements. One example involved a contract with peasants from the village of Putilov. The palace had employed men from this village in nearby Shlisselberg district seasonally for a long time, but in November 1867 the court signed a detailed annual contract with the Putilov elders to supply "sober people" who were "healthy and strong" for work in various court buildings. Workers themselves were to pay for the cost of traveling to the assigned workplaces, but the court would provide housing and a daily wage, varying per type of work performed and "paid every month for not more than 29 days."[13]

The new arrangements caused friction with longtime employees. In February 1868 a Winter Palace linen matron, Varvara Korzhukova, penned a complaint to her superiors. She noted that the four workmen who had served in the laundry with her for twenty-seven years had proved themselves to be thoroughly responsible people, but "now I learn that instead of these workers I'm getting others from the village of Putilov. I request that you let me have the people I've had before because we need to have reliable people living on the premises to wash the underwear of the imperial family, not day laborers."[14] Korzhukova may have been successful in deflecting the incursion of the Putilov day laborers, because soon the court was imploring garden masters at the Summer Garden and other palaces to take on some of these contracted workers. Even though the court assured the supervisors that the peasants were forbidden to get drunk, none of the garden masters would have anything to do with the Putilov villagers.[15] Nonetheless, persistent efforts to mitigate labor costs now regularly appeared in palace records. When officials at a given palace or court site requested additional laborers, often when hosting important guests, the Court Office generally complied, but not without protracted negotiations over the number and wages of workers supplied.[16] The self-contained household in which the children of loyal servants were groomed for future employment and long-term service was rewarded yielded to the impersonal world of modern contract labor.

At the same time the employment of temporary and day laborers generated anxiety about the vulnerability of palace treasures, and the records indicate there was more attention paid to regulating the people who came and went. Winter Palace manager (*zaveduiushchii*) Aleksei Petrovich Del'sal' fielded requests to hire guards for special palace events such as balls, dinners, and one occasion on which the empress was honoring women teachers from St. Petersburg.[17] Del'sal' also addressed concerns about so many Winter Palace cupboards lacking doors and posted night guards outside the New Hermitage when its side gate was under repair in May 1872. On another occasion he arranged guards for a public exhibit of ceramic and glass works set up in the Concert Hall over Christmas. In November 1874 the chief of the Employees' Command notified Del'sal' that he was issuing two hundred new badges for peasants hired temporarily to work during balls and similar events, because the old ones were worn out. But the only request for guards that appeared to be directed at the personal security of the imperial family itself was when Del'sal' dispatched guards to accompany the grand dukes as they dined in the city.[18]

THE URBAN AUDIENCE FRACTURED AND DISTRACTED

The mid-century changes in the script and stage management of monarchy paled in comparison to the dramatic shifts taking place in the audience. By the late 1850s St. Petersburg had blossomed into a major metropolis of over 600,000 residents.[19] A stream of newly freed people seeking wage work on their own terms flooded the new factories, steel mills, and shipyards of St. Petersburg. The overall population rose to 667,000 by the end of the 1860s and to 861,000 by the beginning of the 1880s.[20] Newcomers settled in charmless and filthy factory districts far from the city center. At the same time Alexander's reform of city administration allowed male permanent residents of St. Petersburg from all classes to elect the first city Duma in 1873. This body met regularly to address the welfare of citizens, although their needs outstripped available resources.[21]

By the end of Alexander's reign, as Russia's industrial revolution gained steam, over 110,000 people worked in St. Petersburg manufacturing concerns and supported 58,000 dependents. The fact that the city census tracked the proportion of dependents per occupational category indicates official interest in the question of seasonality, which impinged on policing and social stability. For example, the venerable construction trades employed 22,000 mostly young and unattached men, who supported only 9,000 dependents. Among the seasonal or temporary workers (generally younger and certainly poorer), the pattern of overwhelmingly male communities persisted. Tens of thousands of rural migrants arrived each year after Easter to labor in the city's never-ending construction projects as bricklayers, stonecutters, housepainters, roofers, carpenters, and plasterers. Iaroslavl and Tver continued to send the largest numbers, followed by Petersburg, Novgorod, and Kostroma Provinces.[22] Some of them became *pitershchiki*, staying on as tailors or tavern keepers; others were boys who stayed for three to five years before returning to their villages flush with funds and in search of brides.[23]

St. Petersburg continued to attract goods and people from all over the empire, but these were more and more oriented toward provisioning the huge urban population itself than the imperial court. An army of stevedores labored from Easter to mid-November unloading grain at the Kalashnikov docks near Alexander Nevskii Monastery, earning 150 rubles for the season.[24] Poor women repaired the torn bags of grain at a kopek per bag, and gleaners, many of them children, swept up what spilled to sell along the docks.[25] During August and September the glassed-in market at Haymarket Square also offered vegetables grown by Iaroslavl peasants in the city's hundreds of market gardens, along with the fish and dairy products offered by Finnish fishermen and farmers.

Among those categories of employees that served the court and the government, as well as among those who lived on "income from property," the number of dependents equaled or exceeded the number actually employed, indicating that this was the settled part of the urban population. For example, 13,000 "chinovniki in administrative offices" supported 18,000 dependents; 58,000 merchants supported 41,000 dependents; 1,800 clergy supported 2,700 dependents; those living off property income numbered 11,000 and supported 12,000. It is clear that by 1880 the capital city had so far outgrown its roots that the care and feeding of the imperial court occupied a shrinking proportion of the city's residents.[26] By the late nineteenth century, St. Petersburg was no longer the company town Peter had founded nearly two centuries before.

Although the capital city beckoned as a place of opportunity, a poor man's America, it was nonetheless a place where poverty and misery persisted. Fully half of the city's residential buildings lacked running water at the beginning of the 1880s.[27] Finnish peasant women worked as wet nurses for the thousands of abandoned children cast off by prostitutes or impoverished families and a "foster child industry" flourished. Street children peddled cheap calendars and pictures, and street musicians from all over central Europe hoped for donations, along with beggars from the city's large population of homeless people who "on any given day do not know where they will spend the night."[28] Among them, mourned the chronicler of urban life A. A. Bakhtiarov, were many who had not been to church in fifteen years, by their own admission.

"In church our brothers shun us," they claimed. "Fasting is out of the question. And besides, in Piter you can't even get into a church without a ticket."[29]

As the city population skyrocketed and diversified, the capacity of the Winter Palace to serve as a unifying stage ebbed. Even if Alexander II had been inclined to muster prodigious displays of the patriotic bond between soldier and tsar or edifying spectacles of enlightened culture at Palace Square he would have captured the attention of a declining proportion of the sprawling city's people.

As the pageantry of absolute monarchy was seen less and less on the city's central stage, the drama of public civic life replaced it. The last great patriotic convocation of Alexander's lifetime took place in December 1877 when he returned victorious from the long and costly Turkish War. Although the well-publicized limitations of his personal role in the eventual Russian victory preceded him, St. Petersburg crowds welcomed him as the personification and living symbol of national victory. When he arrived in the city on December 10, a formal military deputation greeted him at the railroad station but a capacity crowd of the humble and the great wedged itself into Kazan Cathedral to join him for prayers of gratitude. Foreign newspapers reported that an enormous crowd of the city's people then accompanied Alexander's carriage to the Winter Palace, where "the cheering continued so long and persistently that he had to gratify the people by showing himself again and again at the window of the palace."[30]

Not all of St. Petersburg's increasingly variegated people revered the tsar. A burgeoning part of the city population were students at the city's many institutions of higher education, including the Engineering Institute, the Mining Institute, the military academies, and St. Petersburg University. The number and social composition of university students had been carefully controlled during most of Nicholas's reign, but with Alexander II came swift expansion. By 1856 admission was offered to any applicant who could pass the entrance examination. Subjects previously banned were restored and, most welcome of all to the liberal minded professors and students, the role of bullying inspectors was much circumscribed. Between 1854 and 1859 the student population of St. Petersburg University nearly tripled, from 350 to about 1,000.[31]

Many memoirists attest to a perceptible blossoming of the spirit of social criticism and esprit de corps among students and the large auxiliary of auditors, which now included many women. A. M. Skabichevskii recalled, for example, that "in the course of my five-year stint at the university, it went through such a radical change as to be unrecognizable. Instead of the old dead silence of empty corridors, ... now you had to fight your way through its corridors and lecture halls."[32] The liberalization of the rules permitted a proliferation of student-led organizations and a newly assertive posture. Alexander and his advisers grew increasingly alarmed at what they had unleashed, at precisely the climax of the emancipation legislation. The crackdown that came in 1861 produced confrontation. Although the new regulations forbade it, students met regularly in the university courtyard tucked behind the main university buildings and easily visible from the Neva windows of the Winter Palace. On a late September day, inflamed by rumors of arrests, a group of about one thousand resolved to march to the university curator's house on the Admiralty side, and their very long foot procession took them across the seasonal Palace Bridge and past the lee of the Winter Palace on their way to Nevskii Prospekt. Authorities did not succeed in quelling the students or in imposing the new regulations, so in December Alexander closed the university.

Many elements of the St. Petersburg educated public seemed to sympathize with the students through the winter of 1861–1862, but in the spring there appeared a new disturbance in the city: a series of fires deliberately set and culminating on Pentecost in May. The fires struck both the prosperous and the poor, but particularly the latter, who lived in close quarters tucked behind such great shopping areas as the old Apraksin Dvor, which burned to the ground in the great conflagration. Rumors flew about the city as to the culprits and the chief suspects were two: the Poles and the students. A sense of general panic set in as householders closed the gates to their courtyards and authorities warned against admitting unknown persons to back stairways and alleys. Some feared a campaign to destroy all government buildings and stores. The anxiety turned public opinion against student demonstrators and one memoirist was grateful that "by August the fires had completely ended, thanks to the chief of police."[33] Despite the ebbing of public sympathy, however, the student movement continued apace. For the rest of Alexander's reign the university and other educational institutions persisted as centers of dissent and sedition, and from the ranks of students and their supporters a campaign of political assassination eventually arose.

MONARCH AND PALACE AS TARGETS

Like his predecessors Alexander took daily strolls in his own neighborhood, and city residents were familiar with his habits. He walked along the Palace Embankment or in the nearby Summer Garden, lightly guarded, as befit a monarch at home among the inhabitants of his capital city. It was on one such occasion in April 1866 that the first attempt on his life occurred, when Russian nobleman and sometime student Dmitrii Karakazov took a shot at him as he was leaving the Summer Garden. The shot missed Alexander, purportedly thanks to the quick action of Kostroma artisan Osip Komissarov who was close enough to deflect Karakazov's arm. The event registered as an occasion on which providence and the emperor's faithful subjects had joined forces to save his life, and Alexander sped immediately to Kazan Cathedral to offer prayers as news of the incident raced through the city. By evening the State Council had assembled at the Winter Palace to congratulate Alexander upon his return, and a crowd gathered on Palace Square to cheer the monarch when he appeared on the balcony. A festive mood gripped the city that night, and city officials illuminated Nevskii Prospekt in holiday style. The next day the Senate, nobles, and merchants came to the palace to offer the sovereign their good wishes.[34] The reaction of the palace authorities to this assassination attempt was extremely muted. There were no alterations in palace security or in Alexander's habits, suggesting that it registered as an anomaly rather than as a new reality.

Karakazov had been a lone wolf, but revolutionary activity did not abate, and students were arrested in great numbers after their summer of "going to the people" in 1874. At the end of 1877 the city was treated to a spectacle in which 193 accused revolutionaries went to trial. The most dramatic trial was that of Vera Zasulich, the woman who had shot St. Petersburg's governor-general, because the jury acquitted her in March 1878 to the general approval of the press. This was the atmosphere in which, on the day after Easter, the sometime student Alexander Soloviev shot at the tsar as he took his daily stroll unguarded near the headquarters of the Guard Corps a few blocks from the palace. Hearing shots, a crowd of people ran toward Alexander from the direction of Palace Square and apprehended Soloviev.

This assassination attempt generated a substantial police reaction. Within a few days they required the posting of doormen (*dvorniki*) at all government buildings and at all private buildings in the Admiralty district at the proprietor's or department's expense. The chief of police issued detailed instructions about the conduct of these private doormen, forbidding them, for example, to be assigned any duties other than surveillance at their posts. The most heavily guarded part of town was the first Admiralty district, surrounding the Winter Palace. There every single building was to post a registered doorman. Outlying sections of the city continued to operate under much lighter surveillance. The governor-general of St. Petersburg made it plain, however, that "to protect the tsar no building he is in will be without a responsible doorman at day or at night."[35] The Ministry of the Court allocated twenty-four hundred rubles for the coming year in order to employ contracted peasants at ten rubles per month for service as doormen.[36] Alexander now at long last abandoned his freedom of movement around the city. He did not take walks in the gardens or along the embankments, and city people exchanged stories of seeing the emperor fly past in a closed carriage under Cossack guard.[37] Russia's ruler had become a target, and the stage of monarchy now offered a tableau of the palace under siege.

That same year the underground People's Will Party issued a death sentence against Alexander II.[38] In September they succeeded in placing one of their members inside the Winter Palace as a contract worker. Stepan Khalturin, founder of the Northern Union of Russian Workers, was a talented cabinetmaker from Viatka. He had been hired using a false passport to work on the imperial yacht and was eventually transferred to the palace where he was assigned to live in the workers' barracks. Christopher Ely stresses that Khalturin was able to play the role of naïve peasant well enough to get the palace position. Both Alexander and court officials still cherished the idea that the love of Russia's rural people for the tsar did not wear off when they arrived in the capital.[39]

Over several months Khalturin spirited about one hundred pounds of dynamite into the palace during his evening strolls. The fact that he could do so undetected reveals the reality of police surveillance at the palace as opposed to the official susceptibility of all workers and servants to search at any time. On February 5, 1880, Khalturin positioned his cache of dynamite near a supporting wall in his basement quarters two stories below the tsar's dining room. He had chosen his hour because inside the palace the imperial family's dining schedule was generally known. He lit the slow fuse and calmly walked outside where he joined his associate Andrei Zheliabov on Palace Square to watch the mayhem that ensued.

The *Sankt-Peterburgskie vedomosti* reported two days later that around twenty minutes after six on the evening of February 5, city residents in the vicinity of the Winter Palace heard a tremendous boom and felt the earth shake. "The explosion was so strong and made so much noise that everyone in the area around the Palace ran toward it in complete confusion."[40] Across the river, at the Stock Exchange on the spit of Vasilevskii Island, people ran toward the embankment, thinking there had been an accident on the Palace Bridge. Because the explosion had taken place deep inside the palace, which "thanks to the strength of the load-bearing walls built by the remarkable Rastrelli," showed no outward sign of damage, it was not immediately clear where the trouble was.[41] People gradually came to understand that something had exploded inside the Winter Palace, where the gas lighting had immediately failed.

There was no official word until the following day. On February 7, the newspaper *Sankt-Peterburgskie vedomosti* printed a brief government statement that the explosion had occurred below the quarters of the main palace guard, which was just under the emperor's dining room, killing eight enlisted men of the Finnish Guards Regiment. The report noted that there were several gas pipes running through this room. Throughout the day on February 6, "a huge crowd of people hastened to Palace Square at the Winter Palace" to express their gratitude that the sovereign's life had been spared.[42]

By February 8, the editorialists of the *Sankt-Peterburgskie vedomosti* were reacting indignantly to General Gurko's statement to *Russkii invalid* the day before, which they quoted in full, that the cause of the explosion had not been gas but dynamite: "someone impudent and evil-minded apparently directed this infernal scheme at the Sacred Person of our Sovereign." The paper chastised authorities for putting out the gas explosion story at first, finding the delay in reporting the full horror of the situation inexplicable. The editorialist expressed the solidarity of the whole Russian people, even "we representatives of the educated *sosloviia*, we are also mortal opponents of sedition, and we wait impatiently for them to inform us as to the special means they will employ in the struggle with this secret treason." The writer was particularly alarmed to realize that the entire imperial family could have been killed if they had not been delayed entering the dining room by the tardiness of their foreign guest. It also seemed incredible, and frightening, that the tsar was not even safe inside his own residence, which was guarded by a whole company of guards around the clock. If such a thing could happen there, which was an attack "on the whole blessed Russian land, then how is it possible to feel secure?"[43]

In all, eleven enlisted members of the Finnish Guards Regiment died of their injuries and over fifty suffered wounds. Alexander and his family attended special prayers in the palace church the following day, at which they honored the officers of the Finnish Guards. The paper reported that the uninjured soldiers had insisted on remaining at their posts to the end of their shift even though others arrived to relieve them. The government announced that the widows and families of those killed would be provided for.[44]

Khalturin's attack was unique in the history of the Winter Palace, but it confirmed that opening the palace to contractors brought inherent risks in a city whose people were no longer reliable monarchists. The attack undermined the durable assumption among members of the Romanov family that they would always be loved and protected by Russia's "simple people." It also revealed an element of civic division, in that those who worked inside the palace themselves became collateral damage. When revolutionaries attacked the monarchy they attacked fellow Russians in its entourage as well as members of the patriotic public. Whether people realized it at the time the contest over monarchy's future had been joined, and Russia's people were protagonists on each side of the struggle.[45] The battle for the hearts and minds of the public was subsequently engaged by the tsarist government, which sought public input about how to combat terrorism in the city, and the People's Will, which sought the support of the liberal middle class.[46] Each side understood the attitude of the St. Petersburg public to be central to the survival or destruction of Russia's monarchical regime.

New security practices regarding palace workers took effect almost immediately.[47] When a St. Petersburg silver manufacturer was engaged to restore items from Nicholas Hall, he was required "per the new instructions about workmen in the Palace" to supply the names of all workmen who would be entering to undertake the work.[48] Palace authorities rejected one of them, described as an infantryman, because too little information had been provided. Some sense of how cumbersome the new security process rendered palace housekeeping is suggested by the fact that this matter apparently consumed five weeks before the restoration work could begin. Other rules tightened up the amount of advance information required about temporary workers hired for masquerade balls before palace uniforms could be issued. The authorities in the Court Office no longer took for granted the loyalty of prospective palace servants.

In the city, news of the "explosion in the Winter Palace" gripped everyone's imagination. The artist Alexander Benois recalled those years of his childhood when the tsar was under constant threat as marked by a feeling of menace and, retrospectively, of twilight, although he did not remember the public events especially impacting his own life. He did recall a sense of foreboding among capital residents and rumors that took on a life of their own. Many of these revealed public perceptions of the great palace as a kind of golden prison penetrated by spies. Benois recounted the story that, after the explosion, the emperor found a threatening letter on his desk every day, placed there by unknown hands. Such a thing was thought possible, Benois wrote, because apparently "there are so many hallways, corridors, and secret passageways in the Winter Palace that to supervise everything that went on inside that colossal labyrinth was utterly impossible."[49] Even that tale was not as fantastic as the rumor spread by "buffoons" that, in the aftermath of this grievous attack, a thorough inspection of the palace revealed that servants were keeping a cow in some garret or other in order to provide their children with fresh milk.[50] In the urban imagination the Winter Palace was ceasing to be the venerable abode of an exemplary imperial household and was taking on the ominous atmosphere of disorders both comic and monstrous.

The disarray inside the imperial household was now widely publicized. Two weeks after the explosion, officials of the court went ahead with plans to commemorate the twenty-fifth anniversary of Alexander's accession to the throne. The public events were canceled, but the tsar received delegations and gifts, including a gilded chest containing twenty-five watercolors of important events and places of his reign, from the City Duma.[51] Otherwise, the celebration was subdued. Lanterns and illuminations brightened the evening sky on public buildings and grand homes, but those closest to the imperial court were saddened by the critical illness of the tubercular empress for whom, it was said, a specially sealed chamber had been created inside the Winter Palace.[52] Nonetheless, in the evening the emperor greeted a large crowd assembled on the Palace Square from the palace balcony, all of them serenaded by music from the combined bands of the guards regiments.[53]

Empress Maria Aleksandrovna died three months after the explosion and she was buried without pomp. Rumors now flew about the city that the emperor had granted his young mistress the title Princess Iur'evskaia, that he had legitimized their three children, and that in fact he had already married her. In truth the morganatic marriage occurred in July, in violation of church standards, and Benois recalled his youthful feeling that "it seemed completely impossible that our 'good and tender' ruler could commit such a deed."[54] Within a few months, though, the air of scandal began to dissipate, and "there were even some people who chose to attend the great 'reception' on January 1 at the Palace, because it was said that [Princess Iur'evskaia] would appear among the city ladies ... but she did not show up at all."[55]

The denouement to this period of ominous twilight that many had anticipated came on Sunday, March 1, 1881. Good news of the arrest of People's Will leader Andrei Zheliabov buoyed Alexander, as did the as-yet-unpublicized planning for his wife's coronation. After church the emperor signed off on the final version of a long-gestating constitutional reform and prepared for the weekly review of guards regiments at the imperial stables, which was one of his favorite duties. This event normally included a parade, but the security situation in the capital precluded that. Minister of the Interior M. T. Loris-Melikov attempted to dissuade Alexander from conducting this widely publicized ritual at all, but the tsar insisted. It was upon his return that the eighth attempt on the life of Alexander II succeeded in its aim. People's Will member Nicholas Rysakov hurled a bomb at the emperor in his "bomb-proof" vehicle, a gift of Napoleon III. Rysakov's bomb wounded members of the emperor's entourage but left Alexander unharmed. As the tsar got out of the carriage to console a wounded Cossack and inspect the pit left by the explosion, Ignatii Grinevitskii threw a second bomb, which tore off one of Alexander's legs and damaged the other. Mortally wounded, the tsar expressed his wish to die at the Winter Palace, a few blocks away. He lost consciousness as police placed him on a sleigh. They were able to fulfill his last wish, placing Alexander on a camp bed in his palace office. The court medic on duty (*vrachebnoe pri Vysochaishim Dvore dezhurstvo*) was F. F. Markus, who attended to the wounded ruler.[56] The heir and his wife arrived, and in the corridors of the palace a small army of palace and court employees crowded about.[57]

By that time a crowd had assembled on Palace Square, in what had almost become a ritual of awaiting news of yet another miraculous escape from death. Now the imperial Life Guards showed themselves in force, both inside and outside the palace. Inside, the Preobrazhenskii Guards lined up in the hallways, with live ammunition. Cossack units presented a line of defense outside the southern façade of the palace, facing the square. Units summoned while still in parade uniform from the just concluded review stood at posts before each palace entrance. The assembled public learned of the emperor's death when they saw the imperial standard lowered over the palace; presumably few of them would have understood the announcement given from the balcony by Adjutant-General Alexander Suvorov, in French. Benois recalled, "the story went that when the standard over the main gate was lowered the throng of people that had gathered on the square of the Winter Palace fell to its knees, and the square resounded with the sound of sobs."[58] This was at about 3:30 in the afternoon.

According to witnesses, large crowds of people remained on the Palace Square into the night. People in the throng were purportedly on the lookout for "students" and actually did seize one unfortunate young man "of the Jewish type, in the uniform of a medical student or veterinarian," who was only rescued by the intervention of Cossacks and gendarmes. The authorities carried him off to the General Staff building for his own safety.[59]

When the new monarch with his family returned later that evening to their home in the Anichkov Palace, their carriage was able to move down Nevskii Prospekt only with difficulty, despite the Cossacks deployed to protect them, as the crowd pressed in with shouts of "Hoorah!" City and court authorities implored the new Alexander III to leave his home of over fifteen years and move into the Winter Palace, where he might be spared the danger of traveling several times a day up and down the avenue between the two palaces. He complied after that first night but only for the week before his father's funeral.

Needless to say in this atmosphere the public was not invited into the palace to view the tsar-liberator's remains. Courtiers and ranking merchants attended the formal viewing of the body in the Great Palace Church, crushing each other to squeeze into the cramped space. On March 8 a funeral procession conveyed Alexander's body from the palace to the Peter and Paul Fortress. For the first time an imperial funeral procession included representative members of the peasant estate, several of whom, it was said, cried as they marched at the end of the parade.[60]

MONARCHY DECENTERED

After the assassination, Russia's security services rounded up revolutionaries and cracked down on university students. Still, to many Russian subjects who lived through the 1880s, the reign of Alexander III appeared to be not a time of repression and decay but of renewal: a return to pre-Petrine values, including a full-throated assertion of the precedence of Slavic Russia, pious Orthodoxy, and a monarchy rooted in the bond between tsar and people, unmediated by the ineffective staff of the Westernized state. The 1880s and 1890s also ushered in an era of rapid economic growth based on coal, steel, and railroad building. The mining engineer Alexander Fenin, who was a student at St. Petersburg's Mining Institute in the 1880s, felt fortunate to have been a student not in the violent and monstrous 1870s but in a period characterized by "exultant national pride. It was a pride in Russia; in her talents; in the strong, unyielding calm of her government; in her might among other nations; in her tsar powerful and just, with his Olympian serenity; these were not just the impressions of greenhorns such as we, but also of a large circle of society in this unjustly overlooked era."[61]

Yet, just as Alexander III's reign invoked traditional Russia it also inaugurated an intentional decentering of the governing monarchy, which the new tsar moved away from the Winter Palace, away from the Neva embankment, and increasingly away from St. Petersburg itself.[62] This decentering was not only ideological. It was also enabled by new distance-conquering technologies such as the railroad and the telegraph.[63] The new medium with the greatest potential for projecting monarchy at a distance, however, was the photograph. Alexander II had been the first Russian ruler to take a keen interest in photography, and by 1860 Alexander had retained Russian photographic pioneer Sergei Lvovich Levitskii, who produced several famous portraits of Alexander III and his siblings, later achieving renown as court photographer for Nicholas II.[64] The long-term effect of the diffusion of the monarchical word and image was to render it more abstract, reducing monarchy's concrete role in holding the civic center.

With the death of Alexander II the Winter Palace ceased to be the primary place of residence of Russia's imperial family, although its formal designation as such never changed: the imperial standard flew over the building even when the last two emperors in fact lived elsewhere.[65] When Alexander III and his family were in the capital they continued living in the "cozy" Anichkov Palace, where Alexander and Maria Fedorovna had resided for the first fifteen years of their marriage. Alexander III was not the first Romanov to prefer life away from what he called the "constant cotillion" at the Winter Palace, but he was the first to simply move across town. This ruler whose family life might have proved as exemplary as his grandfather's displayed it much less regularly than Nicholas I had done, and he preferred to do so via photograph.

Much of the time Alexander III was not in St. Petersburg at all. Throughout his thirteen-year reign he lived and governed primarily from his suburban palace at Gatchina. He broke up this routine frequently by taking his family to Livadia, the newest imperial estate located on the Black Sea, and he came and went by rail. Most years he also sojourned in the summer to Denmark, home of his wife's family, a vacation he relished. The new distance-conquering technologies allowed Alexander to direct an increasingly complex government from further and further away. His ancestor Emperor Paul had also loved Gatchina, but Paul had been compelled to move into the heart of the city when he took the throne. While Alexander and family retreated to Gatchina, the court as such was not required to follow. Most courtiers disliked this distant and charmless palace town, and only actual government officials had to make the regular trek back and forth.[66] For those required social events of the dacha season Alexander took up residence at Tsarskoe Selo, in spite of the fact that it reminded him of his father's courtship with Katia Dolgorukova.

In fin-de-siècle Russia the search for a functional absolutism rendered the face-to-face presentation of monarchical grandeur to the citizens of the capital city less essential. The city on which Alexander turned his back was associated with the Westernized monarchy that he now rejected. Alexander embraced a full-throated monarchical populism tinged with ethno-racism. Eschewing extravagant urban pageants mounted at the Winter Palace and the Palace Square, Alexander weakened the bond that had existed since the beginning of the eighteenth century between St. Petersburg and the monarchy, and he did not replace this bond with a link to any other concrete place, although Moscow took on additional symbolic weight. He demonstrated that court ceremonies were malleable and moveable, dependent only on the body of the monarch himself.[67]

He observed the first, somber, Epiphany ceremony of his reign, in January 1882, at Gatchina. The *Sankt-Peterburgskie vedomosti* described this ceremony a few days later, noting that the liturgy took place in the Gatchina palace church, followed by the procession of the cross and blessing of the waters at Silver Pond on the estate.[68] The Epiphany ceremony had returned to the Winter Palace by 1884. The newspaper noted that "a mass of people covered the Palace embankment, Palace Bridge and the banks of Vasilevskii Island," but there was no mention of city residents exuberantly converging on the hole in the ice.[69] Court memoirists recalled balls of the winter season, over which Alexander's popular Danish wife presided, that seemed to represent a return to the joyful galas of the past, but even these were not necessarily hosted at the Winter Palace. The imperial couple held balls and musical evenings at Anichkov, but for the very large events where they hosted between twenty-five hundred and eight thousand guests, they exploited the great halls of the Winter Palace.[70] The enormous "all-class" New Year's masquerades of Nicholas's reign, which Alexander II had replaced with brief midday palace receptions for notables, did not return.

While the tsar made use of the Winter Palace for large court occasions, its demotion as the center of family and court life made way for certain economies, which suited the frugal ruler. He evicted the innumerable grand dukes who were living at court expense in the Winter Palace's reserve apartments.[71] When the tsar further forbade the grand dukes to help themselves to palace furnishings as they were accustomed to doing, he came close to mimicking the conviction of the Imperial Hermitage staff that these items constituted a collection of property that did not belong exclusively to the imperial family and should remain intact. He also eschewed his ancestors' habit of constant remodeling and augmenting, preferring to make do with essential repairs such as modernizing the palace heating system. It was on his watch, however, that the court installed electricity in all the imperial palaces.[72] Alexander did consider altering the exterior color scheme of the Winter Palace, which had continued in the general palette inherited from Rastrelli, but in the end he settled for a deeper version of the historic hue.[73]

During Alexander's reign the entire Winter Palace housekeeping staff finally crossed over to being paid wages in cash. This trend had encouraged staff reductions since his father's time, and the decline in numbers accelerated when the new imperial family moved away. Alexander did preside over an increase in the wages of the reduced number of court servants, while insisting that they should all be Russians. A smaller number of working people lived permanently in the palace, but the staff was supplemented with temporary workers when great events did take place at the palace and with the personal servants of visitors and the imperial family when they stayed there.[74]

While he exercised careful stewardship over the great Winter Palace on the Neva, Alexander III simply did not consider it necessary to put up with life on the grand stage any longer. Not only had the assassins' bombs made it plain that the venerable bond between the emperor and his city had frayed fatally but, perversely, the assassination also finally vanquished the ghost of 1789—the monarch's murder in his own neighborhood did not produce either revolution or constitutionalism. Alexander III thus subtly directed the locus of monarchy away from the center of the imperial capital and back toward the body of the monarch. In the age of speed and electricity that body could be anywhere, and where it was absent it could be represented photographically.

Simultaneously, the tsar assumed something of the aura of a modern governing executive, presiding over proliferating ministries and oriented toward economic expansion. Thus the Winter Palace was divorced more and more not only from the monarchy but also from the government. Offices directly connected to government such as the emperor's cabinet were moved either to the Anichkov Palace or to buildings in its vicinity.[75] In 1885 both the Council of Ministers and the State Council moved out of the Winter Palace to new quarters in the Mariinskii Palace on St. Isaac's Square.

MONARCHY'S USABLE LEGACY

If Alexander III relinquished this part of his inheritance, other heirs were waiting in the palace wings. What remained in the palace from which Alexander and his government retreated was the imperial court and its quasi-public appendages—that is, the "state" cultural institutions that had taken on a life of their own: the Imperial Library, Imperial Archaeological Commission, and Imperial Hermitage. The Ministry of the Imperial Court still had its main chancellery in the Winter Palace, its telephone number helpfully listed in the 1894 city directory, which also publicized the minister's availability to receive delegations on Wednesday mornings between ten and half past eleven. The administrators of these cultural institutions gradually expanded their grip on the palace terrain and deployed its resources for their mission of popular uplift.

A visitors' registry from 1909 reveals the members of the public who came and went via the "Committee entrance" of the Winter Palace on the Neva side. Many distinguished guests called there for the Archaeological Commission including a representative of the "Asiatic Jews of Turkestan" and the emir of Bukhara. Artists, art experts, and photographers also signed in at this palace entry, including many who were visiting the office of antiquities expert B. V. Farmakovskii. Others who signed in at this "back door" entrance included art students, art school administrators, and delivery boys from all sorts of St. Petersburg stores and bakeries, the latter supplying the commission's cafeteria.[76]

Although they occupied impressive facilities, the overseers of the Imperial Hermitage itself went about their business in the waning decades of Russia's old regime under persistent fiscal constraints and acquiring relatively little. Ranking official of the Ministry of the Imperial Court V. S. Krivenko recalled that in these years the budget of the Hermitage was "pitiful."[77] At the same time the museum's collection was gaining international publicity thanks in part to the decision in 1881 to publish photographic reproductions of works in the Hermitage collection.[78]

Meanwhile, members of the city's cultural elite who were interested in public enlightenment intensified their efforts to publicize the Hermitage artworks within the capital itself. For example, in 1891 the writer Dmitri N. Mamin-Sibiriak penned a long article in the newspaper *Novosti: Birzhevaia gazeta* (News: Stock Exchange gazette) describing the museum's delights. A native of Perm, Mamin-Sibiriak wrote that, "it is a peculiar characteristic of the Petersburger that he is very poorly acquainted with Petersburg, particularly with the treasures that he can see, study, and in which a cultured person can delight." People hurried past those cultural artifacts that were numerous and always at hand. "I am sure," Mamin-Sibiriak continued, "that there are many native Petersburgers who have either never been inside the Hermitage or who haven't been there for ten or fifteen years. Thus it is the 'naïve provincial' visiting Petersburg who considers it his duty to fill up every free minute paying calls on the capital's museums, and above all, of course, on the Hermitage." Mamin-Sibiriak concluded his piece by proclaiming the Imperial Hermitage to be a "national treasure."[79]

No one did more to publicize this treasure than the editors of the new art and preservation journal *Starye gody* (Bygone years), an enormously popular publication that began in 1906 in hopes of raising awareness of the old paintings and art objects collected in museums and private collections of St. Petersburg and other cities.[80] Peter Veiner was the principal editor for many years, but his editorial staff included the great art publicists of the age— Benois, S. K. Makovskii, V. A. Vereshchagin, N. N. Vrangel', A. A. Trubnikov, among others. Within a few years of launching, the editorial committee expanded to include a somewhat younger group, many of whom continued their careers well into the Soviet period: V. Ia. Kurbatov, E. E. Lanceray, and G. K. Lukomskii. Between 1907 and 1916 *Starye gody* kept the Hermitage in the spotlight, carrying at least a note about its activities and collections in the "Chronicle" section of each edition and publishing numerous lengthy studies of its various holdings over those years. No other museum or private collection attracted as much attention in this publication as that of the Imperial Hermitage.[81]

One of the most successful, if unlikely, populizers of the Imperial Hermitage was Count Dmitrii Tolstoy, the last prerevolutionary director of the Hermitage. Scion of a noble clan, Tolstoy became the master of ceremonies of the imperial court in 1889. In 1901 he assumed his first arts position as deputy administrator of the Imperial Russian Museum, and he became director of the Imperial Hermitage in 1909. He stayed in the latter role until he handed over the keys to his Bolshevik successors in 1918. Like his predecessor Tolstoy occupied an apartment in the Winter Palace.[82]

An able administrator with the right kinds of connections Tolstoy raised the museum's international profile and made important acquisitions such as the *Benois Madonna* of Leonardo da Vinci.[83] But Tolstoy knew how to attract visitors as well. He exhibited antiquities recently discovered near the Black Sea coast.[84] His most intuitive move was to embrace the intense public interest in the crown jewels. Other art experts had bemoaned visitors' supposedly lowbrow preference for such items, but Tolstoy made the Imperial Hermitage the premier venue exhibiting Romanov treasures. He managed to get a popular collection of money and medals from the Tsarskoe Selo Arsenal transferred to the Hermitage, which he displayed in the great hall of the Large Hermitage building, recently freed up by the departure of the State Council. Tolstoy also acquired a spectacular trove of silver and porcelain from the Winter Palace, along with permission to exhibit it on the top floor of the palace itself. When visitors crossed from the Small Hermitage into the palace proper to look at the plates and spoons of the tsars, an internal barrier between the private world of the rulers and the civic life of the urban public was quietly breached. Square foot by square foot, the entire ensemble of Hermitage buildings was taking on the mission of public display and cultural enlightenment.[85]

The reign of Alexander II thus ushered in a protracted period of monarchical decline. His efforts to reform what remained an absolutist system had muddied monarchy's script. Not only did his performance of monarchy broadcast mixed messages but Alexander also found it impossible to deploy the palace stage as his father had done. His own family was disordered, and the serving people in his household were reduced in number and increasingly transient. The city to which he wished to project his scenario had grown unwieldy—populous, diverse, less focused on the monarch, and his court rebellious.

After his father's assassination Alexander III rejected both the Winter Palace and increasingly the city it anchored. Alexander's son Nicholas II (1894–1917) briefly experimented with family life inside the Winter Palace, even going so far as to build a private enclosed Winter Garden for his wife on the Admiralty side of the building in 1896.[86] After traumatic events early in his reign, however, Nicholas retreated to his own Versailles and lived most of the year at Tsarskoe Selo. Meanwhile, Palace Square had insinuated itself into the city's collective civic consciousness as a place connected to moments of national triumph, thanksgiving, anxiety, mourning, and finally revolt. What commenced there in the twentieth century was the process of creating a national scenario that left monarchy behind.

9
TO THE PALACE

The long-forestalled collapse of Russian monarchy finally played itself out between 1905 and 1917. The Russian Revolution took place throughout the Russian Empire, in all of its cities, in the countryside, and among the troops fighting World War I. Yet when this tale is told, as it often is, the story of what happened in the imperial capital is often the primary plot line. The culminating event in the transfer of power to the Bolsheviks was seen even by Lenin to be the proverbial storming of the Winter Palace. The fact that the imperial family was not there at the time was quite beside the point. Russian monarchy's primary legacy was control of the sprawling country's political center, and no symbolic action could more forcefully dramatize the transfer of political power than the occupation of the Winter Palace by representatives of St. Petersburg's public. At the same time the new masters of the scene came face-to-face with the cultural administrators who struggled with all their might to preserve and protect the treasures they saw as monarchy's tangible bequest to the nation. Having seized it the Bolsheviks soon dared to transfer the representational power of the old tsarist center to Moscow, but when they did so they left intact the cultural treasures on the Palace Embankment.

We can best articulate the significance of the events that transpired on the Winter Palace stage during Russia's revolutionary decade by considering what the place meant to those cast in the leading roles. The *dramatis personae* include Nicholas II, the St. Petersburg public when it convened on the Palace Square, leader of the Provisional Government Alexander Kerensky, Bolshevik leader V. I. Lenin, and finally one of the revolution's great border crossers, the artist and preservationist Alexander Benois.

CONTESTING PALACE SQUARE, 1905

At the beginning of the twentieth century St. Petersburg was not only the country's capital but also its largest city and primary industrial center. Nearly one and a half million people lived there, two-thirds of them occupying the legal status of peasant. Nearly 80 percent of these urban peasants had been born outside the province of St. Petersburg, but the great majority did not any longer return seasonally to rural villages. The 1890s had seen an explosion of steel and machine factories including shipyards and locomotive plants. A quarter million new laborers had flocked to the city in that decade alone.[1]

There was considerable diversity of living standards from one category of work to another. Metalworkers and artisans formed a labor elite, but even at their average annual wage of 450 rubles most of them lived constantly in debt to shopkeepers. Textile workers, women, domestic laborers, and cabbies earned much less and lived in shockingly poor conditions. Most of St. Petersburg's poor—which is to say most of its working population—could afford to rent only corners of rooms for their families, sharing both cooking and sleeping space with others. Such people accounted for about one-third of the city's population in 1900. Moreover, the industrial workers of St. Petersburg not only lived but also worked in close quarters. In 1905 twelve thousand men worked at the Putilov Factory, the city's largest.

These thousands of working people lived in the sprawling city's outlying industrial regions near factories in the southwest or southeast of the capital or on the northern fringes of Vasilevskii Island or the Petrograd and Vyborg Sides. They socialized when they could at church squares and open spaces in their own neighborhoods, rarely traveling to the ceremonial center of town in the upscale Admiralty district. Nonetheless, when there arose a serious political effort to attract attention to the needs of workers, its leaders focused on Palace Square, a place of historical contact between the monarch and the people.

In response to political agitation by parties of the underground left, the Interior Ministry had given clandestine assent to police efforts to create a working-class association that could provide mutual aid through legal channels. In St. Petersburg this experiment in so-called police socialism was primarily the work of a remarkable priest, Father Georgii Gapon.[2] By the fall of 1903 Father Gapon's Assembly of Russian Factory and Mill Workers of the City of St. Petersburg was meeting in a clubroom in the workers' neighborhood on the Vyborg Side.[3] By the end of 1904 the worker assembly had expanded to ten associated branches across all of working-class St.

Petersburg including the largest of all, the Narva branch, which encompassed the Putilov Factory in the city's southwest.

In the last months of 1904 the combustible fuel for the Revolution of 1905 had nearly finished drying out. Many months of war against the supposedly inferior forces of Japan had gone from bad to worse and exposed government incompetence. Professionals and members of the educated classes gathered in the capital during November 1904 around a banquet campaign and a national zemstvo congress. At the same time leaders of Gapon's assembly sought to publicize the economic grievances of its members while distinguishing them from the more political demands of the liberals. They could not hit upon a plan about how to do so until a strike at the Putilov Factory created an opportunity. The Putilov strike spread to other large factories across the city in the first week of January 1905.

The January 6 Blessing of the Waters fell on a Thursday that year. By now the ceremony was a pale shadow of what it had been sixty years before, even though working people still had the day off. That year many of those who eschewed the observance on the Neva attended all-day meetings about organizing a general strike. Authorities in the city were on edge because of the work stoppages, which now involved nearly one hundred thousand people. In this atmosphere, untoward events looked like frightening omens, and when one of the artillery pieces saluting the emperor from Vasilevskii Island accidentally fired a spray of grapeshot in the direction of the Jordan ceremony, injuring a capital police officer, felling a flagpole, and breaking four windows in the Winter Palace, many suspected foul play. Although the empress dowager, watching from the palace window with the other ladies, was sprayed by window glass, Tsar Nicholas II himself was unhurt on the ice and not overly concerned.[4]

The emperor returned to his suburban palace at Tsarskoe Selo at the end of Thursday's rites and had no immediate plans to return to the city. Meanwhile, the strike continued to mushroom. Gapon was aware that Nicholas had left town but at some point on Thursday he apparently conceived the idea that workers from all of the worker assembly's branches should converge on Palace Square on Sunday afternoon in order to present their monarch with a respectful petition stating their needs. Gapon's collaborator N. M. Varnashev recalled that on Thursday afternoon Gapon drew him aside and whispered: "Tell me, what do you think, would it not be better if we all were to go to deliver the petition? We will inform the tsar and the appropriate authorities that we will assemble on Sunday, let us say, at the Winter Palace, and that the people want to see the tsar and nobody else!"[5] The idea first struck Varnashev as wild, but he quickly concluded it was brilliant. Instead of the predictable petering out of the strikes, the return to work, the inevitable arrests, and restoration of faith in the "little father," a procession to the Winter Palace would amount to "taking the bull by the horns! Tearing off the mask! The blind would see! For the people or against them?"[6] In this telling Varnashev suggests that Gapon had hit upon the symbolic power of the Winter Palace as a zone where St. Petersburg's desperate working people could either induce their ruler to hear them out or, more ominously, where they would confront the fact that their monarch could not be compelled to listen to them.

The idea resonated broadly and quickly. Gapon took his idea directly to the Narva branch of the worker assembly later that evening. By now he seemed convinced that taking workers' demands directly to the tsar was the only hope: "Let us all go with our wives and our children to the Winter Palace on Sunday at 2:00 p.m. Let us go quietly and peacefully, and we will be heard," one eyewitness recorded him as saying.[7] Another heard him say that, if they were not impeded, "we will enter onto the palace square and call the tsar out of Tsarskoe Selo. We will wait for him until evening. When he comes, I will approach him with a deputation of several workers, give him the petition, and say 'Your Highness, you must give the people their freedom.'"[8]

Memoirists record the debate about what to expect on Palace Square. Rumors were rife. Some people anticipated that soldiers would meet them there. There were those who assented tearfully to Gapon's so-called invitation, crying out "we will all give our lives at the Square."[9] Others believed their sovereign would welcome them, confident that soldiers only fired at hooligans and those who waved red flags. One rumor had it that Tsar Nicholas was prepared to host forty to sixty chosen representatives of the workers inside his palace.[10]

The officials in charge of maintaining order were aware of the contents of the petition and of the growing plans to converge in the city center on Sunday. Authorities decided to dispatch troops to various city locations to prevent workers from advancing to the square. Interior Minister Sviatopolk-Mirskii went out to Tsarskoe Selo to report to the tsar late that night, and Nicholas felt reassured that matters were well in hand. Authorities believed spreading the word that the tsar was not in the city and the presence of troops in the streets would deter the demonstrators.

What officials were overlooking, however, was the popular mood. In the previous two days Gapon had flitted about the city rousing assembly members at the various branches, speaking to meetings so large that they overflowed into the streets.[11] At each of them he drove home the idea that, if the tsar would not receive the people who came to him with peaceful petitions, then "for us there is no tsar!"[12] On Saturday night Gapon informed both Nicholas and

Sviatopolk-Mirskii by letter that on the next day thousands would converge on Palace Square. Gapon appears to have expected Nicholas to consent to travel the thirty minutes by train from Tsarskoe Selo on Sunday, but Nicholas never considered doing so.

The troops assigned to the streets of the city on January 9 included about nine thousand infantry and three thousand cavalry. Most took up their positions in the early morning hours, but the reservists assigned to Palace Square were not required to assemble there before eleven o'clock in the morning. Things seemed calm in the city during the morning hours and many people gathered on the square anticipating the arrival of marchers from the various branches in the city's outskirts.

Some marchers had a considerable distance to travel on foot. Most remarkable was the procession of workers that set out from the Kolpino branch, which was located south of the city only five miles from the imperial palace at Tsarskoe Selo where the tsar was actually in residence. Apparently full of faith that Nicholas would travel by train into the city the Kolpino workers set off before dawn in frigid weather to march fifteen miles to the heart of St. Petersburg. If Tsarskoe Selo represented a Russian Versailles, this action by the Kolpino marchers essentially reversed the movement of French revolutionaries in October 1789. The Russian marchers were determined to meet their sovereign on the shared civic plaza of the nation's capital, even if approaching him in his suburban retreat—where he actually remained throughout the fateful day—would have been far more convenient. But Tsarskoe Selo was a place devoid of civic meaning even if it had become the primary residence of Russia's ruler.

Marchers from other branches also began making their way toward the Palace Square early in the morning but most of them encountered troops. Cossacks turned back sixteen thousand marchers from the Neva branch near the Nevskii Monastery but, by following the advice of scouts, about two-thirds of them eventually made it to the square.[13] Other branches sent small groups in separate detachments, seeking open paths to wend their way toward the square. The large contingent attempting to cross from Vasilevskii Island was turned back at the bridge by Cossacks, although a few of the leaders snuck across the ice and made it to the square by late afternoon.

Gapon himself led the all-important Narva branch. Although his lieutenants informed him early in the morning that large detachments of troops were massing near the bridges, Gapon persisted, urging the marchers to procure sacred objects from a nearby chapel with which to indicate that this was a religious procession. Singing "God Save the Tsar" the great crowd proceeded toward the Narva Gates. When the workers did not stop advancing in the face of infantry and Horse Guards, troops fired on them, killing around forty people and wounding sixty-five.[14] The shooting at Narva was repeated in other parts of the city. Nonetheless, by early afternoon thousands of people had managed to converge on the Palace Square from all directions—the frozen river allowed broad access despite military presence on the bridges.

At the square marchers encountered troops, some of whom had been in place since around nine o'clock. Soldiers blocked access routes and tried to disperse those who found their way through the cordon, the largest group of whom came at the square from the Alexander Garden next to the Admiralty. These were the people who took the brunt of the armed assault. A company of the Preobrazhenskii Guard was put into position here, and after a bayonet advance and cavalry whips failed to disperse the marchers, commanders ordered troops to fire. Two volleys killed about thirty people, apparently including some children who had climbed trees to get a better view. One eyewitness sent a telegram to the tsar reporting that, "many women were killed. I saw as they carried off three. . . . They killed a child. . . . And all this without warning. . . . Not one voice shouted: 'Disperse!'"[15] This development unleashed the fury of people who had believed the monarch would never permit a massacre of working people in front of his palace. Crowds now thronged the streets surrounding the square, and troops killed additional demonstrators on nearby Morskaia Street. Only by nightfall did the crowds of people disperse, many converging on city hospitals in search of relatives and friends.[16] Gapon survived the day, but his worker assembly did not.

Nicholas shared the conviction that the confrontation had been a tragedy but he failed to grasp its political significance. In his diary for January 9 he recorded a "painful day! In Petersburg serious disorders occurred following the workers' desire to go to the Winter Palace. Troops had to fire in various parts of the city, and many were killed and wounded. Lord, how painful and hard! Mama came to us from the city and directly to church. We had lunch with everybody."[17] This strange detachment not only elides a political disaster and a peaceful family Sunday. It also suggests that Nicholas did not equate himself with the object of the public's aspirations—the Winter Palace. He understood that people had wanted to go "to the palace." He did not seem to grasp that what they expressed by going there was a memory of mutual regard, a hope that justice would be served when ruler and ruled encountered each other at this symbolic place. As he explained several days later as he lectured a hand-picked delegation of workmen on his own turf at Tsarskoe Selo: "The lamentable incidents, which had the deplorable but inevitable consequences of all disorder, occurred because you permitted yourselves to be led away and deceived by traitors and enemies of the

Fatherland. When they urged you to address a petition to me with regard to your needs they induced you to revolt against me and my Government."[18]

If Nicholas did not comprehend the political shift that was now occurring, many other Russians did. One of the emperor's uncles was aghast that Nicholas had not received the workers' deputies, because "we would have been saved!"[19] But another defended the troops' lamentable actions to an Associated Press reporter, referencing the historical episode that surely resonated most in monarchical circles: "We saved the city from the mob. Unfortunately, before this could be done, innocent and guilty alike had to suffer, but suppose that 140,000 men had reached the gates of the Winter Palace. They would have sacked it as the mob sacked Versailles."[20]

In the wake of Bloody Sunday, all hell broke loose in Russia. Strikes persisted and new ones erupted, ebbing and flowing in St. Petersburg, Warsaw, Moscow, the Donets Basin, and elsewhere for the first half of 1905. Thereafter, strikes flowed without ebbing. With his back to the wall Nicholas finally conceded a written constitution and an elected Duma in October. In December disorders began to subside, and 1906 ushered in Russia's belated, fleeting experiment with constitutional monarchy.

Nicholas II has often been characterized as vacillating, but his public statements and ceremonial acts at the time of the Revolution of 1905 reveal a firmly fixed idea of the righteousness and durability of absolute monarchy in Russia. His political ideas were out of step with his times but they were not unformed. When the emperor refused to receive a delegation of St. Petersburg workers at Palace Square on Sunday, January 9, 1905, he indicated plainly his conviction that no political action could legitimately emanate from the people, that subjects could not compel him to meet them on their terms, and that ruler and ruled had no shared civic space. Even more, he indicated that the St. Petersburg public had no special claim on his attention as representatives of the broader nation.

These were also the political ideas he embodied when it came time to open the first popularly elected national legislature in Russian history on April 2, 1906. It was a novel event that required ceremonial innovation. Some advisers thought the tsar should not condescend to attend this event but should send the prime minister to meet with the people's delegates in their own assembly hall at the Tauride Palace. More liberal members of his government suggested that Nicholas cross town himself to meet with the Duma. What the tsar chose to do, however, was to summon the Duma deputies to the Winter Palace and to convene this unique assembly from the imperial throne. The ceremony thus concocted marshaled as many trappings of imperial monarchy as the Court Office could muster.

On the appointed day Nicholas made his way from Tsarskoe Selo to the city. There he made no effort to be charming and the event was by no means festive. Enacting his understanding of Russia's new constitution the tsar decreed that the delegates would assemble in the great throne room of the Winter Palace, St. George's Hall, where they would stand caps in hand on one side of the gallery while courtiers, officers, and members of the State Council stood across from them. Nicholas and his family processed to the throne between these two phalanxes, and he assumed a seat on the dais beside a table that displayed ancient regalia of monarchy brought from Moscow for the occasion.[21]

Alexander Iswolsky, who attended the ceremony as court chamberlain, recollected the novelty of the scene but thought the emperor's speech made a favorable impression because it contained the word "constitution." To him, the trappings and setting were familiar but he wondered about the impact this resplendent palace must be making on "a crowd of the most democratic aspect" entering its precincts for the first time. "Here and there in the throng one could see a few provincial lawyers or doctors in evening dress, and an occasional uniform was to be noticed; but that which predominated was not even the simple dress of the bourgeois, but rather the long *caftan* of the peasant or the factory-workman's blouse." On the faces of the old courtiers Iswolksy registered consternation and "even anger." The faces of the people's representatives "were lighted by triumph in some cases and in others distorted by hatred. . . . The Russia of yesterday found itself face to face with the Russia of to-morrow," on the parade floor of the Winter Palace.[22] Perhaps some of the Duma deputies were simply tired by the three-mile walk along the embankment from the Tauride to the Winter Palace.[23]

The tsar recorded his satisfaction with the events of the day in his brief diary entry, noting that the family traveled into the city by boat, arriving at the palace for breakfast at eleven o'clock. At one o'clock they processed to St. George's Hall, and "after prayers, I said a word of greeting. The State Council stood on the right, and the Duma stood on the left of the throne. We returned in the same order to the Malachite Hall. At three we boarded the cutter and returned via the 'Alexandria.' We were home by 4:30." Nicholas wrote that he worked that evening with a "light heart thanks to the satisfactory conclusion of the ceremony."[24] The ambiguous convocation of Russia's constitutional experiment augured disappointment. By the middle of 1907 Nicholas had twice deployed his prerogative to close down the Duma and had changed the electoral laws in order to assure a chamber nearly free of socialists. City people of all ranks paid scant attention to the institution after that.[25]

If inaugurating the Duma in the Winter Palace throne room served to remind delegates of their subordinate status in constitutional Russia, Nicholas proved unwilling to deploy the Palace Embankment and Palace Square ceremonially in the wake of the traumatic confrontation of 1905. When it came to the Blessing of the Waters officials innovated. They moved the celebration of the liturgy away from the Great Palace Church to St. Isaac's Cathedral, and the blessing took place on the river at the Peter the Great statue near Senate Square. Thereafter the military procession went from St. Isaac's all the way out to Tsarskoe Selo, sixteen miles away.[26] Nicholas conducted his own version of the New Year's reception at the great Tsarskoe Selo Palace, restricting attendance to courtiers, officials, and foreign dignitaries, the cast of the court monarchy of old.[27] Even though the tsar turned his back on the Winter Palace, however, he did not formally cede it or its treasures to any others.

CONTESTING THE HERMITAGE

In the years since Nicholas I had created the public Imperial Hermitage Museum its leaders had gradually acquired the sense that they oversaw national public property under the sympathetic tutelage of the Ministry of the Imperial Court.[28] In fact, however, Winter Palace and Hermitage treasures continued to be court property, and court property was not easily distinguishable from the personal property of the monarch. Nicholas II's immediate predecessors had taken comparatively little interest in their art collection, which had allowed Hermitage overseers to impose administrative control and order on the collection as such. The last tsar likewise was not overly interested in art but he was keen on several occasions to assert his personal ownership of Hermitage and Winter Palace property. Thus the great contest for Russia's political future included subtle arm wrestling within the gilded halls of the Imperial Hermitage.

Early in his reign, for example, Nicholas decided to celebrate the rebuilt Hermitage Theater by mounting a series of ballets and other performances for the imperial family and selected courtiers, followed by dinners in the halls of the museum. The director of the picture gallery, A. I. Somov, wrote to his son about the "great fuss" this caused: "Because of this decision the Hermitage is closed to the public, electricity is being installed in three of its biggest galleries, the Spanish, the Italian, and the Flemish, tables are set up in them and they are being decorated with plants. There are weekly gatherings of multitudes of people in there . . . and this court outrage is going to continue all the way to Lent."[29]

Another case involved the transfer of objects pertaining to the reign of Peter the Great from the Hermitage to a specially designated division of the Kunstkamera. Nicholas had consented to this transfer as part of a trend toward establishing memorial museums to the heroes of Russia's past. Still, when touring the new exhibit in 1909 Nicholas reminded the Kunstkamera staff that all of the exhibited Petrine objects belonged to him personally and could not be moved without his permission.[30]

Nonetheless, the staff of the Imperial Hermitage labored to advance its mission of public edification in the face of puny budgets. Director Tolstoy tackled a widespread sense of disrepair and neglect head-on. A special commission began in 1911 to inscribe rules for the protection of artistic property in all the imperial museums, including the Hermitage. The commission noted with dismay that far too few guards were employed in the galleries of the Russian Museum and the Hermitage, the latter deploying forty-four employees to oversee forty-eight exhibition halls.[31] Furthermore, the low pay failed to elicit quality work and many of the employees were disabled or chronically ill veterans.

The commission concluded: "These museums represent our own national [obshchegosudarstvennoe] property, which must be reverently guarded by all citizens.... But lately because of moral confusion and disregard for the duty to protect public property, there are more frequent instances of theft of various objects, especially pictures, from the museums."[32] In many cases what the commission called theft were decisions by members of the extended imperial family to move pictures from one palace to another. Labeling such actions as theft amounted to a revolutionary claim: artworks long considered the property of the court or the imperial family actually belonged to the nation, and the nation's leaders had a moral duty to preserve and protect that property. In early 1914 a new auxiliary organization, the Friends of the Imperial Hermitage, envisioned generating an endowment and promoting the museum but thanks to World War I this endeavor never got off the ground.

PALACE AND MUSEUM IN WARTIME

By 1914 the wave of industrial strikes had returned in full force to St. Petersburg, summoned by an economy on the upswing after 1910. The labor movement in Russia's capital city was among the best organized and most politicized in Europe, and in the first half of 1914 the number of strikes and strikers there was on a path to exceed the numbers in 1905.[33] But with the outbreak of war, the sacred union of tsar and people asserted itself one more time. Confronted with so grave a moment in the life of the country, Nicholas now saw fit to return to the Winter Palace and thence to summon the nation.

The French ambassador witnessed the "majestic" solemnities marking Russia's acknowledgment of Germany's declaration of war, on July 20 (OS), 1914. Ambassador Maurice Paléologue recalled that some six thousand people assembled in the Neva galleries of the Winter Palace including members of the court in full dress and officers of the Petersburg Garrison. An altar had been erected in the middle of the Nicholas Gallery and the icon of the Virgin of Kazan had been brought from Kazan Cathedral. "In a tense, religious silence the imperial cortege crossed the gallery" and throughout the following service the emperor and empress prayed fervently. At the conclusion of the liturgy Nicholas swore to pursue the war until the last enemy soldier had been expelled from Russia and cheers erupted inside the hall. Crowds lined up along the riverbank outside added their voices to the clamor.

Thereafter Nicholas and his wife went out onto the balcony facing the thousands of people who had gathered on Palace Square. The crowd stood there in good order, men with hats off, everyone arrayed neatly behind a dispersed row of soldiers. Members of the crowd displayed patriotic signs such as "God Save the Tsar" and "Long Live Serbia" and some waved the flag of the Russian Empire.[34] When the tsar appeared, the crowd erupted in cheers and patriotic enthusiasm, and one observer thought the public exuberance caught the imperial couple by surprise. Within a few months this scene caught the imagination of postcard artists and souvenir makers. Thus the flame of popular monarchism flashed brightly one last time before it was extinguished.[35]

With the outbreak of war the Hermitage director Tolstoy took immediate steps to send the crown jewels to the Kremlin Armory in Moscow for safekeeping. There were similar plans to dispatch items of great value from the ancient and medieval collections, and workers packed up 178 containers. At the last minute, however, authorities decided to hold off shipping these items out, citing the panic such a step might induce in the city population. Tolstoy kept the items packed up and under special guard pending later evacuation, but in the meantime the Hermitage stayed open for visitors throughout the war.[36] Eventually antiaircraft guns were stationed on the palace roof and other important factories and government buildings in the city.[37]

The unity of summer gave way within months to the old political tensions, now exacerbated by food shortages, inflation, mounting evidence of government incompetence, and rumors of scandal at court.[38] The only issue on which crown and public could consistently agree was the need to care for wounded soldiers whose numbers climbed sharply in the middle of 1915. From the start of the war, public buildings and charitable institutions were repurposed as hospitals, but by June the government realized it needed to convert available palaces in the Petrograd area as well as in the provinces.[39]

The Ministry of the Imperial Court now proposed establishing a surgical hospital in the Winter Palace and the Hermitage, and Tolstoy successfully deflected them from the latter citing the inadequacy of the electrical, water, and sewage systems in the museum buildings. The palace, however, underwent a significant transformation in which all of the major parade halls except for the great throne room (St. George's Hall) were readied to receive gravely injured troops of the lower ranks. The court contributed eighty-five thousand rubles to the needed renovations and the Red Cross, which was to manage the facility, covered the costs of supplies and equipment.[40] The renovation began in August 1915.

While some of the paintings and statues were moved out of the prospective wards, and dishes and small objects were packed into chests, many large vases and candelabra were simply covered up where they stood. The remodelers covered the tapestried walls with white calico and the parquet floors with linoleum. They situated the operating theater in the Columned Hall of

FIGURE 9.01   Hospital room in the Nicholas Hall of the Winter Palace. October 1915. The State Hermitage Museum, St. Petersburg.

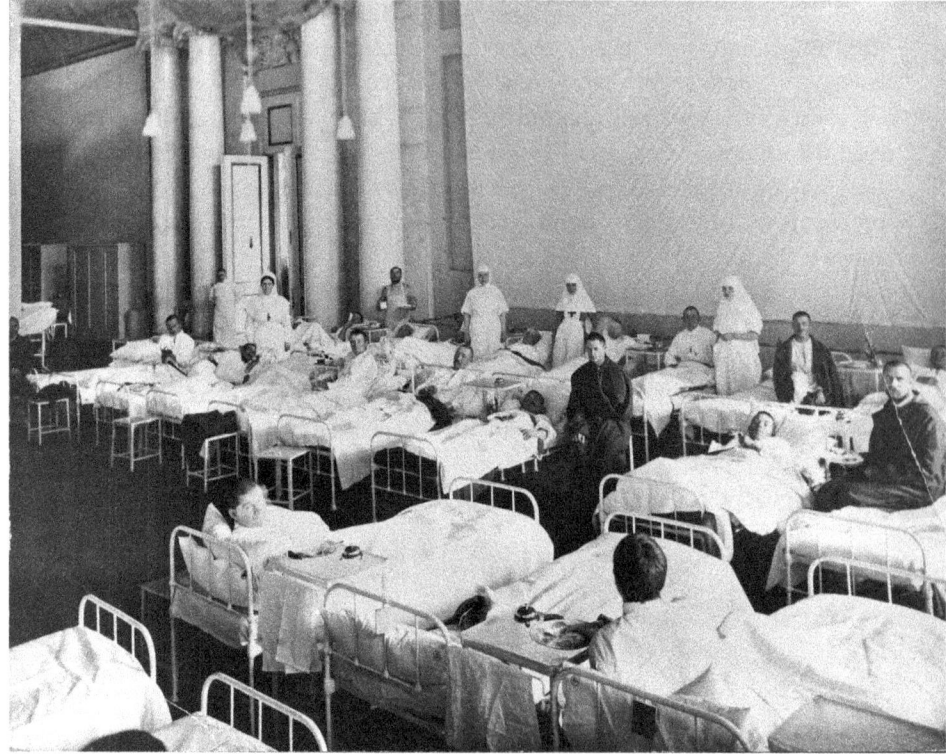

FIGURE 9.02   The wounded in the Field-Marshals' Hall of the Winter Palace. 1915–1917. The State Hermitage Museum, St. Petersburg.

the Second Reserve apartment, with protective iron trays placed under the operating tables to protect the floors. The palace apothecary was entrusted to the hospital. In both the Jordan entryway and the enclosed Winter Garden outside the Admiralty entrance they situated *banyas* and showers. Nurses stored linens in the 1812 Gallery, at one end of which a modern X-ray chamber was set up. This necessitated removing four rows of portraits from each side of Emperor Alexander's portrait, which itself was removed from its frame and stored.[41]

Widely known as the "Hospital in the Winter Palace," it was officially dedicated in October 1915 as the Hospital of His Imperial Highness the Tsarevich Alexei Nikolaevich. The hospital boasted beds for nearly one thousand and specialized in treating serious head wounds. Chief of operations was eminent Chief Surgeon N. N. Petrov, who oversaw a staff of some 30 doctors, 50 nurses (sisters of mercy), 120 orderlies, 26 housekeepers, and 10 clerical workers.[42]

FIGURE 9.03 Medical personnel on the Jordan Staircase of the Winter Palace. December 1915. The State Hermitage Museum, St. Petersburg.

One woman who served as a nurse in the Winter Palace Hospital recalled her time there with mixed feelings. The Red Cross transferred N. V. Galanina and several others from a city infirmary where they had been tending the wounded. With imperial and noble patrons including a handful of nurses from the nobility, the palace hospital employed only the most respectable people. Galanina felt honored and enjoyed working with such an illustrious staff of surgeons at such a well-equipped facility. She had never before cared for such gravely wounded patients and the recovery rate at the palace hospital was nonetheless much higher than at more humble facilities. She slept on the luxurious premises and relished the abundant provision of "cocoa, wine, sour cream, and eggs."[43]

On the other hand Galanina believed that much that went on at the Palace hospital impeded the patients' convalescence, especially the constant stream of visiting dignitaries including members of the imperial family, foreign luminaries, Russian notables, and "endless foreign delegations of the Red Cross—French, Belgian, English, Dutch, and on and on. It was obligatory for every delegation to our country that they visit the Winter Palace hospital. It was not only a model hospital, but also a display hospital."[44] Photographers were constantly roving about the wards and reception areas. Pictures of the patients and facilities appeared during the war in many publications.[45] Being constantly on display made for an exceedingly formal atmosphere governed by strict etiquette, and Galanina pined for the much warmer environment she and her colleagues had been able to create for patients at her former post. However modern and exemplary the hospital, the Winter Palace itself impressed the nurses mostly by its inhuman scale and chilly opulence. The days when its great halls might have been warmed by a personal encounter with a gracious mistress or master of the household were a thing of the past.

THE PALACE IN FEBRUARY 1917

Urban revolution finally caught up with the Romanovs who had avoided it for so long. The year 1917 dawned ominously in Russia's capital: factory workers in critical defense industries were poised to strike over the lack of food and fuel in the city; Petrograd's military garrisons were staffed by raw recruits from nearby districts; and the city's working-class women had reached a breaking point. International Women's Day, February 23 (OS), brought thousands of women into the street demanding an end to the war and even to the monarchy. From military headquarters at the front Nicholas ordered city officials to restore order. This they attempted to do, without success, for three days, by which time it became clear that the available troops were unreliable and were going over to the side of the strikers.

The final act of Romanov Petrograd opened on the Palace Square on the evening of February 27, 1917. The tsar's cabinet resigned. Throngs of people were milling about the entire city with thousands converging on the center where a growing number of guards units were going over to the side of revolution. After being kept standing on Palace Square in subfreezing weather for three hours some of the Preobrazhenskii Regiment defected.[46] The commander of the Petrograd military district, General Sergei Khabalov, saw that the small number of loyal troops on Palace Square was vulnerable to attack from all sides. He ordered them to move to the Admiralty, where most of the General Staff had taken refuge. Discontent among these troops continued to mount, not least because they had received nothing to eat during many hours on duty. The Pavlovskii Regiment, a pillar of monarchy, refused orders to disperse the crowd. At about eleven o'clock at night Major General M. I. Zankevich, chief of the General Staff, ordered the men still under his command at the Admiralty to move to the Winter Palace. If he believed that a last stand in the emperor's palace would prove inspiring to his men or simply that his troops might be fed there he miscalculated.

Some units melted away during the move across the street. Not more than two thousand of the troops entered the palace and they now suffered the ultimate humiliation. The palace commandant General V. A. Komarov complained bitterly to Zankevich about the filthy troops now invading the immaculate precincts of his palace. Komarov was worried that a pitched battle for the palace would destroy its treasures. Zankevich insisted that the soldiers be permitted to stay for the night. This stalemate dragged on until midnight when the tsar's brother Grand Duke Michael Aleksandrovich arrived, stranded in the city overnight. He ignored the troops who cheered his arrival and went directly to his room. There the palace commandant persuaded the grand duke to order the soldiers out of the palace immediately. When the soldiers were ordered back to the Admiralty, still without any food, it was the last straw.[47] As Soviet historian E. I. Martynov put it, "this order made a painful impression on the troops. It seemed that the tsar's own brother was evicting the defenders of the monarchy from his home. The soldiers said, 'They've booted us out like dogs. If they treat us like that come on brothers, let's go home.'"[48]

Thus the last act of the Romanovs' resilient urban monarchy revealed the regime's decadence and unworthiness. The regiments to whom galleries of the Winter Palace were dedicated and whose sacred bond with the monarchy had earned them imperial invitations in bygone years were now ordered out of the building. By the next morning, the emerging Provisional Government in turn ordered those troops who had remained overnight to leave the palace. At this point Grand Duke Michael decamped to a friend's apartment nearby on Millionaia Street.[49] Not long after this the Pavlovskii Regiment, now under command of noncommissioned officers, occupied the Winter Palace in good order. They lowered the imperial flag and raised a red one.[50]

Even as Nicholas thus anticlimactically lost control of the building that more than any other symbolized Russian monarchy, the life of wartime Petrograd went on inside its walls. Galanina recalled the strong impression all the commotion downstairs made on medical staff in the Nicholas Hall: "We listened to the din of a crowd of hundreds (or thousands?) of feet moving around downstairs. It was the soldiers of the Pavlovskii Regiment, gathering from their barracks on the Field of Mars, entering as they had been ordered via the ground floor palace entrance."[51] In the midst of these revolutionary proceedings wounded and convalescing soldiers continued to receive care at the hospital for the rest of the year, and for the nurses life in the wards went on much as before. Many of them received orders from their superiors to remain at the palace despite their desire to depart, and during the days of the February Revolution itself they were actually forbidden to leave the building.

Galanina remembered the intense days and nights around February 27 and 28 when little encounters in the palace galleries mirrored the social divisions of the city itself. One palace guard had been wounded at his post on the embankment during random shooting from the crowds along the bridges. The nurses treated him and gave him a bed, but later that night a band of armed soldiers appeared in the wards demanding that the guard be thrown out the window—an entreaty the nurses were able to repel. Several times that night armed troops appeared demanding that the nurses reveal the hiding places of the tsar's ministers. Soldiers searched under the beds and in the wardrobes but to no avail as the ministers had already fled. Galanina recalled the eeriness of the empty halls at night where more than once she felt tempted to try out the great throne in St. George's Hall. When she passed through the Romanov Gallery it always seemed empty, but from time to time there suddenly appeared "an old palace servant, in his electric blue livery. His face was impassive and he remained silent. But his sudden appearances were surprising and therefore unnerving."[52]

In the city itself the abdication of Nicholas II and the end of monarchy in Russia on March 2 came as an anticlimax. That night a group of drunken soldiers burst into the Hermitage entrance on Millionaia demanding access to the roof, from which they believed shots were being fired on the crowd. The guards of the Second Reserve Battalion of Sappers were able to block this crowd. On March 4 Tolstoy sent a letter to the Provisional Government acknowledging its authority and, implicitly, seeking its protection.[53] Outside, people covered up emblems of monarchy on the Winter Palace main gates with red banners and decorated the fence surrounding the Winter Garden with red flags.[54]

Museum workers scrambled to safeguard treasures of the Winter Palace and the Hermitage, some of which were still packed for possible evacuation. General Komarov, who was also head of the Petrograd imperial palace administration, procured permission from the Provisional Government on May 10 to transfer the items of greatest value to the protection of "the former cabinet of his imperial majesty," which included many treasures under lock and key on the top floor of the palace. This cache of valuables included the famous imperial collection of Fabergé eggs, which were housed in Empress Alexandra's corner office.[55] Over the next several months as the political situation in the capital grew more uncertain and with it the fate of Russia's armies, the Provisional Government gradually yielded to Komarov's entreaties to evacuate the priceless objects to the Kremlin Armory. The first such shipments, including the Fabergé eggs, departed in the middle of September.

BENOIS AND KERENSKY

In the first days of the new regime the official who took the keenest interest in the Winter Palace was the newly appointed minister of justice, Alexander Kerensky, whose brief included responsibility for government property. During that first week Kerensky toured the Hermitage and proclaimed to fearful palace servants assembled in the throne room that the palace was now national property.[56] He designated P. M. Makarov commissar for the protection of the imperial palaces.[57]

Much of what we know about the fate of the Hermitage during 1917 comes from the memories of Alexander Benois, painter, preservationist, founder of the influential journal *Mir iskusstva* (World of art) , and Hermitage advisor.[58] Scion of a wealthy French Russian family of artists, Benois was also an arts visionary consumed by a vision of popular enlightenment that rendered him both hopeful and anxious about the change of power. He was the most influential member of the early twentieth-century Preservationist movement in St. Petersburg. The Preservationists advanced a new, positive vision of their city, which had long suffered the negative appraisal of nineteenth-century writers and intellectuals who considered its founding a fundamental mistake. Benois and his artist associates formed the St. Petersburg Society for the Protection and Preservation of Russian Monuments of Art and Antiquity, a lobbying group that wrote approvingly of the "harmony" of neoclassical St. Petersburg. The painters among them portrayed a lovely, habitable, and elegant city in sharp contrast to the gloomy literary and artistic renderings of several decades earlier.[59]

During the war Benois's general prominence as a spokesman for the arts had been enhanced by his appointment to a special commission organized by the Office of the Emperor in late May 1916 to recommend necessary remodeling for the Winter Palace and the suburban palaces, which had not been undertaken since the 1860s. In the last months of 1916 and early 1917 Benois toured the Winter Palace where he was shocked to find it in substantial disrepair.[60] International Women's Day (February 23, 1917) found Benois peering out the window of the French embassy on the Palace Embankment, where he and other dinner guests watched demonstrators crossing from the Vyborg Side.[61]

For Benois the Revolution meant both peril and promise. He was distressed to think that revolutionary politicians through ignorance might endanger the Winter Palace and the country's artistic heritage. In late February Benois was alarmed to learn of Kerensky's visit because he feared that as a novice in the art world the minister would resist the recommendations of experts like himself. But Benois also saw in the events of late February the opportunity to realize his cherished dream—the creation of a "Museum of Historical Life inside the Winter Palace." When revolution came he was anxious to seize the moment lest it pass unproductively, and he waited expectantly for a summons from Makarov. In a clear statement of his mood one week after the tsar's abdication he confided to his diary on March 10:

> I was lost in conjectures about the silence of Makarov. I finally decided to call Dima (Filosov) and talk it over with him. Not so that I could "direct" our whole undertaking, but knowing Makarov's character I simply wanted to ensure that at such a time energy was not expended pointlessly or dispersed in vain. That old tempo that Russians are accustomed to had already crept in, that powerful slowing down, so that one can "think it over," in which the blues set in. And that isn't far from the psychology of "Oh the hell with it." In those days the Academy [of Arts] was already succeeding in strengthening its lost position, et cetera. "The spirit of the revolution" in the art world was growing faint, and after a few days it was already becoming difficult to see our way clear to achieving all that had suggested itself to us.

So Benois produced a proposal "to reform the Hermitage. The main thing for me," wrote Benois, "would be to create more public access to our museum. With this in mind the first duty is to fundamentally reform the Printing Department." Benois intuited that publicizing the artworks could also take place in print.[62]

It was the writer Maxim Gorky, trusted by both the Provisional Government and the Petrograd Soviet, who assumed the leading position in the arts world during 1917, however. On March 4 Gorky assembled some fifty artists and writers in his apartment, including his good friend Benois.[63] Gorky's group discussed the urgency of protecting monuments of art and antiquity in the capital. In short order they organized a group that became widely known as the Gorky Commission, which petitioned both the Petrograd Soviet and the Provisional Government about its concerns. Both halves of the dual government eventually granted this commission official status, and it worked actively in the ensuing months to establish orderly oversight of the city's artistic inheritance, including palaces, museums, and private collections.[64] The commission dispatched letters to both bodies advising them of the artists' willingness to undertake the work of preserving old monuments and designing new ones and of helping to create new "public holidays, theaters, hymns of freedom, and so on."[65] Benois made his views known at this early meeting: "This is the people's art, our own property, and we must do everything in our power in order that the people realize that and that they take possession of what is rightfully theirs. The national character of all art, through which people of the nation have asserted their own ideals of beauty—this is the idea that must now be revived and proclaimed with exceptional vigor."[66]

In the heady days of 1917 the artistic and civic missions of the Winter Palace complex sometimes conflicted. An immediate danger presented itself when leaders of the Petrograd Soviet proposed to conduct a funeral ceremony for the martyrs of the February Revolution on Palace Square and to further honor them by erecting a monument there. The architects among Gorky's collaborators applauded this proposal but Benois shuddered to think of the "danger that could materialize if a crowd of one hundred thousand attracted to the funeral procession were influenced by some mad demagogues to storm the Palace itself and the Hermitage beyond it."[67] He suggested Kazan Square as a more appropriate site for such a memorial but Gorky proposed to the Soviet that the victims of the February Revolution be interred on the Field of Mars, "where the first shots of the revolution were fired."[68]

Here is a fascinating little moment in the life of Palace Square. The first instinct of the new workers' government was to sanctify a plaza where workers had been slaughtered among shrines to past monarchs. But the new arbiters of culture, protective as they were of the city's artistic heritage, rather instinctively closed ranks to protect the historic architectural ensemble of the old imperial center. Benois wanted the public to claim its cultural heritage but in a preservation-minded way that combined civic innovation with reverence for the past.

A few days later he finally received Makarov's invitation to visit the palace with him and ascertain with his own eyes that it was intact.[69] They toured the main halls of the palace including the hospital wards. The palace's remaining residential servants, "still sporting their beautiful livery," made a melancholy impression on him. Ascending the Jordan Staircase Benois and Makarov startled an elderly lady-in-waiting who was frozen with fright to see them on the premises. Further, along the Palace Square side of the parade floor, rooms had already been assigned to Makarov and Fedor Golovin, newly appointed overseer of all court property.[70] The servants' choice to continue wearing their palace uniforms even as the monarchy's enemies settled in among them suggests they were intentionally siding with their deposed masters in the first days after the monarchy's collapse.

For its part the Gorky Commission took up quarters in the northwest corner of the ground floor. From this vantage point its members resolutely asserted that oversight of the Winter Palace and other imperial palaces properly belonged to experts in art and museum management. Gorky and the others deferred to Benois as the resident expert on the Hermitage collection and the palace itself. This corner of the palace continued as the headquarters for artistic affairs up to the October Revolution and beyond.

Benois observed that the "so-called Gorky Commission" quickly gave way to "the Golovin Commission" as Gorky and his colleagues learned an early lesson in the practice of popular rule.[71] Although both the Petrograd Soviet and the Provisional Government sanctioned their group, a nascent Artists' Union almost immediately challenged the Gorky Commission's precedence. At a meeting on March 9 more than a thousand people interested in the arts gathered at the Mikhailovskii Theater where several of them rose to criticize the agenda of the self-appointed protectors of Petrograd's imperial relics. Gorky, Benois, and their group continued their inventory and advocacy work for two months before disbanding in the face of continued opposition from their brother artists. The tension meant that between April and July little got done, but then Golovin appointed the preservationist Vasilii Vereshchagin to head a new commission charged with completing the inventories. Vereshchagin was especially successful in documenting the furnishings of the Winter Palace, including items believed stolen since the collapse of the monarchy.[72]

Between February and October 1917 the life of the Winter Palace carried on this way as a wartime military hospital and the hub of an emerging ministry of enlightenment. To these purposes was eventually added that of housing the executive organs of the Provisional Government itself. As the public grew impatient with the lack of military progress or land reform, Kerensky's star rose. Originally the only socialist in the new government, he became minister of war in the spring and after major strikes and protests in July he became prime minister. As soon as that happened Kerensky made the decision to move into the Winter Palace with his mistress.[73]

Critics who thought this bold move revealed Kerensky's "Bonapartist" mannerisms felt vindicated by his decision to occupy the quarters assigned to the last Romanovs and to be photographed in Nicholas II's study. Meetings of his cabinet took place in the Malachite Hall, and Kerensky had a red flag raised and lowered at the palace to mark his coming and going.[74] He found time that summer to sit for the renowned portraitist Ilya Repin in the palace. By late summer Petrograd wits had dubbed him "Alexander IV."[75] Kerensky himself did not shed light on this decision, although his memoirs attest that he had attached special significance to the Winter Palace since his student days when he took in its impressive expanse from his university dormitory on Vasilevskii Island. He had been close to Palace Square on Bloody Sunday and had eagerly rushed there after Nicholas announced the creation of the Duma in 1906, disappointed to find that almost nobody else was there.[76]

If we cannot be sure of Kerensky's personal motivation for moving into the palace and conducting government business from its parade floor, we can appreciate that this move refocused public attention on a building that had not been the center of government since the assassination of Alexander II. Kerensky's move was a gesture that unmistakably reconsolidated Petrograd's civic center now sanctified by the blood of martyrs and dignified by the presence of the government's executive branch and the man who was the head of the government. The combined weight of these elements was perhaps meant to prevent the city's center of gravity from drifting off toward either the Tauride Palace where the Petrograd Soviet met, the Mariinskii Palace where other officials of the Provisional Government had offices, or the Smolnyi Institute, in which Lenin had established the Bolshevik Party. At any rate, for reasons he never thought it necessary to state, Kerensky believed that the Winter Palace was the right place for the Romanovs' successor government.

Even before Kerensky officially moved into the Winter Palace, leaders had exploited it for receiving foreign delegations, further disrupting ongoing hospital operations. There, for example, the Provisional Government received members of US President Woodrow Wilson's Root Commission and the US Railroad Commission, each dispatched to shore up and spy on the new Russian leaders. As a member of the YMCA's International Committee, American Edward Heald toured the building in early June. He visited the wounded and registered the contrast between the palace and the poor neighborhoods of the capital. Later in the month US dignitaries including Cyrus McCormick and Charles R. Crane joined John Mott and other YMCA leaders for a conference there. Heald considered the Winter Palace "a dramatic setting for a YMCA conference."[77]

THE STORMING OF THE WINTER PALACE

By the end of October the tide of revolution rose again. Within both the citywide Soviet and the All Russian Congress of Soviets then assembling in the capital, Lenin's Bolsheviks had become masters of the hour. Their consistent opposition to the war now appeared prescient. They took on as their own the popular slogans of the street: "Land, Peace, Bread" and "All Power to the Soviets." The great urban consensus of the fall was that the Provisional Government could neither conclude the war nor defend against counterrevolution. Suspicion of its collusion with the bourgeoisie intensified.

The saga of the October Revolution has been told countless times. But what do these storied events indicate about what the old palace of monarchy had become? It was Kerensky who had restored the building's function as an active center of the governing executive, claiming the luster of tradition for his novel government. This move revitalized the civic bond between the palace and the city and sealed the building's fate in October. For his part Lenin would insist on waiting several painful hours before announcing the victory of the Bolsheviks to the Second All Russian Congress of Soviets so that he could tell delegates the Winter Palace had fallen. Among the events of October 25 and 26 (OS), 1917, the lightly resisted entry into the Winter Palace by detachments of troops loyal to the Bolsheviks was militarily inconsequential. Yet nearly every account of the October Revolution takes the proverbial storming of the Winter Palace as its political climax. At the time the symbolic power of that place was felt universally and required no explanation.

In the second half of October it became clear that most of the military units in Petrograd were under the authority of the Bolshevik-dominated Petrograd Soviet. The Provisional Government summoned to the palace the troops it considered reliable, including the Cossacks Third Corps, cadets from the region's elite military academies, a bicycle battalion, and a women's detachment. A memoirist from the famous First Petrograd Women's Battalion revealed later that the women troops had been awaiting assignment north of the city since completing their training and believed that when they were summoned on October 24 it was for a review in advance of being dispatched to the Rumanian front. They were dismayed to be ordered to defend the Provisional Government, but they spent the night in the palace preparing to do so. They received ammunition and assumed positions in south-facing rooms of the parade floor, sitting on the floor rather than dirtying the furniture. The next morning they received the blessing of a priest in the palace church.[78] In all, about eighteen hundred troops prepared to defend the Provisional Government in the palace.[79] On October 24 Kerensky went across town seeking political support for his shaky government from delegates to a "pre-parliament," but this endorsement was slow in coming. Meanwhile, despite quiet in the streets, Kerensky learned that a unit of troops loyal to the Bolsheviks had commandeered the central telegraph and telephone office. In the middle of that night he left the palace for the General Staff building across the square.

For the defense of the palace loyal troops had erected mountains of firewood to barricade the entrances from Palace Square. Throughout the morning hours of October 25 the Provisional Government attempted to organize a defense of the palace, and such forces as it could muster surrounded government buildings on Palace Square and the embankment. Many eyewitnesses to the October Revolution noted the jumble of automobiles on Palace Square on the afternoon of October 25.[80] Although it was already getting dark, Benois recalled that while he was crossing Palace Square by tram around three o'clock, he could make out that there was some kind of crowd gathering there among the mountains of firewood. "Little did I know," he wrote, "that we were living through the very last hours of our 'bourgeois existence.'"[81] Sometime during that day Kerensky accepted the offer of an American embassy automobile and left town, ostensibly to meet troops heading into the city to defend his government.[82] Now under the leadership of Alexander Konovalov the other ministers assembled in the Malachite Hall to await their fate.[83]

Across town at the Smolny Institute the Bolsheviks were in control of the Congress of Soviets and much of the city, but Lenin insisted on waiting, impatiently, for word that Bolshevik troops controlled the palace before announcing that all power had been transferred to the Soviet. The battle for the Winter Palace took place in the evening of October 25. It was a drawn-out, dilatory affair in which combatants on both sides seemed far from eager to shed blood or to damage the palace. Most of the garrison units in the city now sided with the Bolsheviks. V. A. Antonov-Ovseenko deployed these units at the Peter and Paul Fortress across the river from the palace and others in a ring around Palace Square. Sailors brought the cruiser *Aurora* up the Neva, where its guns also threatened the palace. The defenders of the palace posted sentries at each of the entrances and staircases, and other troops milled about in the galleries along the Neva and in the courtyard inside the main palace gates. The Bolshevik plan called for troops at the fortress to dispatch an ultimatum when they were prepared to commence shelling, but a protracted set of problems establishing the viability of their artillery pieces caused a long delay. Over the several hours during which Bolshevik forces on the *Aurora* and Palace Square awaited the signal to commence firing, most of the defenders of the Provisional Government melted away.[84]

Petrograd governor-general P. I. Palchinskii was on the scene but between ten and one o'clock contingents of armed men found their way inside the building through various entrances. The largest contingent made its way in on the Hermitage side, where servants reportedly let them in.[85] Cadets inside the building disarmed many of the intruders at first but the balance of forces shifted as more of the besiegers found their way in, reversing the process later on. Firing did finally commence from the fortress following a volley of blanks from the *Aurora*. There were also a few field pieces on Palace Square. Whether because of human ineptitude, the poor condition of the guns, or a reluctance to damage the building, very few shells struck the palace from the river and none from the square. On the other hand the southern façade was pocked by hundreds of bullet holes. There were also a few confrontations between opposing troops inside the palace, and at some point sailors threw two grenades into Nicholas II's old suite, wounding two military cadets.

Around one o'clock in the morning a contingent led by Red Guards found its way up the main stairway on the Palace Square side (ever after to be known as the October Stairway) and eventually to the family dining room behind the Malachite Hall where the ministers were seated around a table. After a brief negotiation through the closed door the remnants of the Provisional Government gave up without a fight. To most who tell the story of the Bolshevik Revolution this was the culminating event, and when the leaders at Smolny received this news Lenin went onto the floor of the Congress of Soviets to declare that the government of Russia was in its hands. Before dawn troops transported the arrested ministers out of the palace and across the Trinity Bridge to the Peter and Paul Fortress. By the time the rest of the city awoke, the palace and the government had changed hands.[86]

Several commentators discuss the behavior of the troops who entered the palace in the wee hours of October 26. In some parts of the building there were a few hours of general chaos. Some soldiers found the wine cellars and others ransacked some of the rooms. John Reed, an American journalist who entered the palace armed with papers from the Bolshevik leadership, described the scene at the Palace Square entrance where looting began right away as soldiers began breaking open the packing crates ready for evacuation to Moscow. Reed recorded that "somebody cried, 'Comrades! Don't take anything. This is the property of the People!' Immediately twenty voices were crying, 'Stop! Put everything back! Don't take anything! Property of the People!' . . . Roughly and hastily the things were crammed back in their cases, and self-appointed sentinels stood guard. It was all utterly spontaneous."[87] Bolshevik commanders quickly posted guards, the Kexholm Regiment proving especially reliable for this duty. By morning the stormers of the Winter Palace had mostly returned to their barracks. A typical assessment is that of Soviet scholar A. V. Sivkov who attributed the limited damage to the "exceptional organization of the uprising and the revolutionary consciousness of the participants in the storming."[88]

Reed's fellow journalist Louise Bryant recalled filing in through a small door behind Bolshevik troops around one o'clock in the morning. The great palace was lit up as for a celebration; the defending cadets and women's battalion were being disarmed and sent home. Bryant contends that there was no looting owing in part to the fact that everyone leaving the palace was searched, "no matter on what side he was."[89] She quotes the young Bolshevik lieutenant guarding the door when he declared to those departing, "Comrades, this is the people's palace. This is our palace. Do not steal from the people. . . . Do not disgrace the people." This speech caused a number of items that the soldiers had hidden in their pockets to be placed upon a table by the door, and it amused Bryant that none of the things surrendered had any real value: "the broken handle of a Chinese sword, a wax candle, a coat-hanger, a blanket, a worn sofa cushion."[90] Bryant read the troops as being ashamed to have been caught pilfering. But if her description of the items confiscated is accurate it is interesting to consider what the soldiers meant by taking them. The things she lists seem more in the order of souvenirs than actual loot. What she and others, including Benois, attributed to naïveté may have reflected a reluctance to risk stealing real valuables as well as a desire to preserve some memento of this extraordinary night. For 150 years most people who got inside the palace had carried out only memories. These men had hoped to procure tangible reminders of their visit, and it seems likely that some of them did.

BENOIS AND THE BOLSHEVIKS

On October 27 the newly appointed Bolshevik commissar of enlightenment, Anatolii Lunacharsky, summoned Benois to tour the palace with him, and they were relieved to find the damage limited and superficial. The worst ravages appeared in the offices of Nicholas I, Alexander II, and Nicholas II. Nicholas I's ground floor office and bedroom facing the Admiralty had been preserved since the time of his death with its knickknacks, family portraits, and famously Spartan camp bed. A succession of palace commandants had used it as an office, including both Volkov and Makarov. When Benois visited it the room had been ransacked, the walls were bare, and papers were strewn everywhere. There was a similar scene in the office of Alexander II, one of the few rooms in the palace that retained its eighteenth-century décor. Now all was chaos there as papers were strewn across every surface. Still, a large collection of valuable glass and other items being prepared for evacuation to Moscow stood unmolested, which caused Benois to speculate about what kind of taboo might have saved them. It seemed to him that the early liberators of the palace had been searching for gold or money but, finding none, had left other objects alone.[91] Valentin Serov's portrait of Nicholas II had been smashed and disfigured but it was later restored. When the painter Constantine Somov accompanied Benois on a tour of the palace on November 3 he observed "huge damage" to the suite of Nicholas II in the northwest block recently occupied by Kerensky, which Somov attributed to having been struck by an artillery shell.[92]

Reed summarized the damage and looting at the palace as amounting to far less than reported by the Socialist Revolutionary press, which claimed that thieves had taken five hundred million rubles' worth of goods. He pointed out that many of the most valuable things had already been shipped to the Moscow Kremlin in September (where they survived the Bolshevik attack, as well). But he estimated that because the general public had been "allowed to circulate freely through the Winter Palace for several days after its capture" people had made off with "table silver, clocks, bedding, mirrors, and some odd vases of valuable porcelain and semi-precious stones, to the value of about 50,000 dollars."[93] The new authorities published two proclamations on November 14 (NS) asking citizens and sailors to "exert every effort to find whatever possible of the objects stolen from the Winter Palace on the night of 7–8 November, and to forward them to the Commandant of the Winter Palace."[94]

The comparatively light damage to the Winter Palace stands in marked contrast to that inflicted by Bolshevik units on Moscow's Kremlin, where there was much more real fighting. A contingent of anti-Bolshevik troops managed to occupy the Kremlin briefly, and they offered enough resistance to elicit two separate artillery barrages. It is hard to know whether the damage to the Kremlin represented true revolutionary iconoclasm directed at the many ancient churches and religious institutions within its walls, but it clearly embarrassed Bolshevik leaders. Lunacharsky actually resigned his commission as the new education commissar (temporarily as it turned out) when he learned about the shelling in Moscow: "The Kremlin," he wrote, "where are gathered the most important art treasures of Petrograd and of Moscow, is under artillery fire . . . I can bear no more."[95]

As it turned out the Winter Palace and the Hermitage passed seamlessly to the control of the new Commissariat of Enlightenment, which energetically tackled the administrative tasks inherited from the old Ministry of the Imperial Court. As early as October 30 the Bolsheviks decreed that the Winter Palace was now a state museum on par with the Hermitage itself. Seeing themselves as propagators of cultural uplift the new political masters reached out immediately to "the elders of the artistic intelligentsia."[96] Somov had found the

Bolsheviks "sympathetic and respectful" to the artists during their tour of the palace just after the revolution.[97] Since the collapse of the Gorky Commission in the summer Benois had been excluded from the upper echelons of museum work, but now he and the Bolsheviks found common cause. Despite his semi-aristocratic background Benois had a democratic approach to the arts, and he enjoyed the respect of both Gorky and Lunacharsky. Emily Johnson notes the unexpected affinity of these upper-crust arts figures and the Bolsheviks but observes that men like Benois had also often found it distasteful to work with their old imperial patrons. She quotes preservationist Peter Veiner who defended their decision to cooperate "with a party that was alien to us."[98] Veiner considered the art world's mission to be nonpolitical and stressed his colleagues' urgent conviction that they would never be able to recover treasures lost in those early days.

Benois quickly assented when Lunacharsky prevailed upon him to join the Commission on Art and National Palaces.[99] In this capacity Benois supervised an inventory of the imperial mansions being seized around Petrograd and its suburbs.[100] Other members of the old Gorky and Golovin Commissions were also quick to join the Bolsheviks' preservation projects. Over the ensuing months Benois was inside the palace almost daily, struggling to work out his relationship to the new masters of the scene. He declined an offer, supposedly emanating from Lenin himself, to oversee a newly created ministry of arts and a few months later to replace the retiring Tolstoy as Hermitage director. But Lunacharsky was able to keep him engaged, and he finally joined the Soviet of the State Hermitage in July 1918, accepting an appointment in August 1918 to become the head of the picture gallery, the printing office, and the division of modern sculpture. He remained in that post until his emigration in 1926.

The projects that most engaged Benois centered on how best to deploy the palace complex in the great project of cultural uplift that he and the Bolsheviks envisioned. While many of the Winter Palace and Hermitage personnel were wholly preoccupied with attempting to stave off sales of artifacts during the starvation years of the Civil War and to hasten the return from Moscow of treasures sent there for safekeeping in 1918, Benois worked to mount public exhibits, lectures, and training programs. Like his nineteenth-century predecessors he strained to attract more of the city's people to the museum—after the number of visitors fell to a low point of two thousand in 1918, ten times as many visited the State Hermitage in 1920.[101]

He and his colleagues managed in these early years to achieve a remarkable reversal in the relationship between the Hermitage and the palace. Whereas Catherine had envisioned the Hermitage buildings as annexes to her palace, by 1920 the status was reversed. When Benois mounted a very popular exhibit of seventeenth- and eighteenth-century French paintings in October in the former Second Reserve Apartments of the palace overlooking Palace Square, it was "the first, very successful, occasion on which palace premises were used for the goals of the museum."[102] Thus the sunlit rooms facing Palace Square admitted the sons and daughters of peasants into the suite first designed for the palace's progenitor, Elizabeth Petrovna, and occupied most famously by Catherine the Great. No doubt Benois chose these rooms for the same reason Catherine had preferred them: since the 1760s these palace rooms had been connected by a bridge to the Hermitage.[103]

Between them Benois and the Bolsheviks had intuited the buildings' meanings. Monarchs had first deemed St. Petersburg's "upper embankment" the absolute center of the Russian polity. Over time the space had accumulated a verdigris of civic meaning, layered with patriotic commemoration, disciplined encounter between ruler and ruled, popular protest, the blood of martyrs, the transfer of power. It was these political meanings that then attracted Lenin's attention. But for Benois it was the second heritage of the palace complex that mattered: the tangible objects created and maintained by anonymous hands, by the countless stagehands of monarchy, who had built and maintained a venue for monarchy marked by beautiful things that monarchy's heirs could preserve. Under Benois's tutelage the palace opened its doors to the people of Petrograd. Over the next few years thousands of visitors took center stage as they streamed into a complex of buildings now united by public ownership and shared mission. At the end of 1922 a suite of historical rooms opened to the public. As they trudged up the October Staircase to the living quarters of Nicholas I, Alexander II, Alexander III, and Nicholas II the people of Petrograd came face-to-face with the usable remnants of Russia's monarchical past.

CONCLUSION

No act of revolutionary iconoclasm destroyed either the Winter Palace or the Hermitage. That such a thing was possible had been demonstrated at the climax of the Paris Commune in May 1871 when the Parisian Fédérés set fire to the Louvre, the Tuileries Palace, and Notre Dame, along with other buildings. Advancing government troops put out some of the fires, sparing the great art museum. But the adjacent Tuileries Palace burned to the ground, and it has never been rebuilt. This was the central Paris palace abandoned by Louis XIV when he moved to the chateau at Versailles, later irrevocably associated with monarchism in France, as it passed from one would-be dynasty to the next. In the heat of urban revolution in 1871 some Parisians were prepared to destroy this symbol of a hated form of government, which had acquired little civic value. They were even willing to incinerate all of the artworks confiscated from the Bourbons in the name of the people in 1793.[1]

By contrast, when the Bolsheviks claimed the Winter Palace on October 26, 1917, no one thought of fire. Even artillery and gunfire was long delayed and kept to a minimum. The leading Bolsheviks who entered the palace that night exerted quick control over those men bent on pillage or destruction. They posted guards at the Hermitage, which passed the dangerous night unharmed. No place in Russia spoke more of the imperial regime recently dispatched than Petrograd's Winter Palace and its adjoining art museum, and no one despised that regime more than the Bolsheviks, who eventually murdered the entire imperial family. In the coming days crowds knocked imperial eagles and other Romanov symbols off of every building that sported them including the gates of the Winter Palace itself, before draping them in red banners. But these were gestures of confiscation, not destruction. Petrograd's people claimed what their predecessors had built for Russia's monarchs. By 1917 Palace Square was incontrovertibly the people's space. And now that the palace was also theirs they treated it with both deference and familiarity. Despite its imposing formality the palace had come to stand for Russia. Before long schoolchildren would line up to take a look inside.

The study of a particular place concentrates our attention on the process of meaning-making. All of the words expended in this book attempt to capture an inchoate feeling, an often-unarticulated perception of generations of St. Petersburg people about the Winter Palace. It would be illuminating to know what parents have told their children about the dramatic building as they take their hands to walk them across the square, but this we cannot know. What I hope has become clear, however, is that the significance that accrues to a place like this is the work of many hands, the product of accumulated labor and lived experience. Moreover, the building up of significance is not only vertical—that is, of erecting a taller and taller mountain of meaning. It is also horizontal, back-and-forth, a contest, a negotiation. And as long as the building stands the process of making meaning does not end.

For an interpreter of Russian history asking of the Winter Palace what it can reveal about the long endurance of absolute monarchy in Russia the place yields insight about the kind of monarchy Russian rulers meant to embody as well as their notion of the kind of country they ruled. The practitioners of Russian absolutism long believed that they ruled not only by the grace of God but also because they justly enjoyed the love of Russia's people. If their administrators and police were manifestly unloved, Romanov monarchs felt vindicated by the disciplined and carefully staged interactions with those subjects closest to the throne, those who served the palace household, who lined up along the Neva, who assembled at the edge of Palace Square, who were admitted to the palace as merchants, Grenadiers, veterans, Easter worshipers, New Year's revelers. Such interactions convinced empresses and emperors that they were loved by humble folk as well as, if not better than, by courtiers. The fragmentary historical record gives reason to believe that many Russians who experienced these direct encounters with their rulers were, in fact, overcome with admiration for them. When such people told their stories and wrote their memoirs, monarchism was reproduced.

The other characteristic interaction between ruler and ruled at the Winter Palace was between imperial patrons and talented artists or craftsmen. This encounter, in which the masters of the imperial household combed the country for untapped talent and then provided training and opportunity in the bosom of the palace, exemplifies a premodern (and not only Russian) relationship between patron and protégé. While many aristocrats were no doubt dilettantes when it came to the arts and crafts, across many reigns the Romanov monarchs were true connoisseurs. The objects past which armies of museum visitors troop in our day were once procured at great cost, admired, thoughtfully displayed, and carefully preserved by the palace's ruling family. The Winter Palace and Hermitage complex was a haven for foreign arts but especially for native crafts and later, through the Imperial Hermitage, it became the headquarters for art collecting and preservation. This role proved durable, and when the overtly political significance of the palace melted away this fine residue remained.

So we see something of how Russian monarchy worked in its last 150 years, and we see the elements that some might dare to consider reasons for its durability. Those who wanted absolutism to survive—and they were not all Romanovs—succeeded here longer than anywhere else in Europe. The study of monarchy on its main stage demonstrates reasons for its popularity and reveals savvy political intuition that served the Romanovs well for a long time. Not the least of these sound instincts was the monarchy's disposition to turn away from a court-centered performance in order to ingratiate itself with the residents of its capital city.

In the end the Winter Palace yielded to a public aroused by government incompetence, monarchical decadence, and an imperial family so convinced of the righteousness of their mission that they could not bring themselves to modernize Russian government. In fact, at the turn of the twentieth century the Russian emperor showed little interest in governing, but he was nonetheless loath to share power with representatives of the nation. The disadvantages of such a posture were exposed vividly once World War I began. At the same time each of the last two monarchs attempted to manifest his role as representative of the state and nation, not at close range but from a distance. Photographs and postcards pictured them as fathers, husbands, and officers but a much smaller circle of St. Petersburg's public than previously experienced them in these roles directly. As life for St. Petersburg's exploding industrial population grew more difficult, the comings and goings of the tsar had less and less to do with the people. The modern metropolis grew steadily more diverse and complex. Even if Nicholas had endeavored to show himself to the people of the capital he would have had to play multiple roles—and would the palace have been the proper stage for such performances?

In its final act as the stage of monarchy the Winter Palace played itself. Symbol and instrument were one. The palace was penetrated literally and figuratively by the city's public: by wounded soldiers and nurses, by armed troops, by the champions of popular enlightenment and artistic preservation, by revolutionaries, by people dying of curiosity to see what lay behind the rows of windows. When these newcomers got inside they encountered the epigones of monarchy: liveried footmen, cooks, servants, ladies-in-waiting, invariably described in memoirs as silent and elderly. These people could not or did not choose to explain themselves. Thus in 1917 the Winter Palace housed the revolution. On its great parade staircases, monarchist and revolutionary eyed each other curiously, each giving the other a wide berth. In the background a few hundred soldiers convalesced from their brush with the terrors of the Great War. With or without the tsar, the palace unambiguously represented the most concentrated point of central authority in the Russian Empire. Whatever difficult contests lay ahead, to hold that place—and as Kerensky saw it, to occupy it personally—was to claim authority over all the Russias. When he fled before the Bolsheviks in October 1917 it became clear that just holding it was sufficient. Having seized it the new masters could turn their backs on it and on the city it anchored.

In the end the intimate bond between the fate of the Winter Palace and the fate of its supporting city was thrown into brittle relief by the events of 1917. What was cataclysmic for the monarchy presented to many who staffed the palace complex not a disaster but a new mission. And the new mission grew organically out of what had been the reality of the buildings on the Neva embankment for many years: they had come to house an imperial museum and a museum of monarchy. When the fledgling Soviet government eventually created the new State Museum of the Hermitage there was no need for the keys to change hands. A space erected jointly by court and city passed from the one to the other with impressive continuity of mission and even of personnel. Nonetheless, in commandeering the Winter Palace and evicting the monarchical family, the revolutionaries of Petrograd had prepared the path by which their city would cease to be the nation's political center. What remained was the imperial bequest that made St. Petersburg Russia's cultural center, at the heart of which stands an old building, tended still by loving hands.[2]

Notes

Introduction

1. Monarchy has survived to the present in nine European countries, where all are constitutional. In Asia and Africa there are a few monarchs today, some constitutional and some still absolute. Almost all modern nation-states have a monarchical past, however.

2. Richard S. Wortman, *Scenarios of Power: Myth and Ceremony in Russian Monarchy,* vol. 1, *From Peter the Great to the Death of Nicholas I* (Princeton, NJ: Princeton University Press, 1995); Richard S. Wortman, *Scenarios of Power: Myth and Ceremony in Russian Monarchy,* vol. 2, *From Alexander II to the Abdication of Nicholas II* (Princeton, NJ: Princeton University Press, 2000); and the combined, abridged edition, Richard S. Wortman, *Scenarios of Power: Myth and Ceremony in Russian Monarchy, from Peter the Great to the Abdication of Nicholas II* (Princeton, NJ: Princeton University Press, 2006). Unless otherwise noted, citations hereafter will refer to the combined edition.

3. Monarchy in Europe has attracted a lively and gigantic historiography, a representative sample of which includes the foundational Ernst Kantorowicz, *The King's Two Bodies: A Study in Mediaeval Political Theology* (Princeton, NJ: Princeton University Press, 1957); Paul Kléber Monod, *The Power of Kings: Monarchy and Religion in Europe, 1589–1715* (New Haven: Yale University Press, 1999); Jeroen Deploige and Gita Deneckere, eds., *Mystifying the Monarch. Studies on Discourse, Power and History* (Amsterdam: Amsterdam University Press, 2006). A seminal work that considered the role of ceremony and ritual in modern monarchy was David Cannadine, "The Context, Performance and Meaning of Ritual: The British Monarchy and the 'Invention of Tradition,' c. 1820–1977," in *The Invention of Tradition, ed.* E. J. Hobsbawm and Terence Ranger (Cambridge: Cambridge University Press, 1983), 101–64; Lynn Hunt, *The Family Romance of the French Revolution* (Berkeley: University of California Press, 1992); John Plunkett, *Queen Victoria: First Media Monarch* (Oxford: Oxford University Press, 2003); Simon Schama, "The Domestication of Majesty: Royal Family Portraiture, 1500–1850," *Journal of Interdisciplinary History* 17, no. 1 (Summer 1986): 155–83; Sean Wilentz, ed., *Rites of Power: Symbolism, Ritual, and Politics since the Middle Ages* (Philadelphia: University of Pennsylvania Press, 1985).

4. The imperial court is monarchy's great intermediary institution, or interlocking network of institutions, and it also has a vast literature, representative examples of which will be cited when we discuss the Russian court per se, below.

5. The idea of examining history through the story of important buildings is not unprecedented. A few recent examples include Catherine Merridale's *Red Fortress: History and Illusion in the Kremlin* (New York: Metropolitan Books, 2013); and the brilliant history of the Christ the Savior Church and site in Moscow by Konstantin Akinsha et al., *The Holy Place: Architecture, Ideology, and History in Russia* (New Haven: Yale University Press, 2007). A related idea is to examine exceptional public art, as in Alexander M. Schenker, *The Bronze Horseman: Falconet's Monument to Peter the Great* (New Haven: Yale University Press, 2003).

6. There is an enormous literature in many languages on the architectural history of the Winter Palace and the lives of its principal inhabitants. Much of this has been produced and beautifully illustrated by the State Museum of the Hermitage. Many of these works are cited in subsequent chapters and in the bibliography, but the principal works include V. I. Piliavskii, *Zimnii dvorets* (Leningrad: Gosud. Izd. Lit. po stroitel'stvu, 1960); V. I. Piliavskii and V. F. Levinson-Lessing, eds., *Ermitazh. Istoriia*

i arkhitektura zdanii (Leningrad: Izd. Avrora, 1974); M. B. Piotrovskii et al., *Ermitazh: Istoriia zdanii i kollektsii* (St. Petersburg: Gosud. Ermitazh, 2001); Igor' Zimin, *Zimnii dvorets. Liudi i steny. Istoriia imperatorskoi rezidentsii, 1762–1917* (Moscow: Tsentrpoligraf, 2012); Gosudarstvennyi Ermitazh, *Zimnii dvorets: ocherki zhizni imperatorskoi rezidentsii*, vol. 1 (St. Petersburg: Liki Rossii, 2000); N. Iu. Guseva, "Zimnii dvorets." *Tri veka Sankt-Peterburga. Entsiklopediia v trekh tomakh* (St. Petersburg: St. Petersburg State University, 2003), 1:379–81; Emmanuel Ducamp, ed., *The Winter Palace, St. Petersburg* (St. Petersburg: State Hermitage Museum, 1995).

7. W. Bruce Lincoln, *Sunlight at Midnight: St. Petersburg and the Rise of Modern Russia* (New York: Basic Books, 2002), 81.

8. The term "autocratic" (*samoderzhavnyi*) is typically applied to absolutism in Russia. Its early use in Muscovite Russia referred primarily to the tsar's claim to rule by his own authority, rather than by formal conferral of power from an external institution such as the church. In the imperial period the terminology persisted, but its meaning shifted somewhat, to stress the independence of the Russian emperor (a term first applied to Peter the Great, who added it to a list of titles that also included "tsar") from independent corporations or estates such as guilds, cities, and the like. Although the term aptly accentuates the extraordinary concentration of political authority in Russian imperial rulers, by the eighteenth century it exoticizes a system of government that was not functionally different from that of Europe's other absolute monarchies. Therefore with relevant exceptions the term "absolutism" will be used in this work.

9. All of Europe's great royal art collections eventually became public property, and several are displayed in royal palaces. Philip II's (1556–1598) El Escorial, originally a palace complex surrounding a rural monastery, came to house an important collection of paintings, although these were not displayed to the public for centuries. Francis I (1515–1547) aimed to reassert control over Paris by settling down in the old Louvre, and began filling it with masterpieces, establishing that palace as the home of French academic and court arts even when Louis XIV decamped for Versailles. Louis XVI's director of royal buildings, the comte d'Angiviller, produced a plan to create a public museum in the Grand Gallery of the Louvre, but it was not realized before the French Revolution. The Imperial Hermitage is unique in that it was adjacent to the principal formal residence of Russia's monarch in the heart of the country's largest city.

10. Examples of each of these approaches, respectively, include Jane Burbank et al., *Russian Empire: Space, People, Power, 1700–1930* (Bloomington: Indiana University Press, 2007); Olga Maiorova, *From the Shadow of Empire: Defining the Russian Nation through Cultural Mythology, 1855–1870* (Madison: University of Wisconsin Press, 2010); Catherine Evtuhov, *Portrait of a Russian Province: Economy, Society, Civilization in Nineteenth-Century Nizhnii Novgorod* (Pittsburgh: University of Pittsburgh Press, 2011). Francis W. Wcislo, *Tales of Imperial Russia: The Life and Times of Sergei Witte, 1849–1915* (New York: Oxford University Press, 2011).

11. In his study of seventeenth- and eighteenth-century peasant rebellions, Paul Avrich showed that with each successive popular outbreak between 1607 and 1774 the rebels were stopped further from the center, indicating the steadily expanding zone effectively controlled by the monarch. See Paul Avrich, *Russian Rebels, 1600–1800* (New York: Norton, 1976).

12. Alexander I demonstrated the extent to which the scene of the French king's execution worked on his own imagination when he prayed at the site in 1814; see Wortman, *Scenarios of Power*, 113.

13. References to the dangerous vagrancy in west European cities abound in the analyses produced by both tsars' advisors. See, for example, Nikolai S. Mordvinov, "Osvobozhenie ot zavisimosti," *Arkhiv Grafov Mordvinovykh*, ed. V. A. Bil'basov (St. Petersburg, 1901–1903), 5:145.

14. As he put it most succinctly in his introduction, "(social) space is a (social) product." Henri Lefebvre, *The Production of Space*, trans. Donald Nicholson-Smith (Oxford: Basil Blackwell, 1991), 30. Delores Hayden fleshed out the significance of Lefebvre's notion about how "the production of space" relates the "sense of place" to "the inner workings of the political economy." See Delores Hayden, *The Power of Place: Urban Landscapes as Public History* (Cambridge, MA: MIT Press, 1995), 18–19.

15. *Istoriia dorevoliutsionnoi Rossii v dnevnikakh i vospominaniiakh*, 5 vols. in 13, ed. and intro. P. A. Zaionchkovskii (Moscow: Kniga, 1976–1989).

Chapter 1

1. The institutions and practices of royal courts have become the subject of a large historiography, of which Norbert Elias is generally considered the progenitor. See Norbert Elias, *The Court Society* (New York: Pantheon Books, 1983). Each European court has its own extensive literature, and generalization remains problematic. See the clarifying introductory essay in Jeroen Duindam, *Vienna and Versailles: The Courts of Europe's Dynastic Rivals, 1550–1780* (Cambridge: Cambridge University Press, 2003), 3–20. Duindam traces the beginning of the process by which the monarchical household separated from the more public entities of the court, a process that did not commence in earnest before the eighteenth century.

2. The centralization I am thinking of is administrative, political, and financial. The new formal center was nowhere near the geographical center of Russia, a fact that attracted increasing attention over the course of the nineteenth century. St. Petersburg's relationship to the old capital, Moscow, as well as its setting in the midst of non-Russian populations is considered in Leonid Gorizontov, "The 'Great Circle' of Interior Russia: Representations of the Imperial Center in the Nineteenth and Early Twentieth Centuries," in Burbank et al., *Russian Empire*, 67–93. On the succession of capitals, see Olga Gritsai and Herman van der Wusten, "Moscow and St. Petersburg, a Sequence of Capitals, a Tale of Two Cities," *GeoJournal* 51 (2000): 33–45; Alexander Shevyrev, "The Axis Petersburg-Moscow: Outward and Inward Russian Capitals," *Journal of Urban History* 30, no. 1 (Nov. 2003): 70–84. James Cracraft characterizes the founding of St. Petersburg as a central feature of Peter the Great's "revolution," in *The Revolution of Peter the Great* (Cambridge, MA: Harvard University Press, 2003).

3. Lewis Mumford described the paradoxical process by which, even as the country grew larger, the territories outside the center declined in political and (often) economic significance. See Lewis Mumford, *The City in History* (New York: Harcourt, Brace Jovanovich, 1961).

4. For example, Paul Miliukov described the empress as generally less prone to judicial cruelty than her father, except when her "reputation as a beautiful woman" was at stake. See Miliukov's account of her major domestic and international achievements in Paul Miliukov et al., *History of Russia*, vol. 2, *The Successors of Peter the Great: From Catherine I to Nicholas I*, trans. Charles Lam Markmann (New York: Funk and Wagnalls, 1968), 32. On rising expenditures, see O. G. Ageeva, *Imperatorskii dvor Rossii 1700–1796 gg.* (Moscow: Nauka, 2008), 134–36. On Elizabeth's reign and her court, see Evgeny V. Anisimov, *Rossiia v seredine XVIII veka. Borba za nasledie Petra* (Moscow, 1986), which appears in English translation as *Empress Elizabeth: Her Reign and Her Russia, 1741–1761*, trans. John T. Alexander (Gulf Breeze, FL: Academic International Press, 1995); Paul Keenan, *St. Petersburg and the Russian Court, 1703–1761* (Basingstoke: Palgrave Macmillan, 2013); Konstantin Pisarenko, *Povsednevnaia zhizn' russkogo dvora tsartvovanie Elizavety Petrovny* (Moscow: Molodaia Gvardiia, 2003); Konstantin Pisarenko, *Elizaveta Petrovna* (Moscow: Molodaia gvardiia, 2014). More general studies of the Russian court include L. E. Shepelev, *Chinovnyi mir Rossii XVIII–nachalo XX v.* (St. Petersburg, 1999); N. E. Volkhov, *Dvor russkikh imperatorov v ego proshlom i nastoiashchem* (St. Petersburg: P. Golike, 1900); and the recent collection of highly original essays in Andreas Schönle et al., eds., *The Europeanized Elite in Russia, 1762–1825* (DeKalb: Northern Illinois University Press, 2016).

5. The most famous example of royal flight to the suburbs was Louis XIV's Versailles, built twelve miles outside of Paris in 1682. Erected on the site of a prized royal hunting ground, Versailles differed from the summer hunting lodges of other peripatetic monarchs when Louis made it his primary formal residence and induced his principal courtiers to settle on the rustic site. The Austrian Habsburgs also built a grand palace on suburban hunting land when Maria Therese created Schoenbrunn Palace in the 1740s and 1750s. But this remained a summer palace, with the Habsburgs

returning generally each winter season to the cramped Hofburg in Vienna. Peter, Elizabeth, and their successors built several beautiful suburban palaces—at Peterhof and Tsarskoe Selo, among others—and moved around among them particularly in the summer. St. Petersburg's Winter Palace, however, was their primary court residence for most of the year and for all important court ceremonies apart from coronations, which still occurred in the Moscow Kremlin.

6. See the architectural summary of Elizabeth's Petersburg building program by William Craft Brumfield, "St. Petersburg and the Art of Survival," in *Preserving Petersburg: History, Memory, Nostalgia*, ed. Helena Goscilo and Stephen M. Norris (Bloomington: Indiana University Press, 2008), 5–8.

7. Victor-L. Tapié, *The Age of Grandeur: Baroque Art and Architecture*, trans. A. Ross Williamson (New York: Frederick A. Praeger, 1960), 15.

8. Tapié, *The Age of Grandeur*, 39.

9. Lewis Mumford, *The Culture of Cities* (New York: Harcourt, Brace Jovanovich), 80–88. See also Mumford, *The City in History*, 375–382.

10. Dmitry Shvidkovsky, *Russian Architecture and the West*, trans. Antony Wood (New Haven: Yale University Press, 2007), 76.

11. Shvidkovsky, *Russian Architecture*, 93–97. While the interior of this palace is wholly Russian in design, its façades were something "completely new in Russian architecture," and reminiscent of contemporary projects in Venice and Urbino (96–97).

12. Shvidkovsky, *Russian Architecture*, 198–200. Despite his Italian roots, most scholars see Trezzini's chief influences as Danish and Dutch.

13. Francesco Rastrelli's birth date is given variously as 1699 and 1700. P. N. Petrov, citing a letter from Rastrelli's father, gives it as 1700. P. N. Petrov, "Materialy dlia biografii grafa Rastrelli," *Zodchii: Arkhitekturnyi i khudozhestvenno-tekhnicheskii zhurnal* (1876): 55. Not only is the great architect's birthdate disputed, but his name also appears in a variety of forms. Soviet and Russian scholars most commonly refer to him as Bartolomeo Francesco, or Bartolomeo Bartolomeevich (which in transliterated Russian would read as V. F. or V. V., respectively), but it is also the case that first and middle names are sometimes reversed. By convention the son is referred to as Francesco and the father as Carlo (Karlo). Most often Russian scholars refer to the pair as "Rastrelli-father" and "Rastrelli-son." The architect himself did not provide much assistance here, as he customarily signed the many drawings he left behind simply "de Rastrelli."

14. Petrov, "Materialy dlia biografii," 55. See also Iu. Ovsiannikov, *Franchesko Bartolomeo Rastrelli* (Leningrad: Isskustvo, 1982), 5–10.

15. G. V. Mikhailov, "Zimnie dvortsy Petra I," *Tri veka Sankt-Peterburga*, 366.

16. See http://rusmuseum.ru/eng/museum/complex/let_sad/let_palace/.

17. And here Peter married Ekaterina Alekseevna, the mother of his two daughters, in 1712.

18. See Piotrovskii et al., *Ermitazh*, 8.

19. For example, in 1725 the office of the Winter Palace command (*Hof-intendant* of the Imperial Court) ordered the architect M. Zemtsov to examine the work of "father and son Rastrelli" at the home of Shafirov on the Neva embankment, perhaps in anticipation of awarding a court commission. See the document in "Hof-intendant. Kontor. Min. Imp. Dvora," RGIA, f. 470, op. 5, d. 22 (1725), l. 122.

20. It is not possible to ascertain the younger Rastrelli's exact itinerary in the late 1720s. Many commentators have reported that he was in Italy between 1727 and 1730, but Ovsiannikov points out persuasively that Rastrelli's own list of his activities in those years suggests he was working in Russia the whole time. See Ovsiannikov, *Rastrelli*, 21–22.

21. Details of Rastrelli's biography are known to us through only a small file of his own letters and papers preserved in the Special Collections Division of the National Library of Poland (hereafter NLP): Wil. Kat. Akc. 2189/66e; and extant drawings also held in Warsaw, now available electronically and published recently in Russian: Zigmunt Batowski, *Arkhitektor Rastrelli o svoikh tvoreniiakh. Materialy deiatel'nosti mastera s 65 illiustratsiiami. Pervoe russkoe izdanie* (St. Petersburg: GMZ "Tsarskoe Selo," 2000). This volume is a Russian edition of Batowski's Polish publication from

1939. The editor's notes narrate the almost unbelievable fate of Rastrelli's papers after his dismissal by Catherine at the beginning of her reign. It was apparently one of the Counts Potocki who purchased a collection of Rastrelli's drawings, with a few notes and letters, which found their way eventually to the National Library of Poland—and back again, after being removed to Berlin by the Nazis. The Warsaw documents are published as an appendix to Cornelia Skodock, *Barock in Russland: Zum Oeuvre des Hofarchitekten Francesco Bartolomeo Rastrelli* (Wiesbaden: Harrassowitz Verlag, 2006). See also Iu. Denisov and A. Petrov, *Zodchii Rastrelli. Materialy k izucheniiu tvorchestva* (Leningrad: Gosud. Izd. Lit. po Stroitel'stvu Arkhitektury i Stroitel'nym Materialam, 1963). Many parts of Rastrelli's biography and career remain obscure.

22. Ovsiannikov, *Rastrelli*, 30. The extant records are not entirely clear but his inference is reasonable.

23. Ovsiannikov, *Rastrelli*, 202–4. Which of the two Counts Rastrelli played the leading role in this building is not easily determined. Francesco noted later that he helped his father on this project between 1734 and 1736. Elsewhere he wrote that, upon his return from Courland, the empress directed him to build her a large stone winter palace. See the discussion in Iu. M. Denisov, "Zimnii dom Anny Ioannovny," *Tri veka Sankt-Peterburga*, 1:372.

24. The phrase comes from Feodor Dostoevsky, *Notes from the Underground*, and finds its way into the title of George E. Munro's *The Most Intentional City: St. Petersburg in the Reign of Catherine the Great* (Madison, NJ: Fairleigh Dickinson University Press, 2008). Munro concedes the fact of planning in the origins of St. Petersburg but demonstrates in his book that "the planned city is not always the city that results." See *Most Intentional City*, 17.

25. The childless Apraksin bequeathed his home and its prime real estate to Peter II.

26. Petrov, "Materialy dlia biografii," 55.

27. Denisov, "Zimnii dom Anny Ioannovny," 371.

28. This version of the palace contained over two hundred rooms not counting servants' quarters, according to Rastrelli's notes. See Piliavskii, *Zimnii dvorets*, 14.

29. Denisov, "Zimnii dom Anny Ioannovny," 371–73.

30. Anisimov, *Empress Elizabeth*, 83–109.

31. Volkhov, *Dvor russkikh*, 15–16.

32. Kirill Ospovat, *Terror and Pity: Aleksandr Sumarokov and the Theater of Power in Elizabethan Russia* (Boston: Academic Studies Press, 2016), xi. Ospovat sees tragedy as particularly suited to consideration of the relationship between monarchs and their courtiers, since the power in that relationship was displayed as tableaux not only of harmony but also of "fear instilled by constant and often spectacular judicial terror" (xiii).

33. Keenan, *St. Petersburg*, 60. See also Richard Stites, *Serfdom, Society, and the Arts in Imperial Russia: The Pleasure and the Power* (New Haven: Yale University Press, 2005).

34. Denisov, "Zimnii dom Anny Ioannovny," 373.

35. Francesco Rastrelli, "Relation générale de tous les edifices, palais et jardins, que moy Comte de Rastrelli, Ober-Architecte de la Cour, a fait construire pendant tout le temps que j'ai eu l'honneur d'etre au service d Leurs Majestés Imperiales, de toutes les Russies, à commencer depuis l'année 1716 jusqu'à cette année 1764" (NLP Special Collections, Wil. Kat. akc. 2189/66e), 3.

36. Rastrelli, "Relation générale," 3. There is an extensive discussion of Elizabeth's attention to the style of each of these projects in Pisarenko, *Elizaveta Petrovna*, 388–95.

37. Ovsiannikov, *Rastrelli*, 206–8. Ovsiannikov discusses Rastrelli's *gostinnyi dvor* (159). Although the empress approved his design it was the merchants who were to pay for the construction, and they apparently decided that Rastrelli's plan was too luxurious and expensive. In 1761 they agreed to a plan by de la Mothe, according to the "new French style," that is, classicism—a decision that pointed to the approaching decline of Rastrelli's position and the end of baroque building in the capital.

38. T. L. Pashkova, "Bolshoi Zimnii dvorets," *Tri veka Sankt-Peterburga*, 1:375.

39. Rastrelli, "Relation générale," 5.

40. Ageeva, *Imperatorskii dvor Rossii*, 137, citing RGIA, f. 466, op. 1, d. 91, ll. 16–39. These figures excluded "office employees" but included "73 people receiving partial funding."

41. In 1739, the year before she ascended the throne, the total expense for room, board, and livery of court staff amounted to 112,899R. Now the sum had risen to 171,177R "counting the additional sums requested by the servitors." Ageeva, *Imperatorskii dvor Rossii*, 137, citing RGIA, f. 466, op. 1, d. 89, ll. 81 ob., 86 ob., 90, 94 ob., 95.

42. Besides Louis XIV's retreat to Versailles, the Austrian court abandoned the Hofburg in Vienna to spend most of the year at the remodeled suburban summer palace, Schönbrunn, after the middle of the eighteenth century. This was the palace in which the very young Mozart played the piano, the Congress of Vienna danced, and Charles I ended the Austro-Hungarian monarchy.

43. P. N. Petrov, *Istoriia Sankt-Peterburga s osnovaniia goroda do vvedeniia v deistvie vybornago gorodskago upravleniia, 1703–1782* (St. Petersburg: Izd. Glazunova, 1885), 401.

44. Pisarenko, *Povsednevnaia zhizhn'*, 21.

45. An authoritative description of the design process based on the preserved drawings is Piliavskii and Levinson-Lessing, *Ermitazh*, 39–44.

46. Piliavskii and Levinson-Lessing, *Ermitazh*, 40. Rastrelli, himself, was apparently the builder of at least one of the buildings whose destruction he now proposed, the so-called house by Empress Anna's Winter Palace, built in 1746 between the home of General G. P. Chernyshev and the Admiralty meadow (that is, the current Palace Square). See the drawings in Gosudarstvennyi Muzei Istorii S.-Peterburga, *Katalog, Franchesko Bartolomeo Rastrelli: Arkhitekturnye proekty iz sobraniia*, comp. G. B. Vasil'ev et al. (St. Petersburg, Gosud. Muz. Ist. S.-Peterburga, 2000), 49.

47. Although it must be said that the Summer Palace Rastrelli had already built for her in the Summer Garden did follow the Versailles plan. There is an extensive discussion of Elizabeth's attention to the architectural nuances in each of her palace commissions in Pisarenko, *Elizaveta Petrovna*, 388–95.

48. Piliavskii and Levinson-Lessing, *Ermitazh*, 41; Ovsiannikov, *Rastrelli*, 155.

49. Francesco Rastrelli, "Bâtiments et edifices construits sous le regne de l'Impératrice Elisabeth" (NLP Special Collections, Wil. Kat. akc. 2189/66e), 11.

50. The project cost over three times this amount before it was complete. This account draws heavily from Petrov, *Istoriia Sankt-Peterburga*, 385–493. According to Petrov, Nicholas I ordered a history of the Winter Palace to be composed by the 1830s patriotic writer Nestor V. Kukol'nik. Kukol'nik conducted interviews, but he did not complete the project because "it was not possible to gather all the necessary material." *Istoriia Sankt-Peterburga*, 644–45n653. Likely the 1837 fire destroyed much of the material upon which this history could be based, but some of Kukol'nik's notes found their way to Petrov from the "not yet destroyed *dela* of the *Hof-intendant's* Office" (645).

51. Like other Europeans, Russians count floors of a multistory building differently than Americans do. Here I have used the Russian style, considering the palace to have a ground floor (which is actually accessed by a short set of stairs and worked generally as service floor), a "parade" floor (which Americans would call the second, accessed by the Jordan or other staircase, and on which all the great public galleries, throne rooms, and imperial residences were located) and a second (to Americans, third) floor.

52. Piliavskii, *Zimnii dvorets*, 28–33; William Craft Brumfield, *A History of Russian Architecture* (Cambridge: Cambridge University Press, 1993), 247.

53. Like all great buildings, this one has elicited a variety of responses from architectural critics. William Brumfield concluded that "whatever its faults the Winter Palace represents the quintessence of St. Petersburg's monumental style, an assimilation of Western principles applied in a manner and on a scale uniquely Russian." Brumfield, *Russian Architecture*, 248–49. John Summerlin thought its length and theatricality "would be impossible anywhere in Western Europe," but that it achieved what Russia's rulers needed, "an effect of absolute, grim, and careless dominion." John Summerlin, *The Architecture of the Eighteenth Century* (London: Thames and Hudson, 1986), 34. Bruce Lincoln found it to be

"perhaps the most stunning eighteenth century architectural creation in Russia." Lincoln, *Sunlight at Midnight*, 40.

54. Anisimov, *Empress Elizabeth*, 114–17.

Chapter 2

1. The paper was originally produced by the College of Foreign Affairs and appeared in German. By the late 1720s its publication was taken over by the newly created Academy of Sciences, which began to issue a Russian edition. At the end of the 1740s renowned academician M. V. Lomonosov became the first Russian editor, and the paper's popularity gradually grew. See Dmitrii Iu. Sherikh, *Golos rodnogo goroda: ocherk istorii gazety "Sankt-Peterburgskie vedomosti"* (St. Petersburg: Lenizdat, 2001), 13–38.

2. Sherikh, *Golos*, 41, 47.

3. Miliukov asserted that Elizabeth's court strained equine resources severely. Because she transported most of her household goods with her when she traveled between Moscow and St. Petersburg, those trips required "at least twenty thousand horses." See Miliukov, *History of Russia*, 2:31.

4. *Sankt-Peterburgskie vedomosti* (hereafter *SPV*), no. 6 (Jan. 21, 1754). Trees of up to fourteen inches in diameter fetched 29.50R per hundred; those between sixteen and eighteen inches went for 49.90R.

5. *SPV*, no. 16 (Feb. 25, 1754).

6. *SPV*, no. 54 (July 8, 1754). The challenges of accurately measuring and cutting wood in Russia attracted comment from Rastrelli, who noted that the two extremes of Russia's climate, heat and cold, caused the wood to expand and contract. Rastrelli found the very short building season to be frustrating, especially since part of the spring and summer had to be used repairing the previous winter's damage to the prior year's construction. See Francesco Rastrelli, "Reflexions sur la maniere et les difficultés qu'il y a en Russie pour bâtir avec la même exacitude et perfection comme dans les autres pais de l'Europe" (NLP, Special Collections, Wil. Kat. akc. 2189/66e), 13.

7. L. D. Burim et al., *"Odin otvetstvovat' dolzhen . . .": Ocherki o direktorakh Izhorskikh zavodov* (St. Petersburg: OAO "Izhorskie zavody," 2001), 4.

8. P. G. Liubomirov, "Iz istorii lesopil'nogo proizvodstva v Rossii v XVII, XVIII i nachale XIX vv.," *Istoricheskie zapiski* (Moscow: Ak. Nauka, 1941), 222–49. Liubomirov demonstrates that Russia's lumber milling industry developed relatively late, with most construction through the seventeenth century dependent upon ax-hewn timbers. At the turn of the eighteenth century increased demand for timber exports induced some noble landowners and entrepreneurs to establish sawmills near Narva and Archangel. Growing demand for milled boards for shipbuilding in St. Petersburg led Peter's government to set up the mill at Izhor, southwest of the city, where a Dutch director presided over 135 masters and their apprentices to produce 20,000 boards a year. In 1758 there was a renewed demand for finished and semi-finished pine boards for completing the Winter Palace interiors. *SPV*, no. 41 (May 22, 1758), no. 51 (June 26, 1758).

9. While Catherine II issued a similar decree a few years later neither seems to have been enforced. See Munro, *Most Intentional City*, 203, 324n.

10. Liubomirov, "Iz istorii lesopil'nogo proizvodstva," 222–49.

11. *SPV*, no. 22 (Mar. 15, 1756).

12. *SPV*, no. 6 (Jan. 19, 1759).

13. *Polnoe sobranie zakonov Rossiiskoi Imperii 1649–1913*, 40 vols. (St. Petersburg: Gos. Tip., 1830–1916 [hereafter *PSZ*]), 14, no. 10369 (March 7, 1755), and *PSZ* 14, no. 10373 (March 9, 1755). These decrees particularly concern allocation of funds, payable upon demand to Fermor.

14. *SPV*, no. 21 (March 14, 1755): 2–4; Petrov, *Istoriia Sankt-Peterburga*, 385–86.

15. *SPV*, no. 71 (Sept. 6, 1754). Silicate consists of a mixture of sand and lime, instead of the clay used in red brick. It is less expensive to produce than clay bricks, bears loads well, and does not

yield the variety of colors that different batches of ceramic bricks produce. However, the silicate bricks cannot be used for chimney interiors or where water is present.

16. Rastrelli, "Reflexions sur la maniere et les difficulties," 12.

17. *Posad* people were small merchants and artisans residing in towns and liable to taxation.

18. N. V. Voronov, "O rynke rabochei sily v rossii v XVIII v.: po materialam kirpichnoi promyshlennosti," *Voprosii istorii* 3 (1955): 95.

19. S. P. Luppov, *Istoriia stroitel'stva Peterburga v pervoi chetverti XVIII v.* (Leningrad: Izd. Akademii Nauk SSSR, 1957), 100–101. Brickworks were generally located outside the city limits, because they posed a fire danger while also consuming great quantities of wood for fuel.

20. Ol'ga Kosheleva, *Liudi Sankt-Peterburgskogo ostrova Petrovskogo vremeni* (Moscow: OGI, 2004), 96–97.

21. Kosheleva, *Liudi*, 427. She also concluded that in the first quarter of the century foreign workers were a minute segment of the working population, despite the flowering of Western tastes in the northern capital.

22. V. M. Paneiakh, "Masterovye i rabotnye liudi vo vtoroi polovine XVIII v.," in *Istoriia rabochikh Leningrada*, vol. 1, ed. S. N. Valk et al. (Leningrad: Izd. "Nauka," 1972), 50.

23. G. E. Kochin, "Naselenie Peterburga v 60–90-kh godakah XVIII v.," in *Ocherki istorii Leningrada* vol. 1 (Moscow-Leningrad: Institut Istorii, Ak. Nauk SSSR, 1955), 301.

24. Voronov, "O rynke," 96.

25. "Brick Works," *St. Petersburg Encyclopedia*, ed. the Committee of Culture of St. Petersburg. http://encspb.ru/object/2855710245?lc=en.

26. *SPV*, no. 29 (April 11, 1755).

27. *SPV*, no. 15 (Feb. 21, 1757). At the same time, it notified anyone wishing to buy "broken bricks for floor covering" to apply at the Palace Construction Office.

28. *SPV*, no. 59 (July 25, 1757). Munro suggests that as a principal brick producer itself the government was keen to maintain profitable brick prices, however. See *Most Intentional City*, 325n35.

29. Even before the war started, Russia's treaty with Great Britain at the end of September 1755 obligated Russia to supply fifty-five thousand troops and forty galleys in return for a subsidy of one hundred pounds sterling per annum, although when the war began it was France, not Britain, who provided Russia this subsidy and to whom Russia supplied troops. See Daniel Marston, *The Seven Years' War* (Oxford: Osprey Publishing, 2001), 15. In the long run, however, the quantity of bricks grew. By the 1780s St. Petersburg area kilns were producing fifteen million bricks annually. See Munro, *Most Intentional City*, 323n15.

30. Luppov, *Istoriia stroitel'stva*, 71. Luppov reports that in 1706 the government demanded forty thousand workers from every province to serve in the building of Narva and St. Petersburg, requiring them to travel, often by foot, to the city at their own expense for a term of two months. They received bread and fifty kopeks per month in pay, money supplied as payments from households that did not send men. The actual number of workers that arrived per these levies, however, was usually not more than thirty-four thousand. See Luppov, *Istoriia stroitel'stva*, 78.

31. Luppov, *Istoriia stroitel'stva*, 90.

32. Luppov, *Istoriia stroitel'stva*, 87.

33. Luppov, *Istoriia stroitel'stva*, 89. Luppov refutes the high death toll among the original builders of the city often repeated by foreigners; in the absence of documentary evidence, he estimates that thousands of people perished from disease and hunger, but not the tens of thousands often reported without citation.

34. V. S. Diakin et al., *Istoriia rabochikh Leningrada: 1703–1965* (Leningrad: Izd. "Nauka," 1972), 1:27. For example, the government enlisted 700 obligated laborers from Iaroslavl, Kostroma, and Novgorod to work on reconstructing the Peter and Paul Fortress in the early 1740s; officials were complaining in 1742, however, that when this group was subsequently dispatched to work on the Kronstadt Canal they discovered that only 136 had the necessary skill and experience. The rest "were only a human burden that bore no fruit." See *PSZ* 11, no. 8744,1st ser.

35. Elise Kimerling Wirtschafter, *Structures of Society: Imperial Russia's "People of Various Ranks"* (DeKalb: Northern Illinois University Press, 1994), 21.

36. Wirtschafter, *Structures of Society*, 19–26. On the lowly status of the soldiers and soldiers' sons assigned to these jobs, see Kochin, "Naselenie Peterburga," 307.

37. *SPV*, no. 21 (Mar. 14, 1755).

38. *SPV*, no. 21 (Mar. 14, 1755).

39. *SPV*, no. 21 (Mar. 14, 1755).

40. *SPV*, no. 81 (Oct. 11, 1754).

41. Luppov, *Istoriia stroitel'stva*, 72–73; Kochin, "Naselenie Peterburga," 310.

42. Luppov, *Istoriia stroitel'stva*, 74–75.

43. An October 1756 decree announcing a new military recruitment levy specifically exempted skilled workers and laborers from the Nerchinsk and Kolyvanovoskresensk Factories. *SPV*, no. 83 (Oct. 15, 1756).

44. *SPV*, no. 91 (Nov. 13, 1758) and no. 103 (Dec. 25, 1758.)

45. One such lengthy negotiation with Iarovlavl peasants is recorded in "O vyvoze zhelaiushchikh na postavku chernorabochikh liudei," RGIA, f. 469, op. 14, d. 142 (May 1826). This contract makes it clear that the agreement for peasants to cut wood for the palace during the winter was of long standing.

46. The town and province of Iaroslavl had been the primary suppliers of skilled and unskilled labor for the building and staffing of St. Petersburg ever since Peter founded the new capital. A full analysis of this phenomenon is in Evel G. Economakis, "Patterns of Migration and Settlement in Prerevolutionary St. Petersburg: Peasants from Iaroslavl and Tver Provinces," *Russian Review* 56, no. 1 (Jan. 1997): 8–24. Great landowners such as the mighty Sheremetev clan in Iaroslavl Province encouraged male peasants to go away for work seasonally, or even semi-permanently, as long as these out-migrants paid for their own passports as well as annual *obrok*. See Tracy Dennison, *The Institutional Framework of Russian Serfdom* (New York: Cambridge University Press, 2011).

47. *SPV*, no. 21 (Mar. 14, 1755).

48. Petrov, *Istoriia Sankt-Peterburga*, 387. A *sazhen* equals seven feet. A copy of Rastrelli's drawing for this foundation work, indicating long wooden pilings driven into the sloping embankment with cut stone filling in around their exposed upper sections, is reproduced in Gosudarstvennyi Muzei Istorii S.-Peterburga, *Katalog*, 58–59. This foundation supported the brick foundation of the building itself. The price of the stone was reportedly sixty-five hundred rubles.

49. Piliavskii, *Zimnii dvorets*, 20.

50. *SPV*, no. 29 (April 11, 1755).

51. *SPV*, no. 84 (Oct. 19, 1761).

52. *SPV*, no. 15 (Feb. 21, 1757).

53. A. L. Shapiro, "O roli Peterburga v razvitii vserossiiskogo rynka v XVIII-pervoi polovine XIX v.," *Goroda feodal'noi Rossii: Sbornik statei v pamiati N. V. Ustiugova*, ed. V. I. Shurikov (Moscow: Nauka, 1966), 394.

54. *SPV*, no. 39 (May 15, 1761): one *pood* equals 36.11 pounds, so about 722,200 pounds of stone.

55. *SPV*, no. 51 (June 26, 1761).

56. *SPV*, no. 6 (Jan. 21, 1754) and no. 9 (Feb. 1, 1754).

57. *SPV*, no. 86 (Oct. 28, 1754). Putilov stone continued to be required even into the 1760s.

58. Petrov, *Istoriia Sankt-Peterburga*, 408; *SPV*, no. 15 (Feb. 22, 1760), no. 23 (Mar. 21, 1760), no. 38 (May 11, 1761), no. 92 (Nov. 16, 1761), no 97 (Dec. 1761).

59. *SPV*, no. 27 (Apr. 4, 1755); Anthony G. Cross, *"By the Banks of the Neva": Chapters from the Lives and Careers of the British in Eighteenth-Century Russia* (Cambridge: Cambridge University Press, 2007), 70–71. These modern wallpapers offered a less expensive alternative to the French Gobelin-style tapestries, though the palace consumed both kinds of wall covering. Peter the Great had contracted with French masters to build an imperial wallpaper factory, requiring in 1722 that the imperial works select ten promising Russian apprentices for training. Among the Russian masters who eventually

excelled in Gobelin manufacture under Begal's supervision were Filat Kadyshev, Ivan Kobyliatnikov and Mikhailo Akhmanov. Galina Dregulias, "Shpalernaia manufaktura v Sankt-Peterburge." http:// opeterburge.ru/history_142_158.html.

60. Petrov, *Istoriia Sankt-Peterburga*, 408–10.

61. Petrov, *Istoriia Sankt-Peterburga*, 408–10.

62. Rastrelli originally painted the building a color described as sandy with a tinge of yellow, or "ochre," detailing his extravagant rococo decorations and columns by painting them white. The first complete repainting of the palace occurred in 1786, with several other repaintings in the course of the nineteenth century. Although the pigment changed somewhat over those years, the color remained basically the same until a major change took place in 1901 when both the facades and the columns were painted a dark red. Considerable confusion reigns about the color of the palace in various accounts, but for the final word, see Igor' Zimin, *Zimnii dvorets: liudi i steny: istoriia imperatorskoi rezidentsii, 1762-1917* (Moscow-St. Petersburg: Tsentropoligraf, 2012), 465–69.

63. *SPV*, no. 5 (Jan. 15, 1762), no. 7 (Jan. 22, 1762), no. 16 (Feb. 22, 1762), no. 23 (Mar. 19, 1762). Elizabeth had ordered police to arrange for the sale of surplus construction materials at a fair price "to respectable and honest people," as early as 1760. See Petrov, *Istoriia Sankt-Peterburga*, 410.

64. Andrei Bolotov, *Zhizn' i prikliucheniia Andreia Bolotova*, vol. 2, *1760-1771* (Moscow-Leningrad: Akademiia, 1931), 109.

65. Bolotov, *Zhizn' i prikliucheniia*, 110.

66. Catherine the Great had the church rededicated in honor of the Icon Not Made by Human Hands in July 1763. See Simon Dixon, "Religious Ritual at the Russian Court," in *Monarchy and Religion: The Transformation of Royal Culture in Eighteenth-Century Europe*, ed. Michael Schaich (Oxford: Oxford University Press, 2007), 226 n45.

67. *SPV*, no. 29 (Apr. 9, 1762).

68. *SPV*, no. 50 (June 21, 1762). Fireworks had been deployed regularly in imperial celebrations since Peter's time and, as elsewhere in Europe, demonstrated both scientific and literary refinement. Anna Ioannovna had decreed a regular cycle of fireworks to celebrate her own birthday, name day, and coronation anniversary, as well as New Year's. In 1732 Baron Munnich had erected a permanent "fireworks theater" on the spit of Vasilevskii Island. See Simon Werrett, *Fireworks: Pyrotechnic Arts and Sciences in European History* (Chicago: University of Chicago Press, 2010), 114–15. At Warsaw's Rituals of Power Conference in 2016, Andrei Kostin pointed out that only people situated on the palace embankment or looking out of the palace windows were in a position actually to see the pictorial allegories produced by the fireworks. Descriptions of fireworks were printed well in advance of their actual detonation in order to explain the complex symbolic images, but often what was produced did not much resemble what had been painstakingly designed and reported in advance.

69. Skodock, *Barock in Russland*, 78.

Chapter 3

1. Munro, *Most Intentional City*, 17.

2. Luppov, *Istoriia stroitel'stva*, 33. This settlement pattern persisted: census data for 1762 indicate that 55 percent of Petersburg residents lived in the Admiralty, Moskovskii, and Liteinyi sections of the city, that is the sections south of the Neva. See Petrov, *Istoriia Sankt-Peterburga*, 463–64. The Petrograd side continued to attract a sizeable population of working people, however.

3. Luppov, *Istoriia stroitel'stva*, 54. Bowing to this reality, officials set in motion plans to build several dozen houses for ferrymen there in 1725. A few years later, when new plans called for the destruction of these houses so that a new street could be built, the ferrymen and their families were just out of luck.

4. V. I. Piliavskii, *Dvortsovaia ploshchad'* (Leningrad-Moscow: Isskustvo, 1958), 11.

5. Helpful in reconstructing the social and legal milieu of eighteenth-century St. Petersburg are A. V. Darinskii and V. I. Startsev, *Istoriia Sankt-Peterburga: XVIII-XX vv.* (St. Petersburg: Glagol,

2000); *Tri veka Sankt-Peterburga*, 1:366–81; P. G. Ryndziunskii, *Gorodskoe grazhdanstvo doreformennoi Rossii* (Moscow: Ak. Nauk, 1958); B. N. Mironov, *Russkii gorod v 1740–1860 gg.* (Leningrad: Nauka, 1990).

6. Piliavskii, *Dvortsovaia ploshchad'*, 12.

7. E. Iu. Baryshnikova et al., *Panorama Millionoi ulitsy serediny XVIII v.* (St. Petersburg: Vsemirnyi Klub Peterburzhtsev, 2002), 24. This remarkable study reproduces drawings of buildings on the embankment and Millionaia collected by Swede Franz Wilhelm von Bergholts in the first half of the eighteenth century, which have been matched to available data about the buildings' proprietors and inhabitants recorded in the 1738 map by I. B. von Zicheim.

8. Baryshnikova, *Panorama*, 8.

9. Pisarenko, *Povsednevnaia zhizn'*, 18.

10. See Paul Keenan, "The Summer Gardens in the Social Life of St. Petersburg 1725–61," *Slavonic and East European Review* 88, nos. 1–2 (2010): 134–55; he reports that over the course of Elizabeth's reign the number of other city residents periodically admitted to the Summer Garden gradually expanded, but at no point in her reign were servants or working people admitted to its precincts. See also anecdotes in M. I. Pyliaev, *Staryi Peterburg. Razskazy iz byloi zhizny stolitsy* (St. Petersburg: Suvorin, 1887), 67–68.

11. Bolotov describes the extent of the Admiralty Meadow in early 1762 in *Zhizn' i prikliucheniia*, 2:108. See also the 1753 map of St. Petersburg by Makhaev viewable at http://rumsey.geogarage.com/maps/g5669010.html.

12. *PSZ* 13, no. 10032, 1st ser. (Oct. 14, 1752): 707–8. The same decrees were reiterated again the next year. See *PSZ* 13, no. 10145 (Oct. 19, 1753): 921.

13. Iu. M. Denisov, "Zimnii dvorets Rastrelli," in ed. Piliavskii and Levinson-Lessing, *Ermitazh*, 26–27. Denisov notes that turning the palace away from the Neva broke with Petersburg tradition.

14. Denisov, "Zimnii dvorets Rastrelli," 40.

15. Batowski, *Arkhitektor Rastrelli*, 38n1. In fact, both the Olsuf'ev Palace and the Shepelev Palace survived until the building of Large Hermitage (1770) and the New Hermitage (1839) respectively.

16. Rastrelli's drawings of the square, with his proposed amphitheater and equestrian statue, is reproduced in Batowski, *Arkhitektor Rastrelli*, 102.

17. Denisov, "Zimnii dvorets Rastrelli," 40. See the drawings in Gosudarstvennyi Muzei Istorii S.-Peterburga, *Katalog*, 49.

18. Denisov, "Zimnii dvorets Rastrelli," 41; Ovsiannikov, *Rastrelli*, 155.

19. A drawing of this plan appears in Gosudarstvennyi Muzei Istorii S.-Peterburga, *Katalog*, 56–57. Elizabeth approved this scheme in July 1753, according to a note in the catalogue.

20. N. Veinert, *Rossi* (Moscow: Gosud. Izd. Iskusstvo, 1939), 86; Viktor Buzinov, *Dvortsovaia ploshchad'. Neformal'nyi putevoditel'* (St. Petersburg: Izd. Ostrov, 2001), 36–37.

21. Keenan, *St. Petersburg*, 60.

22. See, for example, Ministerstvo Imperatorskogo Dvora, *Kamer-fur'erskii Tseremonial'nyi zhurnal* (*KfTsZh*), Jan. 1, 1737, which indicates that the cannon salute accompanying Empress Anna's observance of New Year's Day emanated from "cannons arrayed opposite Her Imperial Majesty's palace on the ice of the Neva."

23. Keenan, *St. Petersburg*, 68–69. Keenan lists the holidays with an "Orthodox foundation" that the eighteenth-century empresses overlaid with civic significance.

24. Munro deftly reviews Catherinian city planning in *Most Intentional City*, especially ch. 8. Although she strongly disliked Moscow, Catherine also launched urban reform and infrastructure projects in the old capital. For a full consideration of these, see Alexander M. Martin, *Enlightened Metropolis: Constructing Imperial Moscow, 1762–1855* (Oxford: Oxford University Press, 2013).

25. These were the homes of important people, however, including the sculptor Johann-Gotlieb Shwarts, one of the main creators of marble decorations in the palace, and Countess Alexandra Stroganova, née Golitsyn. It is possible to gain some insight as to how this looked from the 1810

painting, "Dvortsovaia ploshad," by I. V. Bart. http://walkspb.ru/zd/gl_shtab.html (accessed July 1, 2015).

26. Pyliaev, *Staryi Peterburg*, 202–3. The bridge over the Moika at this corner was henceforth known as Police Bridge.

27. P. N. Petrov, *Sbornik materialov dlia istorii Imperatorskoi Sanktpeterburgskoi Akademii Khudozhestv za sto let eia sushchestvovaniia* (St. Petersburg: Tipografiia Kommisionera Imp. Akademii Khudozhestv Gogenfel'da, 1864), 1:237–38: Pyliaev, *Staryi Peterburg*, 204. The competition took place in 1778.

28. This incarnation of Palace Square was short-lived, but some idea of what it looked like can be gleaned from http://walkspb.ru/zd/gl_shtab.html. See the painting by I. G. Maier, "Razvod karaula na Dvortsovoi ploshchadi" (between 1796 and 1803). When Carl Rossi received Alexander I's commission to create the famous General Staff building in this spot a few decades later he retained the scale and silhouette, incorporating many of these edifices into his new, and still extant, creation. A view of the eastern side of Palace Square c. 1810 can be seen in the painting by I. V. Bart at http://walkspb.ru/component/option,com_lightgallery/act,photos/cid,2112/Itemid,218/.

29. Pyliaev, *Staryi Peterburg*, 204.

30. Pyliaev, *Staryi Peterburg*, 175.

31. Kochin, "Naselenie Peterburga," 294.

32. Kochin, "Naselenie Peterburga," 294; A. G. Rashin, *Naselenie Rossii za 100 let, 1811–1913 gg.; Statisticheskie ocherki* (Moscow: Gos. Stat. Izd., 1956), 111.

33. After the 1837 fire the pediment figures were reproduced in a lighter material.

34. Pyliaev, *Staryi Peterburg*, 208.

35. Vera Proskurina has interpreted this singular event as a reference to Catherine's imperial pretensions and demonstrates that for contemporaries such as the poet V. P. Petrov the tournament with its female knights referenced Amazons. See Vera Proskurina, *Mify imperii. Literatura i vlast' v epokhu Ekateriny II* (Moscow: Novoe Literaturnoe Obozrenie, 2006), 11–18.

36. See the detailed description in a letter by English eyewitness Thomas Newberry reproduced by Anthony Cross, "Professor Thomas Newberry's Letter from St. Petersburg, 1766, on the Grand Carousel and Other Matters," *Slavonic and East European Review* 76, no. 3 (July 1998): 490; Ol'ga Eliseeva, *Povsednevnaia zhizn' blagorodnogo sosloviia v zolotoi vek Ekateriny* (Moscow: Molodaia Gvardiia, 2008), 201–10.

37. Pyliaev, *Staryi Peterburg*, 205; Munro, *Most Intentional City*, 80.

38. Pyliaev, *Staryi Peterburga*, 205.

39. Cross, "Professor Thomas Newberry's Letter," 491.

40. Paul A. Bushkovitch, "The Epiphany Ceremony of the Russian Court in the Sixteenth and Seventeenth Centuries," *Russian Review* 49, no. 1 (Jan. 1990): 1.

41. Bushkovitch, "The Epiphany Ceremony," 9.

42. Wortman, *Scenarios of Power*, 15–17.

43. Bushkovitch, "The Epiphany Ceremony," 16–17.

44. *SPV*, no. 3, Jan. 9, 1756.

45. *SPV*, no. 4, Jan. 11, 1762.

46. See, for example, *KfTsZh*, Jan. 6, 1778.

47. Simon Dixon says that Catherine never attended the outside portion of the ceremony after 1766, preferring to participate only in the indoors procession and then to observe from the windows. See Dixon, "Religious Ritual," in Shaich, *Monarchy and Religion*, 238.

48. See *KfTsZh*, Jan. 6, 1797.

49. *KfTsZh*, Jan. 6, 1803. One of Emperor Paul's Epiphany ceremonies, which featured a military review, is described in Adam Czartoryski, *Memoirs of Prince Adam Czartoryski and His Correspondence with Alexander I*, ed. Adam Gielgud (Orono, ME: Academic International, 1968), 1:150–51.

50. John Quincy Adams, *Memoirs*, ed. Charles Francis Adams (New York: AMS Press, 1970), 2:334.

51. Adams, *Memoirs*, 2:334.

52. Adams, *Memoirs*, 2:335. Czartoryski had reported incurring permanent injury from frostbite at the ceremony a few years earlier; Cartoryski, *Memoirs*, 1:151.

53. John T. Alexander, *Catherine the Great, Life and Legend* (New York: Oxford University Press, 1989), 261.

54. *PSZ* 22, no. 16561, 1st ser. (Aug. 8, 1787).

55. Munro, *Most Intentional City*, 229–30.

56. In Catherine's time, military parades took place a few blocks away, on Tsaritsyn Meadow (later the Field of Mars). Her husband had reviewed guards regiments arrayed before the new palace, but it was Catherine's son and grandsons, solidifying the male monopoly on the Romanov monarchy that set in after her reign, who orchestrated some of the most famous public spectacles ever beheld on Palace Square when they reviewed thousands of troops there.

57. Munro, *Most Intentional City*, 80.

Chapter 4

1. Ageeva, *Imperatorskii dvor Rossii*, 360. Ageeva's meticulous mining of scattered figures from the Palace Chancellery (*Dvortsovaia Kantseliariia*) of Peter's time and the later Court Office (*Pridvornaia Kontora*) further suggest that if all of the court institutions of the late eighteenth century, such as the Court Stables, were included, that figure would rise to three million rubles annually (see Chapter Six for the life of servants in the palace).

2. Liveried servants, such as lackeys and footmen, hailed early in the century from the lesser nobility, but over the course of the eighteenth and early nineteenth century demand for their services and the swelling number of children born into the imperial household meant that men of more humble origin found their way into this service. Wearing the costumelike uniforms was a requirement but also a perk, because staff members received a uniform allowance to procure them.

3. The great majority of court-centered entertainments at the palace were shielded from public scrutiny, as in the dramatic example of a 1790 masquerade at the Hermitage in which Catherine had men dress as women and women as men. For this occasion special curtains were hung over all the windows, "especially those facing the front," so that no one outside could see what was going on. See Proskurina, *Mify imperii*, 55.

4. Peter the Great had convoked the earliest antecedents of these public events, generally to commemorate military victories and generally outside on streets and squares. Elizabeth greatly expanded the number of "masquerades" held inside her palaces, which became elaborate court dramas in which her costumed courtiers participated in celebrating the virtues of their empress. Some courtiers adopted the European carnival tradition of wearing a black "domino," a satin robe that covered one's entire outfit, while others had special costumes made for the occasion. On the tradition of "masquerade" and how it came to Russia during Elizabeth's reign, see Jelena Pogosjan, "Masks and Masquerades at the Court of Elizabeth Petrovna (1741–1742)," in *Russian and Soviet History from the Time of Troubles to the Collapse of the Soviet Union*, ed. Steven A. Usitalo and William Benton Whisenhunt (Lanham, MD: Rowman and Littlefield, 2008), 34–50.

5. For example, in 1784 the Sardinian ambassador was impressed that Catherine moved through her palace at New Year's among a throng of "commoners." See David M. Griffiths, "Catherine II: The Republican Empress," *Jahrbücher für Geschichte Osteuropas* 21, no. 3 (1973): 340.

6. A full discussion and chart of the Table of Ranks appears in Shepelev, *Chinovnyi mir Rossii*, 131–38. There were three parallel sets of ranks, with equivalent positions: civil service, military service, and court ranks. Begun by Peter the Great, in each set the lowest rank was number 14 and the highest was number 1. The top four court ranks, those invariably included in important social and ceremonial events, included *kamerher, hof-meister, hof-marshal, shtalmeister, egermeister, obertseremoniimeister, ober-kamerher, ober-hofmeister, ober-hofmarshal, ober-shenk, ober-shtalmeister, ober-egemeister*. Female court ranks in their own right included *shtatsdam, kamerfreilin, pridvornyi freilin*, and *hof-meisterina*.

7. See Munro's discussion of these urban categories in *Most Intentional City*, 61.

8. Robert E. Jones, *Bread upon the Waters: The St. Petersburg Grain Trade and the Russian Economy, 1703–1811* (Pittsburgh: Pittsburgh University Press, 2013), 127.

9. For a fuller discussion of social categories in St. Petersburg and their influence on Catherine's provincial and town legislation between 1775 and 1785, see Janet Hartley, "Governing the City: St. Petersburg and Catherine II's Reforms," *St. Petersburg, 1703–1825*, ed. Anthony Cross (Basingstoke: Palgrave Macmillan, 2003), 99–118.

10. *KfTsZh*, Jan. 11, 1778. This contrasted with the order of Empress Elizabeth, who had decreed in 1755 that, unlike other public masquerades given in Moscow or St. Petersburg, she would not permit, "bawdy dress, sabers, daggers … crystal resembling diamonds and other stones," and "tawdriness" in general. *KfTsZh*, Jan. 9, 1755.

11. See William Coxe, *Travels in Poland, Russia, Sweden and Denmark* (London: T. Cadell and W. Davies, 1802), 139; Guseva, "Zimnii dvorets," 380. Besides the fact that foreigners may not have understood the subtle distinctions among city people, part of the issue may be that the line between townsmen and lower guild merchants did not harden until later in Catherine's reign, and that artists belonged to the ranks of the townsmen. See G. N. Komelova, "Pridvornye publichnye maskarady v Zimnem dvortse," Gosudarstvennii Ermitazh, *Zimnii dvorets: ocherki zhizni imperatorskoi rezidentsii* (St. Petersburg: Liki Rossii, 2000), 1:136.

12. Komelova, "Pridvornye publichnye maskarady," 139. It was no doubt easier for guards to exclude the uninvited at the smaller and more numerous balls held just for ranking courtiers; at these events the clothing requirements and the need for men to bear swords or daggers would have helped unmask interlopers.

13. Komelova, "Pridvornye publichnye maskarady," 140.

14. *SPV*, Jan. 9, 1755.

15. Admission to the balls was free of charge (*bezplatnyi, po biletam, poluchennym v pridvornoi kontore*), and there is no mention of any fee throughout the eighteenth and early nineteenth centuries, except for the fine for nonappearance mentioned in 1755. See Guseva, "Zimnii dvorets," 380.

16. Komelova, "Pridvornye publichnye maskarady," 134. The current Military Gallery eventually replaced these east side galleries. The suite of rooms facing the Neva received a complete makeover between 1791 and 1793, when Catherine took advantage of her grandson Alexander's impending marriage to commission her favorite architect, Giacomo Quarenghi, to transform them in the latest neoclassical style. Quarenghi reduced the total number of rooms in the Neva Suite to three, including the Antechamber, the Great Gallery, and the Concert Hall. After the fire of 1837 these rooms were restored to the same dimensions, and when Nicholas I died in 1855 his son had a large portrait of him hung in the Great Gallery. Ever since that time this room, the largest in the palace, has been known as Nicholas Hall. See Ducamp, *The Winter Palace*, 42–45. A watercolor painting of Nicholas Hall by Konstantin Ukhtomsky depicts the room as it was in 1866. See Ducamp, *The Winter Palace*, 45. We lack a visual depiction of the Rastrelli galleries as they were prior to the 1790s.

17. The Cavaliers' Hall, as it was known in Catherine's time, was the smallish room leading to "the Lantern," the windowed belvedere that protrudes from the southern façade overlooking Palace Square. In her day, performances were held in this room, and the congregation assembled here before moving into the Great Palace Church. Eduard Hau painted it as it stood a century later. See Ducamp, *The Winter Palace*, 226–27.

18. Simon Dixon, *Catherine the Great* (New York: HarperCollins, 2009), 230.

19. During Paul's brief reign, the court journals do not refer to any public masquerades in connection with New Year's, but an event that seems to follow the general pattern, hosting "notable and other persons of both sexes," took place on January 1, 1799, and was attended by both the emperor and his consort and his son, Alexander, and his wife, Elizabeth. *KfTsZh*, Jan. 1, 1799.

20. Translated by David L. Ransel, in *A Russian Merchant's Tale: The Life and Adventures of Ivan Alekseevich Tolchënov, Based on His Diary* (Bloomington: Indiana University Press, 2009), 56–57. The

original is in Ivan A. Tolchenov, *Zhurnal ili zapiska zhizni i prikliuchenii Ivana Alekseevicha Tolchenova* (Moscow: Akademiia Nauk SSSR, 1974), 64.

21. Ransel, *A Russian Merchant's Tale*, 57.

22. Ransel, *A Russian Merchant's Tale*, 58. As Ransel notes, this episode reveals the special concern of police officials to preserve public order in the capital by restraining grain prices, even as the government also backed merchants in labor disputes along the shipment route.

23. *KfTsZh*, Jan. 8, 1778. A *namestnichestvo* was a region ruled by a governor-general.

24. Each of these receptions is recorded in *KhTsZh* for the dates given here.

25. Clifford Geertz, *Negara: The Theatre State in Nineteenth-Century Bali* (Princeton, NJ: Princeton University Press, 1980), 13.

26. *SPV*, Aug. 2, 1762, contains an announcement that Rastrelli and his family would soon depart Russia for his native land and invited those who had business with the architect to visit him at his home on Nevskii Prospekt, "across from Gostinyi Dvor." Rastrelli lived at 46 Nevskii Prospekt, adjoining the site of the famous future shopping arcade Passazh.

27. Skodock, *Barock in Russland*, 79–81. Rastrelli's assignment, apparently, was to complete the decorating of the two Courland palaces he had built in the 1740s. He also completed designs for an Orthodox church in Jelgava and corresponded with Frederick the Great, perhaps in hopes of a commission.

28. NLP, Special Collections Wil. Kat. Akc. 2189/66e, 15.

29. A. F. Krasheninnikov, "Pervye gody posle Rastrelli," in Piliavskii and Levinson-Lessing, *Ermitazh*, 65.

30. *SPV*, no. 14 (Jan. 14, 1771); Skodock, *Barock in Russland*, 82.

31. Today these rooms stand essentially as Rastrelli left them, as they were restored to his specifications after the 1837 fire.

32. Krasheninnikov, "Pervye gody," 66.

33. This throne room and its antechambers no longer exist and are known only through partial drawings. The suite stood in the vicinity of the current Alexander Hall. See Krasheninnikov, "Pervye gody," 70–72. The Opera House, no longer there, lay in the southwestern corpus of the palace.

34. Krasheninnikov, "Pervye gody," 71.

35. R. D. Liulina and V. I. Piliavskii, "Malyi Ermitazh," in Piliavskii and Levinson-Lessing, *Ermitazh*, 185. At some point stables reappeared, east of the Small Hermitage, only to be finally removed in the 1840s, in connection with the building of the New Hermitage.

36. Dixon, *Catherine the Great*, 191–92.

37. Krasheninnikov, "Pervye gody," 67.

38. Krasheninnikov, "Pervye gody, 72.

39. Igor' Zimin, *Detskii mir imperatorskikh rezidentsii: byt monarkhov i ikh okruzhenie* (Moscow–St. Petersburg: Tsentrpoligraf, 2011), 438.

40. V. I. Piliavskii and R. D. Liulina, "Novyi Ermitazh," in Piliavskii and Levinson-Lessing, *Ermitazh*, 223.

41. Antoine Chenevière, *Russian Furniture: The Golden Age, 1780–1840* (New York: Vendome Press, 1988), 26. A similar restriction hit other imported decorative objects in 1778, which encouraged St. Petersburg's bronze smiths to advance their technique. In his capacity as president of the Academy of Arts, Count Alexander Stroganov promoted local craftsmen, particularly those who worked in native hard stone. Catherine's son, Paul, briefly removed these tariffs when he was building his new residence, the Michael Castle, in the city. See Emmanuel Ducamp, "The Production of Russian Bronzes in the Late Eighteenth Century," at http://christies.com/lotfinder/LotDetailsPrintable. aspx?intObjectID=5461768.

42. Munro, *Most Intentional City*, 219–20.

43. Chenevière, *Russian Furniture*, 40–41. One fantastic piece created by an unknown St. Petersburg master in the 1760s is a four-drawer writing desk with engraved ivory plaques. There were over fifty craftsmen working in carved ivory in the city at that point.

44. Chenevière, *Russian Furniture*, 38.

45. Chenevière, *Russian Furniture*, 83–85. One of the most famous extant Meyer pieces was commissioned in 1797 by Catherine's son, Paul: one of six giltwood copies of Peter the Great's silver throne, which is depicted in an 1863 painting by Eduard Hau. See Ducamp, *The Winter Palace*, 54–55.

46. Chenevière, *Russian Furniture*, 100–101.

47. Chenevière, *Russian Furniture*, 83. Chenevière's book provides photographs of several of Maria Fedorovna's pieces, often part of creations made in the workshop of Heinrich Gambs. The book also reproduces a remarkable document written by the future empress, "Description of the Palace of Pavlovsk," in which she inventoried with a detailed description many of the treasures she had collected. She described her own work on several of the pieces, indicating that she worked in grisaille, ivory, amber, and steel engraving. Chenevière, *Russian Furniture*, 296–301. One of the desks the future Alexander I made with Christian Meyer in 1790 is depicted in a painting by Eduard Hau, standing in the study of Tsar Alexander II in the 1860s. See Ducamp, *The Winter Palace*, 140–41.

48. The most spectacular thing Roentgen brought along as an introduction to the Russian empress was the "Mechanikus," a mahogany desk whose hidden mechanisms produced music. See Wolfram Koeppe, "Gone with the Wind to the Western Hemisphere—Selling Off Furniture by David Roentgen and Other Decorative Arts of the Eighteenth Century," *Canadian-American Slavic Studies* 43, no. 4 (2009): 248–50; Chenevière, *Russian Furniture*, 72–74.

49. Chenevière, *Russian Furniture*, 143.

50. Chenevière, *Russian Furniture*, 147–48, 291–92.

51. Chenevière, *Russian Furniture*, 26.

52. I. G. Georgi, *Opisanie rossiisko-imperatorskogo stolichnogo goroda Sankt-Peterburga i dostopamiatnostei v okrestnostiakh onogo, s planom* (St. Petersburg: LIGA, 1996), 195. Georgi was best known for his explorations of Siberia, particularly the Baikal region. He became an academician of the Russian Academy of Sciences in 1783 and first published his survey of St. Petersburg in German in 1790. The Russian edition came out in 1794, and Georgi died in the city in 1802.

53. Georgi, *Opisanie*, 204.

54. Georgi, *Opisanie*, 197.

55. Chenevière, *Russian Furniture*, 30.

56. The suite is depicted in an 1864 painting by Eduard Petrovich Hau. See Ducamp, *The Winter Palace*, 196–97. Bauman's chairs were salvaged from the fire and restored in 1839.

57. Chenevière, *Russian Furniture*, 291, http://muzmebeli.ru/ist-meb/mebmastera.htm. As a bronze smith, Bauman created large chandeliers of patinated bronze in the form of classical urns. See Ducamp, "Russian Bronzes." The term "patinated" refers to the common practice in bronze and other metalwork of applying a finish to a piece at the initial time of fabrication, often to add visual interest and to make the piece appear old.

58. Chenevière, *Russian Furniture*, 277. For beautiful pictures and a thorough history of the decorative stone in the Winter Palace and elsewhere, see Chenevière, *Russian Furniture*, 259–81.

59. Krasheninnikov, "Pervye gody," 82. This new corpus solved a long-running problem about how to create a sufficiently splendid throne room in the Winter Palace. For many years Felten and others tried to redesign the Great Neva Gallery (*Belyi zal*) to accommodate rows of massive marble columns. But all of the plans necessitated substantial retrofitting of the lower floor to accommodate the added weight—which would have profoundly upset palace housekeeping, as the kitchens were located below this room. See Krasheninnikov, "Pervye gody," esp. 78.

60. There are many brief descriptions of Catherine's exuberant pan-European art collecting and the important acquisitions that were the foundation of the Hermitage museum. See, for example, Piotrovskii et al., *Ermitazh*, 18–21; Pierre Descargues, *Art Treasures of the Hermitage* (New York: Harry N. Abrams, 1977), 21–25. Cynthia Whittaker summarizes Catherine's most significant acquisitions and her motives for collecting, which included projecting wealth and imperial good taste to rival monarchs. See Cynthia Hyla Whittaker, "Catherine the Great and the Art of Collecting: Acquiring the Paintings that Founded the Hermitage," in *Word and Image in Russian History: Essays in Honor of Gary Marker*, ed. Maria di Salvo et al. (Boston: Academic Studies Press, 2015): 147–71.

61. A. Somov, *Kartiny Imperatorskago Ermitazha* (St. Petersburg: Tip. A. Iakobson, 1859), 10. Somov reports that Catherine had been dismayed to discover a recently acquired painting, "Descent from the Cross," locked away in a storage room on the palace's upper floors while she was scouting premises for the Legislative Commission. This sparked her determination to find room to display the Romanov art collection. Although Somov says this was a Rubens, the painting in question was almost certainly Nicolas Poussin's "Descent from the Cross," acquired in 1769, long before Alexander I acquired both the Rubens and the Rembrandt paintings by the same name in 1814.

62. S. A. Kasparinskaia, "Muzei Rossii i vliianie gosudarstvennoi politiki na ikh razvitie (XVIII–nach. XXv.)," in S. A. Kasparinskaia, ed., *Muzei i vlast': sb. nauchniykh trudov* (Moscow: Nauchno-issl. In-t kultury, 1991), pt. 1, 15–17.

63. Z. E. Mordvinova, "Smol'nyi Institut v epokhu Imperatritsy Ekateriny II (1764–1796)," *Istoricheskii vestnik* 136, no. 6 (June 1914): 987–1001. http://historydoc.edu.ru/catalog.asp?ob_no=14836&cat_ob_no=12316. Catherine, having acquired complete collections of Voltaire and Diderot, also made the Winter Palace an impressive library.

64. A. B. Kamenskii, "The Congress of People's Deputies of 1767," *Russian Studies in History* 33, no. 4 (1995): 40–41. Odnodvortsy were state peasants who owned small homesteads, in contrast to the larger group of state peasants who owned and worked communal land. The groups omitted from this assembly were the private serfs, the clergy, and members of the military—that is, about 26 percent of the population. See also Oleg A. Omel'chenko, "The 'Legitimate Monarchy' of Catherine the Second: Enlightened Absolutism in Russia," *Russian Studies in History* 33, no. 4 (1995): 82–83.

65. Paul Dukes, *Catherine the Great and the Russian Nobility: A Study Based on the Materials of the Legislative Commission of 1767* (Cambridge: Cambridge University Press, 1967), 82. The predominant theory, which Dukes suggests, is that the particularly vexed question of the rights of the Baltic noblemen was coming to a head in December 1767.

66. Cathcart to Weymouth, 19 Aug. 1768 (OS), *Sbornik Imperatorskago russkago istoricheskago obshchestva* 12 (St. Petersburg, 1873): 357. The committees met separately in different rooms of the palace.

67. Cathcart to Weymouth, *Sbornik Imperatorskago russkago*, 357.

68. Cathcart to Weymouth, *Sbornik Imperatorskago russkago*, 358; see also Dixon, *Catherine the Great*, 181–82.

69. Cathcart to Weymouth, *Sbornik Imperatorskago russkago*, 358 Like many English observers Cathart disparaged the low status of these men admitted to the palace, who reminded him of "the most ignorant of our petty merchants and shopkeepers in Great Britain and Ireland," assembled as though they were "deputies of those nations in America . . . unacquainted with the general principles, which constitute the basis of good government."

70. Among those arguing that the work of this commission was, in fact, important for later eighteenth- and nineteenth-century legislation is Isabel de Madariaga, in *Catherine the Great: A Short History* (New Haven: Yale University Press, 2002), esp. 26–27.

71. Dixon, *Catherine the Great*, 232.

72. Catherine to Potemkin, after April 10, 1774, in *Ekaterina II i G. A. Potemkin. Lichnaia perepiska, 1769–1791*, comp. V. S. Lopatin (Moscow: Nauka, 1997), 23.

73. Elisabeth Vigée Le Brun, *Memoirs*, trans. Lionel Strachey (New York: Doubleday, Page, 1903), 117–18.

74. Wortman insists that, between the deaths of Peter the Great and Alexander I, Russia's rulers did not make a great show of imperial funerals, more often seeking to suggest deliverance from than commemoration of past reigns. The one exception was the elaborate display that Paul mounted to dignify the memory of his murdered father. See *Scenarios of Power*, 130.

75. Dixon, *Catherine the Great*, 318–19. Dixon attributes the "temple" to Rinaldi, but if Rinaldi was its designer it was not built for this purpose originally, as he had died in 1794. See Lindsey Hughes, "Funerals of the Russian Emperors," in Schaich, *Monarchy and Religion*, 413–14. Hughes surveys all of the eighteenth-century lyings in state and confirms that before 1796 only courtiers and selected citizens paid respects to the remains of a deceased monarch. Catherine's body was in fact transferred

from the throne room, where family and intimates had paid respects for several days, to the Great Gallery, in order to accommodate the masses.

76. See, for example, Ransel, *A Russian Merchant's Tale*, 193–94; V. N. Golovina, *Memoirs of Countess Golovine, a Lady at the Court of Catherine II* (London: D. Nutt, 1910), 130–32.

Chapter 5

1. Dixon, *Catherine the Great*, 301.

2. Bruce Lincoln makes the point that "looking at how the Winter Palace figured into the lives of the people of St. Petersburg can reveal the ways the Romanovs worked to shape the contours of their world," but he also claims that by the early nineteenth century the palace had become more separate from the life of the city than formerly. Examples of public use to which Nicholas put the Winter Palace offered in this section suggest that just the opposite was true. See Lincoln, *Sunlight at Midnight*, 79.

3. Heinrich Storch, *The Picture of St. Petersburg* (London: Longman, 1801), 86. He estimated this number at 230,000 in 1800, which apparently did not include soldiers, who probably numbered at least 35,000.

4. Karl F. German, *Statisticheskaia izsledovaniia otnositel'no Rossiiskoi imperii*, pt. 1, *O Narodonaselenii* (St. Petersburg: Imp. Ak. Nauk, 1819), 17.

5. Storch, *Picture of St. Petersburg*, 85; German, *Statischeskaia izsledovaniia*, 269

6. It is true, however, that if Stepan Khalturin's bomb had achieved its goal, Alexander II would have succumbed there in 1880 (see Chapter Eight below). Alexander Kerensky's Provincial Government was overthrown when hostile troops entered the palace to arrest its members in November 1917 but Kerensky had already fled by that time.

7. Igor' V. Zimin, *Liudi Zimnego dvortsa. Monarshie osoby, ikh favority i slugi* (Moscow: Tsentrpoligraf, 2015), 395, 404. From the earliest days of the Winter Palace there was a guardhouse (*gauptvakhta*) in the western corpus, near the exit to the great courtyard in the center of the building. Nearby, just outside the Admiralty side entrance to the palace, there was a parade ground for the guards.

8. Marie-Pierre Rey, *Alexander I: The Tsar Who Defeated Napoleon* (DeKalb: Northern Illinois University Press, 2012), 70–71. From the Guards' perspective, the new monarch's most objectionable innovation was his decree that they, along with all other regiments, must perform "full-time service under iron discipline," meticulously scrutinized by his new inspection corps.

9. Czartoryski, *Memoirs*, 1:141.

10. Wortman, *Scenarios of Power*, 86. These changing of the guards ceremonies commenced the day after Catherine's death.

11. Wortman, *Scenarios of Power* 94–95.

12. Rey, *Alexander I*, 73.

13. This was not the currently standing version of St. Isaac's Cathedral but, rather, the third of the four churches that have stood approximately on this site. The church that stood on Senate Square in 1803 had been commissioned by Catherine, designed by Antonio Rinaldi, and summarily finished by Paul after he diverted much of the marble to build his "castle." By all accounts the edifice was an ugly pastiche, and Alexander opened an architectural competition for its replacement in 1809. The current St. Isaac's was built between 1818 and 1858, to a design by Auguste Montferrand.

14. *KfTsZh*, May 16, 1803.

15. Munro carefully evaluates the population figures available and concludes that in 1801 there were 13,200 nobles of both sexes living in St. Petersburg. This is a much easier figure to arrive at than that for "merchants." Munro comes up with a number of 14,300, inclusive of family members, for people engaged in commercial activity. He cites Storch and German to the effect that there were 1,750 (male) merchants registered in all three guilds as of 1790, but he suspects that the number was somewhat higher. If we guess that each merchant family may have included three people eligible to

attend this ball, by 1801 there were at least 5,000–6,000 Russian "merchants" in the city strictly by *soslovie*. Since fewer than one-third of these people would have been first guild merchants, it seems that the majority of those eligible to attend from the first merchant guild did so, particularly when we consider that some of the merchants counted by the court officials were foreigners. See Munro, *Most Intentional City*, 57–64.

16. Quarenghi built this room to connect the Winter Palace to the Small Hermitage building along its eastern flank, and it was inaugurated on St. George's Day in 1795. One of the largest rooms in the palace, it served Emperor Paul as a throne room, the title by which it is best known today. Paul installed Anna Ioannovna's throne there in 1797. Konstantin Ukthomsky's painting of the room in 1862 appears in Ducamp, *The Winter Palace*, 63.

17. *KfTsZh*, Jan. 1, 1803.

18. Rey, *Alexander I*, 298.

19. The original Narva gate grew more and more dilapidated before Nicholas I commissioned a permanent structure, which was designed by Vasili Stasov and erected between 1827 and 1834.

20. A. D. Zakharov was commissioned in 1806 to undertake a complete remodeling of the old building, which no longer sufficed to house the navy and whose wharves were inadequate to handle the ships now arriving at the northern capital. The wharves moved downstream. The clean lines of the classical building complemented the Winter Palace and General Staff building. See Piliavskii, *Dvortsovaia ploshchad'*, 17–18.

21. Iu. A. Egorov, *The Architectural Planning of St. Petersburg* (Athens: Ohio University Press, 1969), 193–95. See also W. Bruce Lincoln, *Between Heaven and Hell: The Story of a Thousand Years of Artistic Life in Russia* (New York: Viking, 1998), 109–14. On the role of the parade ground in Nicholas I's reign, see Wortman, *Scenarios of Power*, 146–48.

22. http://www.rusartist.org/stepan-stepanovich-pimenov-1784-1833/#.Wi7MUoU3su0. The statue was the work of Vasili Demut-Malinovsky and Stepan Pimenov, the son of a Petersburg customs official who had been admitted to the Academy of Arts at age eleven on signs of artistic promise. Pimenov's sculptures portray patriotic themes and allegories in nearly all the great St. Petersburg buildings of the early nineteenth century: the Mining Institute, Kazan Cathedral, Elagin Palace, and the Admiralty. Nicholas I later hired him to reprise his victory chariot atop the new Narva Gate, but the emperor grew dissatisfied with his "independence and boldness of opinion" and fired him in 1830. Demut-Malinovsky worked on many of the same buildings as Pimenov and also won commissions for several patriotic pieces after the war, including Barclay de Tolly's tomb and the Alexander Column.

23. Richard Stites, *The Four Horsemen: Riding to Liberty in Post-Napoleonic Europe* (New York: Oxford University Press, 2014), 245–47; Rey, *Alexander I*, 318–23.

24. Rey, *Alexander I*, 308–9.

25. Alexander I. Mikhailovskii-Danilevskii, *Imperator Aleksandr Pervyi i ego spodvizniki: Voennaia galereia Zimiago Dvortsa* (St. Petersburg: P. Pechatkin, 1845–1849), ii.

26. Rastrelli had designed this building for D. A. Shepelev, Elizabeth's *ober-hofmarshal* in the late 1740s. It was razed in 1839 in order to build the New Hermitage on that site. See Piliavskii and Liulina, "Novyi Ermitazh," 223.

27. The painting by A. Martynov depicting a visit from the emperor amid several of the military gallery paintings is reproduced in V. Glinka and A. Pomarnatskii, *Voennaia galereia Zimnego dvortsa* (Leningrad: Izd. Avrora, 1974), 18–19.

28. Glinka and Pomarnatskii, *Voennaia galereia*, 15–16, 20. Glinka maintains that many of Dawe's private customers returned their portraits for correction of the color shortly after they were completed.

29. Stites discusses this society in *Serfdom, Society, and the Arts*, esp. 37.

30. Lincoln, *Between Heaven and Hell*, 124–25; Glinka and Pomarnatskii, *Voennaia galereia*, 30. A recent study of George Dawe explicates more thoroughly the problem of copyists and their role in the studios of established painters. See Galina Andreeva, *Genii voiny, blaga i krasoty: Pisal*

Korolevskii Akademik Dzhordzh Dou (Moscow: IKOM Rossii, 2012), 176–78. Andreeva writes that Golike remained grateful for the support of the famous artist throughout his life. Andreeva, *Genii voiny*, 181.

31. Glinka and Pomarnatskii, *Voennaia galereia*, 22; Stites, *Serfdom, Society, and the Arts*, 340. Stites says Poliakov was freed by Nicholas himself.

32. Mikhailovski-Danilevski, *Imperator*, ii; Piotrovskii et al., *Ermitazh*, 89. Dawe's last painting was completed in 1828, at which point Nicholas made him first portrait painter of the Russian Imperial Court. Alexander's contemporary Mme. Choiseul-Gouffier observed that the emperor disliked sitting for portraits and rarely did so. An exception was the portrait for which he sat in 1814 at the Paris studio of the renowned François Gérard. See Sophia de Choiseul-Gouffier, *Historical Memoirs of the Emperor Alexander I and the Court of Russia* (Chicago: McClurg, 1900), 1:83.

33. Ducamp, *The Winter Palace*, 16–17.

34. Alexander died in mid-November at Taganrog, and the circumstances of his death gave rise to rumors that he had staged his death in order to undertake the life of a monk.

35. A. M. Bulatov, letter dated Dec. 25, 1825, cited in M. V. Nechkina, ed., *Vosstanie Dekabristov: Dokumenty* (Moscow: Izd. Nauka, 1984), 18:299.

36. Nechkina, *Vosstanie Dekabristov*, Bulatov letter, Dec. 25, 1825, 299.

37. M. V. Nechkina, ed., "Vsepodanneishii doklad vysochaishe uchrezhdennoi Sledstvennoi komissii ot 30 maia 1826 gg.," in Nechkina, *Vosstanie Dekabristov*, 17:57; this remark is attributed to N. A. Panov.

38. Eventually the commission of inquiry outgrew its quarters in the palace and moved across the river to the fortress. The commission members began planning this move during the breaking of the ice in March 1826 but did not complete it until May. See the record of Session 77 in Nechkina, *Vosstanie Dekabristov*, 16:128. Some officials had objected in the first place to interrogating the conspirators inside the palace.

39. Testimony of Lt. A. S. Gorozhanskii of the Life Guards, in Nechkina, *Vosstanie Dekabristov*, 18:263, and others. The room Decembrists referred to as the White Hall (*Belyi zal'*) was the large Neva-side reception hall in which balls were held, known after Nicholas's death (and today) as Nicholas Hall. The room that is today referred to as the White Hall was not yet built; it is located in the southwest corpus of the palace, part of a beautiful suite of rooms created for the bride of Alexander II in 1841. It can be seen in the 1865 painting of Luigi Premazzi, in Ducamp, *The Winter Palace*, 154–55.

40. M. V. Nechkina, ed., "Vsepodanneishii doklad vysochaishe uchrezhdennoi Sledstvennoi komissii ot 30 maia 1826 gg.," in Nechkina, *Vosstanie Dekabristov*, 17:52.

41. Nechkina, *Vosstanie Dekabristov*, 17:52.

42. Nicholas Riasanovsky elaborates on this political doctrine in *Nicholas I and Official Nationality in Russia, 1825–1855* (Berkeley: University of California Press, 1959).

43. Richard Wortman, "National Narratives in the Representation of Nineteenth-Century Russian Monarchy," in Richard Wortman, *Russian Monarchy: Representation and Rule: Collected Articles* (Boston: Academic Studies Press, 2013), 154–56.

44. Ducamp, *The Winter Palace*, 60. Edouard Hau's 1862 painting depicts the Military Gallery. See Ducamp, *The Winter Palace*, 61.

45. Ducamp, *The Winter Palace*, 17. It is not clear what painting of Alexander was first hung in this gallery. Although he did not sit for Dawe in St. Petersburg, there is some possibility he did so when visiting London in 1814. Also by 1826 it is likely that the Gérard portrait completed in 1817 was hanging in the foyer of the Hermitage Theater; some authorities state that Dawe produced an equestrian portrait of Alexander for the gallery's opening, though not from life. See https://commons.wikimedia. org/wiki/File:Alexander_I_by_Fran%C3%A7ois_G%C3%A9rard.jpg; and http://historicalportraits. com/Gallery.asp?Page=Item&ItemID=909&Desc=Emperor-Alexander-I-%7C-George-Dawe. This picture no longer exists because, apparently, it was the only one not rescued during the great fire of 1837. During the reconstruction Nicholas commissioned his favorite portraitist, Franz Kreuger, to paint a new likeness of Alexander, and this equestrian portrait was placed on the site of the ruined picture after the restoration of the gallery in 1838. See Piotrovskii et al., *Ermitazh*, 89. Kreuger also

produced portraits of the Prussian king Frederick William III (the empress's father), and P. Krafft provided a painting of the Austrian emperor Francis I. These three new portraits brought the total in the gallery to 332.

46. *Russkii invalid* 325 (28 Dec. 1827): 1300–1301.

47. *SPV*, no. 306 (Dec. 30, 1832). See below for a discussion of the Palace Grenadiers.

48. Mikhailovskii-Danilevskii, *Imperator*, vi. For a full description of Mikhailovskii-Danilevskii's historical works, see Alexander Mikaberidze, *Russian Officer Corps of the Revolutionary and Napoleonic Wars, 1792–1815* (New York: Savas Beatie, 2005), 254–55.

49. Plunkett, *Queen Victoria*, 146–47.

50. See paintings of the Grenadiers in the palace, including one Mikhail Kulakov, by Vladimir Poiarkov from 1915. See https://img-fotki.yandex.ru/get/205820/375901008.23/0_152153_53c1c791_orig.jpg.

51. S. A. Grinev, *Istoriia roty dvortsovykh grenader* (St. Petersburg, 1912), 1. In later years Nicholas's special unit included veterans of Guards units who had served honorably for at least twenty years and who had been recognized for exceptional service. After 1900 all army veterans with such a record were eligible. Officers had to be recipients of the St. George's Cross who had been promoted from the ranks of enlisted men.

52. Grinev, *Istoriia roty*, 216.

53. Although the architectural ensemble of Palace Square was complete, Nicholas nonetheless commissioned some substantial reconstruction and remodeling including, most dramatically, a new headquarters for the Guards that incorporated the old Exercisehaus on the east edge of the square. Alexander Briullov designed this building, which went up between 1837 and 1843. See I. E. Grabar', *Istoriia russkogo iskusstva* (Moscow: Izd. "Nauka," 1964), vol. 8, bk. 2, 472–73.

54. P. N. Stolpianskii, *Peterburg: Kak voznik, osnovalsia i ros Sankt-Piterburkh* (Petrograd, 1918; repr., St. Petersburg: Nauchno-izdatel'skii tsentr NeGA, 1995), 204.

55. *SPV*, no. 205 (Sept. 1, 1832). The erection of the column took place on August 30.

56. The State Hermitage Museum: Exhibitions. http://hermitagemuseum.org/html_En/05/hm5_7_13_1.html.

57. I. V. Roskovshenko, "Peterburg v 1831–1832 gg.," *Russkaia starina* 101 (Feb. 1900): 489.

58. Grinev, *Istoriia roty*, 219–22.

59. Grigory Kaganov, *Images of Space: St. Petersburg in the Visual and Verbal Arts*, trans. Sidney Monas (Stanford: Stanford University Press, 1997), 98–99.

60. Wortman, *Scenarios of Power*, 149.

Chapter 6

1. The relationship between mystification and demystification of monarchy is intelligently addressed, and the notion of linear chronology between them challenged, in Deploige and Deneckere, *Mystifying the Monarch*, 9–21; Cannadine, "The Context."

2. Rebecca Friedman asserts that "patriarchy and domesticity were intimately connected within Nicholas's Russia," in her study of the university system. See Rebecca Friedman, *Masculinity, Autocracy, and the Russian University* (Basingstoke: Palgrave Macmillan, 2005), 101. There are more biographies of Nicholas I than of any other nineteenth-century Russian ruler. The main works are N. F. Dubrovnin, ed., *Materialy i cherty k biografii Imperatora Nikolaia I i k istorii ego tsarstvovaniia* (St. Petersburg: Sbornik Imperatorskogo russkago istoricheskago obshchestva, 1896); N. K. Schilder, *Imperator Nikolai Pervyi: Ego zhizn' i tsarstvovanie* (St. Petersburg: A. S. Suvorin, 1903); Riasanovsky, *Official Nationality in Russia*; A. E. Presniakov, *Emperor Nicholas I of Russia: The Apogee of Autocracy, 1825–1855* (Gulf Breeze, FL: Academic International Publishers, 1974); W. Bruce Lincoln, *Nicholas I: Emperor and Autocrat of All the Russias* (DeKalb: Northern Illinois University Press, 1989). A recent collection of memoirs and archival materials usefully annotated is A. N. Tsamutali, Andreeva, T. V., eds., *Nikolai I: lichnost' i epokha. Novye materialy* (St. Petersburg: Nestor-Istoriia, 2007).

3. Schama, "Domestication of Majesty," 155, 183.

4. Wortman stresses the familial aspects of Nicholas's "domestic" and "dynastic" scenario of power, noting the positive impression his family sentiment made on foreigners, including his detractor the Marquis de Custine, who believed the emperor's domestic virtues helped him to govern; see Wortman, *Scenarios of Power*, 1:314–31.

5. This summary is drawn from the daily journal of court activities. See, for e.g., *KfTsZh* for the years 1810, 1812, 1821.

6. Nicholas did take care with artistic portrayals of his family. He did not sit for a portrait *en famille*, as his grandson Alexander III and great-grandson Nicholas II would do photographically. But he commissioned several portraits of his wife, children, and grandchildren, sometimes in family groupings such as, for example, George Dawe's portrait of the empress and two of her children and Christina Robertson's 1849 painting of his daughter, the Grand Duchess Maria Nikolaevna, and her four children. He was the first tsar to issue a "family ruble," in 1835. The commemorative coin, issued not to the public but to ranking noblemen, was engraved on one side with his own visage and on the reverse with the face of the empress, surrounded by the couple's seven children. See http://coins-auctioned.com/auctions/coins/russia/.

7. Ducamp, *The Winter Palace*, 14–15.

8. Piotrovskii et al., *Ermitazh*, 78.

9. Piotrovskii et al., *Ermitazh*, 78. The peregrinations of the family inside the palace can be traced from reproduced paintings of interiors from the mid-nineteenth century, reproduced in Ducamp, *The Winter Palace*, and in publications of the State Museum of the Hermitage, including L. E. Torshina and E. Trubkina, *Zhilye pokoi. Imperatorskoi rezidentsii* (St. Petersburg: State Museum of the Hermitage, 2009).

10. On their family life, see I. N. Bozherianov, *Zhizneopisanie imperatritsy Aleksandry Fedorovny, Suprugi Imperatora Nikolaia Pervogo* (St. Petersburg: Tip. Tov. "Obshchestvennaia Pol'za," 1898); Grand Duchess Olga Nikolaevna, "Son iunosti: zapiski docheri Imperatora Nikolaia I velikoi kniagini Ol'gi Nikolaevny, korolevy Viurtembergskoi (otryvki)," in *Nikolai pervyi i ego vremia. Dokumenty, pis'ma, dnevniki, memuary, svidetel'stva sovremennikov i trudy istorikov*, ed. B. N. Tarasov (Moscow, Olma-Press, 2000): 2:155–91; Lincoln, *Nicholas I*, 156–59. In the late 1830s Nicholas befriended Varvara Neliudova, the niece of his father's mistress. The younger Neliudova was appointed a lady-in-waiting to Alexandra Fedorovna during what daughter Olga termed a "seventeen-year friendship" and what other courtiers whispered was a very discreet affair. Neliudova continued her post, living in the palace for the rest of her life, long after Nicholas's death. See "Son iunosti," 248–49.

11. Torshina and Trubkina, *Zhilye pokoi*, 7–9.

12. Charlotte Disbrowe, *Old Days in Diplomacy: Recollections of a Closed Century* (London: Jarrold and Sons, 1903), 127, 128.

13. I. N. Rybnikov, "Imperator Nikolai i moskovskoe kupechestvo na obede v Zimnem dvortse 13 Maia 1833 g.," in *Nikolai pervyi i ego vremia*, 2:106–12.

14. Rybnikov, "Imperator Nikolai," 108.

15. Rybnikov, "Imperator Nikolai," 106.

16. On the tsarevich's majority ceremony, see Wortman, *Scenarios of Power*, 1:359; Grand Duchess Olga Nikolaevna, "Son iunosti," 162.

17. Grand Duchess Olga Nikolaevna, "Son iunosti," 280.

18. Pushkarev, *Opisanie*, 1:370. Obviously, Pushkarev exaggerates here, as Petersburg's poor people came nowhere near this ball.

19. Pushkarev, *Opisanie*, 1:370.

20. Pushkarev, *Opisanie*, 3:134. The official announcement in *SPV* still offered tickets to "all nobles and merchants." See *SPV*, no. 1 (Jan. 3, 1830).

21. Pushkarev, *Opisanie*, 3:135.

22. Nicholas I, Emperor of Russia, "Imperator Nikolai Pavlovich v ego pis'makh," 6; the letter was dated Jan. 4/16 1832. Nicholas was probably thinking of the Polish rebellion of 1830–1831, only

recently subdued by Russian troops under the command of Paskevich; the French Revolution of 1830; and cholera epidemic that had ravaged Russia throughout 1831.

23. G. T. Polilov-Sievertsev, *Nashi dedy-kuptsy: bytovyia kartiny nachala XIX stoletiia* (St. Petersburg: A. F. Devrien, 1900s [*sic*]), 132.

24. Court Araps, described by Zimin, *Detskii mir*, 410–18, were the most famous of costumed palace servants. Many paintings depict Araps guarding vestibules, staircases, and the corridors outside the children's suites and other rooms, such as the painting of the Arab Dining Room by K. A. Ukhtomskii in Ducamp, *The Winter Palace*, 79. According to Zimin it was members of Russian high society who first brought to Russia the European court custom of employing tall, costumed African palace guards, in the late seventeenth century. Their status was already customary in Russia by the time of Peter the Great. In his famous dictionary, V. I. Dal' insists that "araps" were not Arabs but, rather, dark-skinned men of African descent.

25. Polilov-Sievertsev, *Nashi dedy-kuptsy*, 135.

26. Polilov-Sievertsev, *Nashi dedy-kuptsy*, 136–37.

27. The carnival tradition of celebrating during the final week before Lent by presenting elaborate puppet and other shows at temporary theaters was widespread across Russia, and by the nineteenth century professional and semi-professional impresarios staged such productions in the capital. The Shrovetide festival in St. Petersburg took place in Admiralty and Palace Squares between 1827 and 1872, when they moved to the less traffic-snarling Field of Mars. The festival was not held in the city after 1898. The 1869 painting by Konstantin Makovsky gives an impression of the scene. See A. Leifert, "Balagany," in *Peterburgskie balagany* (1922; repr., St. Petersburg: Giperion, 2000), 36, 107.

28. Roskovshenko, "Peterburg v 1831–1832gg.," 486.

29. Roskovshenko, "Peterburg v 1831–1832gg.," 486. Many memoirists and writers of sketches described the outlandish gaiety and shenanigans of both performers and audience at the Shrovetide Festival in the Admiralty and Palace Squares. For example, see Dmitri Grigorovich, "The Petersburg Organ-Grinders," in Nikolai Nekrasov, ed., *Petersburg: The Physiology of a City*, trans. Thomas Gaiton Marullo (Evanston, IL: Northwestern University Press: 2009), 90–91n26.

30. Roskovshenko, "Peterburg v 1831–1832gg.," 486.

31. John Reynell Morell, *Russia as it is; and Turkey, Past and Present; Their History, Resources, Court, and People* (London: Geo. Routledge, 1854), 95.

32. Morell, *Russia as it is*, 95.

33. Polilov-Sievertsev, *Nashi dedy-kuptsy*, 137.

34. Rashin, *Naselenie Rossii*, 111. Among the more useful of the many guidebooks and surveys of early nineteenth-century St. Petersburg are P. P. Svinin, *Dostopamiatnosti Sanktpeterburga i ego okrestnostei* (St. Petersburg, 1816–1828); A. P. Bashutskii, *Panorama Sanktpeterburga* (St. Petersburg: Pliushar and Sons, 1834); Ivan Pushkarev, *Nikolaevskii Peterburg* (1839–1842; repr., St. Petersburg: "Liga-Plius," 2000).

35. Rashin, *Naselenie Rossii*, 112. According to this reckoning, St. Petersburg's average birth rate between 1764 and 1860 was 28.4 per thousand while the average death rate over the same period was 31.8 per thousand. The 1840s and 1850s were especially deadly decades, with an average annual death rate of 42–43 per thousand; in 1848 the rate was 65.5 per thousand.

36. *SPV*, no. 6 (Jan. 9, 1838). According to this compilation, males numbered 328,719 and females 139,906. We have no way of knowing how many of these men were married, but the great majority lived in the city without their wives, if they had them. Among people who earned more money or who were registered members of permanent urban *sosloviia*, the proportion of females residing in St. Petersburg was much higher, suggesting a more settled domestic life. See Rashin, *Naselenie*, 278.

37. *SPV*, no. 6 (Jan. 9, 1838).

38. Rashin, *Naselenie*, 279. Storch offers a colorful firsthand account of the city from a few decades earlier in *Picture of St. Petersburg* .

39. Evgeny Grebenka sketched out those who did ascend a few rungs up the ladder to settle permanently in the poor quarters across the river from the palace. Among those he found, there were

temporary and junior clerks in the lower echelons of the civil service, unsuccessful actors, bankrupt merchants, "foremen without apprentices or workers, servants without masters, masters without servants." See Evgeny Grebenka, "The Petersburg Quarter," in Nekrasov, *Petersburg* 107.

40. "Spisok povarennym sluzhitelei glavnoi i pervoi kukhon," RGIA, f. 469, op. 14, d. 62, l. 20. The remuneration figures include the court's estimated costs of providing room, board, possibly clothing, and probably a small amount of actual money, paid sporadically. There is no evidence that the imperial family's own appanage estates supplied palace servants except, perhaps, as nursemaids. The Winter Palace did not belong to the Department of Appanages but to the Office of the Court. See *Svod udel'nykh postanovlenii* (St. Petersburg, 1843), pt. 1, 4.

41. Ageeva, *Imperatorskii dvor Rossii*, 346. Employees who committed crimes might still be turned over to the police, and those who broke rules might face punishments ranging from being fed only bread and water to being dismissed.

42. "O ne zameshchenii nikakikh po dvortsam vakansii krest'ianami i ob opredelenii na onyia pridvornosluzhitel'skikh detei," PSZ 2, no. 1596, 2nd ser. (Dec. 6, 1827). An explicit prohibition on employing peasants was probably meant to limit the transfer of people from a taxpaying to a nontaxpaying status as well as to preserve court positions for members of the court household.

43. Zimin, *Detskii mir*, 396–400.

44. "Alfavitnyi spisok gof. vrachei, fel'dsherov, i.t.d.," RGIA, f. 469, op. 15, d. 490 (1803–1850). This file records the names and occupations of palace employees and family members who received pensions, passports, or release from service.

45. "Alfavitnyi spisok gof. vrachei, fel'dsherov, i.t.d.," RGIA, f. 469, op. 15, d. 490 (1803–1850), l. 19. Ageev was typical of those servants who earned the affection of the imperial family, receiving monetary awards from Grand Duchess Olga Nikolaevna and Grand Duke Constantine Nikolaevich. When Ageev married in 1847 he moved out of the palace and received "rent money at the married rate."

46. "Alfavitnyi spisok gof. vrachei, fel'dsherov, i.t.d.," RGIA, f. 469, op. 15, d. 490 (1803–1850), ll. 17, 27.

47. "Alfavitnyi spisok gof. vrachei, fel'dsherov, i.t.d.," RGIA, f. 469, op. 15, d. 490 (1803–1850), l. 27.

48. One such lengthy negotiation with Iaroslavl peasants is recorded in "O vyvoze zhelaiushchikh na postavku chernorabochikh liudei," RGIA, f. 469, op. 14, d. 142 (May 1826). Signature appears on l. 22–22 ob.

49. Bashutskii reported that a typical Petersburg artel' pooled from eight to twelve rubles a month for food, which allowed all members to eat fairly well. Bashutskii, *Panorama*, 3:23.

50. "Spisok povarennym sluzhitelei glavnoi i pervoi kukhon," RGIA, f. 469, op. 14, d. 62, ll. 7–51. Field Marshal Kutuzov had provided recommendations for a number of personal chefs procuring palace appointments in July 1813.

51. Laws issued at different points throughout the tsarist period specified the terms for appointment to the Table of Ranks for certain categories of palace servants, generally after at least ten years of exemplary service, with a statutory upper rank beyond which promotion was forbidden. See, for example, "O nedache Pridvornykh sluzhiteliam, pri proizvodstve ikh v ofitsianty, klassnykh chinov, poka ne prosluzhat oni v sem zvanii 10 let," PSZ 2, no. 834, 2nd ser. (Jan. 21, 1827). Ageeva offers a summary of the expanding categories of ranks and servants in the eighteenth century in *Imperatorskii dvor Rossii*, 188–91.

52. "Spisok povarennym sluzhitelei glavnoi i pervoi kukhon," RGIA, f. 469, op. 14, d. 62, ll. 1 ob.–2.

53. "Alfavitnyi spisok gof. vrachei, fel'dsherov," RGIA, f. 469, op. 15, d. 490 (1803–1850), l. 27. Grebenka tells an unverifiable story about a retired palace servant whose "unusual pallor . . . made him look very much like an albino," but who still retired as a court "Arab"—that is, as a specialized palace servant of African descent. When asked how a white person could have been a court Arab, he explained that "I became an Arab solely by favor of the authorities. . . . I was working as a simple stoker when the time came for me to retire." His wife suggested that he try to retire as an Arab, since the pension was twice as large. When the retiring stoker made this request, his boss "put me down on the

rolls as an Arab," after which three more men did the same thing. Grebenka, "The Petersburg Quarter," in Nekrasov, *Petersburg*, 105–6.

54. "Attestat pridvornogo lakeia Aleksandra Andreeva," RGIA, f. 469, op. 14. d. 1264 (1826).

55. Nicholas expanded *hof-fur'ers'* duties when he grew frustrated during his first remodeling project. See "O peremeshchenii vsekh Kamer-Tsalmeisterskikh Komissarov i sluzhitelei v shtat Gof-Intendantskoi Kontory," *PSZ* 1, no. 728, 2nd ser. (Dec. 5, 1826).

56. Ducamp, *The Winter Palace*, 19.

57. "O revizi i opisanii imushchestva nakhodivshegosia v pomeshchenii zaniatoi poloterami i masterovoi rotoi Zimnego dvortsa," RGIA, f. 490, op. 15, d. 24 (Dec. 3, 1859–Dec. 31, 1859), l. 2 ob.

58. Pushkarev, *Opisanie*, 1:368.

59. Zimin, *Detskii mir*, 449–50. These salaries are very low. Some indication of just how low comes to us from Gogol's fiction: readers of "The Overcoat" may recall that the beleaguered Akaky Akakyevich earned 400 rubles a year in the 1830s—an amount that was, famously, not enough to provide him with a winter coat. Despite the lack of paid salaries the court did make an effort to account for per-employee costs. One mid-eighteenth-century accounting indicates that chefs and maîtres d'hotels attracted annual total remuneration in the range of 150 to 300 rubles per year, footmen around 100 rubles, and cooks' apprentices around 50 rubles. See *Obshchii arkhiv Ministerstva Imperatorskago Dvora. Opisanie del i bumag* (St. Petersburg, 1888), 90–94.

60. Zimin, *Detskii mir*, 438.

61. There were more slots for artisans' children because they were not eligible to attend the local district school as were the children of palace servants; see "Polozhenie o shkole dlia detei pridvornosluzhitelei i masterovykh 24 Marta 1852," RGIA, f. 469, op. 14, d. 1268 (1852), l. 2. Parents in the latter category could choose to send their children to the district school or the court school but not both. The palace estimated that feeding each student cost eight kopeks per day.

62. "Polozhenie o shkole dlia detei pridvornosluzhitelei i masterovykh 24 Marta 1852," RGIA, f. 469, op. 14, d. 1268 (1852), ll. 3, 5.

63. *SPV*, no. 6 (Jan. 9, 1838). Twenty-three thousand people were listed as artisans in registered craft organizations (*tsekovye*). An indication of their permanent status as city residents, women exceeded men in this group. But there were no females at all among the over more than sixteen thousand people listed as holding temporary status as registered craftsmen.

64. Zimin, *Detskii mir*, 439. Male graduates neither gifted, industrious, nor handsome might work as floor polishers, lamplighters, or garden laborers. See "Polozhenie o shkole dlia detei pridvornosluzhitelei i masterovykh 24 Marta 1852," RGIA, f. 469, op. 14, d. 1268 (1852), ll. 2–7.

65. Although evidence of criminal behavior by palace servants is rare, it was recorded in fine books and the court journals in various years. See Ageeva, *Imperatorskii dvor Rossii*, 344–45. One such case detailing the arrest of a barber and a stoker for theft is recorded at RGIA, f. 469, op. 14, d. 731 (1864), l. 6. Even though police did not find the items reported stolen, the accused were excluded henceforth from all court-owned housing.

66. In the eighteenth century no term of service was specified, so most people died while still in service, although there were cases of people being retired due to poor health, "madness," and "grief." The destitute among such people could hope to be housed in a special home for former court workers. See Ageeva, *Imperatorskii dvor Rossii*, 348–51. Although nineteenth-century servants could aspire to a retirement at age forty-five, albeit an impoverished one, this was old age for working people.

67. Mervyn Matthews, *The Passport Society: Controlling Movement in Russia and the USSR* (Boulder, CO: Westview Press, 1993), 3–8. Richard Stites described a variety of circumstances that brought provincials to the capital, observing that "a surprising level of economic mobility combined with relative social immobility meant that poor folks often had rich relatives in the capitals." Stites, *Serfdom, Society, and the Arts*, 18.

68. Zimin, *Detskii mir*, 440–41.

69. About 13 percent of the city's residents in 1837 fell into the "townsman" category (*meshchanstvo*). As a category of taxpaying urban residents, the townsmen included casual laborers

as well as "retired soldiers, vagrants, orphans, foundlings and persons of illegitimate birth" who were subject to conscription. The number of female townsmen actually exceeded the number of males (28,292 to 20,680), indicating the more normal gender distribution of a permanent settled community. See *SPV*, no. 6 (Jan. 9, 1838).

70. "Svidetel'stvo o rozhdenii detei pridvornykh sluzhitelei (1811–1836)," RGIA, f. 469, op. 14, d. 60, ll. 6–24.

71. See Julie A. Buckler, *Mapping St. Petersburg: Imperial Text and Cityshape* (Princeton, NJ: Princeton University Press, 2005), 5–8.

72. Cholera, prevalent in India, made its very first appearance in the Russian Empire at Astrakhan in September 1823, but that incident was isolated. It reappeared with a vengeance at Orenburg in August 1829, recurring in two more serious outbreaks in that city during 1830. From August of that year cholera appeared broadly across the South, finally striking Moscow in September. After reaching Novgorod, Vologda, and Archangel by November 1830 the epidemic subsided during the winter months of 1830–1831 but reappeared in many cities during the spring of 1831. It arrived in St. Petersburg in June of that year. See Roderick E. McGrew, *Russia and the Cholera, 1823–1832* (Madison: University of Wisconsin Press, 1965).

73. *SPV*, no. 150 (June 28, 1831).

74. Grinev, *Istoriia roty*, 21–22.

75. McGrew, *Russia and the Cholera*, 108–10.

76. Nicholas had watched 1830 developments in France carefully and reputedly advocated that the increasingly unpopular French king Charles X dismiss his hated minister Polignac and adhere to the constitutional charter in order to avoid popular disturbances. See Vera Mil´čina, "Nicolas Ier et la politique intérieure de la France à l'époque de la Restauration: deux épisodes," *Cahiers du Monde Russe* 43, no. 2 (2002): 355–74.

77. Count Benkendorf, "Zapiski Benkendorfa," *Russkaia starina* 88, no. 10 (Oct. 1896): 88; McGrew, *Russia and the Cholera*, 112–13.

78. Emily Johnson, *How St. Petersburg Learned to Study Itself: The Russian Idea of Kraevedenie* (University Park: Pennsylvania State University Press, 2006), 34–35.

79. Eyewitness accounts of the fire appear in "Razskazy ochevidtsev o pozhare Zimniago dvortsa v 1837 g.," *Russkii arkhiv* 3 (1865): 1088–113. See also Piotrovskii et al., *Ermitazh*, 76–77; Dolli Fikel'mon (Ficquelmont), *Dnevnik, 1829–1837* (Moscow: Minuvshee, 2009), 362–63; Richard M. Haywood, "The Winter Palace in St. Petersburg: Destruction by Fire and Reconstruction, December 1837–March 1839," *Jahrbücher für Geschichte Osteuropas* 27, no. 2 (1979): 161–80.

80. The loss of the thirteen, which included five members of the palace fire brigade, was noted in several editions of *SPV*, e.g., no. 291 (Dec. 22, 1837).

81. A. F. Orlov to D. P. Tatishchev, 24 Dec. 1837, in *Russkii arkhiv* 3 (1865): 1093.

82. Pyliaev, *Staryi Peterburg*, 91–93. The emperor had been present on Palace Square while firemen fought the 1836 blaze and was said to have become manifestly distraught as it became known that 126 people had perished.

83. S. S. Tatishchev, *Imperator Aleksandr II, ego zhizn' i tsarstvovanie* (St. Petersburg: Suvorin, 1903), 1:90.

84. Haywood, "The Winter Palace," 164. The temperature was reported to be five degrees Fahrenheit. Haywood has pieced together a careful chronological account of the night of December 17 from all available sources.

85. Haywood, "The Winter Palace," 166–67.

86. Pyliaev, *Staryi Peterburg*, 97.

87. Nicholas to Pashkevich, in Nicholas I, Emperor of Russia, "Imperator Nikolai Pavlovich v ego pismakh," 23. The word for what Nicholas would treasure is *podvig*, often translated in other contexts as "spiritual undertaking."

88. Haywood, "The Winter Palace," 168.

89. Piliavskii, *Zimnii dvorets*, 67.

90. The story of the engineering, construction, and redecoration involved in this remarkably speedy effort has been told in great detail. See, for example, *SPV*, no. 76 (Apr. 7, 1839); A. Bashutskii, *Vozobnovlenie Zimniago dvortsa v Sanktpeterburge* (St. Petersburg: Guttenburg Press, 1839).

91. Bashutskii, *Vozobnovlenie Zimniago dvortsa*, 3. Konstantin Akinsha notes the pairing of this dramatic reconstruction of St. Petersburg's great Western style palace with the Moscow project launched at the same time—Konstantin Ton's "Byzantine" Kremlin Palace (1838–1849)—and observes that, "Where the idol of the state was concerned, Nicholas was both a Slavophile and a Westernizer." See Akinsha, *The Holy Place*, 65.

92. See Grinev, *Istoriia roty*, 284, for the story of the widow of one of the Palace Grenadiers.

93. Bashutskii, *Vozobnovlenie Zimniago dvortsa*, 3. Nicholas was so pleased with the reconstruction and remodeling that he commissioned an extensive series of watercolors depicting the palace interiors. These paintings—executed in the 1850s and 1860s by K. A. Ukhtomskii, E. P. Hau, and L. Premazzi—are the only record of what the palace looked like at that time. They are reproduced in Ducamp, *The Winter Palace*.

94. *PSZ* 19, no. 18398, 2nd ser. This law came in 1844, stating that no building could surpass eleven *sazhens*; the Winter Palace stood at twelve *sazhens*. See Grabar, *Istoriia russkogo iskusstva*, vol. 8, bk. 2, 480. One sazhen equals 7 feet or 2.1 meters.

95. Kaganov, *Images of Space*, esp. 114.

Chapter 7

1. The modern art museum differs from its baroque and princely antecedents largely because of this self-consciously educational mission. It was in late eighteenth-century Paris that theorists first worked out enduring principles by which art is arranged so as to instruct visitors on the history of art and so-called national schools. See Andrew McClellan, *Inventing the Louvre: Art, Politics, and the Origins of the Modern Museum in Eighteenth-Century Paris* (Berkeley: University of California Press, 1999), 3–4.

2. Antonio Paolucci, *Great Museums of Europe: The Dream of the Universal Museum* (Milan: Skira Editore, 2002), 11. Very few European art museums in this era were originally open to the entire public. An exception was the British Museum, a universal museum that housed curiosities and books but few paintings at first, which opened in 1753. Although it was from the beginning a public museum, access to the book collection was at first open only to scholars, and members of the general public needed to procure a ticket weeks in advance. The ticket requirement was dropped in 1810. See Jonathan Conlin, *The Nation's Mantelpiece: A History of the National Gallery* (London: Pallas Athene, 2006), 10.

3. Britain's great art museum, the National Gallery, offers a different kind of contrast to the European trend. The country's original royal art collection had been dispersed to the four winds after the execution of Charles I in 1649. Unlike other national collections, therefore, Britain's collection arose from public and private institutions and out of a national desire to surpass its defeated enemy after the Napoleonic Wars. Thus the National Gallery in Britain was not based on a royal collection, and in fact Queen Victoria declined to donate any of her works. See Conlin, *The Nation's Mantelpiece*, 5, 12–47.

4. Peter the Great had first imported antique marble statues from Italy, which he had displayed in specially constructed grottos in the Summer Garden. The reception of these figures in Russia is analyzed in Caspar Meyer, *Greco-Scythian Art and the Birth of Eurasia: From Classical Antiquity to Russian Modernity* (Oxford: Oxford University Press, 2013), 39–51. Early in the nineteenth century there also arose proposals for a universal museum of the fatherland, which would include an "Antiquities Hall" that linked Russia to the ancient world through objects discovered near the Black Sea. See Kevin Tyner Thomas, "Collecting the Fatherland," in Jane Burbank and David L. Ransel, eds., *Imperial Russia: New Histories for the Fatherland* (Bloomington: Indiana University Press, 1998), 91–107.

5. In 1859 Alexander II formally rendered the archaeological commission a branch of the Ministry of the Imperial Court headed by Count S. G. Stroganov.

6. Vitaly Suslov, ed., *The State Hermitage: Masterpieces from the Museum's Collection* (London: Booth-Clibborn Editions, 2001), 37. Nicholas's major purchases occurred in 1829, 1831, 1836, 1845, and 1850. See S. Frederick Starr, "Russian Art and Society, 1800–1850," in Theofanis George Stavrou, ed., *Art and Culture in Nineteenth-Century Russia* (Bloomington: Indiana University Press, 1983), 100.

7. Nicholas's father, Emperor Paul, had actually assigned the Hermitage and its collections to the oversight of the palace *ober-hofmarshal* during his own reform of the court administration.

8. When C. L. Eastlake, director of London's National Gallery, appealed to Parliament for support in building a bigger and better gallery in 1845, for example, he referred to the skylights at the Pinakothek. See C. L. Eastlake to Robert Peel, published separately as The National Gallery, "Observations on the Unfitness of the Present Building for its Purpose. In a Letter to Rt. Hon. Sir Robert Peel," May 1845, 9.

9. Nicholas may also have been influenced indirectly by the poet and lover of German painting V. A. Zhukovskii, his son's tutor, who wrote to two of the emperor's children about the desirability of assembling an educational art museum at the palace. See V. F. Levinson-Lessing, *Istoriia kartinnoi galerei Ermitazha (1764–1917)* (Leningrad: Iskusstvo, 1985), 173.

10. Piliavskii and Liulina, "Novyi Ermitazh," 223–31; Piotrovskii et al., *Ermitazh*, 79; Levinson-Lessing, *Istoriia kartinnoi galerei*, 292–93n215. After construction of the New Hermitage, this "Large Hermitage" became known colloquially as the "Old Hermitage," a term that confuses the issue considerably, since it was not as old as the Small Hermitage. See P. D. Liulina, "Bol'shoi Ermitazh i korpus Lodzhii Rafaelia," in Piliavskii and Levinson-Lessing, *Ermitazh*, 201–12.

11. Piliavskii and Liulina, "Novyi Ermitazh," 237.

12. Meyer, *Greco-Scythian Art*, 82–87. This ideological arrangement of the galleries was very short-lived as a German art critic found few traces of it in 1860. Not only did the rapid expansion of the sculpture collection promote rearrangement but so too did shifting monarchical interpretations of Russian history, which later in the century was recast in a "national" vein rooted in early Muscovy as opposed to the emphasis on Byzantium to which Nicholas I was inclined. See Wortman, "National Narratives," 165; Wortman, "Solntsev, Olenin, and the Development of a National Aesthetic," in *Visualizing Russia: Fedor Solntsev and Crafting a National Past*, ed. Cynthia H. Whittaker (Leiden: Brill, 2010), 17–40.

13. Piliavskii and Liulina, "Novyi Ermitazh," 236.

14. Piotrovskii et al., *Ermitazh*, 112. Labenskii died in 1849 and was replaced by Bruni. To the latter fell the task of overseeing the selection and transfer of paintings to the New Hermitage as well as the details of administrative organization and public access. See Levinson-Lessing, *Istoriia kartinnoi galerei*, 180–81.

15. Gosudarstvennyi Ermitazh, *Sotrudniki Imperatorskogo Ermitazha 1852–1917* (St. Petersburg: Izd. Gosud. Erm., 2004), 5–6. Generally it is unwise to assume that people with German names were foreigners in imperial Russia. Many were people whose families had been in Russia for two or three generations. But in the 1780s and 1790s many German and French scholars received appointments in the Russian academies and elsewhere at court. Here I am just crudely counting the names, which suggests a trend toward fewer foreigners being appointed to leading posts at the museum.

16. Mitrokhin was a portraitist, the painter of a famous picture of Emperor Paul. Tabuntsov's name appears in restoration records of works by Rembrandt and Jacopo Palma. http://artsalesindex.artinfo.com/auctions/Jacopo-Palma-4486526/The-Madonna-and-Child-with-Saints-John-the-Baptist-and-Paul; http://arthermitage.org/Mitrokhin/Portrait-of-Paul-I.html; J. Bruyn et al., *A Corpus of Rembrandt Paintings* (Dordrecht: Martinus Nijhoff, 1989), 3:103.

17. Gosudarstvennyi Ermitazh, *Sotrudniki*. I have included in this "first generation" all those who died before 1900. The twenty-one include two men who immigrated to Russia as children, graduated from Russian educational institutions, and lived the remainder of their lives in Russia. The

others included two Baltic Germans, two Poles, and five Russified Germans from families of long duration in Russia. Ten were Russians.

18. Gosudarstvennyi Ermitazh, *Sotrudniki*, 6–7.

19. Gosudarstvennyi Ermitazh, *Sotrudniki*, 33.

20. Gosudarstvennyi Ermitazh, *Sotrudniki*, 51.

21. Gosudarstvennyi Ermitazh, *Sotrudniki*, 113. There is more information about Mytkin's accommodation in M. B. Piotrovskii, ed., *Istoriia Ermitazha. Kratkii ocherk; materialy i dokumenty* (Moscow: Izd. "Iskusstvo," 2000), 266–67, although there he is referred to as Metkin.

22. Gosudarstvennyi Ermitazh, *Sotrudniki*, 128.

23. Gosudarstvennyi Ermitazh, *Sotrudniki*, 124–26.

24. Piotrovskii et al., *Ermitazh*, 112.

25. Piotrovskii, *Istoriia Ermitazha*, 213–17.

26. Piotrovskii, *Istoriia Ermitazha*, 213. The "Rules" were published in St. Petersburg in 1853 "v tipografii Eksbertsa" and can be found in RGIA, f. 466, op. 1, d. 389, ll. 130–51. They are published in Piotrovskii, *Istoriia Ermitazha*, 205–14. When the Louvre opened to the people of Paris in 1793 there was a similar effort to regulate behavior and to post guards against theft. McClellan, *Inventing the Louvre*, 9.

27. Piotrovskii, *Istoriia Ermitazha*, 217. Apparently the guards at first admitted many people without tickets, although this was against the rules.

28. Piotrovskii, *Istoriia Ermitazha*, 218.

29. Ekaterina Pravilova, *A Public Empire: Property and the Quest for the Common Good in Imperial Russia* (Princeton, NJ: Princeton University Press, 2014), 188–96. Pravilova argues persuasively that the idea of public property developed broadly in the second half of the nineteenth century across a variety of areas and that this notion contrasted with both private property and property of the imperial court or family, which was often thoroughly entangled with "state" property.

30. In the 1840s, records of palace property created a new category for paintings listed as the personal property of the ruler or his family. See Levinson-Lessing, *Istoriia kartinnoi galerei*, 192. On the subtle distinctions between crown and court property, see Arcadius Kahan, *The Plow, the Hammer and the Knout: An Economic History of Eighteenth-Century Russia* (Chicago: University of Chicago Press, 1985), 336–37. The nationalization of property after the Bolshevik Revolution erased all of these fine distinctions in one fell swoop.

31. Hermitage director A. A. Vasi'lchikov, in particular, was able to acquire twenty-two paintings in 1882 from suburban palaces as well as many treasures for the Department of Crown Jewels from the Winter Palace. He took this route because his meager acquisition budget did not allow him to purchase as much as his predecessors. See Gosudarstvennyi Ermitazh, *Sotrudniki*, 34; Pravilova, *A Public Empire*, 358 n51.

32. In 1804 Alexander received a proposal from Count D. P Buturlin, Hermitage overseer, to open the collection to the public, "according to inviolable rules and under the supervision of employees appointed for the role, so that [the collection] might present itself as a source of education." The young ruler did not act on Buturlin's recommendation but he did add curatorial staff. See Gosudarstvennyi Ermitazh, *Sotrudniki*, 4–5.

33. J. G. Kohl, *Russia, St. Petersburg, Moscow, Kharkoff, Riga, Odessa* (London, 1844), 110.

34. This point is developed by Starr, "Russian Art and Society," in Stavrou, *Art and Culture*, 91–93.

35. Katia Dianina, *When Art Makes News: Writing Culture and Identity in Imperial Russia* (DeKalb: Northern Illinois University Press, 2013), esp. 4–7.

36. The Hermitage had begun collecting important Russian paintings in 1825 but continued to concentrate on other European works.

37. P. D. Boborykin, *Vospominaniia v dvukh tomakh* (Moscow: Izd. "Khudozhestvennaia Literatura," 1965), 1:311.

38. Kasparinskaia, *Muzei i vlast'*, pt. 1, 28.

39. McClellan argues that even the revolutionary Louvre did not aim its instructional program at "the *sans-culottes*" when it first opened, eschewing genre pictures and popular arts and providing no written guides. He considers the "fractured public" of the first public art museums an enduring legacy: "the museum bequeathed to us by the Revolution continues to operate on the paradoxical principle of an institution ostensibly open and populist but infused by the exclusive tastes of an Old World elite and full of art fit for kings." McClellan, *Inventing the Louvre*, 12.

40. The collection's first catalogue was written in French in 1773, and sixty copies of it were issued the following year. Paul's reign saw the first Russian-language catalogue of the Hermitage paintings. Gosudarstvennyi Ermitazh, *Sotrudniki*, 5; Kasparinskaia, *Muzei i vlast'*, pt. 1, 17. For a fuller discussion of the genre of Petersburg guidebooks more generally, see Johnson, *How St. Petersburg Learned to Study Itself*, 38–41.

41. Gosudarstvennyi Ermitazh, *Sotrudniki*, 136–37. In that position Somov oversaw a scholarly three-volume catalogue of west European painting in the museum. He served several times as interim director of the Hermitage. Somov's son Konstantin became a prominent painter in the World of Art circle.

42. Somov, *Kartiny Imperatorskago Ermitazha*, 5, 16.

43. Gosudarstvennyi Ermitazh, *Sotrudniki*, 49; N. Iu. Miasoedova, "S. A. Gedeonov i Imperatorskii Ermitazh," *Peterburg i Moskva: Dve stolitsy Rossii v XVIII–XX vekakh*, ed. Iu. V. Krivosheeva et al. (St. Petersburg: St. Petersburg University, 2001), 62–69.

44. The Norman controversy addresses the ninth-century invitation by the Eastern Slavs to the Varangians (Normans, Vikings) to come and rule over them, recorded in the medieval *Povest' vremennykh let* (Russian primary chronicle). By the nineteenth century many patriotic Russians rejected this tale. Gedeonov wrote a two-volume study addressing the Norman controversy and published the heart of his argument in 1862, the year of the big millennial celebration of the founding of Rus'. Gedeonov's complete book, *Variagi i Rus'*, was published in 1876. In it he staked out a complex position, arguing that the Varangians (Normans) were actually a West Slavic people themselves, who had nearly been destroyed by their German neighbors. Thus, for Gedeonov, the invitation to the Varangians satisfied Pan-Slavic and anti-German currents of the day. He cast the Slavs' invitation to a Slavic Riurik as the wise summoning of a new dynasty from among their kin, implying that monarchy was both ancient and natural to the Slavs. See Maiorova, *From the Shadow of Empire*, 82–87.

45. Maiorova notes that Gedeonov shared the views of "Auguste Comte and especially Henry Thomas Buckle, two thinkers, immensely popular in Russia, who saw education, knowledge, and intelligence as the prime forces for progress." See Maiorova, *From the Shadow of Empire*, 86.

46. Piotrovskii et al., *Ermitazh*, 113; Gosudarstvennyi Ermitazh, *Sotrudniki*, 8; Miasoedova, "S. A. Gedeonov," 67. The two-month downtime casts today's venerable "*sanitarnyi den'*" in a somewhat more favorable light.

47. *Severnaia pchela* 78 (March 22, 1863): 1. The commission, appointed by the Ministry of Public Instruction, concluded that what was most needed to increase public access was more funding with which to hire more maintenance staff.

48. Miasoedova, "S. A. Gedeonov," 67–68.

49. Gosudarstvennyi Ermitazh, *Sotrudniki*, 8.

50. Vladimir Mikhnevich, *Peterburg: Ves' na ladoni, s planom Peterburga, ego panoramoi s ptich'iago poleta, 22 kartinkami* (St. Petersburg: Izd. Knigoprodavtsa K. N. Plotnikova, 1874), 202–7.

51. Piotrovskii, *Istoriia Ermitazha*, 57; Gosudarstvennyi Ermitazh, *Sotrudniki*, 9. For the authorities, one consequence of ending the ticket regime was the necessity of increasing the number of guards in the building, the cost of which necessitated a reduction in hours of operation. Throughout the 1870s court officials resisted calls from Hermitage administrators to further increase the number of guards, insisting that it was not the quantity but the quality of personnel that mattered most.

52. Vladimir Nabokov, *Speak, Memory: An Autobiography Revisited* (New York: G. P. Putnam's Sons, 1966), 235. Baedeker also noted that the pink sarcophagus of this Egyptian patron saint of craftsmen graced Room One on the ground floor of the Imperial Hermitage, immediately to the left of the main vestibule. See Karl Baedeker, *Russia with Tehran, Port Arthur, and Peking: A Handbook for Travellers* (Leipzig: Karl Baedeker, 1914), 132.

Chapter 8

1. Wortman, *Scenarios of Power*, 1:346.

2. P. A. Valuev, "Dnevnik Ministra Vnutrennykh Del," March 5, 1861, in *Aleksandr Vtoroi: Vospominaniia, Dnevniki*, ed. V. G. Chernukha (St. Petersburg: Pushkinskii Fond, 1995), 144.

3. Wortman, *Scenarios of Power*, 2:72.

4. Richard Wortman, "Moscow and Petersburg: The Problem of Political Center in Tsarist Russia, 1881–1914," in Wilentz, *Rites of Power*, 246.

5. Wortman, "Moscow and Petersburg," 245. It was also the later Romanovs, especially Alexander III and Nicholas II who embraced the old title of "tsar" more enthusiastically, often preferring it to "emperor [*imperator*]." In popular usage the old term had always prevailed in reference to male rulers.

6. *SPV*, no. 1 (Jan. 1, 1871).

7. To disrupt this behavior, the tsar's son was dispatched for a long sojourn in the United States: see Lee Farrow, *Alexis in America: A Grand Duke's Tour, 1871–1872* (Baton Rouge: Louisiana State University Press, 2014).

8. Wortman, *Scenarios of Power*, 224.

9. Plunkett, *Queen Victoria*, 144–46.

10. "O vydache deneg vmesto prodoval'stviia," RGIA, f. 469, op. 14, d. 770 (1868–1869), ll. 24, 37.

11. See Zimin, *Detskii mir*, 446–47.

12. "O revizi i opisanii imushchenii nakhodivshogosia v pomeshchenii zaniatom poloterami i masterovoi rotoi Zim. dv," RGIA, f. 469, op. 15, d. 24 (Dec. 3, 1859–Dec. 31, 1859), ll.1–5.

13. "O zakliuchenii usloviia s krestianami Sankt-Peterburgskoi gubernii Shlissel'burgskogo uezda Putilovskoi volosti, na postavku imi k V. Dv. rabochikh liudei," RGIA, f. 469, op. 14, d. 965 (Nov. 16, 1867–Dec. 30, 1868), ll. 14–18. The workers would earn from forty to sixty kopeks per day, depending upon the type of service. The contract also specified that the community would post a two-thousand-ruble bond with the Court Office against theft by its members. The newcomers were to live at an assigned place and to refrain from playing pitch and toss (*orlianka*) or other forbidden games.

14. "O zakliuchenii uslovia s krestianami," RGIA, f. 469 op. 14 d. 965, l. 43.

15. "O zakliuchenii uslovaia s krestianami," RGIA, f. 469, op. 14, d. 965, ll. 45–55.

16. For example, efforts to supply water haulers for Tsarskoe Selo, day laborers for a visit of the Herzog of Saxon-Weimar to the Winter Palace, and kitchen workers for the palace at Krasnoe Selo. See "O naime rabochikh liudei i postavke lomovykh podvore," RGIA, f. 469, op. 14, d. 967 (Feb. 6, 1868–Dec. 27, 1868), ll. 3–76.

17. RGIA, f. 469, op. 14, d. 1164 (1871–1875), ll. 7–13.

18. RGIA, f. 469, op. 14, d. 1164, ll. 43, 94, 102, 275, 367.

19. Ministerstvo Vnutrenykh Del, Tsentral'nyi Statisticheskii Komitet, *Statistcheskii tablitsy Rossiiskoi Imperii*, vol. 2, *Nalichnoe naseleni imperii za 1858 g.* (St. Petersburg, 1863), 182. The census for 1858 put the population of the capital city at 395,880 men and 208,737 women.

20. Iu. Ianson, "Promysl i zaniatiia Peterburgskago naseleniia po perepisi 1881 g.," *Vestnik Evropy* 11 (1884): 337.

21. Valeriia Nardova, "Gorodskie golovy Sankt-Peterburga, 1873–1903 gg.," *Otechestvennaia istoriia* (2003): 22.

22. A. A. Bakhtiarov, *Briukho Peterburga: Ocherki stolichnoi zhizni* (1888; repr., St. Petersburg: Fert, 1994), 159.

23. Bakhtiarov, *Briukho Peterburga*, 161.

24. Bakhtiarov, *Briukho Peterburga*, 89.

25. Bakhtiarov, *Briukho Peterburga*, 103.

26. Ianson, "Promysl i zaniatiia," 325.

27. Bakhtiarov, *Briukho Peterburga*, 136.

28. Bakhtiarov, *Briukho Peterburga*, 203.

29. Bakhtiarov, *Briukho Peterburga*, 206.

30. Wortman, *Scenarios of Power*, 2:141. Both British and German correspondents judged the popular enthusiasm to be both sincere and general.

31. Abbott Gleason, *Young Russia: The Genesis of Russian Radicalism in the 1860s* (New York: Viking Press, 1980), 118, 138.

32. Cited in Gleason, *Young Russia*, 146.

33. Marina Bardakova, "Dukhov Den' 1862 goda v Peterburge," *Russkii arkhiv* 49, no. 10 (1911, kn. 3): 232; Gleason, *Young Russia*, 166–71.

34. Wortman, *Scenarios of Power*, 220; Maiorova, *From the Shadow of Empire*, 125.

35. "O naeme dvornikov dlia okhran' dnem i noch'iu dvortsa i zdanii vedomstva Pridvornoi e.v. Kontory i o vydache za eto," RGIA, f. 469, op. 14, d. 955 (Apr. 20, 1879), l. 2. Dvorniki culture is memorably characterized in Vladimir Dal', "The Petersburg Yardkeeper," in Nekrasov, *Petersburg*, 57–70.

36. "O naeme dvornikov dlia okhran'," RGIA, f. 469, op. 14, d. 955 (Apr. 20, 1879), ll. 11, 21.

37. Alexander Benois, *Zhizn' khudozhnika. Vospominaniia* (New York: Izd. Im. Chekhova, 1955), 2:163.

38. The story of the revolutionaries who exploited city life and space to pursue and eventually kill Alexander II has been told with new insight in the highly original work of Christopher Ely, *Underground St. Petersburg: Radical Populism, Urban Space, and the Tactics of Subversion in Reform-Era Russia* (DeKalb: Northern Illinois University Press, 2016).

39. Ely, *Underground St. Petersburg*, 215–20.

40. *SPV*, no. 38 (Feb. 7, 1880).

41. *SPV*, no. 39 (Feb. 8, 1880).

42. *SPV*, no. 38 (Feb. 7, 1880).

43. *SPV*, no. 39 (Feb. 8, 1880).

44. Franco Venturi, *Roots of Revolution: A History of the Populist and Socialist Movements in Nineteenth Century Russia* (Chicago: University of Chicago Press, 1983), 685–86. After the explosion Khalturin slipped away unnoticed and eventually joined comrades in Odessa, where he was executed in March 1882 for his part in another assassination but without having been implicated by police in the explosion in the Winter Palace.

45. *Sankt-Peterburgskie vedomosti* continued for several days editorializing about the crisis that had been mounting, mentioning earlier attempts on the tsar's life and the acquittal of Vera Zasulich.

46. Ely, *Underground St. Petersburg*, 246–51.

47. Peter A. Zaionchkovskii, *The Russian Autocracy in Crisis, 1878–1882* (Gulf Breeze, FL: Academic International Press, 1981), 92–99.

48. "O zatrebovani masterovykh dlia chistki," RGIA, f. 469, op. 14, d. 743 (1880–1882).

49. Benois, *Zhizn' khudozhnika*, 2:163.

50. Benois, *Zhizn' khudozhnika*, 2:164.

51. Benois's father, the architect Nicholas, was in charge of organizing this gift, and his brother Leon executed the decorations on the chest itself. Benois, *Zhizn' khudozhnika*, 2:164–65. Benois recounted that years later, when he found himself in Alexander's study in the wake of the "storming" of the Winter Palace by the Bolsheviks in 1917, he found this very chest broken open and damaged and the watercolor paintings strewn all about the room. Benois, *Zhizn' khudozhnika*, 2:166.

52. Benois, *Zhizn' khudozhnika*, 2:166.

53. Wortman, *Scenarios of* Power, 2:149–50.

54. Benois, *Zhizn' khudozhnika*, 2:167. Not surprisingly, this marriage also strained relations between Alexander and his eldest son and heir, Alexander Alexandrovich.

55. M. Murzanova, "Vospominaniia A. A. Bobrinskogo (1880–1881gg.)," *Katorga i ssylka* 76, no. 3 (1931): 85.

56. F. F. Markus recounted this event in "Poslednie minuty Imperatora Aleksandra II. Rasskaz ochevidtsa," *Istoricheskii vestnik* 80, no. 4 (1900): 133–34; see also the notes of his assistant, Kogan

[*sic*], "Konchina Imperatora Aleksandra II (Rasskaz fel'dshera)," *Istoricheskii vestnik* 131, no. 1 (1913): 133–35. It bears mentioning, in light of the anti-Semitic violence that broke out in the aftermath of the tsar's death, that he was attended in his last moments by two medical men who were most likely Jewish. Kogan narrates graphically his efforts to control Alexander's arterial bleeding by hand. See also Wortman, *Scenarios of Power*, 2:154–56.

57. Tatishchev, *Imperator Aleksandr II*, 2:609; Kogan, "Konchina Imperatora Aleksandra II," 133–35.

58. Benois, *Zhizn' khudozhnika*, 2:168.

59. Murzanova, "Vospominaniia A. A. Bobrinskogo," 98.

60. Wortman, *Scenarios of Power*, 2:198.

61. Alexander I. Fenin, *Coal and Politics in Late Imperial Russia: Memoirs of a Russian Mining Engineer*, trans. A. Fediaevsky, ed. Susan P. McCaffray (DeKalb: Northern Illinois University Press, 1990), 31–32.

62. Alexander III bestowed signs of special favor upon the former Russian capital as when, for example, he appointed his favorite brother, Sergei, to be governor-general of Moscow. In connection with his brother's appointment to Moscow, the tsar expelled twenty thousand Jews from that city, apparently to render the city more hospitable to the anti-Semitic grand duke. See Wortman, *Scenarios of Power*, 2:294.

63. In 1841 the Commission for Oversight of the Electromagnetic Telegraph established a line from the new telegraph office inside the Winter Palace to the General Staff building across Palace Square. In the 1860s the General Staff introduced the practice of daily transmitting a precise time signal from the telegraph office of the palace, via the General Staff telegraph line, to all of the country's far-flung cities. Each morning telegraph operators throughout the empire received a signal that announced, "Listen," followed after five minutes by the announcement "clocks set," which permitted for the first time uniform timekeeping throughout the country—emanating from the Winter Palace. See *Gazeta Elektromontazh* (July 2013), at https://electro-mpo.ru/ newspaper/96/1348/; https://Statehistory.livejournal.com/; and http://statehistory.ru/2056/ Izobretenie-telegrafa-v-Rossii/.

64. Levitskii and his son Rafael achieved fame photographing famous writers and artists as well as Romanovs, and many of their important mid-century photographs are held at the Di Rocco Wieler Collection in Toronto: available at http://diroccowieler.com/gallery.html. *Lichnyi al'bom Aleksandra II (1860–1870 gg.)* (The personal album of Alexander II [1860–1870]), now held at the Russian State Archive of Film and Photo Documents, can be viewed via the World Digital Library, at https://wdl. org/en/item/17159/.

65. Stolpianskii, *Peterburg*, 197–98.

66. For local townsmen and peasants the arrival of the emperor in Gatchina brought many inconveniences and generated grumbling. See V. S. Krivenko, *V Ministerstve Dvora. Vospominaniia* (St. Petersburg: Nestor-Istoriia, 2006), 148.

67. Wortman describes Alexander's political ideology as "monarchical nationalism," which sought to "thwart the transition from dynastic to civic nationalism." See Wortman, "National Narratives," 168.

68. *SPV*, no. 8 (Jan. 9, 1882).

69. *SPV*, no. 7 (Jan. 8, 1884). That year the imperial family also hosted the traditional New Year's reception for courtiers, ambassadors, ranking officials, and merchants at the Winter Palace.

70. Wortman, *Scenarios of Power*, 2:272.

71. The so-called reserve quarters were suites of rooms, some in the northeast and northwest blocks and others along the southern enfilade, in the part of the palace originally inhabited by Peter III and Catherine the Great. Later, Nicholas's married daughter Marie had lived there with her family but subsequently the apartments were assigned to uncles, nephews, and younger sons. They are depicted in Ducamp, *The Winter Palace*, 204–76.

72. Wortman, *Scenarios of Power*, 2:277.

73. Zimin, *Zimnii dvorets. Liudi i steny*, 467–68. The ochre color had been getting a bit darker with each repainting from the late 1850s on, and Rastrelli's scheme of painting the columns and window frames in a different color was muted by changing the contrast color from white to a lighter tone of ochre. Alexander III considered a more significant change, even going so far as to have corners of the interior courtyard painted in sample shades, but in the end he did not abandon tradition.

74. Unfortunately we do not know how many permanent staff remained at the palace when the family left, but presumably the number was lower than the 250 employed in Alexander II's time. The need for housekeeping did not abate in their absence, since court offices, institutions, and leading personnel still resided in the building.

75. *Ves' Peterburga na 1894 g. Adresnaia i spravochnaia kniga*, vol. 1 (St. Petersburg: Novoe vremia, 1894), 448–68. Sergeant V. I. Petrov was the court official who managed the Winter Palace as well as the Court Theater building, the warehouse, and the Summer Garden. Captain G. G. Drabatukhin oversaw the palace's movable property. The separation of movable and immovable property in palace administration proved remarkably durable despite the efforts of Nicholas I to overcome it.

76. Piotrovskii reproduces entries from this intriguing document, which he found in a pile of debris, in *Istoriia Ermitazha*, 267–69.

77. Krivenko, *V Ministerstve Dvora*, 157. From time to time Alexander III supplemented the museum's meager acquisitions budget as in the 1880s so as to acquire a collection of French medieval objects valued at five and a half million francs. See Kasparinskaia, *Muzei i vlast'*, pt. 1, 61.

78. Levinson-Lessing, *Istoriia kartinnoi galerei*, 209. The Hermitage had no photographic division of its own before the revolution so the contract for publishing photographs was awarded first to the Brown Company and later to others as well.

79. D. N. Mamin-Sibiriak, "Iz progulok po Petersburgu," *Novosti: Birzhevaia gazeta* (1891), in Piotrovskii, *Istoriia Ermitazha*, 254.

80. Emily Johnson says that subscribers grew from one thousand to five thousand between 1907 and 1914. See Johnson, *How St. Petersburg Learned to Study Itself*, 65.

81. See F. M. Lur'e, *Starye gody: Khronologicheskaia rospis' soderzhaniia, 1907–1916* (St. Petersburg: Iz. Dom "Kolo," 2007), 9–12. Steven Maddox succinctly situates *Starye gody* and its editors within the context of early twentieth-century Petersburg preservationists in *Saving Stalin's Imperial City: Historic Preservation in Leningrad, 1930–1950* (Bloomington: Indiana University Press, 2015), 24–29.

82. The position of Imperial Hermitage director was very well remunerated. In addition to the palace apartment, the position brought a salary of four thousand rubles annually, as well as a dining allowance of two thousand rubles and another two thousand rubles for travel. While this compensation was lavish, it is interesting that structurally it retained the traditional traits of "fiscal" employment by the imperial court: accommodation within the household and personal responsibility for obtaining one's own meals, the latter typical of both contracted and professional staff. See Piotrovskii, *Istoriia Ermitazha*, 241. Hermitage documents also noted that the court paid for the funeral of Tolstoy's predecessor.

83. This purchase represents another intersection of the life of the Winter Palace with the Benois family. In this case the painting, owned by Alexander Benois's sister-in-law, was sold to the Hermitage at a discount price, according to the official story of its acquisition at https://hermitagemuseum.org/wps/portal/hermitage/explore/history/?lng=en. Piotrovskii discusses the controversy over this painting in *Istoriia Ermitazha*, 65–66.

84. Gosudarstvennyi Ermitazh, *Sotrudniki*, 144–45.

85. R. D. Liulina, "Bol'shoi Ermitazh," in Piliavskii and Levinson-Lessing, *Ermitazh*, 211. Liulina says that these spaces were transferred formally to the Imperial Hermitage, although at the beginning of the twentieth century the Tsarskoe Selo Arsenal collection was brought into the New Hermitage building and the rooms of the Large Hermitage were fitted out as guest rooms. The special assembly halls for the State Council and the Council of Ministers had been created in the Large Hermitage in the middle of the nineteenth century during a significant remodeling of that building

carried out by E. A. Shtakenshneider. He created a new entrance from the Neva with a great staircase known as the "Sovetskii," in honor of the State Council, or the Gosudarstvennyi Soviet. See Piotrovskii, *Istoriia Ermitazha*, 50–51.

86. In connection with this project Nicholas decreed the greatest departure in appearance of the palace since its construction when he ordered in 1901 that the whole edifice be painted to match the red sandstone of the new garden wall. Columns and windows were painted the same color. Thus the huge building, and eventually all of the other buildings on Palace Square, took on a dark monolithic appearance. The change in appearance of the palace and the square generated widespread public complaint, but Nicholas did not address this until 1911 when, in preparation for the Romanov tercentenary, the palace was once again repainted, this time in a hue described by contemporaries as "rose." It retained its monochrome color scheme, however. Zimin, *Zimnii dvorets. Liudi i steny*, 467. The current color of the Winter Palace came only with the repainting of the building after World War II.

Chapter 9

1. Walter Sablinsky, *The Road to Bloody Sunday: Father Gapon and the St. Petersburg Massacre of 1905* (Princeton, NJ: Princeton University Press, 1976), 5–11. The census did not specially designate "workers" so most urban workers were counted among the peasantry, from which they hailed.

2. Jennifer Hedda illustrates both the overall milieu of social activist churchmen in St. Petersburg and the elements of Gapon's own personality, which included a deep commitment to the poor, considerable bitterness about the official rejection of several of his proposed projects, and an eagerness to sacrifice himself publicly for the sake of the people. Jennifer Hedda, *His Kingdom Come: Orthodox Pastorship and Social Activism in Revolutionary Russia* (DeKalb: Northern Illinois University Press, 2008), 141–45.

3. Sablinsky chronicles the complex link between the original propagator of "police socialism," S. V. Zubatov (whose project began in Moscow), and officials of the Interior Ministry, including Minister V. K. von Plehve. Gapon, a young theology student who had abandoned his schooling in 1903, began his organizing efforts under Zubatov's tutelage but pursued an independent path after Zubatov left St. Petersburg in August 1903. See Sablinsky, *Road to Bloody Sunday*, 56–70. Hedda concludes that Gapon never formally associated with the primary "Zubatov" organization sponsored by the secret police but, rather, that he aligned with a separate faction. Hedda, *His Kingdom Come*, 135. Gapon's story has been told many times but not better than in Sablinsky's thorough account.

4. Epiphany was one of the rare occasions on which he went into town: "We left for the city before nine.... We got ourselves dressed at Zimnii." After noting the wayward shot he continued, "After breakfast we received ambassadors and delegates in the Golden drawing room. At four we left for Tsarskoe." See Nicholas II, Emperor of Russia, *Dnevnik Imperatora Nikolaia II* (Berlin: Knigoizdatel'stvo Slovo, 1923), 193. His confidence that the shot was entirely accidental belied the ongoing campaign of assassination, which had carried off Minister of the Interior Dmitrii Sipiagin in April 1902 and his successor, Plehve, in July 1904.

5. N. M. Varnashev, "Ot nachala do kontsa s Gaponovskoi organizatsiei v S.-Peterburge (Vospominaniia)," in *Istoriko-revoliutsionnyi sbornik*, ed. V. I. Nevskii (Moscow-Petrograd: Gosud. Izd., 1924), 1:203. Here I have used the translation in Sablinsky, *Road to Bloody Sunday*, 170.

6. Varnashev, "Ot nachala," 204.

7. Sablinsky, *Road to Bloody Sunday*, 171.

8. Hedda, *His Kingdom Come*, 144.

9. L. Ia. Gurevich, "Narodnoe dvizhenie v Peterburge 9-go ianvaria 1905 g.," *Byloe* 1 (Jan. 1906): 209. As for the marchers, at least some of them foresaw the possibility of an armed confrontation.

10. Gurevich, "Narodnoe dvizhenie," 212.

11. The worker assembly branches included Vyborg, Narva (Putilov), Vasilevskii Island, Neva, the Moscow Gates, Kolomna, the Petrograd Side, Gavan (also on Vasilievskii), Rozhdestvenskii, and suburban Kolpino.

12. Varnashev, "Ot nachala," 205.

13. Sablinsky, *Road to Bloody Sunday*, 232.

14. Among the killed were Gapon's bodyguards, but the priest himself was not hit. His associates quickly secreted their leader away to the home of the writer Maxim Gorky. The story of the confrontation at the Narva Gate is recounted in M. Mitel'man et al., *Istoriia Putilovskogo zavoda, 1801-1917* (Moscow: Izd. Sotsial'no-ekonomicheskoi lit., 1961), 186–96.

15. The report of playwright Leon Zhdanov is quoted by Andrew M. Verner, *The Crisis of Russian Autocracy: Nicholas II and the 1905 Revolution* (Princeton, NJ: Princeton University Press, 1990), 153.

16. This account is drawn from Sablinsky's careful chronicle of eyewitnesses in *Road to Bloody Sunday*, 233–67. As to casualty figures for the day Sablinsky puts the most faith in Soviet historian V. I. Nevskii, who fixed the dead at 150–200 and the wounded at 450–800 (267).

17. Nicholas II, *Dnevnik Imperatora Nikolaia II*, 194.

18. "His Majesty's Speech: A Rebuke and a Promise," *The Times* (Feb. 2, 1905), 3.

19. This was Grand Duke Paul, speaking to future French ambassador Maurice Paléologue. Quoted by Sablinsky, *Road to Bloody Sunday*, 276.

20. "Views of the Grand Duke Vladimir," *The Times* (Feb. 2, 1905), 3.

21. Wortman, *Scenarios of Power*, 2:401–3.

22. Alexander Iswolsky, *The Memoirs of Alexander Iswolsky: Formerly Russian Minister of Foreign Affairs and Ambassador to France*, ed. and trans., Charles Louis Seeger (Gulf Breeze, FL: Academic International Press, 1974), 85–86.

23. The future head of the Provisional Government recollected watching this procession from the window of his prison cell across the river. Alexander Kerensky, *The Kerensky Memoirs: Russia and History's Turning Point* (London: Cassell, 1965), 70.

24. Nicholas II, *Dnevnik Imperatora Nikolaia II*, 240.

25. Marc Ferro, *Nicholas II: The Last of the Tsars* (New York: Oxford University Press, 1990), 134–36. In 1911 an assassin felled the architect of this retrenchment, Prime Minister P. A. Stolypin, at a theater performance in Kiev also attended by Nicholas and two of his daughters.

26. *SPV*, no. 4 (Jan. 6, 1909).

27. *Nikolai II nakanune otrecheniia. Kamer-fur'erskie zhurnaly (Dekabr 1916–Fevral' 1917 gg.*, ed. V. I Startsev (St. Petersburg: Skarabei, 2001), 31–33.

28. Kasparinskaia, *Muzei i vlast'*, pt. 1, 80–81.

29. A. I. Somov to K. A. Somov, February 1898, in *Konstantin Andreevich Somov. Pis'ma. Dnevniki. Suzhdeniia*, ed. Iu. N. Podkopaeva and A. N. Sveshnikova (Moscow: Iskusstvo, 1979), 457. Somov also mentioned that he was not invited to the dinners.

30. Kasparinskaia, *Muzei i vlast'*, pt. 1, 69.

31. Kasparinskaia, *Muzei i vlast'*, pt. 1, 80. This was a much higher ratio, however, than at the Russian Museum, which had only thirteen guards for thirty-seven galleries.

32. Kasparinskaia, *Muzei i vlast'*, pt. 1, 80.

33. In the first three weeks of July tens of thousands of factory workers in several sections of the city were on strike and engaging in confrontations with the police. On one occasion orators proposed that strikers move from the Vyborg Side to Nevskii Prospekt, where the tsar was receiving the president of France. Officials had difficulty calming down these strikes but they were able to prevent protestors from reaching Palace Square and the old city center. See M. V. Dzhervis, "Volneniia Peterburgskikh rabochikh nakanune mirovoi voiny," *Deshevaia biblioteka zhurnala Katorga i ssylka* 46 (1926): 3–30.

34. There is both photography and moving footage of these crowds, and of Nicholas and Alexandra on the balcony, for example. https://youtube.com/watch?v=heGpZZe0JWw and https://www.youtube.com/watch?v=5zWDOZ4w8YE.

35. During the war patriotic postcards proliferated, often with officially sanctioned images of the imperial family and in support of various charities directly associated with the Romanovs. See Alison Rowley, *Open Letters: Russian Popular Culture and the Picture Postcard, 1880–1922* (Toronto: University of Toronto Press, 2013), 163–65.

36. Kasparinskaia, *Muzei i vlast'*, pt. 1, 81.

37. E. I. Martynov, *Tsarskaia armiia v fevral'skom perevorote* (Moscow: Narkomvoenmor, 1927), 63.

38. The empress's close connection to the monk Grigorii Rasputin was the stuff of scandal verging on pornography and it permeated all ranks of St. Petersburg society, even after a group of highly placed noblemen murdered Rasputin in December 1916. See Orlando Figes and Boris Kolonitskii, *Interpreting the Russian Revolution: The Language and Symbols of 1917* (New Haven: Yale University Press, 1999), 13–14; Rowley, *Open Letters*, 168.

39. The city's name was changed from the German-sounding St. Petersburg to Petrograd at the beginning of the war.

40. V. F. Marishkina, *Gospital' v Zimnem dvortse 1915-1917. Katalog vystavki* (St. Petersburg: Izd. Gosud. Ermitazha, 2006), 4. The work was overseen by palace commandant General Major V. A. Komarov, and the oversight commission included palace architects N. I. Kramskoi and G. Shreder as well as the chief doctor of the new hospital, A. V. Rutkovskii. The wards were situated in the Nicholas, Shield, and Alexander Halls as well as the Antechamber, Fieldmarshals, and Peter the Great Halls. The upper landing of the Jordan Staircase was made into a dining room for the medical staff. Some people thought opening a hospital in the palace was merely a pretext to allow for evacuating the art without public alarm.

41. Marishkina, *Gospital' v Zimnem dvortse*, 5. The X-ray chamber ("Roentgen cabinet") was first used in World War I and represented the latest medical technology available.

42. Petrov was considered a brilliant surgeon, and he went on to become the founder of oncology in Russia. Marishkina, *Gospital' v Zimnem dvortse*, 5.

43. N. V. Galanina, "Gospital' Zimnego dvortsa, 5 October 1915 to 28 October 1917: Vospominaniia byvshei medsestry gospitalia," reproduced in Marishkina, *Gospital' v Zimnem dvortse*, 77.

44. Galanina, "Gospital' Zimnego dvortsa," 77.

45. Many of these photos are reproduced in Marishkina, *Gospital' v Zimnem dvortse 1915–1917. Katalog vystavki*. They appeared in 1915 in such publications as *Solntse Rossii* and *Letopis' voiny 1914–1915 gg.*, and also as postcards. Images of Empress Alexandra in a nurse's uniform distributing Easter eggs to convalescing soldiers may have backfired, in fact, as the monarch's close association with wounded men drew criticism. See Rowley, *Open Letters*, 167, citing Countess Kleinmichel who claimed that "when a soldier saw his empress dressed in a nurse's uniform, just like any other nurse, he was disappointed."

46. "An account by Colonel Tugan-Baranovskii, head of the War Minister's Chancellery," in Semion Lyandres, ed., *The Fall of Tsarism: Untold Stories of the February 1917 Revolution* (Oxford: Oxford University Press, 2013), 118.

47. Martynov, *Tsarskaia armiia*, 107–9; Tsuyoshi Hasegawa, *The February Revolution: Petrograd, 1917* (Seattle: University of Washington Press, 1981), 306–8.

48. Martynov, *Tsarskaia armiia*, 108–9.

49. Hasegawa, *The February Revolution*, 556.

50. Ferro, *Nicholas II*, 191.

51. Galanina, "Gospital' Zimnego dvortsa," 80.

52. Galaninia, "Gospital' Zimnego dvortsa," 80.

53. Zimin, *Liudi Zimnego dvortsa*, 674–77.

54. V. P. Lapshin, *Khudozhestvennaia zhizn' Moskvy i Petrograda v 1917 g.* (Moscow: Sovetskii Khudozhnik, 1983), 71.

55. Zimin, *Liudi Zimnego dvortsa*, 678.

56. Zinaida Gippius, *Dnevniki. Siniaia kniga* (7 Marta, Vtornik.). http://bibliotekar.ru/gippius-zinaida/46.htm.

57. A. N. Benois, *Moi dnevnik, 1916–1917–1918* (Moscow: Russkii put', 2003), 155.

58. Much has been written about Benois and *World of Art*. Particularly helpful on Benois's role as Petersburg preservationist, publicist, and well-connected spokesman for the fine arts is Johnson, *How St. Petersburg Learned to Study Itself*, 46–62.

59. Katerina Clark, *Petersburg, Crucible of Cultural Revolution* (Cambridge, MA: Harvard University Press, 1995), 59–61. Benois became vice president of the society in 1911 and in many ways it was a predecessor of the wartime and revolution-era commissions on which the new Commissariat of Enlightenment was built.

60. Other members of this commission included E. E. Baumgarten, A. I. Tamanov, and B. A. Shchuko. E. N. Volkov was the Ministry of the Court official who suggested such a committee to the tsar early in 1916. It is remarkable that such a project was even envisioned in the midst of the war. Benois, *Moi dnevnik*, 592–93n52.

61. Benois, *Moi dnevnik*, 109. This was an intimate dinner for twenty-seven guests, including Benois and his wife, as recorded by the French attaché Louis de Robien in *The Diary of a Diplomat in Russia, 1917–1918* (New York: Praeger, 1970), 7.

62. Benois, *Moi dnevnik* 166.

63. Benois's son attests that Gorky was a frequent visitor to his parents' apartment from 1913 on and that Benois and Gorky shared pacifist convictions as well as an interest in opening the city's great private art collections to the public. "N. A. Benois," in *Gorky i khudozhniki. Vospominaniia, perepiska, stat'i*, comp. I. A. Brodskii (Moscow: Iskusstvo, 1964), 79–81. Also see Johnson, *How St. Petersburg Learned to Study Itself*, 73–75.

64. Benois says that the group first wanted him to serve as its head but he demurred. See Benois, *Moi Dnevnik*, 136–39. See also Lapshin, *Khudozhestvennaia zhizn'*, 74–76.

65. Lapshin, *Khudozhestvennaia zhizn'*, 76. See Zimin, *Liudi Zimnego dvortsa*, 677, on the complex decisions involving Romanov property, much of which was confiscated from other palaces and transferred to the Winter Palace in the months following the first revolution.

66. Lapshin, *Khudozhestvennaia zhizn'*, 75.

67. Benois, *Moi dnevnik*, 156.

68. "M. Gorky v Sovete rabochikh deputatov," *Birzhevye vedomosti* 16126 (Mar. 9, 1917).

69. By this date Makarov had already been through the labyrinthine building several times—the first time with Kerensky.

70. The Provisional Government appointed F. A. Golovin, former chairman of the Second Duma, as commissar over the former Ministry of the Court and Appanages, as early as March 8 (OS) but the group he directed continued to be known informally and historically as the Gorky Commission. The Academy of Arts, museums, and theaters were also part of Golovin's portfolio. Benois, *Moi dnevnik*, 605–6nn137, 138.

71. Benois, *Moi dnevnik*, 179.

72. Johnson, *How St. Petersburg Learned to Study Itself*, 76–78. Leaders of the challengers to Benois and Gorky included Vladimir Mayakovsky and Vsevolod Meyerhold. See also Maddox, *Saving Stalin's Imperial City*, 30–31.

73. N. N. Sukhanov, *The Russian Revolution, 1917: A Personal Record* (Princeton, NJ: Princeton University Press, 1984), 498. Sukhanov says Kerensky moved in on July 18; Zimin says July 11; see *Liudi Zimnego dvortsa*, 681.

74. Richard Abraham, *Alexander Kerensky: The First Love of the Revolution* (New York: Columbia University Press, 1987), 244. On the other hand he and his mistress shared the imperial suite with Ekaterina Breshkovskaia, the incorruptible "Babushka" of the Revolution. The silk wall coverings in the Malachite Hall had been covered with canvas to protect them, although this may have occurred when the hospital was set up.

75. Zimin, *Liudi Zimnego dvortsa*, 682–83. They also referred to him as Alexandra Fedorovna, the name and patronymic of the reviled and deposed empress, a sly play on Kerensky's own name and patronymic, Alexander Fedorovich.

76. Kerensky, *Memoirs*, 20, 48, 57.

77. Edward T. Heald, *Witness to the Revolution: Letters from Russia, 1916–1919*, ed. James B. Gidney (Kent, OH: Kent State University Press, 1972), 111.

78. Laurie S. Stoff, *They Fought for the Motherland: Russia's Women Soldiers in World War I and the Revolution* (Lawrence: University of Kansas Press, 2006), 155. Kerensky had organized the Petrograd women's unit along with several others, earlier in the year, to give women a chance to serve and to inspire dispirited male troops to stay in the fight.

79. Sukhanov, *The Russian Revolution*, 594; Zimin, *Liudi Zimnego dvortsa*, 687.

80. For example, Louise Bryant, *Six Red Months in Russia: An Observer's Account of Russia before and during the Proletarian Dictatorship* (Portland, OR: Powell's Press, 2002), 50, who reports that cadets had been seizing cars and taking them to the square in advance of October 25. George Buchanan, the British ambassador, reported that autos on Palace Square awaited Kerensky's escape that afternoon, but that otherwise the area was calm and "relatively normal." George Buchanan, *My Mission to Russia and Other Diplomatic Memories* (Boston: Little, Brown, 1923), 2:205–6.

81. Benois, *Moi dnevnik*, 198.

82. Kerensky himself did not ride in the American car but in another with some members of his party in caravan under the US flag. A rumor subsequently developed that he had fled the palace disguised as a nurse. Kerensky, *Memoirs*, 438.

83. V. B. Stankevich and Iu. V. Lomonosov, *Vospominaniia 1914–1919. Vospominaniia o Martovskoi Revoliutsii 1917 g.* (Moscow: Rossiiskii Gosud. Gumanitarnyi Universitet, 1994), 138–43.

84. Antonov-Ovseenko details the back-and-forth as he crossed between the *Aurora*, the fortress, and the square during the evening of October 25, which culminated in his arrest of the ministers in the palace itself. See V. A. Antonov-Ovseenko, *V Revoliutsii* (Moscow: Politicheskaia Literatura, 1983), 156–61. A detailed reconstruction based on first-person accounts is Robert V. Daniels, *Red October: The Bolshevik Revolution of 1917* (New York: Charles Scribner's Sons, 1967), 178–99.

85. Hermitage director Tolstoy had successfully barricaded the corridors between the palace and the museum several days earlier, and during the "storming" no invaders entered the Hermitage itself. State Hermitage Museum website http://hermitagemuseum.org/html_En/05/hm5_1_33.html (accessed Jan. 30, 2014).

86. Sukhanov, *The Russian Revolution*, 638–42.

87. John Reed, *Ten Days that Shook the World* (New York: Penguin Books, 1985), 108.

88. A. V. Sivkov, "Ot Velikogo Oktiabria do 1941 g.," in Piliavskii and Levinson-Lessing, *Ermitazh*, 246.

89. Bryant, *Six Red Months*, 59.

90. Bryant, *Six Red Months*, 59. Reed recounted the same scene as looting curtailed and observed that the most commonly pilfered item was clothing, "which the working people needed." Reed, *Ten Days*, 110.

91. Benois, *Moi dnevnik*, 202–5. Benois tells the story of his terror during the night of October 25 as he listened to the firing from the fortress and the *Aurora*: "My heart was stricken. Could these be the last moments of the Winter Palace's existence? And likewise the Hermitage, with all of the main collections of the Russian government, all that to me personally was dearest in all the world!" Benois, *Moi dnevnik*, 199. Reed, who wandered around for an hour or so after the arrest of the Provisional Government, confirms this impression that the worst predations were in offices, where valuable goods stood unharmed as desks and cabinets were ransacked. Reed, *Ten Days*, 110.

92. He also commented on the lewd pictures on the walls of the tsar's water closet. Podkopaeva and Sveshnikova, *Konstantin Andreevich Somov*, 183–84.

93. Reed, *Ten Days*, 304–5.

94. Here Reed cites a proclamation attributed to G. Yatmanov and B. Mandlebaum, "commissars for the protection of museums and artistic collections." Reed, *Ten Days*, 305.

95. Quoted by Merridale, *Red Fortress*, 275.

96. Sivkov, "Ot Velikogo Oktiabria do 1941 g.," in Piliavskii and Levinson-Lessing, *Ermitazh*, 246.

97. Podkopaeva and Sveshnikova, *Konstantin Andreevich Somov*, 183.

98. Johnson, *How St. Petersburg Learned to Study Itself*, 80. Veiner was editor of the preservation journal *Starye gody*.

99. Lunacharsky to Benois, Nov. 8, 1917, in Benois, *Moi dnevnik*, 217–18.

100. Benois, *Moi dnevnk*, 200.

101. Gosudarstvennyi Ermitazh, *Zhurnal zasedanii soveta Ermitazha*, pt. 2, *1920–1926 gg.*, ed. M. B. Piotrovskii (St. Petersburg: Gosud. Ermitazh, 2009), 5. After endless petitions the Hermitage and Winter Palace artworks came back to Petrograd in the late summer of 1920, where overjoyed personnel unpacked the whole load in nine feverish hours.

102. Gosudarstvennyi Ermitazh, *Zhurnal zasedanii Soveta Ermitazha*, pt. 2, *1920–1926 gg.*, 17–18.

103. Peter III, Catherine II, and Paul occupied this suite, which thereafter was converted into second-tier apartments for imperial in-laws such as the king of Prussia and for the sons of Alexander II. See the paintings by Edward Hau in Ducamp, *The Winter Palace*, 224–36.

Conclusion

1. Robert Tombs, *The Paris Commune, 1871* (London: Longman, 1999), 10–11. The government of the Commune had briefly embraced a different possibility for the Tuileries when it staged concerts in its gardens for fifteen thousand people, showing that "the setting of Second Empire court entertainment was now open to the people." Tombs, *Paris Commune*, 8.

2. The fascinating story of what happened to St. Petersburg's imperial palaces and monuments under the Soviet regime and the importance that Stalin attached to the historical legacy of the old capital is told well in Maddox, *Saving Stalin's Imperial City*.

Select Bibliography

PRIMARY SOURCES

Unpublished Works

St. Petersburg

Rossiiskii Gosudarstvennyi Istoricheskii Arkhiv (cited as RGIA).

Fond 466	Court administration
Fond 469	Office of His or Her Majesty's Court, 1730–1882 (especially opisi 14 and 15, Palace Housekeeping)
Fond 470	Hof-intendant Office, 1732–1851
Fond 475	Petrograd Palace Administration 1891–1918
Fond 480	Construction Office 1834–1882
Fond 516	Kamer-fur'erskie journals
Fond 1328	Administration of the Palace Commandant, 1881–1917

Warsaw

National Library of Poland, Special Collections

    Wil. Kat Akc. 2189/66e   Francesco Rastrelli

        "Relation générale de tous les edifices, palais et jardins, que moy Comte de Rastrelli, Ober-Architecte de la Cour, a fait construire pendant tout le temps que j'ai eu l'honneur d'etre au service de Leurs Majestés Imperiales, de toutes les Russies, à commencer depuis l'année 1716 jusqu'à cette année 1764"

        "Relation des bâtiments, qui ont été construits sous le regne de l'Impératrice Anne, de glorieuse memoire et celui de l'Impératrice regnante, executes sous les orders du Général Architecte de la Cour, le Comte François de Rastrelli, Italien de nation."

        "Bâtiments et edifices construits sous le regne de l'Impératrice Elisabeth."

        "Reflexions sur la maniere et les difficulties qu'il y a en Russie pour bâtir avec la meme exactitude et perfection comme dans les autres pais de l'Europe"

Published Works

Newspapers, Court Journals, Laws, Statistical Surveys, and Guidebooks

Bakhtiarov, A. A. *Briukho Peterburga: Ocherki stolichnoi zhizni.* 1888. Reprint, St. Petersburg: Fert, 1994.

Bashutskii, A. P. *Nashi: Spisannye s natury russkimi.* 2 vols. 1841. Reprint, Leningrad: "Kniga," 1986.

———. *Panorama Sanktpeterburga*. 3 vols. St. Petersburg: Pliushar and Sons, 1834.

———. *Vozobnovlenie Zimniago dvortsa v Sanktpeterburge*. St. Petersburg: Guttenburg Press, 1839.

Coxe, William. *Travels in Poland, Russia, Sweden and Denmark*. London: T. Cadell and W. Davies, 1802.

Georgi, I. G. *Opisanie rossiisko-imperatorskogo stolichnogo goroda Sankt-Peterburga i dostopamiatnostei v okrestnostiakh onogo, s planom*. 1794–1796. Reprint, St. Petersburg: Liga, 1996.

German, Karl F. *Statisticheskaia izsledovaniia otnositel'no Rossiiskoi imperii*. Chapter 1: *O Narodonaselenii*. St. Petersburg: Imp. Ak. Nauk, 1819.

Gosudarstvennyi Ermitazh. *Zhurnal zasedanii Soveta Ermitazha*. Part 1, *1917–1919 gg*. Edited by M. B. Piotrovsky. St. Petersburg: Gosud. Ermitazh, 2001.

Gosudarstvennyi Ermitazh. *Zhurnal zasedanii Soveta Ermitazha*. Part 2, *1920–1926 gg*. Edited by M. B. Piotrovskii. St. Petersburg: Gosud. Ermitazh, 2009.

Grigorovich, D. V. *Progulka po Ermitazhu*. 2nd ed. St. Petersburg, 1875.

Ianson, Iu. "Promysl i zaniatiia Peterburgskago naseleniia po perepisi 1881 g." *Vestnik Evropy* 11 (1884): 323–62.

Kohl, J. G. *Russia, St. Petersburg, Moscow, Kharkoff, Riga, Odessa*. London, 1844.

Makhaev, M. I. *Plan de la Ville de St. Petersbourg avec ses Principales Vües dessiné & gravé sous la direction de l'Academie Imperiale des Sciences & des Arts*. 1753. http://rumsey.geogarage.com/maps/g5669010.html.

Mikhailovskii-Danilevskii, Alexander I. *Imperator Aleksandr Pervyi i ego spodvizniki: Voennaia galereia Zimiago dvortsa*. 6 vols. in 3. St. Petersburg: P. Pechatkin, 1845–1849.

Mikhnevich, Vladimir. *Peterburg: Ves' na ladoni, s planom Peterburga, ego panoramoi s ptich'iago poleta, 22 kartinkami*. St. Petersburg: Izd. Knigoprodavtsa K. N. Plotnikova, 1874.

Ministerstvo Imperatorskogo Dvora. *Glavnoe Upravlenie Udelov. Istoriia udelov, 1797–1897*. 3 vols. St. Petersburg, 1902.

———. *Kamer-fur'erskii Tseremonial'nyi zhurnal*. 1737–1817.

———. *Obshchi arkhiv*. 2 vols. St. Petersburg, 1888.

Ministerstvo Vnutrenykh Del. Tsentral'nyi Statisticheskii Komitet. *Statistcheskii tablitsy Rossiiskoi Imperii* Vyp. Vol. 2, *Nalichnoe naseleni imperii za 1858 g*. St. Petersburg, 1863.

Morell, John Reynell. *Russia as it is; and Turkey, Past and Present; Their History, Resources, Court, and People*. London: Geo. Routledge, 1854.

Nekrasov, N. A. *Petersburg: The Physiology of a City*. Translated by Thomas Gaiton Marullo. Evanston: Northwestern University Press, 2009.

Polnoe sobranie zakonov Rossiiskoi Imperii 1649–1913. 40 vols. St. Petersburg: Gos. Tip., 1830–1916. [Cited in the notes as *PSZ*.]

Pushkarev, I. I. *Opisanie Sanktpeterburga i uezdnykh gorodov S. Peterburgskoi gubernii*. 4 vols. St. Petersburg: Published by the author, 1839–1841.

Pushkarev, Ivan. *Nikolaevskii Peterburg*. 1839–1842. Reprint, St. Petersburg: Liga-Plius, 2000.

Russkii invalid. 1827.

Sankt-Peterburgskie vedomosti. 1754–1909. [Cited in the notes as *SPV*.]

Somov, Andrei. *Kartiny Imperatorskago Ermitazha*. St. Petersburg: Tip. A. Iakobson, 1859.

Storch, Heinrich. *The Picture of St. Petersburg*. London: Longman, 1801.

Svinin, P. P. *Dostopamiatnosti Sanktpeterburga i ego okrestnostei*. St. Petersburg, 1816–1828.

Svod udel'nykh postanovlenii. St. Petersburg, 1843.

Ves' Peterburga na 1894 g. Adresnaia i spravochnaia kniga. Vol. 1. St. Petersburg: Novoe vremia, 1894.

Memoirs, Diaries, and Letters

Adams, John Quincy. *Memoirs*. Vol. 2. Edited by Charles Francis Adams. New York: AMS Press, 1970.

Aleksandra Fedorovna, Empress of Russia. "Imperatritsa Aleksandra Fedorovna v svoikh vospominaniiakh." *Russkaia starina* 88, no. 10 (Oct. 1896): 5–60.

Antonov-Ovseenko, V. A. *V Revoliutsii*. Moscow: Politicheskaia Literatura, 1983.

Bardakova, Marina. "Dukhov Den' 1862 goda v Peterburge." *Russkii arkhiv* 49, no. 10 (1911, book 3): 225–32.

———. "V Peterburge 60-x godov proshlago stoletiia." *Russkaia starina* 157, no. 3 (March 1914): 686–702.

Benkendorf, Count. "Zapiski Benkendorfa." *Russkaia starina* 88, no. 10 (Oct. 1896): 65–96.

Benois, A. N. *Moi dnevnik, 1916–1917–1918*. Moscow: Russkii put', 2003.

———. *Zhizn' khudozhnika. Vospominaniia*. Vol. 2. New York: Izd. Im. Chekhova, 1955.

Boborykin, P. D. *Vospominaniia v dvukh tomakh*. Vol. 1. Moscow: Izd. "Khudozhestvennaia Literatura," 1965.

Bobrinskii, A. A. "Vospominaniia 1880–81." *Katorga i ssylka* 76 (1931): 73–111.

Bolotov, Andrei. *Zhizn' i prikliucheniia Andreia Bolotova*. Vol. 2, *1760–1771*. Moscow-Leningrad: Akademiia, 1931.

Brodskii, I. A., ed. *Gorkii i khudozhniki. Vospominaniia, perepiska, stat'i*. Moscow: Iskusstovo, 1964.

Bryant, Louise. *Six Red Months in Russia: An Observer's Account of Russia before and during the Proletarian Dictatorship*. Portland, OR: Powell's Press, 2002.

Buchanan, George. *My Mission to Russia and Other Diplomatic Memories*. Vol. 2. Boston: Little, Brown, 1923.

Bulatov, A. M. "Letter dated Dec. 25, 1825." In *Vosstanie Dekabristov: Dokumenty*, edited by M. V. Nechkina, 18:299. Moscow: Izd. Nauka, 1984.

Cathcart to Weymouth, Aug. 19, 1768 (OS). *Sbornik Imperatorskago russkago istoricheskago obshchestva*, 12:357. St. Petersburg, 1873.

Catherine II, Empress of Russia. *Love and Conquest: Personal Correspondence of Catherine the Great and Prince Grigory Potemkin*. Edited and translated by Douglas Smith. DeKalb: Northern Illinois University Press, 2004.

Choiseul-Gouffier, Sophia de. *Historical Memoirs of the Emperor Alexander I and the Court of Russia*. Vol. 1. Chicago: McClurg, 1900.

Chernukha, V. G., ed. *Aleksandr Vtoroi: Vospominaniia, Dnevniki*. St. Petersburg: Pushkinskii fond, 1995.

Cross, Anthony. "Professor Thomas Newberry's Letter from St. Petersburg, 1766, on the Grand Carousel and Other Matters." *Slavonic and East European Review* 76, no. 3 (July 1998): 484–93.

Czartoryski, Adam. *Memoirs of Prince Adam Czartoryski and His Correspondence with Alexander I*. Edited by Adam Gielgud. 2 vols. Orono, ME: Academic International, 1968.

Dallas, George M. *Diary of George Mifflin Davis while United States Minister to Russia 1837–39 and to England 1856–61*. Edited by Susan Dallas. Philadelphia: Lippincott, 1892.

de Robien, Louis. *The Diary of a Diplomat in Russia, 1917–1918*. New York: Prager, 1970.

Disbrowe, Charlotte. *Old Days in Diplomacy: Recollections of a Closed Century*. London: Jarrold and Sons, 1903.

Ekaterina II i G. A. Potemkin. Lichnaia perepiska, 1769–1791. Compiled by V. S. Lopatin. Moscow: Nauka, 1997.

Fenin, Alexander I. *Coal and Politics in Late Imperial Russia: Memoirs of a Russian Mining Engineer*. Translated by Alexandre Fediaevsky, edited by Susan P. McCaffray. DeKalb: Northern Illinois University Press, 1990.

Ficquelmont, Dorothea. *Dnevnik, 1829–1837. Ves' pushkinskii Peterburg*. Moscow: Minuvshee, 2009.

Galanina, N. V. "Gospital' Zimnego dvortsa, 5 October 1915 to 28 October 1917: Vospominaniia byvshei medsestry gospitalia." In *Gospital' v Zimnem dvortse 1915–1917. Katalog vystavki*, edited by V. F. Marishkina. St. Petersburg: Izd. Gosud. Ermitazha, 2006.

Gavril Konstantinovich, Grand Duke of Russia. *Staryi Peterburg: Iubileinyi sbornik vospominanii E. I. V. Velikago Kniaza Gavrila Konstantinovicha*. Paris: N.p., 1953.

Golovina, V. N. *Memoirs of Countess Golovine, a Lady at the Court of Catherine II*. London: D. Nutt, 1910.

Golovine, Ivan. *Russia under the Autocrat Nicholas the First*. 1846. Reprint, New York: Praeger, 1970.

Gurevich, L. Ia. "Narodnoe dvizhenie v Peterburge 9-go ianvaria 1905 g." *Byloe* 1 (Jan. 1906): 200–229.

Heald, Edward T. *Witness to the Revolution: Letters from Russia, 1916–1919*. Edited by James B. Gidney. Kent, OH: Kent State University Press, 1972.

Iswolsky, Alexander. *The Memoirs of Alexander Iswolsky: Formerly Russian Minister of Foreign Affairs and Ambassador to France*. Edited and translated by Charles Louis Seeger. Gulf Breeze, FL: Academic International Press, 1974.

Kerensky, Alexander. *The Kerensky Memoirs: Russia and History's Turning Point*. London: Cassell, 1965.

Kogan [sic]. "Konchina Imperatora Aleksandra II (Rasskaz fel'dshera)." *Istoricheskii vestnik* 131, no. 1 (1913): 133–35.

Konechnyi, A. M., ed. *Progulki po Nevskomu prospektu v pervoi polovine XIXv*. St. Petersburg: Giperion, 2002.

Krivenko, V. S. *V Ministerstve Dvora. Vospominaniia*. St. Petersburg: Nestor-Istoriia, 2006.

Lawrence, Kelly, ed. *St. Petersburg: A Traveler's Companion*. New York: Atheneum, 1986.

Leifert A. "Balagany." In *Peterburgskie balagany*, 25–70. 1922. Reprint, St. Petersburg: Giperion, 2000.

Lyandres, Semion, ed. *The Fall of Tsarism: Untold Stories of the February 1917 Revolution*. Oxford: Oxford University Press, 2013.

Markus, F. F. "Poslednie minuty Imperatora Aleksandra II. Rasskaz ochevidtsa." *Istoricheskii vestnik* 80, no. 4 (1900): 133–34.

Mordvinova, Z. E. "Smol'nyi Institut v epokhu Imperatritsy Ekateriny II (1764–1796)." *Istoricheskii vestnik* 136, no. 6 (June 1914): 987–1001. http://historydoc.edu.ru/catalog. asp?ob_no=14836&cat_ob_no=12316/.

Murzanova, M. "Vospominaniia A. A. Bobrinskogo (1880–1881gg)." *Katorga i ssylka* 76, no. 3 (Moscow, 1931): 73–120.

The National Gallery. "Observations on the Unfitness of the Present Building for its Purpose. In a Letter to Rt. Hon. Sir Robert Peel." NP. May 1845.

Nechkina, M. V., ed. *Vosstanie Dekabristov: Dokumenty*. 23 vols. Moscow: Izd. "Nauka," 1925–.

Nicholas I, Emperor of Russia. "Imperator Nikolai Pavlovich v ego pis'makh k Kniaziu Paskevich." *Russkii arkhiv* 1 (Jan. 1897): 5–44.

———. *Muzh, otets, imperator*. Edited by D. V. Tevekelian. Moscow: Slovo, 2000.

Nicholas II, Emperor of Russia. *Dnevnik Imperatora Nikolaia II*. Berlin: Knigoizdatel'stvo Slovo, 1923.

Nikolai II nakanune otrecheniia. Kamer-fur'erskie zhurnaly (Dekabr 1916-Fevral' 1917 gg). Edited by V. I Startsev. St. Petersburg: Skarabei, 2001.

Olga Nikolaevna, Grand Duchess of Russia. "Son iunosti: zapiski docheri Imperatora Nikolaia I velikoi kniagini Ol'gi Nikolaevny, korolevy Viurtembergskoi (otryvki)." In *Nikolai pervyi i ego vremia. Dokumenty, pis'ma, dnevniki, memuary, svidetel'stva sovremennikov i trudy istorikov*, edited by B. N. Tarasov, 2:155–91. Moscow, 2000.

Orlov, A. F. "Letter to D. P. Tatishchev, dated Dec. 24, 1837." *Russkii arkhiv* 3 (1865): 1093.

Podkopaeva, Iu. N., and A. N. Sveshnikova, eds. *Konstantin Andreevich Somov. Pis'ma. Dnevniki. Suzhdeniia*. Moscow: Iskusstvo, 1979.

Polilov-Sievertsev, G. T. *Nashi dedy-kuptsy: bytovyia kartiny nachala XIX stoletiia*. St. Petersburg: A. F. Devrien, 1900s [sic].

Radziwill, Catherine. *Behind the Veil at the Russian Court*. New York: John Lane, 1914.

"Razskazy ochevidtsev o pozhare Zimniago dvortsa v 1837 g." *Russkii arkhiv* 3 (1865): 1088–113.

Reed, John. *Ten Days that Shook the World*. 1919. Reprint, New York: Penguin Books, 1985.

Roskovshenko, I. V. "Peterburg v 1831–1832 gg." *Russkaia starina* 101 (Feb. 1900): 477–90.

Rybnikov, I. N. "Imperator Nikolai i moskovskoe kupechestvo na obede v Zimnem dvortse 13 Maia 1833 g." In *Nikolai pervyi i ego vremia. Dokumenty, pis'ma, dnevniki, memuary, svidetel'stva sovremennikov i trudy istorikov*, edited by B. N. Tarasov, 2:106–12. Moscow: Olma-Press, 2000.

Sheremetev, S. D. *Memuary Grafa S. D. Sheremeteva*. Moscow: Indrik, 2001.

Stankevich, V. B., and Iu. V. Lomonosov. *Vospominaniia 1914–1919. Vospominaniia o Martovskoi Revoliutsii 1917 g.* Moscow: Rossiiskii Gosud. Gumanitarnyi Universitet, 1994.

Sukhanov, N. N. *The Russian Revolution, 1917: A Personal Record.* Princeton, NJ: Princeton University Press, 1984.

Tarasov, B. N., ed. *Nikolai pervyi i ego vremia. Dokumenty, pis'ma, dnevniki, memuary, svidetel'stva sovremennikov i trudy istorikov.* Vol. 2. Moscow: Olma-Press, 2000.

Tiutcheva, A. F. *Pri dvore dvukh imperatorov. Vospominaniia, dnevnik.* Moscow: Izd. M. i S. Sabashnikovykh, 1928–1929.

Tolchenov, Ivan A. *Zhurnal ili zapiska zhizni i prikliuchenii Ivana Alekseevicha Tolchenova.* Moscow: Akademiia Nauk SSSR, 1974.

Tsamutali, A. N., T. V. Andreeva, eds. *Nikolai I: lichnost' i epokha. Novye materialy.* St. Petersburg: Nestor-Istoriia, 2007.

Varnashev, N. M. "Ot nachala do kontsa s Gaponovskoi organizatsiei v S.-Peterburge (Vospominaniia)." In *Istoriko-revoliutsionnyi sbornik,* edited by V. I. Nevskii, 1:177–208. Moscow-Petrograd: Gosud. Izd., 1924.

Viazemskii, P.A., Prince of Russia. *Staraia zapisnaia knizhka.* Leningrad: Izd. Pisatelei "Leningrad," 1929.

Vigée Le Brun, Elisabeth. *Memoirs.* Translated by Lionel Strachey. New York: Doubleday, Page, 1903.

Zasosov, D. A., V. I. Pyzin, V. A. Vitiazeva, eds. *Iz zhizni Peterburga 1890–1910-x godov.* Leningrad: Leninzdat, 1991.

Secondary Sources

Abraham, Richard. *Alexander Kerensky: The First Love of the Revolution.* New York: Columbia University Press, 1987.

Ageeva, O. G. *Imperatorskii dvor Rossii 1700–1976 gg.* Moscow: Nauka, 2008.

Akinsha, Konstantin, et al. *The Holy Place: Architecture, Ideology and History in Russia.* New Haven: Yale University Press, 2007.

Alexander, John T. *Catherine the Great, Life and Legend.* New York: Oxford University Press, 1989.

Andreeva, Galina. *Genii voiny, blaga i krasoty: Pisal Korolevskii Akademik Dzhordzh Dou.* Moscow: Ikom Rossii, 2012.

Anisimov, Evgeny V. *Empress Elizabeth. Her Reign and Her Russia, 1741–1761.* Translated by John T. Alexander. Gulf Breeze, FL: Academic International Press, 1995.

Arkhitektor Iurii Fel'ten. K 250-letiiu so dnia rozhdeniia. Katalog vystavki. Leningrad: Iskusstvo, 1982.

Baryshnikova, E. Iu., Iu. M. Denisov, A. I. Bashmakov. *Panorama Millionoi ulitsy serediny XVIII v.* St. Petersburg: Vsemirnyi Klub Peterburzhtsev, 2002.

Bassin, Mark, Christopher Ely, Melissa Stockdale, eds. *Space, Place and Power in Modern Russia: Essays in the New Spatial History.* DeKalb: Northern Illinois University Press, 2010.

Bater, James H. "Modernization and the Municipality: Moscow and St. Petersburg on the Eve of the Great War." In *Studies in Russian Historical Geography,* edited by James H. Bater, R. A. French, 2:305–27. London: Academic Press, 1983.

Batowski, Zigmunt. *Arkhitektor Rastrelli o svoikh tvoreniiakh. Materialy deiatel'nosti mastera s 65 illiustratsiiami. Pervoe russkoe izdanie.* St. Petersburg: GMZ "Tsarskoe Selo," 2000.

Benois, A. N., and N. Lanceray. "Dvortsovye stroitel'stvo Imperatora Nikolaia I." *Starye gody* (July–Sept. 1913): 173–97.

Bozherianov, I. N. *Zhizneopisanie imperatritsy Aleksandry Fedorovny, Suprugi Imperatora Nikolaia Pervogo.* St. Petersburg: Tip. Tov. "Obshchestvennaia Pol'za," 1898.

Brumfield, William Craft. *A History of Russian Architecture.* Cambridge: Cambridge University Press, 1993.

———. *Reshaping Russian Architecture: Western Technology Utopian Dreams.* Cambridge: Cambridge University Press, 1990.

———. "St. Petersburg and the Art of Survival." In *Preserving Petersburg: History, Memory, Nostalgia*, edited by Helena Goscilo and Stephen M. Norris, 1–38. Bloomington: Indiana University Press, 2008.

Buckler, Julie A. *Mapping St. Petersburg: Imperial Text and Cityshape*. Princeton, NJ: Princeton University Press, 2005.

Burbank, Jane, Mark Von Hagen, A. V. Remnev, eds. *Russian Empire: Space, People, Power, 1700–1930*. Bloomington: Indiana University Press, 2007.

Burbank, Jane, and David L. Ransel, eds. *Imperial Russia: New Histories for the Fatherland*. Bloomington: Indiana University Press, 1998.

Burim, L. D, G. A. Efimova, N. L. Lopatenko. *"Odin otvetstvovat' dolzhen— . . ." Ocherki o direktorakh Izhorskikh zavodov*. St. Petersburg: OAO Izhorskie zavody, 2001.

Bushkovitch, Paul A. "The Epiphany Ceremony of the Russian Court in the Sixteenth and Seventeenth Centuries." *Russian Review* 49, no. 1 (Jan. 1990): 1–17.

Buzinov, Viktor. *Dvortsovaia ploshchad'. Neformal'nyi putevoditel'*. St. Petersburg: Izd. Ostrov, 2001.

Cannadine, David. "The Context, Performance and Meaning of Ritual: The British Monarchy and the 'Invention of Tradition,' c. 1820–1977." In *The Invention of Tradition*, edited by E. J. Hobsbawm and Terence Ranger, 101–64. Cambridge: Cambridge University Press, 1983.

Chenevière, Antoine. *Russian Furniture: The Golden Age, 1780–1840*. New York: Vendome Press, 1988.

Clark, Katerina. *Petersburg, Crucible of Cultural Revolution*. Cambridge, MA: Harvard University Press, 1995.

Conlin, Jonathan. *The Nation's Mantelpiece: A History of the National Gallery*. London: Pallas Athene, 2006.

Darinskii, A.V., V. I. Startsev. *Istoriia Sankt-Peterburga: XVIII-XIX vv*. St. Petersburg: Glagol, 2000.

de Madariaga, Isabel. *Catherine the Great: A Short History*. New Haven: Yale University Press, 2002.

Denisov, Iu. M. "Zimnii dom Anny Ioannovny." In *Tri veka Sankt-Peterburga. Entsiklopediia v trekh tomakh*, 1:371–73. St. Petersburg: St. Petersburg State University, 2003.

———."Zimnii dvorets Rastrelli." In *Ermitazh. Istoriia i arkhitektura zdanii*, edited by V. I. Piliavskii and V. F. Levinson-Lessing, 39–64. Leningrad: Izd. Avrora, 1974.

Denisov, Iu., and A. Petrov. *Zodchii Rastrelli. Materialy k izucheniiu tvorchestva*. Leningrad: Gosud. Izd. Lit. po Stroitel'stvu Arkhitekture i Stroitel'nym Materialam, 1963.

Deploige, Jeroen, and Gita Deneckere, eds. *Mystifying the Monarch: Studies on Discourse, Power and History*. Amsterdam: Amsterdam University Press, 2006.

Descargues, Pierre. *Art Treasures of the Hermitage*. New York: Harry N. Abrams, 1977.

———. *The Hermitage Museum, Leningrad*. New York: Henry N. Abrams, 1961.

Diakin, V. S. et al., *Istoriia rabochikh Leningrada: 1703-1965*. Vol. 1. Leningrad: Izd. "Nauka," 1972.

Dianina, Katia. *When Art Makes News: Writing Culture and Identity in Imperial Russia*. DeKalb: Northern Illinois University Press, 2013.

Dixon, Simon. *Catherine the Great*. New York: HarperCollins, 2009.

Dubrovnin, N. F., ed. *Materialy i cherty k biografii Imperatora Nikolaia I i k istorii ego tsarstvovaniia*. St. Petersburg: Sbornik Imperatorskogo russkago istoricheskago obshchestva, 1896.

Ducamp, Emmanuel. "The Production of Russian Bronzes in the Late Eighteenth Century." http://christies.com/lotfinder/LotDetailsPrintable.aspx?intObjectID=5461768/.

———, ed. *The Winter Palace, St. Petersburg*. St. Petersburg: State Hermitage Museum, 1995.

Duindam, Jeroen. *Vienna and Versailles: The Courts of Europe's Dynastic Rivals, 1550–1780*. Cambridge: Cambridge University Press, 2003.

Dukes, Paul. *Catherine the Great and the Russian Nobility: A Study Based on the Materials of the Legislative Commission of 1767*. Cambridge: Cambridge University Press, 1967.

Dzhervis, M. V. "Volneniia Peterburgskikh rabochikh nakanune mirovoi voiny." *Deshevaia biblioteka zhurnala Katorga i ssylka* 46 (1926): 3–30.

Economakis, Evel G. "Patterns of Migration and Settlement in Prerevolutionary St. Petersburg: Peasants from Iaroslavl and Tver Provinces." *Russian Review* 56, no. 1 (Jan. 1997): 8–24.

Egorov, Iu. A. *The Architectural Planning of St. Petersburg*. Athens: Ohio University Press, 1969.

Eliseeva, Ol'ga. *Povsednevnaia zhiznn' blagorodnogo sosloviia v zolotoi vek Ekateriny*. Moscow: Molodaia Gvardiia, 2008.

Ely, Christopher. *Underground St. Petersburg: Radical Populism, Urban Space, and the Tactics of Subversion in Reform-Era Russia*. DeKalb: Northern Illinois University Press, 2016.

Ferro, Marc. *Nicholas II: The Last of the Tsars*. New York: Oxford University Press, 1990.

Figes, Orlando, and Boris Kolonitskii. *Interpreting the Russian Revolution: The Language and Symbols of 1917*. New Haven: Yale University Press, 1999.

Friedman, Rebecca. *Masculinity, Autocracy, and the Russian University*. Basingstoke: Palgrave Macmillan, 2005.

Gafifulan, R. R., Liubov Goriacheva, Mikhail Katin-Iartsev, A. A. Shumkov. *Kostiumirovannyi bal v Zimnem dvortse*. 2 vols. Moscow: Russkii antikvariat 2003.

Geertz, Clifford. *Negara: The Theatre State in Nineteenth-Century Bali*. Princeton, NJ: Princeton University Press, 1980.

Gleason, Abbott. *Young Russia: The Genesis of Russian Radicalism in the 1860s*. New York: Viking Press, 1980.

Glinka, V., and A. Pomarnatskii. *Voennaia galereia Zimnego dvortsa*. Leningrad: Izd. Avrora, 1974.

Gorizontov, Leonid. "The 'Great Circle' of Interior Russia: Representations of the Imperial Center in the Nineteenth and Early Twentieth Centuries." In *Russian Empire: Space, People, Power, 1700–1930*, edited by Jane Burbank, Mark Von Hagen, A. V. Remnev, 67–93. Bloomington: Indiana University Press, 2007.

Gorlanov, L. R. *Udel'nye krestiane Rossii, 1797–1865*. Smolensk: Gosud. Ped. Inst., 1986.

Goscilo, Helena, and Stephen M. Norris, eds. *Preserving Petersburg: History, Memory, Nostalgia*. Bloomington: Indiana University Press, 2008.

Gosudarstvennyi Ermitazh. *Sotrudniki Imperatorskogo Ermitazha 1852–1917*. St. Petersburg: Izd. Gosud. Ermitazh, 2004.

Gosudarstvennyi Ermitazh. *Zimnii dvorets: ocherki zhizni imperatorskoi rezidentsii*. Vol. 1. St. Petersburg: Liki Rossii, 2000.

Gosudarstvennyi Muzei Istorii S.-Peterburga. *Katalog, Franchesko Bartolomeo Rastrelli: Arkhitekturnye proekty iz sobraniia*. Compiled by G. B. Vasil'ev et al. St. Petersburg: Gosud. Muz. Ist. S.-Peterburga, 2000.

Grabar', I. E. *Istoriia russkogo iskusstva*. Vol. 8, bk. 2. Moscow: Izd. "Nauka," 1964.

Griffiths, David M. "Catherine II: The Republican Empress." *Jahrbücher für Geschichte Osteuropas* 21, no. 3 (1973): 323–44.

Grinev, S. A. *Istoriia roty dvortsovykh grenader*. St. Petersburg, 1912.

Gritsai, Olga, and Herman van der Wusten. "Moscow and St. Petersburg, a Sequence of Capitals, a Tale of Two Cities." *GeoJournal* 51 (2000): 33–45.

Guseva, N. Iu. "Zimnii dvorets." *Tri veka Sankt-Peterburga. Entsiklopediia v trekh tomakh*, 1:379–81. St. Petersburg: St. Petersburg State University, 2003.

Hamm, Michael. *The City in Late Imperial Russia*. Bloomington: Indiana University Press, 1986.

Hartley, Janet. "Governing the City: St. Petersburg and Catherine II's Reforms." In *St. Petersburg, 1703–1825*, edited by Anthony Cross, 99–118. Basingstoke: Palgrave Macmillan, 2003.

Hasegawa, Tsuyoshi. *The February Revolution: Petrograd, 1917*. Seattle: University of Washington Press, 1981.

Hayden, Delores. *The Power of Place: Urban Landscapes as Public History*. Cambridge, MA: MIT Press, 1995.

Haywood, Richard M. "The Winter Palace in St. Petersburg: Destruction by Fire and Reconstruction, December 1837–March 1839." *Jahrbücher für Geschichte Osteuropas* 27, no. 2 (1979): 161–80.

Hedda, Jennifer. *His Kingdom Come: Orthodox Pastorship and Social Activism in Revolutionary Russia*. DeKalb: Northern Illinois University Press, 2008.

Hobsbawm, E. J., and Terence Ranger, eds., *The Invention of Tradition*. Cambridge: Cambridge University Press, 1983.

Hunt, Lynn. *The Family Romance of the French Revolution*. Berkeley: University of California, 1992.

Istoriia dorevoliutsionnoi Rossii v dnevnikakh i vospominaniiakh. 5 vols. in 13. Edited and introduced by P. A. Zaionchkovskii. Moscow: Kniga, 1976–1989.

Johnson, Emily. *How St. Petersburg Learned to Study Itself: The Russian Idea of Kraevedenie*. University Park: Pennsylvania State University Press, 2006.

Kaganov, G. Z. *Images of Space: St. Petersburg in the Visual and Verbal Arts*. Translated by Sidney Monas. Stanford: Stanford University Press, 1997.

Kamenskii, A. B. "The Congress of People's Deputies of 1767." *Russian Studies in History* 33, no. 4 (1995): 35–65.

Kasparinskaia, S. A., ed. *Muzei i vlast': Sbornik nauchnykh trudov*. Moscow: Nauchno-issl. In-t kultury, 1991.

Keenan, Paul. *St. Petersburg and the Russian Court, 1703–1761*. Basingstoke: Palgrave Macmillan, 2013.

———. "The Summer Gardens in the Social Life of St. Petersburg 1725–61." *Slavonic and East European Review* 88, no. 1/2 (Jan./Apr. 2010): 134–55.

Klokman, Iu. P. *Ocherki sotsial'no-ekonomicheskoi istorii gorodov severo-zapada Rossii v seredine XVIII v*. Moscow: Izd. Ak. Nauk SSSR, 1960.

Kochin, G. E. "Naselenie Peterburga v 60–90-kh godakh XVIII v." In *Ocherki istorii Leningrada*, edited by M. P. Viatkin et al., 1:294–319. Moscow-Leningrad: Institut Istorii, Ak. Nauk SSSR, 1955.

Koeppe, Wolfram. "Gone with the Wind to the Western Hemisphere—Selling Off Furniture by David Roentgen and Other Decorative Arts of the Eighteenth Century." *Canadian-American Slavic Studies* 43, no. 4 (2009): 245–72.

Komelova, G. N. "Pridvornye publichnye maskarady v Zimnem dvortse." In Gosudarstvennyi Ermitazh, *Zimnii dvorets: ocherki zhizni imperatorskoi rezidentsii*, 1:132–43. St. Petersburg: Liki Rossii, 2000.

Korshunova, M. F. *Iurii Fel'ten*. Leningrad: Lenizdat, 1988.

Kosheleva, Ol'ga. *Liudi Sankt-Peterburgskogo ostrova Petrovskogo vremeni*. Moscow: OGI, 2004.

Krasheninnikov, A. F. "Pervye gody posle Rastrelli." In *Ermitazh. Istoriia i arkhitektura zdanii*, edited by V. I. Piliavskii and V. F. Levinson-Lessing, 65–76. Leningrad: Izd. Avrora, 1974.

Lapshin, V. P. *Khudozhestvennaia zhizn' Moskvy i Petrograda v 1917 g*. Moscow: Sovetskii Khudozhnik, 1983.

Lefebvre, Henri. *The Production of Space*. Translated by Donald Nicholson-Smith. Oxford: Basil Blackwell, 1991.

Levinson-Lessing, V. F. *Istoriia kartinnoi galerei Ermitazha (1764–1917)*. Leningrad: Iskusstvo, 1985.

Lincoln, W. Bruce. *Between Heaven and Hell: The Story of a Thousand Years of Artistic Life in Russia*. New York: Viking, 1998.

———. *Nicholas I: Emperor and Autocrat of All the Russias*. DeKalb: Northern Illinois University Press, 1989.

———. *Sunlight at Midnight: St. Petersburg and the Rise of Modern Russia*. New York: Basic Books, 2002.

Liubomirov, P. G. "Iz istorii lesopil'nogo proizvodstva v Rossii v XVII, XVIII i nachale XIX vv." In *Istoricheskie zapiski*, edited by B. D. Grekov, 222–49. Moscow: Ak. Nauka, 1941.

Lotman, Iu. *Semiotics of Russian Cultural History*. Edited by A. D. Nakhimovsky and A. S. Nakhimovsky. Ithaca: Cornell University Press, 1985.

Lukomskii, G. K. *Sankt-Peterburg: Istoricheskii ocherk arkhitektury i razvitiia goroda*. Munich: Orkhis, 1923.

———. *Staryi Peterburg: Progulki po starinnym kvartalam*. Petrograd: Svobodnoe iskusstvo, 1917.

Luppov, S. P. *Istoriia stroitel'stva Peterburga v pervoi chetverti XVIII v*. Leningrad: Izd. Akademii Nauk SSSR, 1957.

Lur'e, F. M. *Starye gody: Khronologicheskaia rospis' soderzhaniia, 1907–1916*. St. Petersburg: Iz. Dom "Kolo," 2007.

Maddox, Steven. *Saving Stalin's Imperial City: Historic Preservation in Leningrad, 1930–1950.* Bloomington: Indiana University Press, 2015.

Maiorova, Olga. *From the Shadow of Empire: Defining the Russian Nation through Cultural Mythology, 1855–1870.* Madison: University of Wisconsin Press, 2010.

Marishkina, V. F. *Gospital' v Zimnem dvortse 1915–1917. Katalog vystavki.* St. Petersburg: Izd. Gosud. Ermitazha, 2006.

Martin, Alexander M. *Enlightened Metropolis: Constructing Imperial Moscow, 1762–1855.* Oxford: Oxford University Press, 2013.

Martynov, E. I. *Tsarskaia armiia v fevral'skom perevorote.* Moscow: Naarkomvoenmor, 1927.

Matthews, Mervyn. *The Passport Society: Controlling Movement in Russia and the USSR.* Boulder, CO: Westview Press, 1993.

McClellan, Andrew. *Inventing the Louvre: Art, Politics, and the Origins of the Modern Museum in Eighteenth-Century Paris.* Berkeley: University of California Press, 1999.

McGrew, Roderick E. *Russia and the Cholera, 1823–1832.* Madison: University of Wisconsin Press, 1965.

Merridale, Catherine. *Red Fortress: History and Illusion in the Kremlin.* New York: Metropolitan Books, 2013.

Meyer, Caspar. *Greco-Scythian Art and the Birth of Eurasia: From Classical Antiquity to Russian Modernity.* Oxford: Oxford University Press, 2013.

Miasoedova, N. Iu. "S. A. Gedeonov i Imperatorskii Ermitazh." In *Peterburg i Moskva: Dve stolitsy Rossii v XVIII–XX vekakh,* edited by Iu. V. Krivosheeva et al., 62–69. St. Petersburg: St. Petersburg University, 2001.

Mikaberidze, Alexander. *Russian Officer Corps of the Revolutionary and Napoleonic Wars, 1792–1815.* New York: Savas Beatie, 2005.

Mikhailov, G. V. "Zimnie dvortsy Petra I." In *Tri veka Sankt-Peterburga. Entsiklopediia v trekh tomakh,* 1:366–70. St. Petersburg: St. Petersburg State University, 2003.

Mil'čina, Vera. "Nicolas Ier et la politique intérieure de la France à l'époque de la Restauration: deux épisodes." *Cahiers du Monde Russe* 43, no. 2 (2002): 355–74.

Miliukov, Paul et al. *History of Russia,* vol. 2. *The Successors of Peter the Great: From Catherine I to Nicholas I,* trans. Charles Lam Markmann. New York: Funk and Wagnalls, 1968.

Mironov, B. N. *Russkii gorod v 1740–1860 gg.* Leningrad: Nauka, 1990.

Mitel'man, M., et al. *Istoriia Putilovskogo zavoda, 1801–1917.* Moscow: Izd. Sotsial'no-ekonomicheskoi lit., 1961.

Monod, Paul Kléber. *The Power of Kings: Monarchy and Religion in Europe, 1589–1715.* New Haven: Yale University Press, 1999.

Mumford, Lewis. *The City in History: Its Origins, Its Transformation, and Its Prospects.* New York: Harcourt, Brace Jovanovich, 1961.

———. *The Culture of Cities.* New York: Harcourt, Brace Jovanovich, 1970.

Munro, George E. *The Most Intentional City: St. Petersburg in the Reign of Catherine the Great.* Madison, NJ: Fairleigh Dickinson University Press, 2008.

Nardova, Valeriia. "Gorodskie golovy Sankt-Peterburga, 1873–1903 gg." *Otechestvennaia istoriia* 3 (June 2003): 20–39.

Nekrasov, Nikolai, ed. *Petersburg: The Physiology of a City.* Translated by Thomas Gaiton Marullo. Evanston, IL: Northwestern University Press: 2009.

Norman, Geraldine. *The Hermitage: The Biography of a Great Museum.* New York: Fromm International, 1998.

Omel'chenko, Oleg A. "The 'Legitimate Monarchy' of Catherine the Second: Enlightened Absolutism in Russia." *Russian Studies in History* 33, no. 4 (1995): 66–94.

Ospovat, Kirill. *Terror and Pity: Aleksandr Sumarokov and the Theater of Power in Elizabethan Russia.* Boston: Academic Studies Press, 2016.

Ovsiannikov, Iu. *Franchesko Bartolomeo Rastrelli.* Leningrad: Isskustvo, 1982.

Paneiakh, V. M. "Masterovye i rabotnye liudi vo vtoroi polovine XVIII v." In *Istoriia rabochikh Leningrada,* edited by V. S. Diakin et al., 1:46–71. Leningrad: Izd. "Nauka," 1972.

Paolucci, Antonio. *Great Museums of Europe: The Dream of the Universal Museum*. Milan: Skira Editore, 2002.

Petrov, P. N. *Istoriia Sankt-Peterburga s osnovaniia goroda do vvedeniia v deistvie vybornago gorodskago upravleniia, 1703–1782*. St. Petersburg: Izd. Glazunova, 1885.

———. "Materialy dlia biografii grafa Rastrelli." *Zodchii: arkhitekturnyi i khudozhestvenno-tekhnicheskii zhurnal* year 5 (1876): 55–57.

———. *Sbornik materialov dlia istorii Imperatorskoi Sanktpeterburgskoi Akademii Khudozhestv za sto let eia sushchestvovaniia*. Vol. 1. St. Petersburg: Tipografiia Kommisionera Imp. Akademii Khudozhestv Gogenfel'da, 1864.

Piliavskii, V. I. *Dvortsovaia ploshchad'*. Leningrad-Moscow: Isskustvo, 1958.

———. *Zimnii dvorets*. Leningrad: Gosud. Izd. Lit. po stroitel'stvu, arkhitekture i stroit. materialam, 1960.

Piliavskii, V. I., and V. F. Levinson-Lessing, eds. *Ermitazh. Istoriia i arkhitektura zdanii*. Leningrad: Izd. Avrora, 1974.

Piliavskii, V. I., and R. D. Liulina. "Novyi Ermitazh." In *Ermitazh. Istoriia i arkhitektura zdanii*, edited by V. I. Piliavskii and V. F. Levinson-Lessing, 223–44. Leningrad: Izd. Avrora, 1974.

Piotrovskii, M. B., ed. *Istoriia Ermitazha. Kratkii ocherk; materialy i dokumenty*. Moscow: Izd. Iskusstvo, 2000.

Piotrovskii, M. B., L. E. Torshina, et al. *Ermitazh: Istoriia zdanii i kollektsii*. St. Petersburg: Gosud. Ermitazh, 2001.

Pisarenko, Konstantin. *Elizaveta Petrovna*. Moscow: Molodaia gvardiia, 2014.

———. *Povsednevnaia zhizn' russkogo dvora tsarstvovanie Elizavety Petrovnya*. Moscow: Molodaia Gvardiia, 2003.

Plunkett, John. *Queen Victoria: First Media Monarch*. Oxford: Oxford University Press, 2003.

Pogosjan, Jelena. "Masks and Masquerades at the Court of Elizabeth Petrovna (1741–1742)." *Russian and Soviet History from the Time of Troubles to the Collapse of the Soviet Union*, edited by Steven A. Usitalo and William Benton Whisenhunt, 34–50. Lanham, MD: Rowman and Littlefield, 2008.

Pravilova, Ekaterina. *A Public Empire: Property and the Quest for the Common Good in Imperial Russia*. Princeton, NJ: Princeton University Press, 2014.

Presniakov, A. E. *Emperor Nicholas I of Russia: The Apogee of Autocracy, 1825–1855*. Gulf Breeze, FL: Academic International Publishers, 1974.

Proskurina, Vera. *Mify imperii. Literatura i vlast' v epokhu Ekateriny II*. Moscow: Novoe Literaturnoe Obozrenie, 2006.

Pyliaev, M. I. *Staryi Peterburg. Razskazy iz byloi zhizny stolitsy*. St. Petersburg: Suvorin, 1887.

Ransel, David L. *A Russian Merchant's Tale: The Life and Adventures of Ivan Alekseevich Tolchënov, Based on His Diary*. Bloomington: Indiana University Press, 2009.

Rashin, A. G. *Naselenie Rossii za 100 let, 1811–1913 gg.; Statisticheskie ocherki*. Moscow: Gos. Stat. Izd., 1956.

Rey, Marie-Pierre. *Alexander I: The Tsar Who Defeated Napoleon*. DeKalb: Northern Illinois University Press, 2012.

Riasanovsky, Nicholas V. *Nicholas I and Official Nationality in Russia, 1825–1855*. Berkeley: University of California Press, 1959.

Rowley, Alison. *Open Letters: Russian Popular Culture and the Picture Postcard, 1880–1922*. Toronto: University of Toronto Press, 2013.

Ruble, Blair. "From Palace Square to Moscow Square: St. Petersburg's Century-Long Retreat from Public Space." In *Reshaping Russian Architecture: Western Technology Utopian Dreams*, edited by William C. Brumfield, 10–42. Cambridge: Cambridge University Press, 1990.

Ryndziunskii, P. G. *Gorodskoe grazhdanstvo doreformennoi Rossii*. Moscow: Ak. Nauk, 1958.

Sablinsky, Walter. *The Road to Bloody Sunday: Father Gapon and the St. Petersburg Massacre of 1905*. Princeton, NJ: Princeton University Press, 1976.

Schama, Simon. "The Domestication of Majesty: Royal Family Portraiture, 1500–1850." *Journal of Interdisciplinary History* 17, no. 1 (Summer 1986): 155–83.

Schilder, N. K. *Imperator Nikolai Pervyi: Ego zhizn' i tsarstvovanie.* 2 vols. St. Petersburg: A. S. Suvorin, 1903.

Schönle, Andreas, Andrei Zorin, and Alexei Evstratov, eds. *The Europeanized Elite in Russia, 1762–1825.* DeKalb: Northern Illinois University Press, 2016.

Shaich, Michael, ed. *Monarchy and Religion: The Transformation of Royal Culture in Eighteenth-Century Europe.* Oxford: Oxford University Press, 2007.

Shapiro, A. L. "O roli Peterburga v razvitii vserossiiskogo rynka v XVIII–pervoi polovine XIX v." In *Goroda feodal'noi Rossii: Sbornik statei v pamiati N. V. Ustiugova,* edited by V. I. Shurikov, 386–96. Moscow: Nauka, 1966.

Shepelev, L. E. *Chinovnyi mir Rossii XVIII–nachalo XX v.* St. Petersburg, 1999.

———. *Tituly, mundiry, ordera v Rossiiskoi Imperii.* Leningrad: Nauka, 1991.

Sherikh, Dmitrii Iu. *Golos rodnogo goroda: ocherk istorii gazety "Sankt-Peterburgskie vedomosti."* St. Petersburg: Lenizdat, 2001.

Shevyrev, Alexander. "The Axis Petersburg-Moscow: Outward and Inward Russian Capitals." *Journal of Urban History* 30, no. 1 (November 2003): 70–84.

Shvidkovsky, Dmitry. *Russian Architecture and the West.* Translated by Antony Wood. New Haven: Yale University Press, 2007.

Sitwell, Sacheverell. *Valse des fleurs: A Day in St. Petersburg and a Ball at the Winter Palace in 1868.* London: Faber and Faber, 1944.

Skodock, Cornelia. *Barock in Russland: Zum Oeuvre des Hofarchitekten Francesco Bartolomeo Rastrelli.* Wiesbaden: Harrassowitz Verlag, 2006.

Sokolova, Tat'iana M. *Zaly Zimnego dvortsa i Ermitazha: kratkii istoriko-arkhitekturnyi ocherk.* Leningrad: Izd. Gos. Ermitaza, 1963.

Stavrou, Theofanis George, ed. *Art and Culture in Nineteenth-Century Russia.* Bloomington: Indiana University Press, 1983.

Stites, Richard. *The Four Horsemen: Riding to Liberty in Post-Napoleonic Europe.* New York: Oxford University Press, 2014.

———. *Serfdom, Society, and the Arts in Imperial Russia: The Pleasure and the Power.* New Haven: Yale University Press, 2005.

Stoff, Laurie S. *They Fought for the Motherland: Russia's Women Soldiers in World War I and the Revolution.* Lawrence: University of Kansas Press, 2006.

Stolpianskii, P. N. *Peterburg: Kak voznik, osnovalsia i ros Sankt-Piterburkh.* Petrograd, 1918. Reprint, St. Petersburg: Nauchno-izdatel'skii tsentr NeGA, 1995.

Summerlin, John. *The Architecture of the Eighteenth Century.* London: Thames and Hudson, 1986.

Suslov, Vitaly, ed. *The State Hermitage: Masterpieces from the Museum's Collection.* London: Booth-Clibborn Editions, 2001.

Tapié, Victor-L. *The Age of Grandeur: Baroque Art and Architecture.* Translated by A. Ross Williamson. New York: Frederick A. Praeger, 1960.

Tatishchev, S. S. *Imperator Aleksandr II: ego zhizn' i tsarstvovanie.* 2 vols. St. Petersburg: Suvorin, 1911.

Tombs, Robert. *The Paris Commune, 1871.* London: Longman, 1999.

Torshina, L. E., and E. Trubkina. *Zhilye pokoi. Imperatorskoi rezidentsii.* St. Petersburg, State Museum of the Hermitage, 2009.

Tri veka Sankt-Peterburga Entsiklopediia v trekh tomakh. 3 vols. St. Petersburg: St. Petersburg State University, 2003.

Veinert, N. *Rossi.* Moscow: Gosud. Izd. Iskusstvo, 1939.

Venturi, Franco. *Roots of Revolution: A History of the Populist and Socialist Movements in Nineteenth Century Russia.* Chicago: University of Chicago Press, 1983.

Verner, Andrew M. *The Crisis of Russian Autocracy: Nicholas II and the 1905 Revolution.* Princeton, NJ: Princeton University Press, 1990.

Volkhov, N. E. *Dvor russkikh imperatorov v ego proshlom i nastoiashchem*. St. Petersburg: P. Golike, 1900.

Voronov, N. V. "O rynke rabochei sily v rossii v XVIII v.: po materialam kirpichnoi promyshlennosti." *Voprosii istorii* 3 (1955): 90–99.

Werrett, Simon. *Fireworks: Pyrotechnic Arts and Sciences in European History*. Chicago: University of Chicago Press, 2010.

Whittaker, Cynthia Hyla. "Catherine the Great and the Art of Collecting: Acquiring the Paintings that Founded the Hermitage." In *Word and Image in Russian History: Essays in Honor of Gary Marker*, edited by Maria di Salvo, 147–71. Boston: Academic Studies Press, 2015.

Wilentz, Sean, ed. *Rites of Power: Symbolism, Ritual, and Politics since the Middle Ages*. Philadelphia: University of Pennsylvania Press, 1985.

Wirtschafter, Elise Kimerling. *Structures of Society: Imperial Russia's "People of Various Ranks."* DeKalb: Northern Illinois University Press, 1994.

Wortman, Richard S. "Moscow and Petersburg: The Problem of the Political Center in Tsarist Russia, 1881–1914." In *Rites of Power: Symbolism, Ritual, and Politics since the Middle Ages*, edited by Sean Wilentz, 244–74. Philadelphia: University of Pennsylvania Press, 1985.

———. "National Narratives in the Representation of Nineteenth-Century Russian Monarchy." In Richard Wortman, *Russian Monarchy: Representation and Rule: Collected Articles*, 152–69. Boston: Academic Studies Press, 2013.

———. *Scenarios of Power: Myth and Ceremony in Russian Monarchy*. Vol. 1, *From Peter the Great to the Death of Nicholas I*. Princeton, NJ: Princeton University Press, 1995.

———. *Scenarios of Power: Myth and Ceremony in Russian Monarchy*. Vol. 2, *From Alexander II to the Abdication of Nicholas II*. Princeton, NJ: Princeton University Press, 2000.

———. *Scenarios of Power: Myth and Ceremony in Russian Monarchy, From Peter the Great to the Abdication of Nicholas II*. Princeton, NJ: Princeton University Press, 2006.

———. "Solntsev, Olenin, and the Development of a National Aesthtic." In *Visualizing Russia: Fedor Solntsev and Crafting a National Past*, edited by Cynthia H. Whittaker, 17–40. Leiden: Brill, 2010.

Zaionchkovskii, Peter A. *The Russian Autocracy in Crisis, 1878–1882*. Edited and translated by Gary M. Hamburg. Gulf Breeze, FL: Academic International Press, 1981.

Zarubin, Ivan. *Almanakh-Putevoditel po Sankt-Peterburga*. St. Petersburg: Muller, 1892.

Zimin, Igor'. *Detskii mir imperatorskikh rezidentsii: byt monarkhov i ikh okruzhenie*. Moscow–St. Petersburg: Tsentrpoligraf, 2011.

———. *Liudi Zimnego dvortsa. Monarshie osoby, ikh favority i slugi*. Moscow: Tsentrpoligraf, 2015.

———. *Zimnii dvorets. Liudi i steny. Istoriia imperatorskoi rezidentsii, 1762–1917*. Moscow: Tsentrpoligraf, 2012.

Index

A

Abraham, Richard
  Alexander Kerensky, 254n74
absolutism
  and Alexander II, 162, 163
  and architecture, 77
  discussed, 95, 115, 140, 149, 151, 214, 215, 281n8
Academy of Arts
  contest, 60, 228n27
  discussed, 84, 147, 153, 154
Academy of Sciences, 153, 223n1
Adams, John Quincy, 66
Admiralty Meadow, 50, 53, 54, 55
Afanasev, Pavel, 128
Ageev, Mikhail, 126–27, 240n45
Ageeva, O. G.
  discussed, 28
  Imperatorskii dvor Rossii 1700–1796 gg, 219n4, 222n40, 229n1
Aix-la-Chapelle, Conference of, 103
Akhmanov, Mikhailo, 226n59
Akinsha, Konstantin
  Holy Place, The, 217n5
Aksakov, Constantine, 163
Alexander Column, 111–14, 135, 137, 237n55. *See also* Alexander I; cult of 1812
Alexander I. *See also* Alexander Column; cult of 1812
  abdication of, 103
  and Blessing of the Waters/Epiphany, 65
  and Buturlin, 245n32
  and centenary of St. Petersburg, 98
  death of, 105, 233n74, 236n34
  as furniture maker, 81, 82, 232n47
  and General Staff building, 228n28
  and Louis XVI, 218n12
  and masquerades, 99–100
  and military reviews, 66
  and monuments, 101, 103
  and Palace Square, 103
  portraits of, 236n45
Alexander I (Rey), 234n8

Alexander II
  and absolutism, 182
  assassination attempts on, 170–72, 248n45
  assumes throne, 162
  children of, 164, 165
  death of, 9, 161, 175–76, 249n57
  discussed, 150, 153, 164, 244n5, 248n39
  funeral of, 177
  and Gedeonov, 153
  and Imperial Hermitage Museum, 151, 154, 156
  and majority ceremony, 119
  marries Princess Iur'evskaia, 175
  and photography, 177
  portraits of, 147
  and Seriakov, 147
  threatening letters to, 174
Alexander III
  and Blessing of the Waters/Epiphany, 179
  discussed, 177, 178, 247n5
  expels Jews from Moscow, 249n63
  and Imperial Russian Museum, 152
  and masquerades, 164, 179
  and palace workers, 179–80
  portraits of, 238n6
Alexander Kerensky (Abraham), 254n74
Alexander Nevskii Monastery, 112
Alexander Palace, 85
Alexandrovsk Iron Foundry, 145
Alexei, Tsar, 65
Alferov, Afonasii, 127
Amazons, 228n35
Andreeva, Afim'ia, 126
Andreeva, Galina
  Genii voiny, blaga i krasoty, 235n30
Angiviller, comte d', 218n9
Anichkov Palace, 176, 178
Anisimov, Evgeny V.
  Empress Elizabeth, 219n4
Anna Ioanovna, 25, 29, 54, 226n68, 227n22, 235n16
anti-Semitic violence, 249n57

X

Y

Z

www.ingramcontent.com/pod-product-compliance
Lightning Source LLC
Chambersburg PA
CBHW020414040426
42428CB00031B/1690